Virtuosity and the Musical Work

This book is about three sets of etudes by Liszt: the *Etude en douze exercices* (1826), its reworking as *Douzes Grandes Etudes* (1837), and their reworking as *Douzes études d'exécution transcendante* (1851). At the same time it is a book about nineteenth-century instrumental music in general, in that the three works invite the exploration of features characteristic of the early Romantic era in music. These include: a composer-performer culture, the concept of virtuosity, the significance of recomposition, music and the poetic, and the consolidation of a musical work-concept. A central concern is to illuminate the relationship between the work-concept and a performance- and genre-orientated musical culture. At the same time the book reflects on how we might make judgements of the 'Transcendentals', of the Symphonic Poem *Mazeppa* (based on the fourth etude), and of Liszt's music in general.

Jim Samson has been a Professor of Music at the Universities of Exeter and Bristol and is now Professor of Music at Royal Holloway, University of London. He has published widely on the music of Chopin and on analytical and aesthetic topics in nineteenth- and twentieth-century music and has recently edited the *Cambridge History of Nineteenth-Century Music*. He is a Fellow of the British Academy and holds the Order of Merit of the Polish Ministry of Culture.

Virtuosity and the Musical Work

The *Transcendental Studies* of Liszt

JIM SAMSON

CAMBRIDGE
UNIVERSITY PRESS

CAMBRIDGE UNIVERSITY PRESS
Cambridge, New York, Melbourne, Madrid, Cape Town, Singapore, São Paulo

Cambridge University Press
The Edinburgh Building, Cambridge CB2 2RU, UK

Published in the United States of America by Cambridge University Press, New York

www.cambridge.org
Information on this title: www.cambridge.org/9780521814942

First published 2003
This digitally printed first paperback version 2007

A catalogue record for this publication is available from the British Library

ISBN-13 978-0-521-81494-2 hardback
ISBN-10 0-521-81494-4 hardback

ISBN-13 978-0-521-03604-7 paperback
ISBN-10 0-521-03604-6 paperback

In memory of my father

Contents

Acknowledgements

Switching from Chopin to Liszt has not been without its perils and insecurities. Fortunately I have been helped by numerous colleagues more experienced than I in Liszt research. They include: Mária Eckhardt, who first suggested that I work on the *Transcendentals*; James Deaville, who advised me on matters of publishing history; Rena Charnin Mueller, who shared her knowledge (second to none) of the sources; Detlef Altenburg, who was generous with his expertise on the prose writings, Rainer Kleinertz, who responded to some of my queries about titles; and Kenneth Hamilton, who was not only free with information, but (to my intense irritation) can actually play the *Transcendentals*. A special thank you must go to Adrienne Kaczmarczyk, who alerted me to several sources and even helped procure copies of some of them. I am grateful to staff at the National Széchényi Library, Budapest, the Goethe- und Schiller-Archiv, Weimar, the Library of Congress, Washington, and the Richard-Wagner-Museum, Bayreuth, for their assistance and courtesy, and to the Leverhulme Foundation and Music & Letters Trust for financial help. My gratitude also to Mark Henry, who processed the music examples, and to Penny Souster, who saw the book through the press in her usual efficient manner. And finally, thanks to Sue, who (reluctantly) spared me some of the farming chores in the final stages of preparing the manuscript.

Introduction

The signature on a musical score claims it, but that claim is not straightforward. This book will examine its nature and status in relation to the *Etudes d'exécution transcendante* by Liszt. It will further ask just what kind of musical work this is, how it relates to its two earlier versions, and even how we might begin to make judgements about it. The *Transcendentals* had a pre-history, well known in general outline. Liszt's youthful *Etude en douze exercices* was reworked as his *Douze Grandes Etudes* and they in turn were reworked as the *Etudes d'exécution transcendante*. The three sets of etudes, together with the symphonic poem *Mazeppa*, based on the fourth etude, make up the body of music addressed by this book. Naturally one of my aims is to examine the music itself. Perhaps the 'naturally' can no longer be taken for granted. Music analysis, the discipline where the specificity of music is most obviously celebrated, has been challenged by several, now-familiar anti-essentialist critiques: that closed concepts of a work, involving such notions as structure, unity, wholeness and complexity, need to be replaced by open concepts whose defining criteria are neither precise nor complete;[1] that what we analyse is a schematic structure which is bound to remain less than its realisation as a work;[2] that the work anyway is collectively authored;[3] that its identity is unstable, shaped anew in multiple receptions.[4] These critiques were salutary. As well as exposing the ideological roots of analysis and de-naturalising some of its assumptions, they opened music up to interpretative strategies that had already proved their worth in other disciplines. Yet they carried with them certain dangers, implicit in the change of 'root-metaphor' from organicism to contextualism.[5] Homologies of compositional and contextual figures can of course be suggestive. But it is evident that they cannot do adequate

[1] Morris Weitz, 'The Role of Theory in Aesthetics', *Journal of Aesthetics and Art Criticism*, 15 (1956), pp. 27–35; also *The Opening Mind: A Philosophical Study of Humanistic Concepts* (Chicago, 1977), and chapter 4 of Lydia Goehr, *The Imaginary Museum of Musical Works: An Essay in the Philosophy of Music* (Oxford, 1992).

[2] See especially Roman Ingarden, *The Work of Music and the Problem of its Identity*, trans. A. Czerniawski, ed. J. G. Harrell (Berkeley and Los Angeles, 1986; orig. edn, 1928).

[3] See, famously, Roland Barthes, 'The Death of the Author', in *Image – Music – Text* (London, 1977), pp. 142–8.

[4] Classic texts in reception aesthetics are Hans Robert Jauss, *Towards an Aesthetic of Reception*, trans. T. Bahti (Minneapolis, 1982) and Wolfgang Iser, *The Act of Reading: A Theory of Aesthetic Response* (Baltimore and London, 1978).

[5] Naomi Cumming's term, in 'Analogy in Leonard B. Meyer's Theory of Musical Meaning', in Jamie C. Kassler (ed.), *Metaphor: A Musical Dimension* (Sydney, 1991), pp. 177–92.

justice to the notoriously elusive meanings of music. More often than not the quest for the plot that will enable the good fit is all too transparent. Worse still, the music may be not just over-interpreted, but appropriated by the politicised and predatory agendas of special interest groups.

I see every reason to value music's commonalities with other disciplines, provided that its specificities are also protected. Likewise, I accept the potency of enriching metaphors, provided that their status as metaphors is not in question. At root, though, I believe that a direct, close-to-the-text engagement with musical materials is likely to prove more revealing than the seductive hermeneutics of the 1980s and 1990s, and that such an engagement need not signal an undeconstructed formalist orthodoxy; on the contrary, it may provide the necessary ballast for a more thoroughly grounded, evidence-based hermeneutics. Accordingly, I will examine the music of all three sets of etudes in reasonably close detail in this book, though I recognise that conventional analytical approaches leave something of a shortfall in explication. In particular it is not obvious to me that existing methods can easily accommodate the concept of virtuosity that is so clearly prescribed by the etudes. Virtuosity brings into sharp focus the relationship between music's object-status and its event-status. It marks out a relational field in which text, instrument, performer and audience are all indispensable to defining significance. It draws the performer right into the heart of the work, foregrounding presentational strategies that are hard to illuminate through the familiar, pedigreed methods of music analysis. And it spotlights the instrument, elevating the idiomatic (the figure), a category much less amenable to analysis than theme, harmony and form.

In any case, what I described as a 'direct, close-to-the-text engagement with musical materials' need not constitute analysis at all, except in a very informal meaning of the term. I do not really intend the detailed examination of music in this book to bolster those well-seasoned ideologies of unity and hierarchy that have been central to music analysis as a discipline. Rather it will be allied to, and will support, critical evaluations of some of the major topics of early nineteenth-century music history, or that at least is my hope. One might characterise this larger ambition as an attempt to place the music within a larger cultural setting. Yet that would not entirely cover it. It would be more truthful to acknowledge that the three sets of etudes were chosen partly because they seem to demand this larger topical approach; indeed the ordering of the components within my bipartite title is significant in this regard. Liszt's recompositions do after all highlight a number of topics that are lodged somewhere close to centre stage in the instrumental repertories of the early nineteenth century. I aim to expose and explore these topics, and in so doing to arrive at useful historical generalisations about the Romantic age in music, and about the special significance of the piano in its characterisation. Moreover, I find it attractive that the topics venture into several specialised corners of our disciplinary field, allowing for points of contact between researches in historical musicology, music theory, and music aesthetics, and within those broad categories between performance studies, genetic analysis and critical hermeneutics. With any luck the three sets of etudes will form a kind of linking thread, forging connections across a range of approaches as well as a range of topics, and in ways that are neither narrowly analytical nor cloudily sociological. The major topics will come into focus as the book unfolds. But it will be helpful at this stage to formalise them, and even to label them.

A composer–performer culture. This topic, exposed in general terms in chapter 1, is the background presence that informs much of my discussion of the *Etude en douze exercices* in chapter 2. I am not concerned here to present a conventional social history as the backcloth against which to discuss these fairly simple pieces, but rather to demonstrate how a repertory can reveal the practice of which it is a part. This involves recovering something of the practice of early nineteenth-century pianism, a performance-orientated rather than a work-orientated practice, and that means filtering out habits and values that are deeply ingrained in our way of thinking today. Everyone knows that the past is unavailable to us, but by examining the ecology that made possible Liszt's youthful composition we may begin to broaden our understanding of its authorship, and in so doing make room for the 'intention' of its text, to borrow Umberto Eco's useful formulation.[6] What interests me here is the intersection between individual and collective creativity, especially as registered through musical materials. An obvious effect of theory-based analysis has been to emphasise musical structures at the expense of musical materials. I hope that by homing in on materials, a category I will explore in chapters 2 and 4, I will not only illuminate the shared culture to which the work contributes, a culture that was less inclined to separate text and performance than we are today, but also allow for some informed speculation about the listening strategies of the historical (early nineteenth-century) subject. To generalise wildly, I suspect that contemporary audiences might well have focused rather more on the material content of a repertory, a content that freely crosses the boundaries of individual works, than we do today. They might have heard, in other words, a succession of familiar genre markers, tonal types, expressive gestures, idiomatic figures and the like, where we tend to focus rather more on work character – on the integration of elements rather than the combination of materials. It is likely, too, that the contemporary listener would have been much more aware of the basis of these materials, or many of them, in popular genres. Our present age may need to rediscover the obvious in this respect.

Methodologically, then, this first topic invites the examination of a cultural practice and its repertory. It is intriguing that the repertory of early nineteenth-century pianism is now eagerly embraced by the 'early music revival'. I accept that this can be genuinely revealing of the kind of sound-world the composer had in mind. But I would argue that placing Liszt's early *Etude* in the context of a cultural practice – both through an archaeological quest and an exercise in historical imagination – is likely to take us closer to original meanings than any attempt to reproduce that sound-world. At the same time I am alive to the dialogical nature of this larger enterprise. I have used the sub-titles 'recovered past' and 'active present' in chapter 2 to focus what I hope may be a productive dialogue (as opposed to a spurious fusion) between the historical Liszt and the present-day Liszt: between, in very rough translation, musical materials and musical structures. In the final part of the chapter I engage in a modest and informal analytical exercise both on the cycle as a whole and on some of its individual exercises. The premise underlying this analytical work is that a focus on form

---

[6] Umberto Eco, *Interpretation and Over-interpretation*, ed. Stefan Collini (Cambridge, 1992).

and design, on a sense of work character and individuation, might usefully complement the quest for musical materials, which is my primary concern at this initial stage of the enquiry. At the same time I acknowledge that both these exercises – recovering materials and finding forms – are inescapably undertaken from the perspective of today's world, complicating any dialogue we might establish between 'now' and 'then'.

The concept of virtuosity. Virtuosity ought to be a subject for today. It brings into focus key questions about the relation of performance to text, and therefore about the limits of what we can usefully say about musical works without reference to their performance – to the act of performance. It spotlights the performance, undervalued in music history: the 'extreme occasion', as Edward Said described it.[7] And also the performer, an individual pursuing personal fulfilment of one sort or another, but also a participant in the larger practice, with unspoken and unwritten obligations and responsibilities. As a very particular exemplification of the burgeoning field of performance studies today, virtuosity will be addressed in chapter 3, in relation to the *Grandes Etudes*. I recognise that the concept of virtuosity has no single congealed meaning, and that its manifestations have not remained invariant through music history; even its definitions, to say nothing of its connotations, have been subject to transformation. And I further recognise that the term should not be confined to music history. If the early nineteenth century was in some special sense an age of virtuosity, it embraced a broad spectrum of skill-based activities, encompassing formal culture, competitive games, culinary arts, public spectacles and even, as Paul Metzner suggests, criminal detection.[8] And if Paris was in some special sense the 'capital' of virtuosity in the early nineteenth century, it was no doubt due to a rather specific set of socio-political circumstances that enabled the celebration of what has been aptly described as 'public man'.[9]

I want to argue that as virtuosity meshed with a Romantic aesthetic, it generated a dialectical relationship with a strengthening sense of the autonomous musical work, involving taste and ideology as well as form and closure. Already in the late eighteenth century keyboard virtuosity had acquired those pejorative connotations of excess, artifice and kitsch that were associated with the virtuosity of the opera house. The language of contemporary criticism is revealing here. It suggests that the extremes of display and sentiment through which executants established their reputations with a larger public were considered if not morally suspect, then at least a violation of taste, itself an elusive quality, but one that often seemed to hinge on the status of individuality. Highly valued when kept within certain boundaries, individuality courted censure when it exceeded them, just as it courted popularity. And often it was a fetishism of the (mechanical) instrument that lay at the roots of both the censure and the popularity, with a consequent sense that the performance exceeded the work. Two subtexts of virtuosity are already suggested here: a surrender to mechanism, and the stigma of the gratuitous. They will be explored in chapter 3, as will a third subtext, the occlusion of reference. But for now we may note, more straightforwardly, the historical sequence described by Dahlhaus, in which the virtuosity of the first half of the nineteenth

---

[7] Edward W. Said, *Musical Elaborations* (London, 1991).
[8] Paul Metzner, *Crescendo of the Virtuoso* (Berkeley, Los Angeles and London, 1998).
[9] Richard Sennett, *The Fall of Public Man* (Cambridge, 1977).

century is presumed to have made room for the affirmation of work character that typified its second half.[10] Virtuosity, in short, gave way to interpretation. We may note, too, Lydia Goehr's similar, if more nuanced, observation of a shift in balance between two competing principles at work in the performance traditions of Western art music as a whole. She characterises them as 'the perfect performance of music' and 'the perfect musical performance', and together they form useful reference points for a study of early nineteenth-century virtuosity.[11] One might go a stage further, and suggest that there are covert values lurking in these categories, bearing on the canonising of some composers and the marginalisation of others.

The significance of recomposition. Arrangement, transcription and recomposition all raise basic questions about compositional process within nineteenth-century pianism. Before Liszt recomposed his own music, he transcribed and 'paraphrased' that of others. In a series of remarkable, and often under-valued, transcriptions or arrangements of everything from Berlioz and Beethoven symphonies to Schubert songs and Donizetti operas, he steered a dangerous and exhilarating path between commentary and tribute. It may be that the line separating categories such as arrangement, transcription and recomposition needs to be looked at in rather broader terms than the legalistic definitions of an analytical aesthetics,[12] and that a more flexible view of roles and motivations would not find an abundance of clear water between them, to borrow a party-political metaphor. In any event, there are issues that arise equally from all of them. One concerns the intersection between age-old processes of compositional borrowing, including self-borrowing, and a Romantic ideology that privileged the singular and the inimitable. Bach was certainly an important exemplary model for the nineteenth century in this respect, not only licensing arrangement and recomposition for an age of individuality, but providing a model for how any apparent incompatibility might be overcome; as Lawrence Dreyfus has potently demonstrated, Bach wrested from his pre-existent materials statements that were not just unique, but were registered 'against the grain' of the model.[13] It is in any case reasonable to ask just where a line can be drawn between composition and recomposition, given that new creative thoughts usually amount to a restructuring of existing figures and systems. The question will be addressed in chapter 4 by way of a sideways glance at etudes by Chopin.

A further issue concerns the relationship between Idea and Form, and specifically if we can reasonably speak of an idea and its several forms. Here we might argue that, despite the difficulty in reconciling recomposition and the Romantic ideology, Liszt's cyclical returns to a common starting-point, by no means unique to the works studied here, belonged to a familiar enough Romantic trope, one in which cyclical return was a measure of difference rather than similarity.[14] That trope, as common in literature as in music, allowed that

---

[10] Carl Dahlhaus, *Nineteenth-Century Music*, trans. J. B. Robinson (Berkeley and Los Angeles, 1989).

[11] Lydia Goehr, 'The Perfect Performance of Music and the Perfect Musical Performance', *new formations*, 27 (Winter 1995–6), pp. 1–22.

[12] For an example of the analytical approach, see Stephen Davies, 'Transcription, Authenticity and Performance', *British Journal of Aesthetics*, 28 (1988), pp. 216–27.

[13] Lawrence Dreyfus, *Bach and the Patterns of Invention* (Cambridge MA, 1996), especially chapter 2.

[14] See Rainer Nägele, *Echoes of Translation: Reading between Texts* (Baltimore and London, 1997), pp. 5–6.

an almost neo-Platonic authorial idea – privileged, inaccessible and embodying a central purpose and intention – might be multiply and imperfectly represented in the world of forms, including sounding forms. Compositional reworking invites an examination of the 'idea', of which (one may hazard) a performance, no less than a recomposition, might be a version. Despite Schoenberg's attempts at elucidation, the musical 'idea' remains a slippery formulation, and one that is often difficult to separate from the piece *in toto*. Nonetheless, I will try to make some sense of it in chapter 4, invoking Liszt's commentaries as well as Schoenberg's. However we understand the idea and its forms, it seems clear that mechanisms of translation are central to this topic. We are encouraged to reflect on what is said and meant (the idea) as against the mode of saying and meaning (the presentation). Indeed where music is concerned, we are invited specifically to consider just what can constitute idea and object within a temporal, performer-dependent and symbolic art. There is of course a qualitative distinction in this respect between the recompositions of 1837 and the revisions of 1851 which resulted in the *Transcendentals*. These revisions will be the subject of chapter 5, which will also examine formal and tonal processes in this, the final, version of the etudes.

Music and the poetic. In 1851, Liszt added poetic titles to ten of the etudes, and at around the same time he turned one of them into a symphonic poem. These decisions need to be considered in light of his understanding of the category 'poetic', which considerably expands the familiar early nineteenth-century usage. Not only does the poetic signal music's putative expressive powers; it places the status and dignity of music on the critical agenda. In chapter 6, which deals exclusively with the *Transcendentals*, Liszt's understanding of the poetic will be examined in tandem with the idea of absolute music. Their rival claims (synthesised in Wagner and also in Liszt) echoed a central debate within the philosophical aesthetics of the early nineteenth century, and it can be argued that the all-important polemic of the 1850s, in which Liszt was heavily implicated, partly recycled that debate, albeit now addressing a rather different agenda (essentially about historicism and the constitution of the new). In light of this, it is tempting to invoke ontological questions associated with programme music, especially as Liszt went on to compose a symphonic poem based on the fourth etude. It is easy to demonstrate, of course, that his choice of titles for the *Transcendentals* (invoking Hugo, the medieval-gothic romance, the cult of nature, the dream-world of the artist) was fairly arbitrary, and then to conclude that their essential significance lies in the material and formal rather than the poetic domain. Yet, however randomly chosen, the title remains part of the piece. At the very least, it influences our listening strategies. Beyond that, it effectively supports and crystallises any existing tendencies of the music to exemplify a topic, genre or affective meaning, and for that reason it encourages excursions into the semiotics of music. Again we cut across the boundaries of the works, opening up their meanings through shared expressive codes. Again we call into question the singular nature of authorship. And again we are obliged to ask how this kind of poetic agenda has fared within the Western tradition.

The musical work. As these topics are introduced successively, they bring into increasingly sharp focus not just questions of authorship, but also of work character. Here my concern is with the work-concept in nineteenth-century music, by which I (and others) mean the assumption that a musical culture is manifest first and foremost in, and is indeed regulated by, self-contained musical works. This topic has been much debated,[15] and it will bear somewhat on the argument of chapter 7, which looks at multiple versions of *Mazeppa*. Since these versions take us from 1826 to 1874, they naturally raise again the issue of authorship, and in particular the extent to which an authorial voice can formulate and sustain its identity through contextually and temporally separated utterances. They also invite us to reflect on the tension – even the opposition – between a gradually strengthening sense of the work as an object of contemplation, independent of contexts, and a performance- and genre-orientated musical culture, to which the work-concept posed something of a threat. My five topics might be regarded in one sense as progressively mediating this opposition, which arguably boils down to a developing opposition between the musical performance and the musical work. At the same time it seems fairly clear that the strengthening of the work-concept was in part a political development, allied not only to the development of a middle-class culture but more specifically to German nationalism and its cultural triumph. The legacy of this remains with us today, and inevitably colours any attempt we make to evaluate Liszt's achievement. I will address his reputation in chapter 7, and I will ask specifically if in the face of so many contingencies there is any room left for an aesthetic judgement of his music. This is tantamount to asking if the aesthetic has standing in our modern world.

---

[15] For a rehearsal of the arguments surrounding the work-concept, see the chapters by Lydia Goehr and Reinhard Strohm in Michael Talbot (ed.), *The Musical Work: Reality or Invention?* (Liverpool, 2000).

Chapter One

—

Ecology by numbers

3 TIMES 12 ETUDES

In 1827, when Liszt was sixteen years old, a volume of twelve exercises, almost certainly composed in the early months of the previous year, was published by Boisselot in Marseilles. Its full title was *Etude pour le piano en quarante-huit exercices dans tous les tons majeurs et mineurs*, Op. 6, and it was therefore intended as the first of four volumes. The other three were not composed, though it has been suggested that a recently uncovered piece in F♯ major may have been destined for No. 13.[1] The work was issued simultaneously by Dufaut et Dubois in Paris, where Liszt and his father had been based since December 1823, shortly after his course of lessons with Czerny came to an end.[2] Liszt's (or Boisselot's) use of 'etude' as a collective term for a group of exercises has attracted attention in the Liszt commentaries. In fact it was a common enough practice in the early history of the genre, though already somewhat outmoded in 1827.[3] By 1839, when the work was reissued by Hofmeister in Leipzig, the usage had completely died out, and its demise is reflected in the double plural of the German publisher's confused and confusing title, *Etudes . . . en douze exercices*, Op. 1.[4] In the preface to his edition of the work, Busoni pointed out that this opus number indicated that the *Etude* was the first work of Liszt to have been published in Germany.[5] The title page of the Hofmeister edition has a rather curious vignette depicting a child in a cradle, together with the explanatory, and apologetic, note: 'Travail de la Jeunesse'. It was published without permission, a form of 'piracy' that was common enough in the nineteenth

---

[1] See the worklist compiled by Rena Charnin Mueller and Mária Eckhardt for the Liszt entry in Stanley Sadie and John Tyrrell (eds.), *The New Grove Dictionary of Music and Musicians*, 2nd edn (London, 2001), vol. 14, pp. 785–872.

[2] Intriguingly, Charles Salaman remembered an amended version of the sixth exercise; see Adrian Williams, *Portrait of Liszt by Himself and his Contemporaries* (Oxford, 1990), p. 31.

[3] See Peter Felix Ganz, 'The Development of the Etude for Pianoforte', diss., Northwestern University (1960), p. 298. Ganz's dissertation is still an invaluable source of information on the early history of the genre.

[4] Lina Ramann gives the erroneous date 1835 for the reissue, and this date has been followed by several later commentators. *Franz Liszt als Künstler und Mensch*, vol. 1 (Leipzig, 1880), p. 87.

[5] Ferruccio Busoni, *The Essence of Music*, trans. Rosamund Ley (London, 1957), p. 157. For a discussion of the rival claims to the designation Op. 1, see Georg Schütz, 'Form, Satz- und Klaviertechnik in den drei Fassungen der *Grossen Etüden* von Franz Liszt', in Zsoltán Gárdonyi and Siegfried Mauser (eds.), *Virtuosität und Avantgarde: Untersuchungen zum Klavierwerk Franz Liszts* (Mainz, 1988), p. 71.

century,[6] and this contributed to a distinct cooling in the relationship between Liszt and the publisher. The Complete Editions give the work as *Etude en douze exercices*, and this is its usual title today.[7]

Liszt himself remarked that he composed these exercises in his thirteenth year (1824), and this was taken by Alan Walker as evidence that he may have begun working on them in that year.[8] We should be less trusting of the composer's memory, given that on another occasion he claimed to have composed them in Marseilles in 1827. It seems likely that the place of publication was more reliably remembered than the date, especially as the work was published in Marseilles. The most plausible date of composition, then, lies between the two dates given by Liszt, in early 1826, when he stayed in Marseilles for a short period, following a concert tour of southern France. This is the date assigned it by most Lisztians, from Peter Raabe onwards,[9] and it is supported, too, by the dedication on the French editions. This was to Lydie Garella, a young pianist who lived in Marseilles, with whom Liszt apparently played duets during his stay there. Much later, in August 1877, he told his biographer Lina Ramann that he had had an adolescent crush on the girl and that the dedication was intended as an act of homage to the object of this early, uncharacteristically innocent, love.[10]

The concerts in southern France were just part of an extensive programme of tours organised for Liszt by his father from early 1824 through to 1828, including several visits to England, as well as to Switzerland and other parts of the French provinces. For a variety of reasons – the death of his father, an unhappy love affair, and no doubt the inevitable ageing of the *petit prodige* – Liszt withdrew from the public platform from around the middle of 1828, supporting his mother, who had by then moved to Paris, largely through teaching. It seems he suffered a kind of depression at this time (oddly enough, just as Chopin was enduring a similar malaise out there in Warsaw), and it was by no means a fruitful period compositionally. It was shortly after this, in the immediate aftermath of the 1830 July Revolution, which inspired his own unfinished 'Revolutionary Symphony', forerunner of *Héroïde funèbre*, that he engaged with the teachings of the Saint-Simonians and Felicité de Lamennais, and began to develop notions of the social and moral obligations of art and the artist that remained with him in one form or another throughout his life. And it was also in the early 1830s that he heard Paganini and began to associate with some of the leading artists and writers domiciled in Paris, as well as with composers such as Berlioz and Chopin. These events 'roused Liszt from his lethargy and morbid brooding', as Frederick Niecks

---

[6] A detailed exposition of publishing practices in the nineteenth century, including the problems associated with variable copyright laws in Europe, can be found in Jeffrey Kallberg, 'Chopin in the Market-Place', *Notes*, 39, 3 and 4 (March–June 1983), pp. 535–69 and 795–824.

[7] By the complete editions, I mean *Franz Liszt: Musikalische Werke*, edited by Busoni, Raabe, Wolfrum and others, and *Franz Liszt: Neue Ausgabe sämtlicher Werke*, where the etudes were edited by Zsoltán Gárdonyi and István Szélenyi.

[8] *Letters of Franz Liszt*, coll. and ed. La Mara, trans. Constance Bache, 2 vols. (London, 1894), vol. 1, p. 231; Alan Walker, *Franz Liszt: The Virtuoso Years 1811–1847* (London, 1983), p. 118.

[9] Peter Raabe, *Liszts Schaffen* (Tutzing, 1968; orig. edn, 1931), p. 242.

[10] Ramann, *Franz Liszt als Künstler und Mensch*, vol. 1, p. 93. See Mária Eckhardt, 'Liszt à Marseille', in *Studia Musicologica Academiae Scientarum Hungaricae*, 24 (1982), pp. 163–97, for an account of the visit to Marseilles, casting doubt on Ramann's claims of a visit in 1825 and discussing reviews of the concerts in 1826.

put it.[11] In April 1832, his well-known response to Paganini contributed to a new burst of creativity, and a resumption (in 1833) of his career as a professional pianist. He also met Marie d'Agoult towards the end of 1832, and their relationship developed in intensity through to the early summer of 1835, at which point she left her husband. In June 1835 the lovers effectively eloped to Geneva, where they remained for well over a year.

Immediately before departing for Geneva, Liszt wrote to Ferdinand Hiller, outlining some of the major projects planned for the immediate future. It is clear from this letter that he was already thinking about a set of *Grandes Etudes* at that time, though there is no indication of their form or character.[12] On the other hand, in a letter to his mother, written in March 1836 from Geneva, he requested 'a copy of my published *Etudes* and, still better, ... the *manuscript* of the 12 *Etudes*,[13] and this suggests that the basic conception of the work – a recomposition of the early exercises – was already in his mind. It is by no means certain, however, that he put anything on paper then, though it is very likely that he played through the early exercises and conceived at least some of the recompositions *in intellectu*. In any event the real work was undertaken in the autumn months of 1837, while he and Marie d'Agoult were staying in northern Italy, after a year based at the Hôtel de France in Paris. The outcome was a set of twelve *Grandes Etudes* based loosely on the early exercises, and completed, according to Marie, in late October.[14] In the new etudes the clean, classical cut of the originals was replaced by a fierce, hugely challenging virtuosity, stretching even the most developed technique of the day (or any day) to its limits. All the same, the links with the early set are clearly perceptible, and the tonal scheme remains the same (pairings of tonal relatives: C major-A minor, F major-D minor, and so on, ending with B♭ minor). The one anomaly is that the original No. 7 was transposed from E♭ to D♭ and was reworked as No. 11, while a new etude in E♭ major replaced it as No. 7. Even the newly composed etude retained a link with the youthful Liszt, however, in that it reworked the introduction of his *Impromptu brillant sur des thèmes de Rossini et Spontini*, Op. 3 (one of the early pieces sent to Geneva by his mother).

There is an extant autograph Stichvorlage for the first of these new etudes, with the title *Préludes* [sic] given in Liszt's hand.[15] Interestingly this was also the title used by Marie d'Agoult in her letter of 23 October announcing the completion of the work. This autograph was destined for the Haslinger edition, though it differs from the published form in several minor respects. There is a further autograph of the newly composed No. 7, and the page numbering of this (fols. 55–66) suggests that it was at some point detached from the complete

[11] Frederick Niecks, *Programme Music in the Last Four Centuries: A Contribution to the History of Musical Expression* (London and New York, [1907]), p. 273.

[12] This letter, published as part of a collection of 'unknown' letters edited by Gerhard Tischler, is quoted by Alan Walker in *Franz Liszt: The Virtuoso Years*, p. 219.

[13] See Adrian Williams (ed.), *Franz Liszt: Selected Letters* (Oxford, 1998), p. 51.

[14] Many commentators, including Raabe, opt for 1838 as the date of completion. However, Marie's letter of October 1837 celebrates the fact that 'Franz has just finished his twelve preludes [sic]'. Moreover in January 1838, Liszt himself wrote to Adolphe Pictet from Milan: 'With the 12 *Etudes* – monsters – and a small volume entitled *Impressions et Poésies* which I have just finished, I am not displeased'. See Williams (ed.), *Selected Letters*, p. 80.

[15] This is held by the National Széchényi Library, Budapest (Ms. Mus. 24). For a description, see Mária Eckhardt, *Liszt's Music Manuscripts in the National Széchényi Library* (Budapest, 1968), pp. 96–9.

set. It seems plausible that this too was part of the Haslinger Stichvorlage, though there are some grounds for uncertainty.[16] The set was published 'simultaneously' by Schlesinger (Paris) and Haslinger (Vienna) in 1839, with the designation *24 Grandes Etudes*, though as before the promise of more to come remained unfulfilled. Indeed it is hard to see what Liszt could have had in mind for the remaining twelve etudes, given that the existing pieces are recompositions of the twelve youthful exercises. It should be added that for the fourth etude there are important textual differences between the Schlesinger and Haslinger editions, and there is also a separate 'corrected' version of pages 23 and 24 of the Haslinger edition of this piece.[17] The cycle also appeared with Ricordi (Milan) and with Mori and Lavener (London). In 1840, shortly after the *Grandes Etudes* were published, Liszt drafted yet another version of the fourth of them, involving a short introduction and a new ending. On this occasion he gave it the poetic title *Mazeppa*, after Victor Hugo, though plans to publish it as a separate piece at this time came to nothing.

Several of the *Grandes Etudes* were performed in the course of the eleven Vienna concerts given by Liszt in April 1838 on behalf of the flood victims in Pest. He himself remarked that it was the success of these concerts that decided him on a career as a virtuoso pianist. Certainly it was from that point that his astonishing series of concert tours really began in earnest, and they lasted for the better part of a decade, during which time he was widely acknowledged as the pre-eminent virtuoso pianist in the world. In the course of that decade of endless travelling, he spent a two-month period of residence in Weimar (in early 1844), and he returned there briefly in 1846. Already during the first of those visits he began to formulate plans for the regeneration of Weimar's once glorious cultural life, and this was the path he chose to follow when the touring was finally abandoned following a concert in Elisavetgrad in September 1847. Much of the impetus for Liszt's decision to withdraw from the public platform no doubt came from his developing relationship with Princess Carolyn von Sayn-Wittgenstein, whom he had met during his concerts in Kiev in February of that year, and at whose estate in Woronince he stayed in March and again in October. It was during this year, with things Ukrainian very much on his mind, that he finally published the version of *Mazeppa* drafted in 1840. It was issued as a separate piece by Schlesinger, with a dedication to Hugo, and shortly after by Haslinger in Vienna.

In June 1848 Liszt moved to Weimar with Carolyne, taking on the post of Court Kapellmeister, and Weimar was to be at the centre of his life through to 1860. Shortly after his arrival he embarked on extensive revisions of several of his earlier compositions, including the *Paganini Etudes*, the *Album d'un Voyageur* and the *Grandes Etudes* (including the 1840 version of *Mazeppa*). The *Grandes Etudes* occupied him during the early months of 1851. Some of his revisions to the earlier versions of the etudes are of a fairly minor nature, and may simply have registered on paper his performing practice of several years. But others were much more significant, affecting the formal design and substance of the music. In any event all twelve etudes were reworked on paper at this time. Liszt used the Haslinger edition of the *Grandes Etudes* as the basis for the Stichvorlage he sent to Breitkopf & Härtel,[18] with cancellations

---

[16] *Ibid.*, pp. 99–100.

[17] These changes concern the later stages of the fourth strophe, and they will be discussed briefly in chapter 7.

[18] This is located in the Weimar archive (D-WRgs J 23).

and paste-overs effecting the revisions in most cases. Following the lead of *Mazeppa*, a further nine etudes were given poetic titles in this new version, leaving only two (Nos. 2 and 10) without titles. The entire set was published by Breitkopf & Härtel the following year (1852) as *Etudes d'exécution transcendante*, and Liszt was careful to point out that this was the 'seule edition authentique revue par l'auteur'. He even secured the rights to Haslinger's plates for the 1839 version.[19]

With the publication of the *Transcendentals*, Liszt effectively produced a second version of the new No. 7 (*Eroica*), a fourth version of No. 4 (*Mazeppa*) and a third version of a further ten etudes (the original No. 11, it will be remembered, was not reworked in 1837). The story of the fourth etude does not, however, finish there. The final page of the Stichvorlage for the *Transcendentals* was signed and dated by the composer 'Eilsen 2 avril 1851'. But by then Liszt had already begun yet another version of *Mazeppa*, this time taking us suggestively beyond the boundaries of the piano medium. One of the draftbooks in Weimar – the so-called 'Mazeppa' draftbook (N2) – begins with a thirty-three page orchestration draft of the well-known symphonic poem, including the final march, which is not present in any of the piano versions.[20] Liszt dated the completion of this draft precisely, writing 'Eilsen 1re Semanie [sic] de 1851'. The symphonic poem was then orchestrated and revised, and was given its first performance on 16 April 1854 at the Hoftheater, Weimar. Liszt arranged it for two pianos in February the following year (published 1857), and the full score of the final form was also published in 1857. Much later (1874) the composer also made an arrangement for four hands (published 1875). This four-hand version represented Liszt's final say about material to which he had returned intermittently over the previous fifty years.

Table 1.1 sets out the chronology of successive versions of the etudes and of the symphonic poem (s.p.). Dates are of composition rather than publication (they mark the completion of the work; the dating of first thoughts will be discussed in the text).

3 COMPOSERS

The dedication on the *Transcendentals* is significant. It reads: 'A Charles Czerny en temoignage de reconnaissance et de respecteuse amitié/son élève F. Liszt'. Liszt's tribute to his first and principal teacher made explicit the link between the *Transcendentals* and those youthful exercises, composed in the shadow of Czerny's teaching (1822–3) and partly inspired by it. Indeed it is rather striking that Liszt should have written 'son élève' at a time when he was himself widely regarded as one of the great musicians of the age, while his teacher's reputation had already faded. In earlier days, Liszt's father had used Czerny's name to promote his son's youthful concerts.[21] But by the 1850s it was rather Liszt who could promote Czerny. Indeed he had never been reluctant to do so. He performed

[19] La Mara (ed.), *Letters of Franz Liszt*, vol. 1, pp. 230–1.
[20] The major study of Liszt's sketchbooks (focusing on N5) is Rena Charnin Mueller, 'Liszt's "Tasso" Sketchbook: Studies in Sources and Chronology', diss., New York University (1986).
[21] Walker, *The Virtuoso Years*, p. 91.

Table 1.1 *The 'Transcendental Studies' and* Mazeppa: *chronological table*

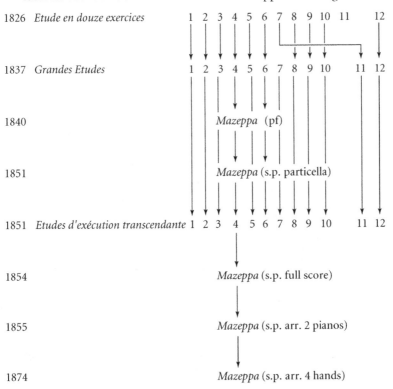

1826 *Etude en douze exercices* 1 2 3 4 5 6 7 8 9 10 11 12

1837 *Grandes Etudes* 1 2 3 4 5 6 7 8 9 10 11 12

1840 *Mazeppa* (pf)

1851 *Mazeppa* (s.p. particella)

1851 *Etudes d'exécution transcendante* 1 2 3 4 5 6 7 8 9 10 11 12

1854 *Mazeppa* (s.p. full score)

1855 *Mazeppa* (s.p. arr. 2 pianos)

1874 *Mazeppa* (s.p. arr. 4 hands)

Czerny's music on his concert tours (mainly concert pieces, but also heavier works such as the Op. 7 Sonata), wrote to him in December 1828 to ask which of his compositions he thought would make 'the best effect in society',[22] and in August 1830 urged him to visit Paris, where 'you are so widely esteemed that without doubt you will be well satisfied with the reception you receive there'.[23] His most explicit tribute to Czerny is found in a letter to Dionys Pruckner, where he commented on his Beethoven playing, his openness to new developments in piano technique, and the quality of some of the earlier music, blaming Viennese social and publishing practices for the 'excessive productivity' that weakened his later music.[24] Michel Sogny has argued that 'creative admiration' was a central impulse underlying Liszt's work.[25] That thesis will be touched on later. What is certain is that Liszt never lost his admiration for Czerny, who disciplined and directed his prodigious youthful talent ('the talent with which nature had equipped him'[26]) through rigorous technical training.

---

[22] La Mara (ed.), *Letters of Franz Liszt*, vol. 1, p. 4.   [23] *Ibid.*, p. 6.

[24] Williams (ed.), *Selected Letters*, p. 401.

[25] Michel Sogny, *L'Admiration Créatrice chez Liszt* (Paris, 1975).

[26] Carl Czerny, *Erinnerungen aus meinem Leben*, ed. Walter Kolneder (Strassburg, 1968; orig. MS, 1842). My excerpts are from the English translation by Ernest Sanders: 'Recollections from my Life', *Musical Quarterly*, 42, 3 (July 1956), pp. 302–17; this quotation from p. 315.

The pedagogue and the prodigy. These labels could serve as literal descriptions of Czerny and Liszt in 1822–3, during the fourteen months of their closest association, and they met almost daily. But the labels resonate more widely. Both terms carry connotative values for an age of emergent Romanticism, and values that point in rather different directions. There was music as a craft to be learned, a discipline to be followed, a set of rules, conventions and practices to be handed down from master to pupil. And there was music as an embodiment of the mystery and magic of individual creative genius, the gift of God or of nature. These values may even have a bearing on the nature and status of virtuosity. On one reading virtuosity would be viewed as the ultimate reward for industry; on another reading it would be the most visible sign of genius. For, ironically enough, a Romantic aesthetic in music, so perfectly attuned to the notion of the prodigy, the Lisztian *Wunderkind*, came to fruition more-or-less in tandem with the growing standardisation and institutionalisation of pedagogical practices. This, after all, was the age of the conservatory, the tutor, the textbook, the classroom; the age, too, when pianist-composers (the *grands pédagogues*), virtually without exception, had their systems, their *Lehrbucher*, and their coteries of pupils; the age, in brief, of the etude and the exercise. And looming behind all of this – behind the conflicting values embodied in the pedagogue and the prodigy – lay a larger, bolder issue. It is to the early nineteenth century that we can trace the beginnings of a perceptible separation of a performance culture and a compositional culture.

Already during the 1830s Czerny the composer was characteristically ridiculed by many of the most representative of the Romantics. He was an 'inkwell', 'bankrupt of fantasy', a production line for etudes and exercises.[27] Liszt the pianist, on the other hand, was eulogised as the archetypal Romantic artist. He was exuberant, spontaneous, intuitive; opposed – or so it seemed – to the conventional, the predictable, even the rational. In the myth-making of the age, it was precisely these qualities, qualities which served the improvising performer almost as a matter of routine, that were elevated to the status of a compositional ideal. In the quest for Czerny's 'beautiful English garden', executed 'according to plan',[28] for a rational, coherent design, the improviser would have spared little thought for that most essential pre-condition of his craft, the spontaneous generation of 'new' musical thoughts. Yet it was just this process that was to be freighted with ideology in the age of Romanticism. An idealised reception of Mozart was partly instrumental in promoting one of the most enduring myths of the century – a near-equation of invention and inspiration, where the latter would appear 'sudden, complete, sublime', and largely untrammelled by the operations of reason. This image of the creative process rapidly took root (notwithstanding documentary evidence – composition sketches, for example – which tells a different story), and it played a major role in the construction of the prodigy. What was new in this was the significance attributed to prodigious talent, not the talent

[27] The 'inkwell' was apparently John Field's description; see H. Dessauer, *John Field: sein Leben und seine Werke* (Langensalza, 1912), p. 76. Schumann referred to the 'bankruptcy of fantasy'; see *Gesammelte Schriften über Musik und Musiker* (Leipzig, 1888), vol. 2, pp. 156–7.

[28] His description of an improvised Fantasy. See Carl Czerny, *A Systematic Introduction to Improvisation on the Pianoforte*, op. 200, trans. and ed. A. Mitchell (New York, 1983; orig. edn, 1829), p. 2.

itself.[29] The fusion of youthful skills and creativity with essentially Romantic concepts of inspiration and genius resulted in a product – almost an institution – that proved eminently marketable in the nineteenth century, and retains much of its spell today.

Czerny, too, had been a so-called 'prodigy', and had been given his own musical direction by Beethoven.[30] The symbolic potency of this succession was not lost on Liszt. Like Czerny, he viewed Beethoven as the pinnacle of creative achievement, and, again like Czerny, he was committed to the serious study and proper interpretation of his music.[31] The point needs stressing, since interpretation was by no means a central concern of the early nineteenth-century pianist-composer. Liszt and Czerny shared other enthusiasms. Both were responsive to the music of Bach and were instrumental in its promotion (Czerny was one of the first to edit and publish the *Wohltempiertes Klavier*, an edition still in use today).[32] Both regarded transcription and arrangement as central categories of musical thought, and here again Czerny proposed a decisive influence from Beethoven. And both were committed to technique and virtuosity. Liszt was happy to acknowledge that much of the technical foundation for his own musicianship had been laid by Czerny. As Czerny put it: 'Since I knew from numerous experiences that geniuses whose mental gifts are ahead of their physical strength tend to slight solid technique, it seemed necessary above all to use the first months to regulate and strengthen his mechanical dexterity....'[33] Czerny's 'solid technique' was in many ways a synopsis of early piano pedagogy, celebrating a 'finger school' whose harpsichord ancestry still glimmered through the multiple piano methods of the early nineteenth century, though it also took on board Beethoven's replacement of short-breathed staccato technique by a longer-phrased legato.[34] Undoubtedly Liszt's later technique and teaching methods represented a significant departure from Czerny's methods. Yet it is clear from accounts of his own early teaching, notably the lessons he gave to Valérie Boissier in 1832, that he rejected those methods only when they had been fully assimilated.[35] Moreover, like his teacher, he never lost faith in the virtues of practice, of endless work on technique, however different the goal.

The *Etude en douze exercices* testifies to the direct influence of Czerny on Liszt's compositional thought. Yet there was clearly a marked divergence of temperament and approach between teacher and pupil, just as there had been between Beethoven and Czerny. In his autobiographical sketch of 1842, Czerny expressed his disapproval of the exploitation of

---

[29] Research in educational psychology suggests that the idea of the prodigy has been overvalued in the past; see, for example, Michael Howe, *The Origins of Exceptional Abilities* (Oxford, 1990). Whatever the truth of that, the potency of the idea in the nineteenth century could scarcely be overestimated; see Peter Kivy, 'Child Mozart as an Aesthetic Symbol', in *The Fine Art of Repetition* (Cambridge, 1993), pp. 200–13.

[30] A useful account of Czerny's transformation of this Beethoven legacy is offered in George Barth, *The Pianist as Orator: Beethoven and the Transformation of Keyboard Style* (Ithaca and London, 1992).

[31] From 1816, Czerny gave or arranged weekly performances devoted exclusively to Beethoven at his home.

[32] Barth (*The Pianist as Orator*) points out that Czerny was a pioneer of the modernising tendency in nineteenth-century editing.

[33] 'Recollections from my Life', p. 315.

[34] Barth, *The Pianist as Orator*. It seems that, for all his reputation as a 'legato' pianist, Clementi had a finger technique that was not dissimilar to Couperin's, and that it was above all through Beethoven and Beethoven interpretation that modern legato playing was developed.

[35] Mine Augrste Boissier, *Liszt pédagogue: Leçons de piano données par Liszt à Mlle. Valérie Boissier em 1832* (Paris, 1927).

Liszt's youthful talent through premature concertising in the early 1820s.[36] A few more years in Vienna would not only have secured his technique, according to Czerny; it would have enabled him 'to fulfil in the field of composition all the high expectations that were then rightly cherished by everyone'. He referred to the loss of many years 'during which his [Liszt's] life and his art became misdirected'. In the years immediately following their early association, the two men were in touch only by letter. Then they met again in the spring of 1837, when Czerny visited Paris on one of his rare excursions from Vienna. He was clearly disconcerted by the radical change in Liszt's piano technique. 'I found his playing rather wild and confused in every respect, the enormous bravura notwithstanding'.[37] This comment neatly identifies the divide that had by then taken place between two fundamentally different approaches to piano technique and style. In a nutshell it was a divide between post-Classical and Romantic virtuosity. A suggestive comment in Liszt's earliest sketchbook, dating from the early 1830s, and almost certainly penned in 1831, is revealing of the underlying shift in impulse and motivation: next to the name 'Czerny', and some fragments of exercises, he wrote 'Celui qui n'a pas souffert/que fait-il?'[38]

It may have been that meeting with Czerny in 1837 that spurred Liszt to turn to the project he had announced in 1835, a set of *Grandes Etudes* which rework material from the *Etude en douze exercices*. He worked on this second version of the etudes in Italy towards the end of 1837 (hence the Ricordi edition), well before he visited Czerny in Vienna the following April. He had almost certainly played at least one of them in Italy without success, and he performed several of them during the Viennese tour.[39] Intriguingly, Czerny decided on this occasion that Liszt's genius had 'received a new impetus' and that his playing had taken on 'that brilliant and yet more limpid style of playing for which he has now become so famous throughout the world'.[40] It is tempting to ask just who had changed. Admittedly Czerny was now on home ground and may have felt more secure about his own standing, but the possibility that he may also have found some measure of accommodation with the new manner is supported by Liszt's comment in another context that 'he [Czerny] did not set himself up against some progress that had been made in technique'.[41] Moreover, when Czerny later sketched a history of performance styles, he identified six schools, of which the last, a 'new style' represented chiefly by Thalberg, Chopin and Liszt, 'may be called a mixture of and improvement on all those which preceded it'.[42]

---

[36] 'Recollections from my Life', p. 316.   [37] *Ibid.*

[38] This is located in the Library of Congress. Compare Liszt's remark in his book on the Hungarian gypsies: 'As soon as Pain makes her appearance in art . . . her influence upon the heart changes character'. *Des Bohémiens et de leur musique en Hongrie* (Leipzig, 1981). This extract from the English translation: *The Gypsy in Music*, trans. Edwin Evans, 2 vols. (London, [1926]), vol. 1, p. 102.

[39] Liszt referred to his performance of a 'prélude-étude' in La Scala in December 1837. See Franz Liszt, *An Artist's Journey*, trans. and annotated Charles Suttoni (Chicago and London, 1989; orig. letters, 1835–41), p. 89.

[40] 'Recollections from my Life', p. 316. For an interesting perspective on Liszt's changing approach to performance in the 1830s, see Katherine Kolb Reeve, 'Primal Scenes: Smithson, Pleyel, and Liszt in the Eyes of Berlioz', *19th-Century Music*, 18, 3 (1995), pp. 211–35.

[41] La Mara (ed.), *Letters of Franz Liszt*, vol. 1, p. 266.

[42] This is found in the fourth volume of the *Complete Theoretical and Practical Piano Forte School*, Op. 500, trans. J. H. Hamilton (London, 1839), where Czerny offers advice on the performance of 'new music'.

And perhaps most telling of all is his contribution to Liszt's *Hexaméron* variations, composed for Princess Belgiojoso probably during his visit to Paris. Here there is stylistic evidence that even as a composer Czerny was far from immune to the attractions of the 'new style'.

This was not the first occasion on which Czerny adopted a modern idiom (his titles not infrequently include the gloss 'in the modern style', though by 'modern' here he often meant simply 'bravura'). But in general he reserved it for more serious works, notably the sonatas, and especially the tenth sonata, Op. 268 (the *Grande sonate d'étude*), whose elaborately decorated slow movement was probably his closest point of stylistic contact with the younger generation.[43] In the context of his output as a whole, such moments are relatively rare. The bulk of his music remains firmly rooted in the idiom of a post-Classical 'brilliant style', to use his own label.[44] Adolph Kullak remarked that his *Pianoforte School* 'closed an era'.[45] This was a reference to Czerny the pedagogue, but it might equally be applied to Czerny the composer, and especially to his contributions to the etude, the genre where these two roles ideally meet. As everyone knows, Czerny wrote etudes in generous quantities. He used them to develop technical prowess, of course, but also to codify and systematise the numerous techniques associated with an instrument whose idiomatic potential was still under exploration. The titles of his etudes also hint at an element of stylistic classification, based principally on categories labelled 'salon', 'brilliant' and 'characteristic'. This taxonomy was reinforced by the categories used in his *Pianoforte School*, and it can speak of real stylistic and aesthetic distinctions, extending well beyond Czerny, and well beyond the etude. Yet for Czerny's own etudes the distinctions remain at best notional. Even those described as 'characteristic' smack of the post-Classical past rather than the Romantic present, of the classroom rather than the salon or concert hall. Seldom, if ever, do they enter the orbit of the new pianism, where they might have rubbed shoulders with the later etudes of his pupil Liszt. Or with those of Chopin.

Liszt's *Grandes Etudes* were dedicated to Czerny in the Schlesinger and Haslinger editions. However the Ricordi edition registered an intriguing change. Here the dedication was shared between Czerny for the first volume (Nos. 1–7) and Chopin for the second (Nos. 8–12). Of course we cannot be entirely certain that this change was instigated by Liszt, but there could have been little reason for the publisher to alter the dedication, and little probability that he would have done so without consulting the composer. However the new dedication came about, it brought into the frame a composer whose career until that point had paralleled Liszt's in interesting ways. It is possible that the two men originally met through Ferdinand Paër,[46] who introduced Chopin to many of Paris's leading musicians when the young composer first arrived there in the autumn of 1830. In any event they were soon part of the same circle of artists and musicians, meeting at restaurants, at one or other of their apartments,

---

[43] Contemporary critics described the sonatas, especially their slow movements, as 'romantic' in character. See Randall Keith Streets, 'The Piano Sonatas of Carl Czerny', diss., University of Maryland (1987) for relevant documentation.
[44] In volume 3 of the *Pianoforte School*, Op. 500.
[45] Adolph Kullak, *The Aesthetics of Pianoforte-Playing* (New York, 1972; based on the 3rd edn, 1889), p. 76.
[46] Serge Gut, *Franz Liszt* (Paris, 1989), p. 250.

or at concerts. The musicians in the circle regularly participated at each other's 'benefits', and there are several documented (as well as numerous fabled) concerts involving both Liszt and Chopin as pianists. The two men may have been temperamental opposites, and to some extent professional rivals, but each had great respect for the other's very different talents, at least in the early days. Chopin exerted a special fascination for Liszt, based less on his prowess as a thinker than on his exceptional musical gifts, allied to the inevitable attractions that attend a personality wrapped in secrecy. As a pianist, his technique had been largely self-acquired, eschewing contemporary orthodoxies, and this translated to a pronounced individuality of playing, and to a no less singular teaching style, hostile above all to 'mindless' mechanical exercises. Anything further from Czerny's approach would be difficult to imagine, and it is likely that Liszt took careful note.

By 1837, when Czerny visited Paris, Chopin was still involved, albeit reluctantly, with the Liszt circle at the Hôtel de France (he had been introduced to George Sand through Liszt and Marie d'Agoult a few months earlier). It is not certain that he and Czerny renewed their earlier brief acquaintance during these months,[47] but it was at least the only time when all three composers almost certainly found themselves in the same place at the same time. Moreover, like Czerny, Chopin contributed a variation to *Hexaméron* in the spring (albeit belatedly), adding another strand to that most remarkable of pianistic documents, itself immensely revealing of collective styles and personal rivalries. It is worth recording too that later in the same year Chopin prepared his Op. 25 etudes for the publisher, that he dedicated them to Liszt's mistress Marie d'Agoult, and that Liszt himself performed several of them in April 1837, prior to publication. Could this have been a further impetus for him to turn again to his own etudes? Already by then he had established a special and recognised affinity with Chopin's etudes. Five years earlier (1832) Op. 10 had been dedicated to him and had made a decisive impression. Liszt had composed nothing of remotely comparable stature at that time, and his new-found creativity in the early 1830s certainly owed something to his contact with Chopin. Such was his feeling for Op. 10 that his readings gained even Chopin's approval, always given sparingly: 'Liszt is playing my studies . . . . I wish I could rob him of the way to play my own studies.'[48] However we interpret the Chopin connection, and more will be said on this in due course, one certainty is that Liszt's admiration for Chopin's etudes perfectly complemented his admiration for Czerny's. He gained a stimulus of quite another kind – poetic rather than technical – from the music of the Polish composer, even if it remained no more than a catalyst to his own, emphatically singular, expressive world.

It is a commonplace of music history that it was through Chopin and Liszt, albeit in very different ways, that the piano found its idiomatic voice. This is not to denigrate earlier or coeval approaches to the instrument (Clementi, Cramer and Beethoven in particular

---

[47] They met in Vienna when Chopin spent eight months there immediately prior to settling in Paris. 'There is more feeling in Czerny himself than in all his compositions' was Chopin's verdict. See *Collected Correspondence of Fryderyk Chopin*, collected and annotated B. S. Sydow, trans. and ed. Arthur Hedley (London, Melbourne and Toronto, 1962), p. 27.

[48] *Ibid.*, p. 117.

transformed the medium through their insistence on a basic legato touch[49]), but simply to argue that Chopin and Liszt crystallised the essential relation between medium and style that so clearly set the Romantic piano apart from Classical and post-Classical antecedents. For both composers the musical idea was inseparably welded to the instrument, determined in every particular by its potentialities and its limitations. Of course a study of Romantic pianism might refer to many names, styles and genres. But, as Walter Benjamin suggested, antithetical exemplary models can often reveal more about a topic than any amount of subject survey.[50] Adorno, following Benjamin, adopted just this approach when he set out to reveal the true nature of Modernism in music through a near-exclusive focus on Schoenberg and Stravinsky rather than an exhaustive survey of individual Modernists.[51] There were undoubtedly casualties of Adorno's approach (not least due to a subtle denigration or marginalisation of composers and materials that failed to conform to canonised procedures[52]), but it did at least mark out provisional boundaries, defining an arena within which later negotiation could take place. And in a rather similar way, I suggest that Chopin and Liszt might serve as plausible exemplary models for a study of the Romantic piano, that the forcefield between them might reveal with greater clarity than any survey of composers and genres what we may call the 'historical moment' of the piano. The polarities between them (of temperament, technique, style and aesthetic) will be explored in a little more detail in chapter 4; for now the comparison will remain at a level of greater generality.

The personalities of the two men could scarcely have been more sharply contrasted: the one extraverted and ostentatious, flaunting convention at every turn, embracing (however insecurely) the most radical intellectual, social and political agendas of the day; the other private and aloof, a stickler for proprieties and innately conservative in all social and political matters. Likewise their musical personalities: the one displaying, the other concealing. Yet for all the contrast, the starting-point was much the same, a world of post-Classical concert music firmly centred on the piano, and designed principally for performance in benefit concerts and salons. This was music designed to be popular, and happy to accept its commodity status. Its basic ingredients were a bravura right-hand figuration that took its impetus from the light-actioned Viennese and German pianos of the late eighteenth century and a melodic idiom, associated in its early stages with English and French instruments, that was rooted either in Italian opera, in folk music or in popular genres such as marches (including funeral marches), dance pieces, pastorales or barcarolles. It was the special achievement of Chopin and Liszt to elevate this popular idiom to a plane where it need concede nothing in stature to more prestigious private and epic musics, chamber and symphonic. But the key point is that they did this in very different ways. For Chopin, it was achieved through a unique blend

---

[49] Beethoven, according to Czerny, felt that the staccato manner was inappropriate to the nature of the piano. See Barth, *The Pianist as Orator*, pp. 42–3. See also note 34.

[50] Walter Benjamin, *Ursprung des deutschen Trauerspiels*, in *Schriften*, vol. I, ed. T. W. Adorno (Frankfurt, 1955), p. 163.

[51] T. W. Adorno, *Philosophy of Modern Music*, trans. Anne G. Mitchell and Wesley V. Bloomster (London, 1973; orig. edn, 1948), p. 3.

[52] By 'canonised procedures', I have in mind especially octatonic and set theory, which have to some extent shaped the analytical agenda for early twentieth-century repertories.

of the Classical and the post-Classical. His music remained firmly anchored in the brilliant style, but the components of the style were transformed through the agencies of Bach and Mozart. Not only did they influence him in precise technical ways; they represented the perfect embodiment of 'taste', Chopin's guiding aesthetic principle.[53] Throughout his life he adhered to an essentially Classical view of the musical work, rooted in the immanent, the real, even the rule-bound. At the same time he responded in his own, muted way to the spirit of an emergent Romanticism, rejecting an Idealist view of the musical work, but admitting compositional criteria derived unmistakably from Idealist values, and I include here notions of originality, subjectivity and nationality.

Liszt, on the other hand, elevated and transformed the ingredients of popular pianism by infusing them totally with a Romantic ideology. Either he adapted them to the demands of a 'transcendental' virtuosity, whose extravagant technical challenges were far removed in scope and nature from the more contained, nuanced technique favoured by Chopin; or he conflated them with a poetic idea, investing them with greater ambition by associating them with high-prestige literary or philosophical ideas. The category 'poetic' will be explored in a later chapter, but we should note here that it extended well beyond any specific literary or musical genre to embrace the concrete (epic) expression of that lofty Idealism to which the Romantics aspired, the attempt to elevate art to a powerful metaphysical status. In this sense it became part of Liszt's renovative programme for an instrumental music that might itself become the highest form of poetry through its association with a poetic idea. For Liszt, then, the piano was a channel; for Chopin a filter. And in narrowly technical terms, the contrast is no less explicit. Where Chopin separated out the bravura figuration and popular melody of the brilliant style in formal juxtaposition, allowing the first to become dense with information and the second to take on an ornamental character (where ornamentation grows from, and is integral to, melody), Liszt drew the two together in superimposition. Typically his figuration took on an explicitly decorative function, either colouring melody, as in those delicate background washes of sonority, or dissolving it, as in those cadenzas that periodically interrupt the flow. Meanwhile the melody itself, 'sweetening' or 'martialing' its post-Classical models, eschewed Chopin's cumulative ornamental variation in favour of a cross between character variation and thematic transformation, at times even adopting a kind of *cantus firmus* approach to repetition and form. These are generalisations of course, but they indicate that the polarity between the two greatest pianist-composers of the early nineteenth century extended to particulars of compositional technique.

At a deeper level, however, those polarities might well be reducible to something like a common denominator, one that draws the popular and the significant into a new accommodation and a new synthesis. It is tempting to invoke again the parallel with Schoenberg and Stravinsky. Here too the elements of sharpest opposition appear in retrospect to dissolve into something approaching a single statement, in this case essentially about defining a creative attitude to the past. Indeed the parallel could be taken one stage further. Just as

---

[53] At the end of his life Chopin compared Mozart and Beethoven in terms which spelt out clearly his commitment to order and balance, his rejection of extravagant rhetoric and theatricality: 'Where [Beethoven] is obscure and seems lacking in unity . . . the reason is that he turns his back on eternal principles; Mozart never'. See *The Journal of Eugène Delacroix*, ed. Hubert Wellington, trans. Lucy Norton (New York, 1948), pp. 194–5.

Stravinsky 'reacted', creatively yet ambivalently, to Schoenberg's death in 1951, so Liszt reacted to Chopin's death a century earlier (1849), and in several capacities: as critic, arranger and composer. In 1852 he published the first book-length study of the Polish composer, and its extravagant language set the compass-reading for later generations of myth-making, especially in France,[54] effectively translating Chopin from a figure of pronounced Classical sympathies into an archetypally Romantic 'poet of the piano'. A few years later he arranged six of Chopin's songs into a cycle, ensuring, as Charles Rosen rightly argues, 'a considerable improvement on the vocal versions'.[55] Then, even more crucially, in the early 1850s he composed two polonaises, a mazurka, a *Valse impromptu*, the second ballade, and a berceuse. Here we have, in Alan Walker's words, 'a body of piano music in which Chopin's personality continues to speak to us, as it were, from beyond the grave'.[56] All this in addition to *Funérailles*, based explicitly on the A♭ major Polonaise, Op. 53. It was also in the early 1850s that Liszt composed the two sets of etudes, including the *Transcendentals*, that rework earlier material in light of a newly defined poetics of instrumental music. This was part of a more general reworking of selected earlier music. But it may also have been part of Liszt's response to Chopin. And if so the timing is of particular interest, since Chopin's death coincided with a determinate stage in Liszt's evolution as a composer, amounting to nothing less than the establishment of a new creative agenda for himself and for his contemporaries. The shared genre titles would serve only to emphasise, then, the ambivalence in Liszt's response, as he carefully measured the space that now separated his own aesthetic from Chopin's, no less than from Czerny's. A tribute, but at the same time a symbolic burial. *Le roi est mort. Vive le roi!*

2 PIANOS

Czerny and Chopin allow us to model the central significance of the piano to the early nineteenth century in two quite different ways. Czerny brings its social history into focus. Even more than Clementi, whose teaching he observed, admired, and learnt from, Czerny might be regarded as the first modern piano teacher, in that he cultivated the 'player and practical musician', developing performance as a highly specialised, professional skill, separated out from composition and from an all-round training in music. Czerny's treatises emphasised the importance to the pianist of supplementary skills (the science of thorough-bass 'ought not to remain unknown'), but the real point is that they were indeed supplementary rather than integral. His piano workshop provided a training for the budding virtuoso, a training that embraced everything from finger technique to dress and deportment. It involved a regime of practice that was positively industrial, a committed testimony to the power and efficacy of a bourgeois work ethic; '*Industry and practice* are the Creators and Architects of all that is great, good, and beautiful on the earth'.[57] For Czerny, anyone could be taught anything, provided the preparation were adequate and the will to learn were there. The

[54] Franz Liszt, *F. Chopin* (Paris, 1852).

[55] Charles Rosen, *The Romantic Generation* (London, 1995), p. 512.

[56] Alan Walker, *Franz Liszt: The Weimar Years 1848–1861* (London, 1989), p. 146.

[57] Carl Czerny, *Pianoforte School*, Op. 500, vol. 2, p. 115.

Czerny etude was the mainstay of a formidable pedagogical programme, a programme, we should note, whose tendency was towards conformity rather than individuality.

There was a wider context for this professionalisation of piano teaching. The rise of the conservatories, like the rise of commercially run theatres and concert-giving music societies, marked a change in the basic structures of musical life, associated with the consolidation of a mercantile musical culture. The piano, lodging itself in the public concert, the salon and the bourgeois home, was to become the single most potent symbol of that culture. It drew to itself both a modern technology that would in due course translate craft to industry, and a new social order that would translate economic success to cultural and political status. In the process it generated interconnected and increasingly specialised roles, all addressing the needs of a new kind of consumer. Piano manufacturer, publisher, promoter, critic, teacher, performer, composer: the interrelation between these roles is an intricate and complex dimension of the social history of the piano in the nineteenth century, and one still in need of adequate exposition. Initially a single musician might embrace all or most of them, and right through the nineteenth century, and beyond, several areas of duplication remained common. But from the 1830s the growing tendency was for such duplication to make room for a greater specialisation of function, and that in turn created a whole new set of vested interests, by no means easily harmonised. The piano, in short, found itself at the centre of, and perfectly epitomised, an immensely competitive mercantile culture, whose components and mechanisms differed essentially from those of a patronal culture. In particular a functional link was created between the vested interests of the amateur in the home and those of the celebrity touring virtuoso. The one depended on the other, albeit indirectly, through the ever expanding market for pianos, for published music, and of course for music instruction. The touring virtuoso drove this market, and the training of virtuosos accordingly became a highly specialised activity, carving a space for keyboard technique outside the general field of musical training.

It is worth emphasising that the practice I am describing here – the practice of pianism – resists easy assimilation into the grand narratives, based on style systems and notional traditions, of more conventional histories. Indeed my use of the term 'practice' is calculated. I borrow it very largely from the philosopher Alasdair MacIntyre, who argues for a separation between the interests of a practice, with its own setting, history, tradition, values and ideals, and those of an institution, structured in terms of power and status.[58] For music historians this is a valuable distinction, even if we decide in the end that the separation is less clean than MacIntyre suggests. Thinking in terms of practices allows us to build the performer – the act of performance – centrally into the historical study of a repertory, and also to register something of the quest for personal authenticity that is promoted by a practice, often in opposition to the institutions that lodge it. Indeed it is sometimes tempting to imagine a history of music which starts from practices rather than composers, works and institutions. Such a history, it need hardly be said, would embrace multiple, often overlapping, practices, each with its institutions, its sub-practices, its enabling agencies, its repertory, its ethos. In the early nineteenth century, for instance, it would encompass the French salon, the English

---

[58] Alasdair MacIntyre, *After Virtue* (London, 1981).

subscription concert, the German choral association, and the Italian opera company. To reduce these monolithically to a single 'movement' of cultural history would be challenging, to say the least.

On the other hand, our alternative history might seek ways of venturing beyond the descriptive in order to attempt bolder, more reductive interpretations. It might, for instance, take the operatic voice, the violin, and the piano as respective starting-points for a narrative which locks together contextual and compositional readings of the tonal tradition. Each of these instruments generated a range of practices sufficiently broadly-based to dominate music's social history at particular times, and in particular places. The instruments themselves became both social components and social agents. At the same time each of them generated vast repertorial cycles, and these cycles in their turn profoundly changed the stylistic history of music through performance-led compositional innovation, fashioned above all by an idiomatic imperative. The piano, of course, takes up the rear in this cyclical history, and there is a real sense in which it retraced many of the well-worn paths of the operatic voice and the violin. Like them it established its own institutions and its own taste-publics, and like them it built its own armoury of idiomatic devices, partly in response to the demands of those taste-publics. Moreover, it arrived at many of these devices by borrowing unashamedly, and then transforming, figures originally associated with the voice and the violin.

Elsewhere I have suggested that in taking a long view of the practice of pianism, we might propose a three-part structural history: pre-recital, recital and post-recital ages.[59] Needless to say, these structures are simplifications. Yet they remain suggestive, and they usefully draw a line between the early nineteenth-century pianism I have been describing and the age of the recital. For it is the institution of the recital that must surely provide the essential reference point for any social history of pianism. Of course there was a lengthy period of induction from Liszt's 'musical soliloquies' or 'monologues' in the late 1830s (concerts 'out of the ordinary run', as he himself put it),[60] to the consolidation of modern programming in the late nineteenth century, a development associated especially with Anton Rubinstein. But the underlying impulse was clear. The recital consolidated a larger tendency within middle-class culture towards stable, settled structures, all of them designed to confirm and authenticate a new status quo. It presented a forum for canon formation, where an 'innocent' repertory, initially centred on Bach, Scarlatti, and the so-called 'Viennese classics', might be manipulated to ideological ends through a massive investment in the musical work, and in its greatness. In short, the rise of the recital formalised the rise of the work. Accordingly, it was the adequate interpretation of the work, involving a careful balance between a liberal realisation of the self and a contractual acknowledgement of collective norms and inherited knowledge – between, in Adorno's phrase, the 'self and the forms' – that provided the ethos underlying pianistic practice during the age of the recital.[61] At risk of forcing the point,

[59] 'The Practice of Early-Nineteenth-Century Pianism', in Michael Talbot (ed.), *The Musical Work: Reality or Invention?* (Liverpool, 2000), pp. 110–27.

[60] La Mara (ed.), *Letters of Franz Liszt*, vol. 1, p. 53. Liszt first used the term 'recitals' (note the plural) of his Hanover Square concert of 9 June 1840. On earlier occasions, he referred to 'monologues'. See *An Artist's Journey*, p. 181.

[61] For the background and context of Adorno's phrase, see Max Paddison, *Adorno's Aesthetics of Music* (Cambridge, 1993), especially p. 16.

my structural history might propose a later *kairos* or point of perfection in the story of the recital, associated with some of the giants of the early twentieth century, just prior to the reification of interpretative forms associated with electronic media.[62] This would be the point, so the argument might run, at which the balance between 'the self and the forms' (between, in a way, the demands of the performer and those of the work) had been optimally achieved. Following it the practice entered a stage of qualitative change which I venture to describe as the onset of a post-recital age.

In light of this, we may return to the first stage of our structural history, the pre-recital age, taking us roughly speaking from the infancy of the public concert in the late eighteenth century through to the mid-nineteenth century. Here we are looking at the practice of pianism prior to that very pattern of music-making whose stability and integrity – I am suggesting – is currently threatened by mass culture. There is even a nice irony in this, for the rise of the recital effectively marked a socially elitist retreat from an earlier form of mass culture, or at least something beginning to approach it. Needless to say we should avoid the retrospective fallacy that would equate this pre-recital age with a pre-history of the recital. Indeed one reason for presenting the whole sequence over-schematically, as I am doing here, is precisely to try to do greater historical justice to the pre-recital practice. It is all too easy for the familiar culture of the piano recital, not excluding its ethical values, to obscure the less familiar culture of the benefit concert and the salon, and thus to compromise any attempts we make to engage with early nineteenth-century piano repertories on anything like their own terms. We need a certain historical sympathy to appreciate fully that in the early nineteenth century the practice of pianism, insofar as it can be generalised geographically, functioned within a very different ecology, a very different configuration of agents and agencies. In particular it was a configuration not yet centred on the musical work and on its interpretative forms.

How, then, might we summarise the essential components of an early nineteenth-century pre-recital practice? For a start, the real home of the piano lay in performance sites (benefits, salons) that are no longer a part of our culture today. Likewise its key supporting agents, the piano manufacturer and the music publisher, were very different from those of today. More-over, unlike their present-day counterparts, early nineteenth-century pianists had themselves to shoulder most of the entrepreneurial burden of planning their tours and 'seasons'. Liszt himself described the 'tiring and ridiculous effort' involved; the artist 'must beg an audience with His Highness the *Impresario* ... he must present himself to the police commissioner ... he must negotiate with the gentleman who distributes the posters . . . he must enquire after some errant soprano . . . He spends days and nights climbing staircases that reach as far as the eye can see, scaling boundless heights step by step.'[63] These remarks (and the further descriptions that follow them) nicely convey a sense of the mutual dependencies of roles and functions within the practice to which I referred earlier. Even more crucially, they hint that the focus of the pre-recital practice was not so much an object and concept

---

[62] Kenneth Hamilton takes the death of Paderewski as a convenient terminal point for the 'virtuoso tradition'. See his chapter 'The Virtuoso Tradition', in David Rowland (ed.), *The Cambridge Companion to the Piano* (Cambridge, 1998), pp. 57–74.

[63] *An Artist's Journey*, pp. 86–7.

(the musical work and its interpretation), as an event (the performance). The repertory and programming practices reflected that distinction, with the borderlines separating categories such as composition, transcription and improvisation by no means clearly demarcated and the formulaic demands of conventional genres in competition with the individuality of the work.

The product of the pre-recital practice was not, then, an interpretation. An interpretation mediates the separate worlds of the composer and the performer, and although it may veer towards one or the other, it remains caught within their force-field. This separation was less obvious in the early nineteenth century, not least because a very high proportion of the pianist's repertory consisted of his or her own music, or alternatively of arrangements and transcriptions of music from other media. To a marked extent, then, there was an immediate identification of the performer with the music performed. The product was a performance rather than an interpretation, a presentation rather than a representation, an act rather than an acted-out concept. Where interpretation played a part its reference point was more to do with general styles than with individual works; it was a component of the product rather than the product itself. And that distinction is vital. A performance, after all, may exemplify or promote many things other than a musical work: a technique, an instrument, a genre, an institution, a direct communicative act. It was in the age of the recital that all of these, including the last, were subordinated to the claims of the work. The tendency of the pre-recital practice, in contrast, was to subordinate the creative to the performative. Moreover, it was a tendency mirrored in some of the values and priorities of the wider cultural world in the early nineteenth century. It is not possible to elaborate on this here, but one may at least offer the pointer that there are stories to tell about how the rise of journalism impacted on literary circles (and their publishing practices), and likewise about how the burgeoning of popular prints began to influence the formal culture of the visual arts.[64]

There was a second sense in which the piano took on special significance in the early nineteenth century, and it was explicitly opposed to the mercantile culture I have just been describing. This second image of the piano highlights aesthetic rather than commercial values, though it is also possible to read it – at least partly – as a means of defining (elitist) social identities and confirming their boundaries. It is more readily associated with Chopin than with Czerny, and is indeed perfectly captured by many a contemporary account of Chopin's salon performances. Already by the 1830s, the piano was gaining ground as the ideal medium through which instrumental music might aspire to the condition of the 'poetic'. In this it touched an essential nerve of the Romantic movement in music. Like earlier keyboard instruments, the piano was of course privileged by its functional range (in a word, its capacity to combine melodic and harmonic roles), but unlike its predecessors it was also deemed to possess a remarkable expressive range and an unprecedented capacity for differentiation and nuance. Attempts to model the new pianism on expressive values represented by the operatic voice and the violin clearly signalled the ambition of the instrument as an agent of expression. There is scarcely a piano method of the early nineteenth century that fails to

---

[64] See Susan Bernstein, *Virtuosity of the Nineteenth Century: Performing Music and Language in Heine, Liszt and Baudelaire* (Stanford, 1998), chapter 1.

direct aspiring performers to the opera house as the model for a *bel canto* style of playing, and an appropriate mode of ornamentation. In other words, the piano, paradoxically enough given the nature of its mechanism, became a symbol of the expressive aesthetic that lay close to the heart of an emergent Romanticism. It became the intimate medium through which the Romantic composer, privileged by his genius, could most clearly express himself, whether in improvisation or composition. Through a single instrument, he could make his commitment to subjectivity, translating rhetorical figure to 'characteristic' gesture, affective *scopus* to expressive *langage*.

This expressive competence was greatly enhanced by the perceived power of the instrument, even the instrument of the 1830s, and by its self-contained status. Indeed in one sense the rise of the piano recital celebrated precisely these qualities. It was a bold step for any pianist-composer to give a public concert without supporting artists, especially the ubiquitous singers, in the early nineteenth century. Liszt spelt out the novelty of it in a letter to the Princess Belgiojoso in 1839. 'I dared, for the sake of peace and quiet, to give a series of concerts entirely alone, affecting the style of Louis XIV and saying cavalierly to the public, "Le Concert – c'est moi".' For the curiosity of the thing, here is the programme of one of these soliloquies'.[65] The piano could apparently say everything in its own terms, could contain its own meaning, could embody in itself (in its very name) the symbolic power of contrast. C. P. E. Bach had already privileged the keyboard in this respect: 'the keyboardist, before all musicians, is especially able *all alone* to practise the declamatory style, that astonishingly swift flight from one affect to another'.[66] He could almost have been describing Chopin, communing with his instrument and independent of all other agencies, as he evoked in rapid juxtaposition the contrasted worlds of pastoral innocence and terrifying aggression in a performance of his second Ballade. The piano, in short, came to be viewed as nothing less than a universal medium of musical experience, capable of translating other musical worlds, including the world of an idealised past, into its own unified terms, 'transfer[ing] them', as Liszt said of Chopin, 'into a more restricted but more idealised sphere'.[67] Indeed, through the resource of transcription, it could effect such translations literally. Again all this resonated with the Romantic ideology, and especially with the 'autonomy character' increasingly assigned to music following the rise of aesthetics. An all-important sense of privilege was beginning to attach itself to so-called 'absolute' music both in the philosophical aesthetics and in the music criticism of the early nineteenth century, and the piano was its embodiment. Representing as it did a self-contained functional and expressive world, the piano could encourage and promote an already developing sense of music as an art form closed off from the world around it, essentially separate and monadic.

There are two contrasted representations here, even if at a deeper level we might identify the one as a precondition of the other; a mercantile culture does, after all, make possible a project of aesthetic autonomy. And if we argue that Czerny and Chopin draw us to one or the other of these two images of the piano, we might further argue that Liszt leads us to both – to

---

[65] Williams, *Portrait of Liszt*, p. 110.
[66] See Barth, *The Pianist as Orator*, p. 4, for further comment on this.
[67] Franz Liszt, *F. Chopin*, p. 32.

the 'real' piano of a mercantile concert life, and to the 'ideal' piano of a symbolic aesthetic universe. Again he himself put it succinctly, describing his efforts to '[steer] a course between the Ideal and the Real, without allowing myself to be overly seduced by the former, nor ever to be crushed by the latter'.[68] This quotation can bear closer scrutiny. In the first place it conveys a strong sense of the ethical choices and dilemmas faced by the participants of a pre-recital pianistic practice. I return to my earlier comments on the nature of a practice. As Liszt implies here, the practice demands of its participants the exercise of virtues as well as skills, and virtues are recognised as such in relation to an underlying ethos. It seems to me that Liszt's quotation actually takes us close to the nature of that ethos for the pre-recital age. Rather than the balance between self-expression and established interpretative forms associated with the age of the recital, the pre-recital practice sought and cultivated a no less delicate balance between the mercantile and the aesthetic values of a developing instrument.

It may be interesting, in light of this tale of two pianos, to attempt some very broad, poster-like characterisations of the journey taken by Liszt through his three sets of etudes. In such an exercise in caricature, the *Etude en douze exercices* would portray him as the youthful pianist-composer, the brilliant prodigy, training in the most rigorous of all post-Classical workshops for a 'typical' career on the concert platforms of Europe. The *Grandes Etudes*, on the other hand, would present him as the archetypal Romantic virtuoso, parading and displaying his prodigious talent (and ego), while at the same time responding to that popular taste for the flamboyant, the acrobatic, and even the vulgar associated with the rise of 'public man'. Finally, the *Etudes d'exécution transcendante* would reveal him as the pioneering composer-thinker, encapsulating through textural and formal simplification and through the addition of poetic titles a much grander vision: a music that draws together transcendental virtuosity and the poetic, while at the same time enacting a kind of withdrawal from the public arena. At this point the rhetoric invades the music. The musical differences between the *Grandes Etudes* and the *Transcendentals* are in some cases relatively slight, and are often motivated as much by pragmatism as by formal or programmatic imperatives. Yet those differences take on new significance in light not just of the titles but of the manifesto implicit in the titles.

These characterisations, distorted but indicative, point to a yet larger history. Like Liszt's career as a whole, they describe a progression from pianist-composer to pianist and composer, and a related progression from the musical performance to the musical work. Of course the reality was nothing like so pat; more a shift in emphasis between co-existing elements. There was undoubtedly a new direction at (roughly) the mid-century, as the 'virtuoso years' made way for the 'Weimar years'.[69] But there was also continuity. Underlying and bridging the change of agenda was a consistently intimate, almost symbiotic relation between composer and instrument, one characterised by a kind of thinking in sound, or better, intuiting in sound. For Liszt, as for Chopin, musical thoughts were pianistic thoughts, and it was this near-perfect equation of substance and idiom that inaugurated the great era of the piano. Whether displaying or communing, improvising or composing, Liszt thought

---

[68] *An Artist's Journey*, p. 88.
[69] The periodisation is Alan Walker's, describing volumes 1 and 2 of his three-volume biography.

with his fingers at the keys, and he did so with a fluency as natural as breathing. 'My piano is myself, my speech, and my life'.[70] The piano was in this sense his 'premier langage'.[71] The display and the poetry, the trivial exercise and the significant work, the public concert and the private *réunion*: all were a part of the same process, the same intuiting in sound. So too were his many transcriptions from other musical worlds – opera, symphony, *Lied* – and even his 'translations' from worlds beyond music – literature, painting, nature. All of these were united in the instrument itself. And on this very fundamental level the two pianos were one.

[70] *An Artist's Journey*, p. 45.   [71] See Sogny, *L'Admiration Créatrice chez Liszt*, p. 39.

Chapter Two

—

Of maps and materials

On the face of it, etude composition should be for teachers, not their pupils, and Liszt's *Etude en douze exercices*, announcing the end of his years as a prodigy, a 'second Mozart', no doubt tells us something about the self-confidence of a fifteen-year-old. Certainly his earlier works were more obviously tailored to the kind of concert tours he had just completed, in Germany, London and the French provinces, and more generally to the world of public pianism. They were also, if anything, even closer compositionally to his piano teacher Czerny, whose many excursions into popular concert genres – variations, fantasies, pot-pourris and the like – are mercifully hidden from view today. In fact it is ironic that, of all things, it was a collection of exercises that helped lift the young Liszt clear of any stylistic dependence on Czerny. It is hardly necessary to flesh out the generic history here, beyond observing that the proliferation of instructional pieces entitled etudes, exercises or *leçons* was closely tied to the rise of modern conservatories in the late eighteenth and early nineteenth centuries. Indeed there is a real sense in which the etude, at least in its present-day sense, was a creation of the Paris Conservatoire in particular.[1] Professors such as Aubert, Baillot, Cartier, Boisière, Lefevre and Hugot had already issued numerous collections for non-keyboard instruments (especially violin) before Cramer went on to secure the genre title for the piano with his *Etude pour le pianoforte, contenant 42 Exercices* of 1804, later to be subsumed by the *84 Etudes* that comprised Part 5 of his *Grosse Pianoforte Schule*. The appearance of Cramer's etudes coincided both with definitive improvements to the mechanism of the instrument, partly in response to music by Clementi and Beethoven, as Czerny himself pointed out,[2] and with the parallel demise of its principal rival, the harpsichord. (I will sidestep for the moment the larger history shaping this, described by Max Weber as a progressive rationalisation of resources in Western music, a process that embraced instruments and instrumental technique.[3] The etude was a product of this larger history.)

Franzgeorg von Glasenapp neatly traced the gradual ascendancy of the piano over the harpsichord by describing the nine successive editions of Löhlein's *Clavier-Schule*, whose

---

[1] See Peter Ganz, 'The Development of the Etude', diss., Northwestern University (1960), p. 20.
[2] Carl Czerny, *Umriss der ganzen Musikgeschichte* (Mainz, 1851), p. 74.
[3] Max Weber, *The Rational and Social Foundations of Music*, trans. and ed. D. Martindale, J. Riedel and G. Neuwirth (Illinois, 1958; orig. edn, 1921).

original text (1765), unsurprisingly, made only the barest mention of the piano.[4] By the fifth edition (1791), prepared by Johann George Witthauer, it was emphasised that 'clavier' meant harpsichord, clavichord or pianoforte, while in the sixth (1804), prepared by August Eberhard Müller and given the title *Clavier und Fortepiano Schule*, the piano was promoted and the harpsichord actively discouraged because of its brittle, unyielding sound quality. Intriguingly, the eighth edition of the *Clavier-Schule* was prepared by Czerny, and it was published in 1825, one year before Liszt composed his *Etude en douze exercices*. Czerny gave it a significant change of title, *A. E. Müller's Grosse Fortepiano-Schule*, and in line with this he downplayed the material dealing with continuo playing and figured bass, and stressed – in his preface – the need for scale-based digital dexterity to do justice to the modern pianoforte. As all aspiring pianists know to their cost, his own etudes and exercises – more than 8,000 of them, though some are mere fragments – responded to that challenge, pursuing their pedagogical aims through a ruthless insistence on technical content rather than artistic value. By 1826, when Liszt composed his exercises, Czerny was in his mid-thirties and had completed, *inter alia*, the *Toccata ou Exercice*, Op. 92, the *100 leichte Übungsstücke*, Op. 139, the *Grosse Uebung durch alle 24 Tonarten*, Op. 152, and the *Grand Exercice de Gammes et Tierces et des Passages Doubles*, Op. 245. These culminated at the end of the decade in *Die Schule der Geläufigkeit*, Op. 299, some of whose exercises were almost certainly composed before the Liszt work. Most of these pieces were designed as functional exercises rather than as 'brilliant' etudes, very much in the tradition of the school etude that had developed at the turn of the century as part of a wider institutionalisation of instrumental pedagogy. That tradition was maintained by composers such as August Klengel and (slightly later) Henri Bertini, but we should note that it already represented a conservative approach to the genre in the late 1820s.

It is hardly surprising that there are correspondences between the figurations of Czerny's etudes and those of Liszt's youthful exercises, for all that their lessons were devoted to the piano rather than to composition. At the same time it is rather clear that Czerny's school etudes were not the principal models chosen by Liszt when he first used the title etude, however much he may have drawn from them in purely technical terms. Even at fifteen his artistic ambition for the genre was very much higher. And in that he was not alone. In the 1820s the etude was beginning its migration from classroom and bourgeois home to concert hall and fashionable salon, and in the process its scope was broadened considerably. Increasingly it was about virtuosity as well as 'solid technique'. Yet it carried with it something of its original earnestness of purpose, and thus avoided some of the pejorative associations of the more obviously public virtuoso genres, such as variations, rondos, fantasies, and even concertos. The etude formed in a way the 'brilliant' counterpart to the emergent lyric or character piece, and the chronology of its inception and early development was broadly similar. Etudes and character pieces moved centre stage as the Classical sonata receded, or at any rate lost something of its monopoly status as the most prestigious genre of pianism. 'A SONATA is indeed a rarity!', cried the critic of *Harmonicon* in 1827.[5] This should not be

---

[4] Franzgeorg von Glasenapp, *Georg Simon Löhlein* (Halle, 1937). For a full account, see Ganz, 'The Development of the Etude', pp. 57–61.

[5] *Harmonicon*, 27 November 1827, p. 228.

overstated. Right through the nineteenth century creative deformations of Classical models kept the sonata in good health. But the tonal and thematic dialectic associated with its Classical archetype began to give way in many quarters to just the kind of neo-Baroque thinking that was most readily associated with miniatures or cycles of miniatures. When Schumann remarked that 'the whole so-called Romantic school . . . is far nearer to Bach than Mozart ever was',[6] he no doubt meant, at least partly, the general tendency for the Romantic generation to reach back across the Classical era to recover something of Bach's formal thinking, a unitary process of departure and return, often marked by the consistency of figuration or unity of mood found in etudes and character pieces.

Earlier, in 1836, Schumann had turned his critical eye more specifically on the etude, preparing a kind of interim assessment of contributions to the genre for *Neue Zeitschrift für Musik*.[7] His central aim was to classify etudes according to their technical features, but he also attempted an evaluation of composers and of individual etudes (partly by assigning asterisks to those etudes exhibiting 'poetic' quality). Much of Schumann's attention was of course given to etudes composed in the 1830s, in other words several years after Liszt's early composition. Thus Chopin, Hummel, Herz, Bertini and Schumann himself are discussed in terms of what he considered to be the ideal in etude composition, and actually, as his writings elsewhere indicate, in musical composition generally: a perfect fusion of technique and art, where 'imagination and technique share dominion side by side'. He was quite clear, incidentally, that Czerny did justice to only one of the pair. And of the sets composed prior to 1826, those by Kessler and Kalkbrenner were also found wanting artistically. On the other hand several of the etudes that merited asterisks had already been composed by the time Liszt published his *Etude en douze exercices*. That work, not surprisingly, escaped Schumann's attention, as did major sets by Daniel Steibelt and John Field. But he found what he described as 'poetic content' in etudes by Ludwig Berger, Maria Szymanowska, Cipriani Potter and Ignaz Moscheles, and of these, the works by Berger and Szymanowska preceded Liszt's *Etude*, while those by Potter and Moscheles were more-or-less coeval with it. It should be added that the music of all these composers, without exception, was widely circulated in the 1820s (we should not be influenced here by the subsequent neglect of several of them), and that many of their etudes, unlike most of Czerny's, clearly aspired towards Schumann's union of pedagogical and aesthetic values. In other words, Liszt was by no means alone when he set out to compose a cycle of exercises 'mit Geist' in the mid-1820s.[8]

Yet the inspiration for his exercises may well have pre-dated such contemporary works. Intriguingly Liszt's title, or his publisher's, returned to the formulation of Cramer's pioneering, controversial, and musically highly regarded work published in 1804, the *Etude pour le pianoforte, contenant 42 Exercices*. This is often characterised as the foundation stone of the modern piano etude, though the issue of chronology was famously and publicly called into question by Clementi.[9] In any case Cramer's title was itself borrowed from several earlier sets of exercises for non-keyboard instruments. Once applied to the piano it was immediately

---

[6] Robert Schumann, *On Music and Musicians*, trans. P. Rosenfeld, ed. K. Wolff (London, 1946), p. 93.

[7] *Neue Zeitschrift für Musik*, 4 (1836), pp. 45–6.

[8] See Karl Borromaüs von Miltitz, 'Exercice und Etude', *Allgemeine musikalische Zeitung*, 8 (1841), cols. 209–13.

[9] See Alan Tyson, 'A Feud between Clementi and Cramer', *Music & Letters*, 54 (1973), pp. 281–8.

taken up by other pianist-composers, notably Daniel Steibelt in a work of 1805 characteristically designed to capitalise on Cramer's success. It was only rather later, incidentally, that the two terms 'etude' and 'exercise' took on the familiar connotations we register today, differentiating pieces with artistic ambition – 'with inspiration' – from purely mechanical practice pieces.[10] An early nineteenth-century usage was very much more fluid, with 'étude en exercices', 'études et exercices', and 'études ou exercices' all commonly found on the title pages. Nor do contemporary dictionaries make any really clear distinction. As late as 1840, Schilling's *Universal-Lexicon der Tonkunst* could carry the entry '*Exercice*, the same as *etude*'. All that said, the usage 'étude en exercices', as noted in the last chapter, was already distinctly outmoded by the mid-1820s (even Cramer's subsequent collections use 'etude' to refer to the individual piece rather than the collection). The publisher in provincial Marseilles may have been a little behind the times. On the other hand, the choice of title might have been a deliberate tribute.

It would be unduly partial to situate Liszt's youthful composition somewhere between Czerny and Cramer; there are transparently ingredients that stem from quite other sources, post-dating the Cramer work and extending well beyond the boundaries of Czerny's various 'schools'. It would be more foolhardy still to propose any direct modelling process in the absence of documentary confirmation. Yet I will venture at least some way down this path.[11] The association with Czerny is so transparent as to need little exemplification, but it is tempting to set the second of Liszt's exercises alongside No. 28 from Book 3 of Czerny's *Die Schule der Gelaüfigkeit*, some of which Liszt must surely have known (Ex. 1).[12] There was undoubtedly an element of common currency about such figures (indeed the point will shortly be elaborated), but the specificity is naturally strengthened by our knowledge of a teacher–pupil relation. All the same, the parallels with Cramer's more intrinsically interesting – indeed seminal – contributions to the genre go deeper, extending beyond the structures of the figures to parallel harmonic and formal schemes. The Cramer etudes were known, praised and emulated by many of the leading practitioners of early nineteenth-century pianism, from Beethoven onwards; they were to be found, as contemporary sources indicate, on every piano. In fact their reputation – unlike that of just about all Cramer's other music, including his later etudes – survived right through into the later nineteenth century, as commentaries by Brendel, Weitzmann and von Bulow indicate.[13] They were valued above all as an important bridge between the keyboard writing of Bach and the modern school of pianism, and that very fact gives them privilege in any discussion of the youthful Liszt.

---

[10] Chopin initially called the first two of the Op. 10 Etudes 'Exercise 1' and 'Exercise 2'. Only when they were published three years later as part of a larger cycle did they become 'etudes'.

[11] In doing so, I incur the ridicule of Michel Foucault, who described such influence-spotting and tradition-placing as 'harmless enough amusements for historians who refuse to grow up'! See *The Archaeology of Knowledge and the Discourse on Language*, trans. A. M. Sheridan Smith (New York, 1972), pp. 143–4.

[12] The precise date of the publication of Czerny's 'School' is uncertain, but it was probably in the late 1820s. Alan Walker refers to its influence on Liszt, though the School would have been as yet unpublished when Liszt wrote his own early exercises. *Franz Liszt: The Virtuoso Years 1811–1847* (London, 1983), p. 66.

[13] See von Bulow's remarks on this in the preface to his edition of the Cramer *84 Etudes*. Tellingly, the critic of *The Musical Standard*, writing on 10 July 1869, described Cramer as the 'founder of the second great pianoforte school'.

Example 1 Liszt, *Etude en 12 exercices*, No. 2 bars 1–4
Czerny, *Die Schule der Gelaüfigkeit*, Book 3, No. 28 bars 1–6

Liszt. *Etude en 12 exercices*, No. 2 bars 1–4

Czerny. *Die Schule der Gelaüfigkeit*, Book. 3, No. 28 bars 1–6

Example 2 is intended to be indicative only, revealing just how closely the head motives of some of the Liszt exercises map on to Cramer's.[14]

Echoes of Czerny and Cramer catch a yet more distant resonance from the early history of the instrument. When Liszt composed his exercises there had been a general smoothing-out of differences between the separate traditions of pianism represented by these two major figures. In very broad stylistic terms we can relate Czerny most clearly to a line of 'Viennese' bravura pianism indebted most of all to Hummel, but also, through Hummel, to Mozart. The light-actioned Viennese-German instrument lay behind this line, and its performance

---

[14] Three of these affinities are also noted by Georg Schütz, 'Form, Satz- und Klaviertechnik in den drei Fassungen der *Grossen Etüden* von Franz Liszt', in Zsoltán Gárdonyi and Siegfried Mauser (eds.), *Virtuosität und Avantgarde: Untersuchungen zum Klavierwerk Franz Liszts* (Mainz, 1988), p. 74.

Example 2 Liszt, *Etude en 12 exercices*, No. 3 bar 1 Cramer, *84 Etudes*, No. 7 bar 1

No. 4 bars 1–2   No. 60 bar 1

No. 5 bar 1   No. 5 bar 1

No. 6 bars 1–2   No. 57 bar 1

No. 10 bar 1   No. 50 bar 1

Liszt. *Etude en 12 exercices,*
No. 3 bar 1

Cramer. *84 Etudes,*
No. 7 bar 1

No. 4 bars 1–2

No. 60 bar 1

No. 5 bar 1

No. 5 bar 1

No. 6 bars 1–2

No. 57 bar 1

No. 10 bar 1

No. 50 bar 1

style was characterised by a staccato, 'equal-finger' action well suited to rapid figurations and elaborate ornamentation. Cramer, on the other hand, owed more to Clementi, and therefore to the heavier English piano, better suited to a legato touch, *sostenuto* melody, and thicker chordal writing. This was never a hard-and-fast separation (Czerny learnt a good deal from Clementi too; and, as von Bulow suggests, Cramer departed from Clementi in certain essentials of technique[15]), but until the 1820s the two lines retained a measure of independence. It was partly the achievement of a younger generation of pianists to draw them together, and in this respect even Liszt's youthful exercises made their modest contribution. By the time of their composition, of course, the real explosion of pianistic virtuosity had already occurred. The pianism of the 1820s and 1830s was nothing if not cosmopolitan, stretching the capacities of instruments and performers alike in ways that drew upon, and cut across, the separate traditions stemming from Mozart and Clementi. All the same, emaciated traces of two distinguishable pianistic styles can still be detected in the bravura repertory, and are indeed detectable in the varied and contrasted exercises of the Liszt *Etude*.

A RECOVERED PAST

To describe Liszt's exercises as 'varied and contrasted' is already to say something, however minimal, about their intrinsic musical value. It would be wrong-headed to make too many claims for these little pieces, and some of the problems associated with them will be identified later. Yet equally we need to resist the temptation to make *a priori* judgements on the products of an apprenticeship, in effect to regret their failure to live up to the later Liszt.[16] Moreover, 'variety' and 'contrast' can embrace the moods, tempos, forms and textures of the exercises, most of which exhibit clearly defined, distinctive characters (the characteristic was an emergent category of the early nineteenth century); or, to use Leonard Ratner's term, 'topics'; or, to use my preferred term, 'genres'.[17] As I hinted in the Introduction, the early nineteenth-century practice would have cultivated a rather greater awareness of the generic contrasts between individual exercises in a collection than a later structuralist age encouraged.[18] On occasion the genres feeding into etudes and exercises were even incorporated in the title, though it is dangerous to infer too much from titles in what was – in that respect at least – a permissive age. Thus we have *Etude formant caprices, Etudes dans le genre fugue, Etude composée de morceaux de différents genres*, or *Etude en forme de rondo*.

Such references were not in any case essential to generic recognition. Musical materials were often quite enough to indicate a generic affiliation. By musical materials I have in mind

---

[15] In the preface to his edition of the Cramer etudes.

[16] They are as undervalued by Charles Rosen (*The Romantic Generation* [London, 1995], p. 493) as they are overvalued by Walker (*The Virtuoso Years*, p. 118).

[17] Leonard Ratner, *Classic Music: Expression, Form, and Style* (New York, 1980).

[18] Much the same was true of variation sets, where successive variations often had a distinctive generic character, and incidentally would on occasion have been individually applauded in early nineteenth-century performances. Following his performance of the *'Là ci darem' Variations*, Chopin wrote that 'everyone clapped so loudly after each variation that I had difficulty hearing the orchestral tutti'. See *Korespondencja Fryderyka Chopina*, ed. B. E. Sydow (Warsaw, 1955), vol. 1, p. 37.

an emphatically plural and historical category, whose antinomy might be the musical idea, a singular and notionally ahistorical category in the sense that it is grounded in subjectivity. Materials might be characterised as the repertory of commonalities that results from composers' negotiations with those abstract partitioning systems that mediate between the idea and nature (I will elaborate on this in chapter 4). They can embrace everything from formal and generic schemata of various kinds to motivic and harmonic archetypes, and conventional figures, imbued with history. My focus here will be on figures, the most neglected of these categories, and the one least likely to be subsumed by analysis and read as a formal function.[19] Figures can signal a genre, and I would like to nominate such genre markers as the first of several 'ideal types' of musical material, analogous in principle to the ideal types of musical form identified by analysis. It has been remarked, by Adorno and Dahlhaus, among others, that the potency of genre declined in the nineteenth century with the rise of aesthetic autonomy and a consequent focus on the individuality of the musical work.[20] Self-contained works, in other words, increasingly resisted the closure and clarity of meaning conventionally offered by a genre title. In contrast, there was rather greater stability of reference in a post-Classical pianistic culture. Genre markers could signify not only a genre, but also, depending on the genre in question, a wide range of functional and aesthetic associations – extra-musical reference, pedagogy, vocal influence, improvisation, virtuosity, and even musical form as form was understood in the early nineteenth century. Here the musical work had a more contingent quality; it exemplified a genre, and that in turn exemplified an aspect of the practice.

It is often instructive to read back from the *Transcendentals* to see just how far the generic characters of the mature etudes might be detected as latent presences in the youthful exercises, whether or not Liszt was aware of this. Thus, the figures in the first exercise are in keeping with those of a prelude, signifying a practice of improvised preluding that was a familiar part of public pianism.[21] The *moto perpetuo* figuration, echoing the characteristic Bachian prelude, is only one part of this story, as is the C major tonality, a sort of *Ur*-tonality for piano pedagogy. The essential mark of a prelude was that the inductive figuration, designed to test the touch and tuning, warm up the fingers, and at the same time prepare the audience for weightier matters, would be subordinated to a strongly marked cadence. Indeed there is a sense in which the prelude as a genre was little more than an elaborated cadence (Czerny's Op. 16 Etudes are actually marked 'en form de Préludes et Cadences'[22]). The first harmony of Liszt's exercise is a pregnant V of IV, and it initiates a standard cadential formula

---

[19] It should be noted that the distinction between materials and forms is not an absolute one; what is 'material' on one level may well be read as 'form' on another.

[20] T. W. Adorno, *Aesthetic Theory*, ed. Gretel Adorno and Rolf Tiedemann, trans. Christian Lenhardt (London, 1983), pp. 285–9; and Carl Dahlhaus, 'New Music and the Problem of Musical Genre', in *Schoenberg and the New Music*, trans. Derrick Puffett and Alfred Clayton (Cambridge, 1987), pp. 32–44.

[21] Aside from Czerny's well-known text (see note 22), we might cite Kalkbrenner's subtitle to his set of *Vingt-quatre préludes*, where he suggests that they 'pouvant servir d'example pour apprendre à préluder'.

[22] The etymological link between 'cadence' and 'cadenza' is obvious enough. At times the terms were all but synonymous. Czerny distinguishes between short improvised preludes and 'longer, and more elaborate' preludes; see *A Systematic Introduction to Improvisation*, op. 200, trans. and ed. A. Mitchell (New York, 1983; orig. edn, 1829), p. 5.

Example 3 (a) Liszt, *Etude en 12 exercices*, No. 1 bars 1–2
(b) cadence structures

Liszt. *Etude en 12 exercices*, No. 1   (a)

bars 1–2

                                                     (b)

cadence structures

(Ex. 3a) which is reinforced by immediate repetition. This repeated cadence is then inflated to different formal levels, underlying subsequent figurations and culminating in a strong intermediate cadence at bars 18–20, and a yet stronger final cadence at bars 29–31 (Ex. 3b). As Example 3 suggests, a cadential function – a chain of cadences – is part of the substance of the piece, right from its opening bar. It is worth noting too that the break in figuration preceding a strong final cadence is characteristic of several of the exercises, and is in the tradition of the composed-out prelude.[23]

Again reading back from the *Transcendentals*, we may consider the third and fourth of the exercises. The third has loose affinities with the pastorale, one of the most popular genre pieces at the turn of the eighteenth and nineteenth centuries, with resonances in opera and oratorio, and more broadly in age-old constructions of a pastoral topos. The genre is suggested by the tonal type of the piece, which links the characteristic key of F major with a repertory of associative devices. These include the fluid, mono-rhythmic quaver movement, the double notes in thirds, the lucid diatonicism of the exposition and the subdominant direction of the larger tonal movement. Such generic associations are common to a wide

---

[23] The 'chain of cadences' was familiar in C major piano etudes; compare, for example, no. 12 from one of the earliest sets, Aloys Schmitt's *20 Etudes*.

Example 4 Liszt, *Etude en 12 exercices*, No. 3 bars 1–2
Berger, *12 Etudes*, Op. 12, No. 4 bars 1–4

Liszt. *Etude en 12 excercices*, No. 3 bars 1–2

Berger. *12 Etudes*, Op. 12, No. 4 bars 1–4

repertory of pianism in the early nineteenth century, ranging from 'pastorales' by Field to innumerable so-called 'pastoral rondos' composed by Cramer, Steibelt, Berger and many others, either as separate pieces or as finales. Nor was the pastoral topic at all uncommon in etude collections; compare No. 4 from Berger's Op. 12 Etudes (Ex. 4).[24] In contrast, the genre markers of the fourth exercise hint at a rather different dimension of pastoral. The *chasse* had a lengthy history in Classical and post-Classical musics when Liszt wrote this exercise. It is found in the popular repertory – in, for example, Steibelt, Dussek, Cramer, Clementi, Bertini, and later Stephen Heller – but also in the four-movement sonata-symphonic cyclic design, either as a characteristic device of the trio sections of Classical minuets, or as a finale topic, notably in the many, hugely popular, hunting symphonies composed in the late eighteenth century. In the case of the fourth exercise, it is only really through the later recompositions that we are likely to register an association with the *chasse* topic. The compound duple metre would be the starting-point for such an association, and the ascending double-note figure would then strengthen it. It may be that this figure, especially in its cadential form (Ex. 5), put Liszt in mind of the archetype of a *cor de signal* when he reviewed the piece for recomposition. At any rate the inversion of the figure from the third exercise highlights the generic contrast between these two pieces, which we might characterise (adapting Empson) as 'soft' and 'hard' pastoral, respectively.[25] Such categories had a wide associative range in late eighteenth- and early nineteenth-century culture generally, extending well beyond the notes and well beyond any explicit intention of the author.

---

[24] See Hermann Jung, *Die Pastorale: Studien zur Geschichte einer musikalischen Topos* (Bern and Munich, 1980). The characteristic 'pastoral' keys were F major and D major. For a discussion of key characteristics, see Rita Steblin, *A History of Key Characteristics in the Eighteenth and Early Nineteenth Centuries* (Ann Arbor, 1983).
[25] William Empson, *Some Versions of Pastoral* (New York, 1974).

Example 5 Liszt, *Etude en 12 exercices*, No. 4 bars 1–2, 17–18

Liszt. *Etude en 12 exercices*, No. 4

bars 1–2   bars 17–18

A later trio of exercises – Nos. 8–10 – further illustrates contrasted generic characters within the collection. A♭ major was a favoured key for lyrical pianism, and Liszt's ninth exercise responds to some of its conventional associations. It might be described as a 'romance' (later a 'nocturne'), which title signified vocal models – French or Italian accompanied songs – in the early nineteenth century. At the same time it pioneered the fully developed character of the nocturne, anticipating that most paradigmatic of nocturnes, Chopin's E♭ major Op. 9 No. 2, in striking ways. As an ideal type, the nocturne style was characterised by a delicate balance between core elements, vocally inspired and even at times literally singable, and decorative extensions and interpolations which are idiomatically pianistic, even if they partly stylise vocal practice. The wide-spread arpeggiation (demanding the sustaining pedal) and closing cadenza were integral to the style, as were the appoggiaturas and the tendency to offset cumulative ornamental variations of the main theme with contrasted material. In fact the nature of the contrasted material in this exercise – the octaves theme at bar 9 and the pulsating chords at bar 29 – is itself typical of the romance or nocturne (compare, respectively, Chopin's Nocturne Op. 9 No. 1 at bar 19 and Field's B♭ major Nocturne at bar 18). The movements flanking this aria are two bravura exercises, in C minor and F minor respectively. The conjunction of a C minor tonality with an impassioned left-hand figuration, fully scored right-hand chording and the characteristic rhythmic fingerprints of a *march brillante* amounted to yet another conventional type in the early nineteenth century, its associations readily apparent from antecedents in Beethoven and Weber, as well as from later etudes by Chopin and Berger. The title 'revolutionary' was not Chopin's, but it does at least serve as a pointer to the relevant affect (compare also No. 8 in C minor from Czerny's *Préludes et cadences*). In contrast, the tenth exercise is a toccata, standing for technical skill, pedagogy and an equal-finger virtuosity. Steibelt's *Etude en 50 exercices* offers one comparator, Kessler's *24 Etudes* another (Ex. 6).[26]

Of their nature genre markers promote intertextual readings of this kind, where the work exemplifies its genre as well as making its own statement. Leonard Ratner's influential study, in which he identified topics in relation to locale, occasion, status and function, gave considerable impetus to such readings, and the value of his typology has not been diminished by a subsequent need to refine and qualify its categories.[27] The main point for now is that Ratner's

---

[26] Other examples include parts of Reicha's *L'art de varier*, Op. 57, a treasure trove of keyboard devices.
[27] See Raymond Monelle, *The Sense of Music: Semiotic Essays* (Princeton and Oxford, 2000).

Example 6 Liszt, *Etude en 12 exercices*, No. 10 bars 1–2
Steibelt, *Etude en 50 exercices*, No. 10 bars 3–4
Kessler, *24 Etudes*, Op. 20, No. 14 bars 1–2

Liszt. *Etude en 12 exercices*, No. 10 bars 1–2

Steibelt. *Etude en 50 exercices*, No. 10 bars 3–4

Kessler. *24 Etudes*, Op. 20, No. 14 bars 1–2

categories, since they focus on shared materials, invite a semiotic approach to the identification of musical meaning, such as that proposed by Márta Grabócz in her several studies of Liszt.[28] Some of the ramifications, and limitations, of Grabócz's approach will be discussed in chapter 6, but we may note here that in identifying two highly reductive organising topics, pastoral and heroic respectively, she points to Liszt's Beethoven inheritance as an important primary source, lending some weight to the proposal that Baroque affections were in a sense reinvented as characteristic or poetic figures in the post-Beethoven generation. This is a persuasive argument, and it is supported by other neo-Baroque features in the early Romantic repertory.[29] At root, the contention is that the affections may have gone underground with the decline of a mimetic aesthetic, but that they never quite disappeared from view, so that there is considerable continuity between eighteenth- and nineteenth-century repertories in respect of a store of common expressive devices.[30] Genre markers were part of this. So were tonal types. And so too were musical-rhetorical figures, even if these were only loosely

---

[28] Notably Márta Grabócz, *Morphologie des Oeuvres pour Piano de Liszt* (Paris, 1996).

[29] For a larger context, see my chapter 'The Great Composer', in Jim Samson (ed.), *The Cambridge History of Nineteenth-Century Music* (Cambridge, 2001), pp. 259–84.

[30] Raymond Monelle differentiates between iconic, indexical and symbolic devices (cuckoo – spring – nature). See *The Sense of Music*, chapter 2.

connected to the *figurae* of Baroque theory (Ratner refers to 'characteristic figures').[31] All worked towards a similar end, highlighting the shared expressive substance of a repertory, though if we were to fine-tune this proposition we would make a functional distinction between Baroque allegory and Classic-Romantic symbol. In brief, the latter, unlike the former, allows for multiply expressive inflections of an independently constituted whole, an intact body.

In proposing musical-rhetorical figures – figures imbued with history – as a second ideal type of musical material, I immediately invite hoary problems not just over their identification but over their notional separation from syntax. Even for seventeenth- and eighteenth-century music the *figurae* are often so generalised in character that they are barely distinguishable from the syntactic constituents of the music: scale figures, schematic harmonic progressions and the like. That in turn begs the question of their authenticity, given that they were never intended as templates for composition, but rather as theoretical abstractions, part of a much larger attempt by music theorists to codify elements of a living language. All the same, the 'shared expressive substance' to which I referred earlier was real enough, even where classificatory devices may be found wanting, and it may well have been more evident to early nineteenth-century ears than to our own, given that, as contemporary theory and criticism testifies, such ears may have been less inclined than ours to draw successive elements into a higher synthesis. Its residue is still present in nineteenth-century music, and even twentieth-century music, for all the subsequent investment in subjectivity and individuality. At the turn of the two centuries, Mahler could engage in an ironic play of meanings that still depended heavily on the connotations attached to genre markers, affections, and rhetorical figures.

There may be some value, then, in testing out the *figurae*, since they point to qualities that may be differentiated from constitutive motives or figurations. Admittedly these qualities are often reducible to rather basic relationships, of a kind whose expressive function (as sensuous surface) is rather easily subordinated by present-day listeners to their analytical function (as formal components), especially when the association with a text is not there to prompt semantic interpretation. The change of mode from major to minor at bar 27 of No. 11 is an obvious case in point, carrying with it traditional affective connotations, but at the same time articulating a major formal division; compare the identical gesture at bar 38 of No. 3, where there is no such caesura.[32] For some of the figures, it is probably not realistic even to attempt a separation of function between rhetorical gesture and formal constituent. We can find numerous examples in the Liszt exercises of melodic variation, and even of immediate repetition, either involving sequential transposition in the same voice or alternatively a transfer from one voice (or hand) to another. These constituted

---

[31] Ratner, *Classic Music*, p. 9. George Barth (*The Pianist as Orator: Beethoven and the Transformation of Keyboard Style* [Ithaca and London, 1992]) identifies several 'layers' in the application of rhetoric to music: gesture and punctuation (Mattheson); affective significance (C. P. E. Bach); harmony and large-scale form (Kirnberger). It is by no means easy to trace a single narrative in which these rhetorical devices make room for the characteristic and the formal.

[32] This change of mode is characteristically 'marked' as an expressive device, to use the terminology of Robert Hatten. See *Musical Meaning in Beethoven: Markedness, Correlation, and Interpretation* (Bloomington and Indianapolis, 1994).

Example 7 Liszt, *Etude en 12 exercices*, No. 3
Berger, *15 Etudes*, Op. 22, No. 11 bars 1–2

Liszt. *Etude en 12 exercices*, No. 3

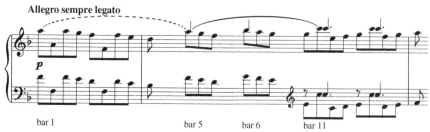

Berger. *15 Etudes*, Op. 22, No. 11 bars 1–2

figures in rhetorical theory, but for instrumental repertories they were processes rather than figures, and it seems unlikely that early nineteenth-century listeners would have been aware of any trace element from earlier traditions of vocal music. The case is somewhat different, however, with figures identifiable by shape, interval or texture. These can range from such simple gestures as rising or falling shapes (expressive of yearning or resignation), to axial figurations (*circulatio*), specific intervallic types, and double note textures, all relatable to traditional figures or variations of them. Such gestures can be found in abundance in the Liszt exercises, and it may be worth identifying a few of them as figures, holding them up for inspection as semi-autonomous features rather than surrendering them to larger contextual functions.

We might, for instance, consider the expressive charge contained within a simple gesture of melodic ascent or descent, such as the appoggiaturas of No. 9, with their ancestry in a Classical *Empfindsamkeit* idiom, or the question and answer built into the theme of No. 12, or the play of third-progressions, descending and ascending, that is thematicised in No. 3; compare No. 11 from Berger's *15 Etudes*, Op. 22, again in F major and again in *fauxbourdon* (Ex. 7). In such cases the figure *qua* figure may make some claims on us, but more likely it will be subsumed by its near-identity with a general vocabulary for tonal music, by its replication of archetypal patterns of tension and release, or by its formal functions. On the other hand, the characteristic melody and associated phraseology of the fifth exercise has a profile that is distinctive enough to suggest more potent intertextual connections, opening the piece out to the practice around it, as brief extracts from Bertini, Potter, Steibelt and Berger suggest (Ex. 8). The sighing thirds in this exercise likewise evoke a common gesture of early nineteenth-century pianism, and so too does the almost operatic dialogue between

Example 8 Liszt, *Etude en 12 exercices*, No. 5 bars 1–2
        Steibelt, *Etude en 50 exercices*, No. 3 bars 12–14
        Cramer, *Dulce et Utile*, Etude No. 1 bars 104–5
        Potter, *Etudes*, Op. 19, No. 2 bars 1–4
        Bertini, *25 Etudes Characteristiques*, Op. 66, No. 15 bars 1–2

Liszt. *Etude en 12 exercices*, No. 5 bars 1–2

Steibelt. *Etude en 50 exercices*, No. 3 bars 12–14

Cramer. *Dulce et Utile*. Etude No. 1 bars 104–5

Potter. *Etudes*, Op. 19, No. 2 bars 1–4

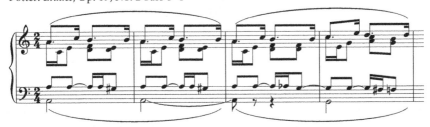

Bertini. *25 Etudes Characteristiques*, Op. 66, No. 15 bars 1–2

Example 9 Liszt, *Etude en 12 exercices*, No. 5 bars 40–3
Beethoven, Sonata in A major, Op. 2, No. 2 bars 130–8

Liszt. *Etude en 12 exercices*, No. 5 bars 40–3

Beethoven. Sonata in A major, Op. 2, No. 2 bars 130–8

the hands, reminiscent of early Beethoven (Ex. 9), and of C. P. E. Bach's 'switching between affects'.[33] An intriguing, seemingly trivial, measure of the affective value of such gestures, incidentally, is their ubiquity in programmatic conversation pieces and battle pieces of the late eighteenth and early nineteenth centuries.[34] Thus, in one of the most popular of the battle pieces, Koczwara's *Battle of Prague*, the left-hand scales and right-hand sighing figures, strikingly reminiscent of gestures in the fifth of Liszt's exercises, are labelled 'running fire' and 'cries of the wounded' respectively, while the rest of the piece offers us trumpet fanfares

---

[33] Such gestures, common in Clementi and Beethoven, resist fixation, according to Barth (*The Pianist as Orator*, p. 52), partly because they carry over the prosody of language and the rules of verbal and sung declamation into instrumental forms.

[34] Battle pieces were especially popular, with examples by, among many others, Abbé Vogler, Steibelt, Méhul, Dussek, Koczwara and Challoner.

Example 10 Liszt, *Etude en 12 exercices*, No. 5 bars 35–8 (reduction)
Berger, *Etudes*, Op. 12, No. 7 bars 53–5 (reduction)
Czerny, *Préludes et Cadences*, Op. 16, No. 12 bars 1–3 (reduction)

Liszt. *Etude en 12 exercices*, No. 5 bars 35–8 (reduction)

Berger, *Etudes*, Op. 12, No. 7 bars 53–5 (reduction)

Czerny. *Préludes et Cadences*, Op. 16, No. 12 bars 1–3 (reduction)

and cavalry charges (*chasse* motives) in plenty.[35] Such pieces present in extreme form the capacity of intertextual figures to disturb an underlying unity of style. It might well be argued, for instance, that Koczwara's battle piece exemplifies a tension between material and form that also characterises, albeit less blatantly, the fifth of Liszt's exercises.

An entire monograph has been devoted to the demonstration that a single musical-rhetorical figure can retain its presence and potency across several centuries of music.[36] Moreover, as Peter Williams has pointed out, *passus duriusculus* (the 'chromatic fourth') may extend beyond the fourth interval without losing its identity as the *lamentoso* figure of Baroque practice. In this broader understanding, it crops up on the surface of Liszt's seventh exercise, and appears again in the fifth, and in modified form in the ninth (compare the extracts from Berger's Op. 12 etudes and Czerny's *Préludes et Cadences* in Ex. 10). Of course, in all these pieces, including the Liszt exercises, the figure is part of a larger functional progression, with a connecting or prolonging role in relation to the underlying structural harmonies. And it need hardly be said that chromatic bass progressions of this kind are part of the common currency of tonal music. Yet, as Williams has demonstrated, this syntactic role by no means disqualifies *passus duriusculus* as an expressive gesture common to many different historical and stylistic contexts. It makes further appearances in the third and

---

[35] Such sections and gestures were highly standardised: the 'cries of the wounded' sub-title, for example, appears time and time again.

[36] Peter Williams, *The Chromatic Fourth during Four Centuries of Music* (Oxford, 1997).

eleventh of the Liszt exercises, and in these instances it takes its place alongside double notes in thirds and sixths, conventionally labelled *fauxbourdon* in rhetorical theory. In parts of No. 11 these double-note patterns offer us a nice illustration of how an expressive figure, translated into the medium of the piano, can take on a quite new idiomatic character, itself in due course rendered conventional, the stuff even of Czerny exercises (for example, of the *Grand Exercise*, Op. 245). And in a slightly different way, the fourth of the exercises illustrates the same point, sharing double-note patterns between the hands to make a composite idiomatic figure, whose execution at this tempo is appropriately challenging.

This leads naturally to idiomatic figures, my third ideal type of musical material, and the one most germane to a study of virtuosity. There is no hard and fast rule that enables us to define materials as idiomatic. One litmus test might be their transferability from one medium to another, and here Liszt more than anyone has shown us the way. We need only consider his reworking of Paganini's *La Chasse* to see how a paragraph of literal transcription can be succeeded by its idiomatic translation to the medium of the keyboard. This is almost tantamount to an object lesson in defining the idiomatic, perfectly exemplifying how the basic characteristics of the two hands on the keyboard, the limitation of compass for each of them and the absence of any such limitation between them, can generate musical materials. And of course it goes beyond this, exploring pianistic figures that were only beginning to glimmer in the pianism of the 1820s. Indeed the truly striking feature of Classical and post-Classical pianism is the surprisingly limited range of idiomatic figures. The tendency was for a modest number of 'patterns of invention', most of them demanding finger, rather than wrist and arm, agility, to be worked and reworked in many different ways. Of their nature, these patterns are welded to the keyboard, and in that sense they signify a performance-orientated (rather than a work-orientated) practice. Almost by definition they are unavailable to structural analysis, of whatever persuasion, for all such analysis – by no means only Schenkerian – is reductive in quality, concerned with formal, motivic or harmonic relations at a level beyond the surface play of figures.

The story of keyboard virtuosity is partly the story of such idiomatic figures. They are among the most transparent embodiments of instrumental thought available to us, and as such they document a medium-sensitive approach to composition which percolates through from the general conception of a work to the specific details of its execution. There is considerable historical continuity in their development. They took their character from a lengthy process of individuation in instrumental media, and their subsequent evolution was increasingly linked to a fetishism of technique which was given expression in such genres as variations or divisions, where figurative patterns acquired considerable brilliance and sophistication, and toccatas, where mono-motivic writing of some concentration was cultivated. For obvious reasons they invoke the ancient craft of improvisation, which played a vital role in the early stages of the practice, epitomising the dual role implicit in today's retrospective term 'pianist-composer', and epitomising too the constructed, formulaic qualities associated with the brilliant style. The essential paradox of improvisation, after all, is that the demand for constant spontaneity ultimately promotes the formula, and at the same time elevates the idiomatic, the capacity to 'think with the fingers'. The historical record is self-evidently sketchy, but it seems likely that in the early nineteenth century

Example 11 Liszt, *Etude en 12 exercices*, No. 1. Figurations

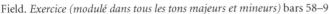

Liszt. *Etude en 12 exercices*, No. 1. Figurations

Example 12 Field, *Exercice (modulé dans tous les tons majeurs et mineurs)* bars 58–9

Field. *Exercice (modulé dans tous les tons majeurs et mineurs)* bars 58–9

improvisation gradually weakened its bonds with composition and strengthened its links with performance. In other words its tendency was increasingly to freeze, rather than to stretch, compositional conventions, pushing the practice towards standardisation by relying on well-tried idiomatic figures. Most of these were variants of scale- or arpeggio-based patterns, just the kind of formulae celebrated by the Czerny exercises, for there is a real synergy here between devices appropriate for training a performer and elements suitable for building a composition. Indeed the whole point about idiomatic figures is that they direct our attention away from the composer towards the performer. They invite us to ask how well they have been executed, where a melody invites us to admire it and a motive invites us to predict what will be done to it.

These latter categories suggest a kind of typology for Liszt's exercises as a whole, distinguishing between motivic-melodic (Nos. 3, 7, 9 and 11), motivic-figurative (Nos. 2, 5, 8 and 12) and figurative (Nos. 1, 4, 6 and 10). This is crude and in need of shading, but it is indicative nonetheless of a basic distinction between motives or melodies, susceptible to variation, transformation or development, and figures, resistant to any of these processes as conventionally understood. And we should note that covert values have attached themselves to this distinction, where motives, signifying (at least to us) work character, are more highly valued than 'mere' figurations, signifying performance. It is partly due to this prejudice that figuration has attracted little analytical scrutiny, and that conventional analytical methods are poorly placed to deal with it. At the very least we may isolate some of its components and in doing so attempt some initial partitioning. At the opening of the first exercise the right hand divides into chord-based, scale-based, and changing-note figures, all of which recur in various forms, since a rather basic contrast between arpeggio and scale is fundamental to the piece and supports its prelude-like character (Ex. 11); compare the last figure to Field's *Exercice modulé en tous les tons* (Ex. 12). Subsequent bars then introduce (broken) octave figures and *Rollfiguren*, the latter a device shared with violin virtuosity, together with characteristic mixtures. These figures – essentially chord divisions activated by the fingers within a fairly constant hand shape – in turn prepare the technical ground for the second exercise, though additional figures are introduced here, including rapid repeated notes.[37] As suggested by my typology, the real contrast between the first and second exercises is that in the latter the figures support – are indeed fused with – a clear top-voice melody. But they are still shaped by, or adapted to, the physical properties of the hands on the keyboard, and as such they establish a continuity with idiomatic keyboard writing through the ages, to say nothing of innumerable correspondences with the wider post-Classical repertory. Intertexts here might include etudes by Aloys Schmitt, Steibelt, Potter and Hiller (Ex. 13). The conformity with Steibelt is strengthened by tonal parallelism (A minor – C major), that with Potter by a transfer of the figuration to the left hand and then to both hands in the coda.

The characteristic deployment by pianist-composers in the 1820s of such idiomatic figures – in myriad combinations, juxtapositions and transformations – was in many ways simply an extension of Classical pianism. In general this music elaborated figurative textures that were all present in Mozart, and it relied too on the extended sequential patterns that were characteristically employed by Mozart to sustain the textures. Since the figures were usually irreducible and functioned as minimal formal units, they courted immediate repetition and resisted assimilation into larger paragraphs, so that a common practice was to allow groups of figures to form a larger unit and then to repeat this larger unit sequentially. One prophetic effect of this, incidentally, was a temporary suspension of harmonic teleology in favour of a symmetrical ordering of tonal space. Figuration ordered in this way was part and parcel of the 'brilliant style', to use a term well recognised in contemporary theory and criticism, where it could signify either a performance style or a compositional style, designed in both cases for the demonstration and display of technical mastery. Demonstrating and displaying are different things, of course, and in the Liszt exercises it is the former that largely prevails. One could almost add some of Czerny's functional sub-titles to some of these exercises, suggesting for instance that Nos. 1 and 2 are designed 'to develop the independence of the fingers in broken chords and broken octaves'. And as this suggests, their virtuosity is relatively contained, certainly when placed alongside contemporary works by, for example, Kalkbrenner, Pixis, or even Moscheles. Performer and composer have equal claims on the *Etude en douze exercices*. Virtuosity and work character are roughly in balance.

It is not always the idiomatic piano, as distinct from the idiomatic keyboard, that is exemplified by the figures in Liszt's exercises. I am not recommending it (!), but a performance of the first and (parts of) the second on harpsichord would not be entirely unimaginable. And even more plausible would be a harpsichord performance of at least part of the tenth, with its toccata-like scalar patterns in third and sixths. What this emphasises is that post-Classical virtuosity was not yet, or not fully, a specifically pianistic virtuosity. It might even be argued that the equal-finger technique cultivated by Czerny and others in their quest for a commanding technique promoted the idiomatic keyboard, but inhibited the idiomatic piano. Paradoxically, virtuosity – in the narrow sense of a display of technical skill through speed, agility and accuracy – could work against the distinctive voice of the piano in this repertory. That voice (and 'voice' is the appropriate term) often emerged at its clearest in moments of sentiment rather than display, as in the

---

[37] Such figures were popular in the immediate aftermath of Erard's double-escapement action.

Example 13 Liszt, *Etude en 12 exercices*, No. 2 bars 1–2
Schmidt, *Etudes*, Op. 16, No. 38 bars 1–2
Liszt, *Etude en 12 exercices*, No. 2 bars 5–6
Steibelt, *Etude en 50 exercices*, No. 2 bars 17
Potter, *Etudes*, Op. 19, No. 16 bars 19–20
Hiller, 24 *Grandes Etudes*, Op. 15, No. 8 bars 1–3

Liszt. *Etude en 12 exercices*, No. 2 bars 1–2

Schmidt. *Etudes*, Op. 16, No. 38 bars 1–2

Liszt. *Etude en 12 exercices*, No. 2 bars 5–6

Steibelt. *Etude en 50 exercices*, No. 2 bar 17

Potter. *Etudes*, Op. 19, No. 16 bars 19–20

Hiller. 24 *Grandes Etudes*, Op. 15, No. 8 bars 1–3

Example 14 Liszt, *Etude en 12 exercices*, No. 7 bars 1–2
Cramer, *Short Studies*, Op. 100, No. 22 bars 1–3
Clementi, *Preludi ed esercizi*, Prelude in C♯ minor bars 1–3

Liszt. *Etude en 12 exercices*, No. 7 bars 1–2

Cramer. *Short Studies*, Op. 100, No. 22 bars 1–3

Clementi. *Preludi ed esercizi*. Prelude in C♯ minor bars 1–3

lyrical pianism of No. 9, where successive textures – accompanied ornamental melody, parallel octaves, and pulsating chords of which the top voice is melodic – all exploit the idiomatic tonal qualities of the instrument; or in the legato chordal syncopations of no. 7, where the tonal quality of the piano, supported by the pedal, allows rhythmically dislocated materials to blend into a uniform texture. This latter texture was again common in the practice; compare the E♭ etude from Cramer's *Short Studies*, Op. 100, or the C♯ minor prelude from Clementi's *Preludi ed esercizi* (Ex. 14).

The idiomatic voice of the piano can also be heard in those pieces that differentiate elements of a broken-chord pattern to create a hierarchy within the figure. The fifth and sixth of the exercises might be considered together in this respect, and again neither of them is a bravura piece. In the opening bars of each, we can identify similar figures embodying similar technical problems. At the same time the texture allows for a blend of theme and figure (No. 5) or ground and figure (No. 6) through a skilful division of the hands. Such composite figures have a Baroque ancestry, but they were redesigned for early

Example 15 Liszt, *Etude en 12 exercices*, No. 6 bars 1–2
Cramer, *Short Studies*, Op. 100, No. 16 bars 1–2

Liszt. *Etude en 12 exercices*, No. 6 bars 1–2

Cramer. *Short Studies*, Op. 100, No. 16 bars 1–2

nineteenth-century pianism to establish a familiar texture of tiny particles in layered counter-point; once more there are countless parallels in contemporary pianism: compare No. 16 from Cramer's *Short Studies*, Op. 100 (Ex. 15), or the Potter and Steibelt extracts in Example 8.[38] The technical challenge in these exercises resides partly in preserving a weighted evenness of touch, so that hierarchies (melody-accompaniment) can be established while fluency is maintained. Thus in No. 5 the melody is confined to the upper (weaker) part of the hand while the accompaniment is in the lower (stronger) part. This differentiated counterpoint (as opposed to the equal-voiced counterpoint of Bach) is moulded to the idiomatic nature of the piano, where there can be a clear hierarchy of voices created by dynamic shading and layering, and where the harmonic resonance of the instrument can even permit the addition or subtraction of voices while preserving a perfect illusion of contrapuntal consistency. And much the same is true in the last of the exercises, which requires notes to be sustained at the extremes of both right and left hands, while the figure is subordinated to the theme on a different dynamic level.

In other words, it is through exercises that eschew display that the idiomatic piano emerges most clearly in the *Etude en douze exercices*. Naturally a great deal of virtuoso music was written for the piano prior to 1826. And naturally that music sounds better on the piano than on the harpsichord. But not all of it responded to an idiomatic imperative, in the sense that it exploited those properties of the piano that differentiate it explicitly from other keyboard instruments. This is not to suggest that bravura writing was totally unresponsive to the singularity of the piano. In the 1820s it responded in two very different ways. On the one hand, bravura figuration was enriched from within through the capacity of the piano to 'bring out' rather than simply imply a linear-contrapuntal working that emerges

---

[38] Again Reicha's *L'art de varier*, Op. 57, is a storehouse of relevant examples.

through the figure. On the other hand, the figures – accompanimental or decorative as well as integral – were themselves opened up through the wide leaps and widespread arpeggiations newly enabled by the resonance of the instrument, and by the pedal. There was also a third way, already intimated by the dramatic sequences and whirling octaves of the eighth of Liszt's exercises. I will elaborate on it in due course. But for now I will say that it exploited both the power and the lightness of the piano, and not only through differentiated dynamics. Massive chordal writing or bravura passages in octaves or double octaves (a 'vertical' technique) could sit alongside finely wrought filigree writing or delicate impressionistic washes of sound shading in the background for thematic substance (a 'horizontal' technique). One of the main changes represented by the 'vertical' technique was a shift from the virtuosity of the fingers to that of the wrist and the arm, a shift that supplemented and in some ways threatened the idiomatic figures of a post-Classical repertory. This amounted to pianistic virtuosity on a new plane, demanding a very different approach to technique than that imparted by Czerny. In due course it would culminate in the *Grandes Etudes* of Liszt.

It may be worth adding a brief postscript to this discussion by proposing a fourth, putative, ideal type of musical material. Formal motives, by definition, are identified by their function within a larger unit, and are thus primarily components of structure. However, they can sometimes also be identified as a class of material. In the first of the Liszt exercises the opening 'prelude' appears to give rise to an expository formal motive at bar 5, albeit still figurative in character. This is defined by its harmonic placement (the first structural downbeat on the tonic), phrase structure, and internal repetition scheme (*aab aab*), such that motivic definition emerges briefly from figuration. In other words we may identify what we take to be a formal motive from its qualities as an ideal type of musical material, and we would then expect it to function accordingly. There can, however, be a rhetorical dimension to the relation of material to function. Just as a popular generic theme (say, a waltz or barcarolle) may become the unexpected basis of a sonata-form movement, as in a Chopin ballade, so a musical idea whose 'cut' is that of a formal motive may in the end fail to function as such. This is precisely what happens in the first exercise, and the fact that the functional implication of the motive is not realised in the formal discourse in no sense annuls our initial identification (even when the opening figuration returns to define the form as rounded binary). In the eleventh exercise, on the other hand, there are no such complications. Here the opening theme is a Classical period, whose phrase structure, internal repetitions (*ab ac*), and schematic accompaniment pattern all identify it as a 'subject' whose formal function will be established by repetition and development. Stylistically, there are parallels with Voříšek and Schubert, but it is telling that, unlike them, Liszt achieved intensification in the middle section through the rhetoric of pianistic devices rather than through motivic working. In any event, the formal motive here points unambiguously to work character rather than to performance. It is less amenable to recomposition as a 'characteristic' melody (try playing it at different speeds, for example) or as a bravura figuration than the motives or figures of the other exercises; and there we may already have the principal reason that Liszt decided to abandon No. 11 in his later recompositions.

AN ACTIVE PRESENT

The identification of a material content in this way privileges the contemporary moment of Liszt's exercises, as also the preceding moment, the world that helped to shape them. It depicts Liszt 'in his time'. In seeking commonalities of musical material, we may hear distant echoes of expressive vocal figures from the remote past, their original meanings all but lost. We may hear more vibrant echoes of popular genres from the recent past, many of them imbued with sedimented social as well as musical meanings. We may hear too materials that direct us away from the music towards its performance, foregrounding skill, technique and virtuosity, and signifying present immediacies, the events and actions (rather than the works) of a pre-recital practice. And finally, we may hear figures that point towards elements of work character within that practice. My representation of ideal types of musical material amounts to little more than a sketch, and one whose limitations should be rather clear. The identification of figures confines our explanation to what Roger Scruton has called a 'recognitional capacity'.[39] It demands that further stage of interpretation that will be essayed in chapter 6. Nonetheless it is a starting-point. Its larger aim in this chapter is twofold. First it seeks to describe the intersection of the repertory and its practice, and that carries with it a caution against collapsing the materials of multiple practices (for all the undoubted overlaps between them) into a single period style. And secondly, it tries to make concrete that sense in which the individual work is, as Barthes memorably suggested, a 'tissue of quotations'.[40] Of course, investigating Liszt 'in his time' already involved a dialogue between ourselves and the past. In turning now to Liszt 'for today', and setting the two perspectives side by side, we enable a further stage of that dialogue.

Liszt 'for today' may not be quite the right slogan, given recent changes not only in scholarship, but in the structures of musical life. However our listening habits are not so quickly changed. Those listening habits have been very largely shaped by the age and ethos of the recital, and by the work-concept embodied in a recital culture. Indeed one of the difficulties in cutting our way through to Liszt 'in his time' is precisely the need to de-naturalise some of these ways of hearing. Music analysis can partly stand for the recital culture. Of course we know that such analysis impinges hardly at all on the listening public, and perhaps only marginally on the professional musician (a point well made by Nicholas Cook in several publications).[41] But the analytical enterprise is without question a celebration of the musical work, of its greatness, and of its autonomy character, which means in practice its goal-directed rather than additive structure. More crucially, analysis, whatever precise form it may take, interprets the musical work as a real presence in our culture today, imbued with meanings that were made concrete only in relatively late stages of its reception. In other words, of its nature it is concerned with an active present rather than a recovered past. It speaks of our world in several ways: in its tendency to adopt the esoteric languages

---

[39] Roger Scruton, *The Aesthetic Understanding* (London, 1983), p. 99. See Robert Hatten's comments on this in *Musical Meaning in Beethoven*, pp. 31–2.

[40] Roland Barthes, *Image–Music–Text* (London, 1977), p. 146.

[41] Notably *Music, Imagination and Culture* (Oxford, 1990).

Example 16 Cyclic associations in the *Etude en 12 exercices*

Cyclic associations in the *Etude en 12 exercices*

promoted by an ethos of professionalism; in its investment in the status of the work as a text rather than a performance; and in its relativistic appropriation of the object of analysis. When we analyse, in other words, we construct the Liszt exercises in the image of our world.

Nothing illustrates this more clearly than our apparent need to view cycles such as this as a whole, a point elaborated by Jeffrey Kallberg in an essay on Chopin's *24 Préludes*.[42] To conceive Liszt's twelve exercises as a unified work is implicitly to elevate their artistic status by attributing to the entire cycle a structural sense of form. Such an enterprise would have been less likely to engage an early nineteenth-century musician, quite apart from its apparent incompatibility with the conventions of the genre. After all, it can be argued that etudes and exercises, almost by definition, were weakly conceived in terms of work character. And the case is hardly strengthened by our knowledge that Liszt anyway intended a further three books of exercises. If he had completed his initial project of forty-eight exercises, or even twenty-four of them, the tonal progression would of course have resulted in closure of a kind, albeit through a (Bachian) principle of chromatic exhaustivity – literally a cycle – rather than one of tonal reprise. As it is, the harmonic structure remains open. The logic of the tonal ordering may create a connecting thread through the twelve exercises, but it falls short of full circle. All the same, for today's listener, and very possibly for Liszt himself, that thread is strengthened by tonal associations forged across the cycle (mediant and submediant relations within an individual exercise will inevitably establish links with neighbouring exercises where the overall key scheme descends in thirds, as in Nos. 1 and 2, and again Nos. 8, 9 and 10), by a three-note motive common to some of the earlier exercises (Ex. 16a), and by a descending *fauxbourdon* scale which appears explicitly at strategic points in several of the exercises, and is arguably present more latently in others (Ex.16b). All of these may be regarded as 'associational structures', and while they may indeed strengthen the cohesion of the cycle for many listeners, they can only be regarded

---

[42] Jeffrey Kallberg, 'Small "Forms": in Defense of the Prelude', in Jim Samson (ed.), *The Cambridge Companion to Chopin* (Cambridge, 1992), pp. 124–44.

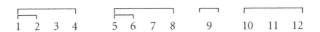

Figure 1 *Etude en douze exercices*. Grouping structures

as hierarchical – and therefore unifying – within an unhelpfully general meaning of the term.

Programming practices today naturally encourage us to hear such collections as single works rather than as self-standing miniatures. In formal terms, therefore, a likely listening strategy of our age – rather less likely in the early nineteenth century – is to group Liszt's exercises into larger units. The strategic placement of the four cantabile exercises encourages such groupings. One possibility, for instance, would be to view the first four exercises as a single group, where No. 1 acts as a prelude to No. 2, making a larger three-part form in which a melody is enclosed within two figurations, or perhaps a pastorale within two etudes. The next four exercises might then form a second group. Like Nos. 1 and 2, Nos. 5 and 6 are closely linked, this time through texture, suggesting another three-part form, where the enclosed melody, marked 'con molta espressiona', would be No. 7. Again it is sandwiched between sections based on figuration. Nos. 10–12 would comprise a final three-part form, this time with a 'Classical' melody – intermezzo-like in its outer sections – enclosed between two contrasted etudes. This leaves No. 9, which stands somewhat apart from the rest of the set as an expansive, self-contained slow movement, acting as the point of repose between groups 5–8 and 10–12 (Fig. 1). This reading is further supported by what we might term the intensity curve of the cycle, which rises through group 2 to reach its maximum intensity in No. 8. The point of greatest contrast in the cycle, then, is between the impassioned bravura of No. 8 and the nocturne-like tranquillity of No. 9. (It might be noted, incidentally, that the cantabile exercises remain on the flat side of the tonal spectrum.) Such 'grouping structures' by definition span the work as a whole, but they are concerned with boundaries rather than territories, with form rather than process, and as such they have a rather limited capacity to unify the cycle.

It is when we come to examine individual exercises that analysis can most helpfully complement history. Here we move from an investigation of musical materials, where the orientation is towards genres rather than works, to a focus on form and structure, strengthening the sense of work character, of individuation, and of singular authorship. Effectively we ask about the individual strategies by means of which common materials have been assembled into a form. In the following account, my aim is modest: a breakdown of the individual etudes into their main formal components, with supplementary observations on phrase structure and harmony. The sectionalisation of music's 'flowing state' in this way would obviously be problematical for anything approaching a more sophisticated analysis, but at least it will prove useful here for later comparative study, given that the main themes of the exercises were taken over by Liszt in his later recompositions. The idiomatic figures of the first exercise, supportive of its generic character, stress the tactile, the technical, the immediate, the performative (Ex. 17). It would be possible to map out the entire piece in such terms, adopting an additive or combinative approach to its musical materials, rather as

Example 17 Idiomatic figures in the *Etude en 12 exercices*, No. 1

Idiomatic figures in the *Etude en 12 exercices*, No.1

a × 3   b × 5
a × 3   b × 5
                        c × 4   d × 3
                        c × 4   d × 3
                                        e × 8   f × 12
        a' × 2   f' × 2
                                                        g × 3   h × 9
                                                        g × 2
                b × 2
        a' × 4
        a × 3   b × 5
        a × 3   b × 25
                                                        g × 20

Figure 2 *Etude en douze exercices*, No. 1. Repetition structures

suggested in Figure 2.[43] Already a clear repetition structure emerges from this map. However the play of figures is subordinated to a larger grouping structure dictated by metrical and phrase-structural relationships which are conventional within the style, and would naturally yield a very different repetition structure. And here we may note that while deviations from the normative pattern established in bars 1–8 are themselves in a sense conventional, they nonetheless direct the music away from regularities of phrase structure and of motivic definition. There is a sense, then, in which the analysis of repetition schemes and phrase structures dissolves a regular periodicity into a complexity of differentiated materials.

Analysis such as this lays out the ground on which further motivic interrelationships (associational structures) might be plotted. As we bind these into a form, however, we note problematical features of a kind that will recur in several of the later exercises. The simplest reading of the larger form is as a rounded binary, where the opening material is recapitulated at bar 20. However, as I observed earlier, this opening material is tonally inductive, and functions as an upbeat to the structural downbeat of bar 5, at which point the tonic is clarified in association with a formal motive that has something of the character of a principal idea or 'first subject'. The oddity here is that, unlike the opening material, this formal motive is not repeated. In any event, it is the underlying harmonic movement that determines the larger shape of this piece, enabling hierarchical relationships that can be registered both at a background structural level and at a more immediate foreground level, and can therefore – in theory at least – help us to relate the part organically to the

---

[43] For a systematic attempt to partition figures in a similar, but not identical, manner, see Tomi Mäkelä, *Virtuosität und Werkcharakter* (Munich and Salzburg, 1989), pp. 42–5.

whole. Such hierarchies are simply not available to associational, metrical or grouping structures, and it is for this reason that harmony offers to many listeners the best hope of hearing a piece as a unified structure. Something of the integration of structural levels through patterns of cadential harmony has already been noted (Ex. 3). It might be added here that prolongations outline third-related harmonic sequences (bars 11–14 and 15–18) in ways that are familiar enough from Classical repertories, but already look to the symmetrical figurations characteristic of Liszt's maturity.

The second exercise has a simple three-part tonal scheme (A minor – C major – A minor), but it is surprisingly difficult to map its figurations and themes on to this structure in a coherent way. Nor should we assume that these are enriching ambiguities, as distinct from youthful confusions. Part of the difficulty flows from the kind of shading between thematic definition and a constantly evolving figuration that can often be characteristic of the etude as a genre, but is here obfuscatory. However, a more problematical feature is the early return of the tonic following the C major section, creating a sense of tonal redundancy in the later stages that is not entirely eliminated even in the subsequent recompositions. The opening 'mirror' theme (the hands in informal inversion and with loose elements of palindrome in the theme itself) is the first part of a bipartite subject, where both parts describe an arc-like shape of scale and arpeggio respectively, while the second part cadences with a strongly characterised arpeggiation figure (bar 8). Yet the relation between the two ideas is oddly gauged. Neither has the internal repetition typical of a Classical period, and the first might almost be regarded as an introduction to the second, except that both affirm the A minor tonic (the first more weakly than the second). There is further ambiguity when the music moves to C major. This is a new theme, but it really amounts to a remoulding of the original octave figuration, and this time the theme is worked in a more conventionally Classical manner, with sequential repetition. Understood in this way, the original bipartite structure is repeated in the new tonal area, with the second part of the subject used to return the music to A minor. From this point the tonic is secure, and we might read the remainder of the form in two ways: as an immediate recapitulation, with a variant of the opening theme in informal invertible counterpoint (a further remoulding of the thematic shape imposed on the figuration), or as a brief middle section followed by the 'real' reprise when the second part of the theme returns in the tonic. The non-thematic, tension-building figuration of bars 21–7 strengthens the latter reading, while the mono-tonality from bar 17 supports the former. Figure 3 outlines the structure diagrammatically.

The expressive motives described in the third exercise are animated by particularities of phrase structure and at the same time structured by a close integration of material, ranging from the ubiquity of the double-note texture to the larger top-voice spans. At the same time they are developed into a surprisingly sophisticated form combining variation and ternary. Since all these features are common to the later recompositions of the etude, it will be worth elaborating a little here. The opening strophe (bars 1–15) presents an irregular phrase structure as in Figure 4. Within this there are further asymmetries – essentially rhythmic syncopations that allow large-scale motives to emerge. For instance, in Example 18a, the placement of the top-voice progression is on the second crotchet beat for the a'' and bb'' and on the second quaver beat for the c'''. Likewise, the phrasing within the two parts of the

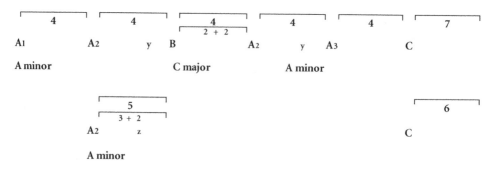

				4			

Figure 3 *Etude en 12 exercices*, No. 2. Formal design

$$a \qquad\qquad b \qquad\qquad c$$

$$2 + 2 \quad + \quad 3 + 3 \quad + \quad 3 + 2$$

Figure 4 *Etude en 12 exercices*, No. 3, bars 1–15. Phrase structure

Example 18 Motivic-rhythmic figures in the *Etude en 12 exercices*, No. 3

Motivic-rhythmic figures in the *Etude en 12 exercices*, No. 3

$$a' \qquad\qquad c$$

$$2 + 2 \qquad\qquad 3 + 3 + 4$$

Figure 5 *Etude en 12 exercices*, No. 3, bars 16–29. Phrase structure

b section is significantly varied. The second strophe thickens and chromaticises *a* (indeed, no two statements of *a* are exactly alike), omits *b*, and develops *c* by sequential repetition to a total of ten bars to allow a modulation to the subdominant (Fig. 5). The middle section or third strophe is a modulating sequence based on *a* and *b* and followed by a transformation of *c* with a new consequent. The colouristic change of mode from major to minor is striking

a	b	a	b	c'
2 + 2	4	2 + 2	2 + 2 + 2	4 + 4

Bb major   Bb minor

Figure 6 *Etude en 12 exercices*, No. 3, bars 30–55. Phrase structure

I	*a b a b*		(2 + 2)
IV	*a b a*	*c c*	(2 + 1 + 2)
I	*b*		(1)
I	*a b*	*d d e e*	(2 + 2 + 2)

Figure 7 *Etude en 12 exercices*, No. 5, bars 1–16. Formal design

here (Fig. 6). The reprise is regular in the main, though with a short coda, and throughout the exercise the third progressions are integrated at several levels over a conventional harmonic schema, rather as sketched in Ex. 18b. It should be noted that both the subdominant (rather than dominant) direction of the harmony and the change of mode are characteristic for a pastoral topic.

The fifth of the exercises is one of the most ambitious of the cycle, and also one of the most difficult to categorise in terms of conventional formal archetypes. Attempts to understand it in sonata-form terms seem to me unhelpful, except in the general sense that it involves relatively large-scale tonal and thematic tensions. The true dynamic of the piece lies in an interruptive quality, where the mono-motivic character of the etude genre is not so much balanced, as interrupted, by contrasted elements. In the process sonata-like materials (as distinct from sonata-form components) do indeed intrude – at times rather oddly – into the generic world of the etude. The first of the four extended sections is unexceptional in this respect, allowing its period structures to play with conventional expectations in interesting but by no means unprecedented ways, rather as Figure 7 suggests. Following this sixteen-bar paragraph the first interruption occurs, initiating the second section of the piece. This comprises a group of unusually constituted elements which alternate with the main theme in textural and registral contrast (Fig. 8). The overall harmonic scheme plotted by this sequence is outlined on Example 19. It describes a progression from I to V with the harmony coloured chromatically at various stages. The arrival at V introduces the third section, a sonata-like (specifically an early Beethoven sonata-like) left-hand melody with answering sighing figure (Ex. 9), to which the basic figuration of the main theme acts as an accompaniment. The sigh motive then takes us through what appears to be a modulating field before circling back to V for the final stage of the piece. Here the alternation of *a* and *x* from section 2 briefly returns in V before the main theme and a 'new' codetta theme round off the etude. The overall effect is rather like a hybrid between an etude and a sonata, with the consistency of the etude broken up by the sonata elements and the dramatic tensions of

Example 19 Harmonic schemes in the *Etude en 12 exercices*, No. 5

Harmonic schemes in the *Etude en 12 exercices*, No. 5

Bars	1	1	1	1	1	4	2 + 2	1	2	1	4	2
Elements	*a*	*x*	*a*	*x*	*a*	*b*	*c*	*d*	*x*	*d*	*x*	*e*

x: the principal theme
a: strident right-hand chords over left-hand scales to which the theme is a
    contrasted echo
b: conventional right-hand scalar figuration in modulating sequence
c: a countertheme with alberti-like accompaniment on V of V
d: a scalar figure in octaves with the character of closural gesture, but here
    functioning (like *a*) as a foil to *x*
e: conventional closural gesture leading to V

Figure 8 *Etude en 12 exercices*, No. 5, bars 17–38. Formal design

the sonata weakened by a diffuse thematic substance and by the absence of clearly defined areas of tonal opposition and synthesis.

In contrast, the sixth exercise conforms more closely to the archetype of the genre. A single configuration is maintained throughout, while the shape of the piece is determined by harmony and its design by internal repetitions of the double-note ground. For all that, the phrase structure is characteristically irregular, and as elsewhere in these exercises it is by no means easy to decide how much of this is purposeful ambiguity and how much youthful inexperience. Thus the five-bar phrase at the opening, in which a Classical top-voice descent elaborates a simple I–II–V pattern, is immediately repeated. By analogy with bar 6, bar 11 is heard as initiating, but comes to be viewed retrospectively as a closure to the second (now six-bar) phrase (Ex. 20a). The material that follows in the dominant minor has a more regular phrasing, as an outline of its melodic repetitions indicates (Ex. 20b). However, the dynamic markings here (presumably Liszt's) break up the phrase structure in ways that can only be described as eccentric. Then, when there is a partial return of the opening idea (confirming the form as a rounded binary), the phrase structure is reversed, with a six-bar phrase in the tonic and a five-bar repetition in the flat submediant. The final section, beginning in a remote F major, varies the melodic ground yet again, but once more the basic unit is a five-bar phrase, with a cadential extension to the repetition, and a characteristic, prelude-like, break before the final cadence.

The seventh exercise, one of the most persuasive of the set, allows its syncopated melodic shape, with informal inversion in the left hand, to emerge from the harmonic resonance of an E♭ major tonic chord, as in Example 14. The melody adopts one of the formal patterns

Example 20 Phrase structures and motives in the *Etude en 12 exercices*, No. 6

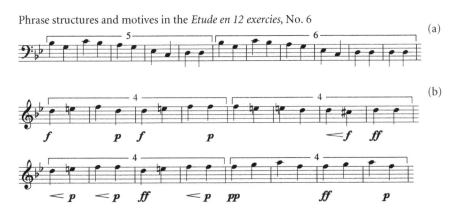

Phrase structures and motives in the *Etude en 12 exercies*, No. 6

conventionally associated with the Classical eight-bar sentence, with two distinct melodic shapes subject to repetition, and a two-bar liquidation picking up the falling scalar pattern of the second shape. The immediate repetition of this opening sentence is diverted into a sequential intensification of the material in a manner familiar enough for the genre (etude or exercise), and here the syncopation is translated into a literal canon at the semiquaver between the two hands, a 'rhetorical' gesture that hints at characteristic tension-building figurations from Liszt's later music. This middle section culminates in a rising chromatic-scalar progression that signals the partial reprise at bar 27. The four-note closing motive, whose layering across the texture produces uncomfortable parallel fifths in the voice lead-ing, is interrupted by a cadenza, again highly characteristic for aria-like pieces within the style, before the final cadence. As the melody unfolds it outlines certain larger implicative structures within a uniform texture-space, all of them depending on stepwise movement that circles around a top-voice 3, and with a conventional underlying harmonic support. Indeed the eccentricities of form and presentation that are marked in the second, fifth and sixth of the etudes are conspicuous by their absence here.

The eighth of the exercises, whose affinity with Beethoven has been noted, is one of the most ambitious of the set in terms of formal organisation. It would be misleading to suggest that it was a full-scale sonata-form movement, but it undoubtedly comes closer than any of the others to that kind of thinking. The most straightforward reading of the exercise is as an extended form of rounded binary, essentially monothematic, but with a modulating middle section and a brief reprise of the opening. Yet the scale of the piece – the main theme has itself a tripartite design describing a large-scale I–V–I progression – and the modulating transition to E major (bars 24–31), based on a motive from the main theme, hint at a background of sonata form, albeit monothematic and with a compressed recapitulation. That move to E major within a C minor context is itself suggestive of the later Liszt, but more importantly it initiates a 'working out' section of a distinctly Classical cut, where the alternation of elements between the hands in a kind of invertible coun-terpoint unfolds through a circle of fifths before a dominant preparation (based on ma-terial from the exposition) returns us to the main theme and key. Here too the shadow

Example 21 *Etude en 12 exercices*, No. 9 bars 2–3, 6–7

Etude en 12 exercices, No. 9

bars 2–3

bars 6–7

of Beethoven is unmistakable. And it is worth noting that in the 1837 recompositions this is the first of the exercises to be translated into a more fully elaborated sonata-form movement.

It is something of a commonplace in Liszt criticism that the ninth exercise is the most mature of the set. As Alan Walker remarks, 'its nocturne-like melody, which so many . . . assume to have been inspired by Chopin, was in fact the creation of the thirteen-year-old [sic] Liszt'.[44] If Liszt took any single general model it must surely have been the nocturnes of Field, several of which follow the same basic procedure, which is to offset the main 'aria' with contrasted melodies, here in the sequence *a b a c a*. Liszt's melody is characteristically vocal in shape, and its ornamentation stylises a typical operatic practice, though such devices were already well rehearsed in piano music. Given that so many aspects of this melody are conventional within the style (its appoggiatura figures, its four-bar phrase structure, and its rhythmic and textural invariance), it is hard to pinpoint the source of its striking appeal. Much of the freshness undoubtedly lies in the detail, and especially in subtle variations in the relation between melody and harmony between the two phrases (bars 1–8). The changes here (the outer bars of each phrase are identical) influence both the larger sweep of the underlying harmony (increasing the sense of movement in the second strophe) and at the same time ensure that the points of dissonance created by the appoggiaturas are varied, as Example 21 indicates. As noted earlier, the foils to this aria are again melodies characteristic of the nocturne style. They are contrasted not only in texture but in structure (*b* is marked by an internal repetition scheme, *c* by a continuously unfolding, non-repetitive line), but they both dissolve into cadenza-like material, with a shared left-hand motive, and that material later forms the basis of extended sections in the recompositions. Likewise, the tonal scheme of the exercise – in which *b* and *c* are in the relative minor and sub-dominant

[44] Walker, *The Virtuoso Years*, p. 119.

Example 22 Motivic and harmonic patterns in the *Etude en 12 exercices*, No. 10

Motivic and harmonic patterns in the *Etude en 12 exercices*, No. 10

respectively, creating a third-related sequence – is taken over more-or-less unchanged in the later etudes.

The toccata-like figurations of the tenth exercise trace characteristic scale-based motives over a conventionally modulating harmonic framework, in which sequential working, with diminutions and extensions, is prominent. The emergence of motivic definition from this *moto perpetuo* figuration is often unpredictable in relation to underlying phrase structures, however. Thus, the opening sixteen-bar paragraph is not a straightforward pairing of two eight-bar sentences, but a characteristically irregular grouping, where the only conventionally constructed eight-bar sentence is the passage from bar 8 to bar 15. The first clearly defined motive is *x* in Example 22, but it yields to a three-note rising scalar pattern (*y*) for the eight-bar sentence at bar 8, which cadences conventionally by way of a diminished-seventh harmony.[45] On repetition, the second part of this extended opening paragraph develops *x* sequentially, moving across third-related harmonies (f, A♭, c and E♭), and the E♭ then functions as the dominant of the relative major, clarified at bar 31. From this point a new figure (inverting the opening) is introduced, and with various extensions it forms the basis of further sequential modulations, taking us through first G♭ major and then B♭ minor (bars 36–48). The dominant is finally approached by way of further diminished-seventh harmonies, and it resolves to the tonic at bar 66 for a brief reprise of the opening material, and a final cadential flourish.

I will pass over No. 11, in some ways the most self-contained and Classically conceived of the set, since it was not used by Liszt in his later recompositions. The last of the exercises

---

[45] Bar numbering here counts the first (incomplete) bar as bar 1.

in B♭ minor, on the other hand, offered Liszt ample opportunity for rethinking, both in terms of its expressive melodic substance (with supporting 'melodic' bass) and its uninterrupted accompanimental figuration. The exercise has a conventional two-part structure, preceded by a four-bar introduction which foreshadows the main theme. It is essentially a varied strophic design, of which the first strophe moves, again predictably, to the dominant harmony, while the second, creeping in on the crest of a chromatic codetta figuration, foreshortens the melody to enable first a brief climactic development of its principal motive and then a coda. However, the melodic structure within this conventional surface is remarkably fluid, offsetting the regular periodicities of the opening 'question and answer' with motivic repetitions (sometimes chromatically inflected) that impose new metrical groupings on the constant flow of the music. Interestingly, the later etudes iron out some of these irregularities, and this is a pattern repeated elsewhere in the cycle. Just as figuration is amplified, so melodies are 'characterised', and that often involved a simplification of their structure.

This kind of commentary, demonstrating the singularity of the pieces with reference to schemata of various kinds, would probably have seemed of limited value to early nineteenth-century theorists and critics. For the most part, the theorist was preoccupied with notionally universal properties of music, of which the work was an illustration. The critic was interested in the work, but was inclined to register this interest as an empirical aesthetic judgement. These differences in perspective hinge partly on concepts of uniqueness and individuality, and such concepts are not entirely neutral. They need very careful handling when applied to the practice of post-Classical pianism. In particular, individuality within this practice was not yet freighted with a Romantic ideology, where it would be associated not just with a characteristic and singular deployment of recognised skills but with the biography and personality of the artist or the interpretative demands of the work. To cultivate individuality in the early nineteenth-century practice was to cultivate qualities of performance as well as of composition, and within the practice the former were admired as much as the latter. Moreover, such individual qualities were intended and understood neither as 'fragments of autobiography' nor as agents of interpretation. For the pianist-composer, they were independent values – ends in themselves – that were regarded as essential to a distinctive profile, and they had to sit alongside those other, no less vital, pre-requisites of success: easy, undemanding communication, a readily assimilable message, clearly defined norms. Individuality, compositional and performative, was invariably grounded in the familiar.

One might go further. Far from describing a progress towards Romantic individualism and subjectivity, post-Classical pianism (rather like Rossini-an opera) actually tolerated a much greater degree of stylistic uniformity than anything we find in so-called Viennese Classical music. It was first and foremost an art of conformity, and for the most part its individuality was a calculated display of novelty, not unlike the kind described, and deplored, by Adorno in relation to popular music (in both cases the public pressure towards conformity was and is considerable). The practice of pianism began to congeal in the 1820s, and as it did so its tendency was to reduce rather than to enhance the diversities and refinements that had differentiated pianist-composers of an earlier generation. The multiple voices of a youthful practice, in other words, made way for more uniform voices, as celebrity pianism was increasingly channelled on to the twin rails of (post-Classical) virtuosity and (pre-Romantic) sentiment. In this sense the brilliant style might be represented as a kind of transition, to use a dangerous word. Compositionally, it amounted to a populist, conformant idiom which developed from, and smoothed out, the individuality of late Classicism in the interests of virtuosity. At the same time, in performance history, it prepared the ground for a rather different quality of individuality, that of the Romantic pianists. This latter, the expression of a sanctioned ideology of subjectivity, whose origins were closely linked to political liberalism and to the rise of an Idealist aesthetics, reached its full fruition rather later in the day, and it will be discussed here in due course.

It will be worth reviewing the general approach adopted by this chapter, an approach that might be loosely related to a critical hermeneutics. The first stage was to isolate fragments of a general language and relate them to qualities of a collective practice. The quest here was for a causal understanding that might enable us at least to begin formulating something like the intention of the text. To describe this as a collectively authored document responsive to a particular ecology would be to pitch it too high; rather my aim has been to hint at the collective voice bearing on the individual voice, and to do so in rather more than just the usual stylistic terms. The second stage was to sketch putative forms, recognising that these represent present-day perceptual constructions, and that my formal descriptions may well be incompatible with other formal descriptions. To represent these approaches starkly as the perspectives of the historical subject and the present-day subject respectively is again to push it too far. Early nineteenth-century listeners were no doubt more alive to figures than we are today, but they would also have heard the figures as part of something larger, taking on new properties in the process. I would argue, however, that in doing so they would have been guided more by generic conventions than by a structural sense of form. Likewise today's listener, as Adorno lamented, is well capable of atomised (as opposed to structural) listening, but will tend to miss the representational and even iconic significance of the individual gesture, isolated from its context. More crucially, the effect of both stages is to problematise intention and authorship, albeit in rather different ways. I will avoid here the ontological debate about the very possibility of creation (as distinct from discovery). It is enough to point out that although the specific arrangement of collectively authored fragments amounts to an individual statement, and may even embody a unity of intention, this is not the same as claiming that the meanings of the fragments lead to the meaning of the whole. On the contrary, their meanings may be dispersed laterally. Likewise, a perceived structure that corresponds to my experience of the music today is separated from authorial intention by multiple, incremental layers of receptional insight. Its meaning incorporates the 'effective history' of early nineteenth-century repertories over the better part of two centuries, and that includes their submission to the scrutiny of analysts. Squeezed by both history and analysis, the voice of the youthful composer struggles to be heard.

Chapter Three

▬

Composing the performance

SOUNDING HISTORY

Traditional modes of analysis implicitly attribute privileged meanings to formal, harmonic and motivic relationships. The underlying assumption seems to be that structural functions of this kind make up the content or substance of the work. Content or substance, in other words, equate roughly with a particular kind of (top-down) structural configuration, a relatively modern equation which paradoxically strengthens both a sense of the work's originality and uniqueness, and a sense of its communion with other music; *semper idem sed non eodem modo* [always the same, but not always in the same way] was Schenker's formulation.[1] Indeed it is precisely through this paradox that the work might be viewed as a form of knowledge, the particular tracing of a universal form, as well as an object of beauty. When analysis was instituted as a discipline in the late nineteenth century, it formalised a growing tendency for the profiles of individual works to emerge sharply from music as a whole, and specifically from larger generic groupings. One might argue about the details of the history here. But at the very least there was a shift of emphasis through the nineteenth century from a position where genres were exemplified by works to one in which works made their own statement. The work, clearly defined against a generic background, would be legitimised by its structure, and that in turn might be revealed by analysis. Hence the antinomy in the preceding chapter between genre and work: between those genre markers and other figures which stress the music's relationship to larger groupings, and those formal, harmonic and motivic functions which translate it – through a reductive, yet integrative process – into a schematic structure. That schematic structure is presumed to stand for the original and durable 'ideal aesthetic object' we call the musical work.[2] It gives it 'work character'.

There is another antinomy highlighted by analysis. We might describe it as an opposition between text and performance, each of which is in a sense contained by the musical work. Analytical functions reveal the properties – the constructedness – of a text, an object made of notational symbols. And since in all cases these functions involve a reduction from explicit

---

[1] The motto to *Free Composition* (*Der Freie Satz*): Volume 3 of *Neue Musikalische Theorien und Phantasien*, ed. and trans. Ernst Oster (New York, 1979; orig. edn, 1935).

[2] See Roman Ingarden, *The Work of Music and the Problem of its Identity*, trans. A. Czerniawski, ed. J. G. Harrell (Berkeley and Los Angeles, 1986; orig. edn, 1928) for this ontology.

surface to implicit structure, they remain a-idiomatic; one might almost say performer-proof, except that a performer may choose to underline or suppress them. Moreover, as I implied at the end of the last chapter, reducing the work to a text strips it of a sense of authorship or ownership, a sense that someone worked to produce it. It de-humanises and neutralises the work. It suppresses its historical nature, its production at a particular historical moment, the outcome of someone's activity, in favour of its a-historical, durable presence in our culture. A performance, on the other hand, is itself an activity; it is time-specific, singular and expressive, asserting the work, but at the same time instantiating it in a unique and particular way. It realises one of the many possible worlds prescribed by the text, and it does so within certain contextual constraints, including the skills and personality of the performer. It is tempting to think of performance, then, as the Saussurian *parole* of a compositional *langue*.[3] But this can be no more than suggestive, for in reality both composition and performance have their *langue* and *parole*, just as both have their 'text' and 'act'.[4] The compositional act is, of course, concealed from us, though we may struggle to recover it. And the performative text, the product of the act, is no less elusive; it vanishes into the ether. All the same, the act is not synonymous with its outcome.

In large part these are present-day concerns. It has been common for our age to view the work as a musical whole, intentionally shaped, its configuration fixed once-and-for-all in its notation. Yet, just as there was a shift from genre to work, or perhaps rather a separation of genre and work, roughly congruent with the separation of 'popular' and 'significant' – formulaic and original – repertories, during the nineteenth century, so too there was a separation of text and performance. Like genre and work, these were far from cleanly divided prior to the nineteenth century; witness figured bass realisation, ornamentation, and other forms of extemporisation. Really performance was widely regarded as the final stage (in rhetorical terms, the execution) of a largely undifferentiated process of making music. However, as the notated text congealed into a fixed form, supposedly representing its author's intentions, so the performer became increasingly an interpreter, subordinated to the work, yet at the same time marked off as special by the uniqueness of his or her interpretation. We need to take a very long view of this to see the pattern emerge. From an intimately related, if not fused, pair in the eighteenth century, performance and text separated out through the nineteenth century and had been well and truly split apart by the early twentieth. Stravinsky and Busoni might be taken to represent polarised responses to this increasingly divided culture, where the one fetishised the text and the other the performance. For Stravinsky interpretation 'got in the way' of the composer's intentions as represented by the text. For Busoni those intentions were imperfectly reflected in the text, but could be accessed by the inspired performer *through* the text. In effect, Busoni reordered a Platonic degenerative sequence, such that the performance, although subsequent to the text, might be closer to the ideal form of the work.

I will not even attempt to trace with greater specificity the origins of a polarity between the work-as-text and the work-as-performance; for one thing, it varied from practice to

[3] See Susan Bernstein, *Virtuosity of the Nineteenth Century: Performing Music and Language in Heine, Liszt and Baudelaire* (Stanford, 1998), pp. 41–51.
[4] My terms are a tribute to Richard Taruskin, *Text and Act* (Oxford, 1995).

practice. Carl Dahlhaus has famously drawn attention to it in relation to Beethoven and Rossini, and one might add that it became even more pronounced in the reception histories of those composers in the later nineteenth century. In the one case there was a developing conviction that the notational form embodied a kind of intentional knowledge – an idea which originated with the composer and was made available to the listener.[5] In the other case, where the text is typically more fluid and often in search of 'completion' by the performer, the listener would be encouraged to focus on the medium as much as the message, to appreciate a sensuous or brilliant surface persuasively and directly communicated by the performer rather than to search out a form of knowledge embedded (concealed) in sound structures by the composer.[6] For the aficionado of Italian opera, today as much as in the early nineteenth century, the great singer can justify the mediocre aria. The performer can make the evening. At risk of reading history backwards, I venture that already during the eighteenth century this division between notational and acoustic forms was plotted and enabled. That century greatly strengthened the work-concept, establishing the relative autonomy of the work by loosening the threads binding it to genre and social function. It also created the modern virtuoso, an international figure in whom the activity of performance gained (or regained) its own measure of autonomy.[7] And it is fair to say that until recently this activity has not been subject to the kind of scholarly scrutiny afforded to musical works. Our instincts as historians, by and large, have been to value composers rather than performers, even to the point of disguising the rather basic condition of music as a performing art. (The study of so-called 'performance practice' is something of a red herring here, for its concern is at least as much with works – doing justice to them – as with performances.)

Jankélévitch is right to remind us that virtuosity is 'as old as music'.[8] The concept, if not the term, was part of Classical Greek writings on music. Yet however long established as a phenomenon, it was institutionalised at determinate stages within the practices of Western music history (its role within non-Western musics is too big a subject to introduce here). The concept of virtuosity seems to offer only a limited yield on medieval repertories in Europe, for example, though it can play a significant role in the presentation of this music to audiences today.[9] Or at least the term itself had a quite different resonance in pre-Renaissance Europe. As Susan Bernstein reminds us, it first came into prominence in the Italian cinquecento, with the sense of 'possessing virtue', and its application was by no means only, or even primarily, associated with the fine arts.[10] Of course, the refinement of vocal and instrumental technique was a dimension of the developing 'profession' of music in pre- and early modern Europe, highlighting a growing tension between art music (an *ars subtilior*) and popular culture (music for the *illiterati*). The history of secular song would be distinctly relevant if

---

[5] The 'musical idea' will be explored in chapter 4.

[6] Susan Sontag urges an appreciation of the 'sensuous surface' of art objects, arguing that this has been a casualty of the quest for multiple layers of meaning and deep structures. See 'Against Interpretation', reprinted in Elizabeth Hardwick (ed.), *A Susan Sontag Reader* (London, 1983), p. 98.

[7] See Sylvette Milliot, 'Le virtuose international: un création du 18e siècle', *Dix-huitième siècle*, 25 (1993), pp. 55–64.

[8] Vladimir Jankélévitch, *Liszt et la Rhapsodie: Essaie sur la Virtuosité* (Paris, 1979, repr. 1989), p. 11.

[9] Gérard le Vot, 'Le Chant médiéval et la virtuosité vocale', in Anne Penesco (ed.), *Défense et illustration de la virtuosité* (Lyon, 1997), pp. 15–50.

[10] For a discussion of the etymology, see Bernstein, *Virtuosity of the Nineteenth Century*, p. 12.

we were to fine-tune this crude history, and we might even (with Liszt) invoke the rhapsodes of Classical culture.[11] But I suggest that it was only really in seventeenth-century operatic and violin repertories in Italy that the ground was tilled for a modern understanding of virtuosity, an understanding that would crystallise in the eighteenth century.[12] At the very beginning of that century (1703), one of the most famous dictionaries of the time (Sébastien de Brossard) offered a telling definition which referred specifically to the Italian lineage:

Virtu veut dire en italien, non seulement cette habitude de l'âme qui nous rend agréables à Dieu et nous fait agir selon les règles de la droite raison; mais aussi cette *supériorité de génie*, d'adresse ou d'habileté, qui nous fait exceller, soit dans la *Théorie*, soit dans la *Pratique* des *beaux-Arts*, au-dessus de ceux qui s'y appliquent aussi bien de nous.[13]

Although he applies the term 'virtuosity' to the *beaux-arts* in general, Brossard points out that it almost always refers to an *excellent musicien*. Far from denigrating virtuosity, he still insists on its association with the virtues, and points out that it may be applied to both theory and practice – to musicus and cantor, perhaps even (echoing the ancients) to *musica mundana* and *musica instrumentalis*.

The century was substantially to reduce this meaning, first removing theory from the embrace of virtuosity, and then allowing the performer to supplant the composer as the archetypal virtuoso. Moreover through this change of meaning Brossard's etymological link to the virtues was weakened. Virtuosity, narrowly associated with display and spectacle, could be viewed in certain quarters as detrimental to music, opposing rather than enabling true creativity. That shift was registered most clearly in opera, where a century-long polemic about Italian and French styles – *opera seria* – *tragédie lyrique* – debated the rival claims of voice and instrument, melody and harmony, music and language. Already during the earliest stages of that polemic,[14] a key distinction was drawn between virtuosity as an essential component of an autonomous art, allowing music to reach beyond the specifics of the text to convey a more generalised sentiment (the aria expressing in music what cannot be expressed in words), and virtuosity as an agent divorcing music from the rhetoric of the text, and thus from meaning and idea.[15] This notion, the occlusion of meaning or reference, continued to resonate in nineteenth-century virtuosity and it will be explored later. But for now we may note that the polemic about opera took on both a more text-specific and a more metaphysical quality through the *querelles* of the second half of the eighteenth century; we need only consider competing pronouncements on accent, where Rousseau's and Garcin's understandings already point to an emergent divide between 'absolute' and 'poetic' music. Indeed metaphysical, ethical and aesthetic issues all mingled in this polemic. It was concerned

---

[11] In *Des Bohémiens et de leur musique en Hongrie* (Leipzig, 1881).

[12] See Gérard le Vot, 'Le Chant médiéval et la virtuosité vocale', p. 15 for a discussion of 'le concept moderne de virtuosité'.

[13] Sébastien de Brossard, *Dictionnaire de Musique* (Paris, 1703); the entry on 'Virtuosité'.

[14] See Michelle Calella, 'La virtuosité italienne et la tragédie lyrique: polémiques et réformes', in Penesco (ed.), *Défense et illustration*, pp. 113–22.

[15] For something of the very early history of this separation of voice and text, see Mladen Dolar, 'The Object Voice', in Renata Salecl and Slavoj Žižek (eds.), *Gaze and Voice as Love Objects* (Durham, NC, and London, 1996), pp. 7–31.

with models of musical substance, with correct and natural musical expression, and with the boundaries of good taste, beyond which (vocal) virtuosity might appear as excess or surplus. The notion of surplus will also be explored in due course.

Throughout the century it was Italy above all that was associated with virtuosity. Right from its inception in the early Baroque era, Italian opera had harnessed the resources of a rich repertory of formalised vocal embellishments, and these demanded in their turn highly specialised performance skills. Already within the relatively narrow catchment areas of a patronal culture the forerunner of the archetypal *diva* began to emerge in response to that demand, to say nothing of the castrato. But as opera went public, the nature of its vocal virtuosity changed. It lost its link with the expressive *agréments* (and therefore with the word), and was channelled rather into the bravura aria, tailor-made (it seemed) to display the skill and dexterity of a small handful of high-profile singers whose careers were promoted and managed in ways that are not altogether unfamiliar today. As the bravura aria developed in figurative and ornamental difficulty, moreover, it drew increasingly upon parallel traditions of instrumental virtuosity. Significantly, it was in Italy that these traditions too were instituted. The remarkable achievements of Italian violin manufacturers were directed initially towards ensemble performance, but in due course they helped make possible the type of the modern instrumental virtuoso. From their bases in Italian cities, the violinist-composers became international figures, crossing the Alps to display their wares and establish their 'schools' in Europe's leading cultural capitals. The wealth of Baroque treatises, with their competing views on many aspects of technique ('le *pizzicato*, le *vibrato*, les doubles cordes; les ornaments obtenus avec la main gauche: trémolos, trilles et mordants; les effets obtenus avec la main droite; coups d'archets divers, jeux sur le chevalet, sur la touche, avec le bois de l'archet; les nuances, la sourdine et l'expression; le *tempo*; les sons harmoniques'[16]), tells its own story.

In one important respect, however, the conditions of modern virtuosity did not yet fully obtain. The audiences for these performer-composers were still restricted for the most part to the courts and the aristocratic salons, a far cry as yet from the popular audiences and large public spaces of early nineteenth-century benefit concerts. As Sylvette Milliot reminds us, this situation began to change when Italian instrumental traditions were transferred to France, notably through the establishment of the 'Concert spirituel' in 1725.[17] In due course the vast *salle des Suisses* of the Tuileries played host to a new taste public. Aristocratic and bourgeois listeners mingled freely on these occasions to hear instrumental performances geared both to the acoustic demands of a larger space and to the aesthetic demands of a more diverse audience. A symbiotic relationship developed here between the needs of an audience (for sensation and spectacle) and the performative modifications made to meet, and even to encourage, those needs. And these were spectacles of the first order. The fleeting, transient and impressionistic quality of spectacle – its focus on impact rather than sustenance – became an in-built dimension of aesthetic effect in the Tuileries concerts. At the same time

---

[16] Janine Cizeron, 'La technique violonistique d'après les traités baroques', in Penesco (ed.), *Défense et illustration*, pp. 75–6.
[17] Milliot, 'Le virtuose international'.

the concerts generated intense competition and rivalry between performers, the more so in that they were regularly 'noticed' in the press, so that reputations could be made and unmade with remarkable speed. A modern cult of personality was built up in this way, fed by audience demand and regulated by the pronouncements of critics, who increasingly functioned as key arbiters of taste. One might add that in the later years of the century the Concert spirituel played a no less seminal role in canon formation (Haydn in particular), firming up the musical work even as it exhibited the virtuoso performer.

Germany's contribution came later, and in some ways it provided the final impetus which forged the type of the international virtuoso. Organology is the important background here, promoting harmony (as Italian makers promoted melody) through the evolution of a variety of keyboard instruments to a point of optimum sophistication. There is a story here about the link between virtuosity and mechanism, about the impersonal drives of technology, and about the human impulse to harness them, that takes us through to the rise of Modernism. Naturally part of that story included the early history of the piano, which reached a defining stage in the 1770s with a select group of makers and performers. The marriage of instruments by Andreas Stein and the exceptional performing and composing talents of Mozart was symptomatic, and it marked a turning-point not only in the history of the piano but in the history of virtuosity. From this point the virtuoso became a truly cosmopolitan figure, an ambassador for music in the courts and cities of Europe and beyond. By the end of the century the concert tour was becoming a fixture (witness the career of Dussek), the 'season' of public concerts in London, Vienna or Paris a necessity. Even the rivalry between Mozart and Clementi played out in rehearsal a leading theme of early nineteenth-century pianism, where competition amongst the growing 'swarm of pianists' was a driving force of concert life. For the drive to outperform all rivals took on greater urgency as the arena of competition steadily widened. There was an element of psychological egoism in this that was well attuned to a coming era of economic liberalism and free enterprise, where specialised professional skills were cultivated in many fields. And we can push that point further. Like the entrepreneur in an industrial age, the individual virtuoso would stand out in sharp relief against the de-personalised 'division of labour' embodied in the nineteenth-century orchestra, where freedom and subjectivity are suppressed.

At the beginning of the nineteenth century, then, the time was ripe for an age of virtuosity, and even for a radical change in its nature. First, there was the instrument. The development of the piano to the point where it could stand alongside, and even supplant, the operatic voice and the violin as the primary medium of virtuosity is a well-charted history. Through a succession of technical improvements, culminating in Erard's double escapement action of 1822, the instrument gained the capacity for power, velocity and expressive range, and above all for contrast and mediation. Second, there was the performer. By the early nineteenth century the pianist-composer (usually, though not always, male) was a competitor on a world stage, an acrobat of the keyboard, aiming for speed, reach, strength, agility and endurance, and a compiler too of the technical devices necessary to the task. Third, there was the audience, expanding both numerically and in terms of social background, but arguably contracting in its knowledge base. To characterise the pre-nineteenth-century audience as informed and participatory, in the sense that it listened actively, is without doubt to idealise it. But we might note that one characteristic of musical virtuosity is that it demands little beyond admiration from its audience; it is in this sense that the audience for a benefit concert would have differed from, for example, the audience for a chess tournament. And fourth, there was the 'making public' symbolised by the public spaces that enabled the spectacles, increasing in size and number as the century turned. If all these factors converged on a single centre, it was post-revolutionary Paris. As Gautier claimed, Paris was the city 'which puts the seal on all reputations and definitely places the golden crown on the heads of young prodigies'.[18] And if any one of them proved to be the decisive catalyst of Romantic virtuosity, it was the proliferation of public spaces, for which the piano would prove to be the ideal medium. In this respect the Concert spirituel, which did not survive the revolution, was especially prophetic.

Public spaces were in turn part of a larger history, which we might characterise as the emancipation of the public sphere in the eighteenth century, where new cultural institutions such as the newspaper, the novel and the coffee house formed the (literally) powerful foci for public opinion. The idea of 'public space' can be understood rather broadly, then. Indeed Paul Metzner understands it metaphorically, arguing that the revolutionary mentality in Paris first 'made government a public space and then used the space for public spectacles'.[19] Metzner's larger point is that social life became public in many spheres of activity in Paris in the late eighteenth and early nineteenth centuries. The public space, in other words, was social as well as physical. The explosion of public concerts was part of this larger development, providing one form of spectacle among many others. Metzner cites in particular the emergence of chess from private to public arenas, as also cuisine, automaton-building, criminal detection, and of course music, and he goes on to demonstrate that each of these practices produced its virtuoso performers, all committed to showmanship, to sleight-of-hand and to the perfection of technical skills. Moreover, as performance (in this wide sense) migrated from private to public spheres, and was transformed from a domestic pursuit to a spectacle, it acquired in the process some of the engines of publicity with which we are familiar today. The public performance, after all, needs to be publicised before it can be brought to the public. The mercantile pianistic culture I described in chapter 1 found its wider context, then, within this expansion of public space, above all in Paris, where it was fed by a lively operatic culture, by an unusually large market of amateur pianists, and by a powerful press. Here we have a large part of the reason that Paris took over from London and then Vienna as the 'capital' of pianism in the 1820s and 1830s.

The separate strands of high art and popular culture in the late eighteenth and early nineteenth centuries can partly be mapped on to these private and public spaces. However this issue is not straightforward. Historically we can trace two interwoven but distinguishable developments. On the one hand there was a steady democratisation of culture as private spaces became public, a development that naturally proceeded hand in hand with political and social change, leading to the ever greater accessibility of high culture through education and social reform, though in practice this could only proceed so far, such were the barriers

---

[18] *The Romantic Ballet*, trans. Cyril W. Beaumont (London, 1932, repr. New York, 1980), p. 49.

[19] Metzner, *Crescendo of the Virtuoso* (Berkeley, Los Angeles and London, 1998), p. 4. See also Jürgen Habermas, *The Structural Transformation of the Public Sphere*, trans. Thomas Burger and Frederick Lawrence (Cambridge, MA, 1991).

of social class in the nineteenth century. On the other hand there was an appropriation by elitist taste publics of a defamiliarised popular culture, defamiliarised in the sense that it had once been deemed available to those publics but had subsequently been removed from their purview (more accurately, they had withdrawn their participation). In the eighteenth century this took the form of aristocratic flirtations with popular culture. But it was steadily transformed in the nineteenth century by the developing ideologies of a middle-class ascendancy, such that definitions of elite and popular themselves began to destabilise. The middle class appropriated popular repertories and practices for ideological, predominantly nationalist, purposes, for example. But it looked in the other direction too, harnessing the sophisticated products of aristocratic art to serve as the primary validators of its own 'invented', and distinctly bourgeois, tradition. By the mid-nineteenth century, or thereabouts, a new middle-class elite was effecting a second stage of withdrawal from popular culture, for the crucial point here is that 'popular culture' by then embraced the arena of public pianism. It was banished to the realm of mass entertainment and as such identified with a debasement and trivialisation of culture.[20] It was at this point that the public spaces contracted, and became at least semi-private.

That, however, was barely on the horizon in the 1820s, when the pianists descended regularly on Paris for the 'season' in a frenzy of competitive concerting, with all the attendant publicity and hype. The adoration of the public and the condemnation of the more high-minded critics, from Cherubini to Fétis, went hand in hand. Cherubini argued that technique could threaten creativity, Fétis described the 'revolt of the instrumentalists against music', and remarked too that 'pianists have made music into silliness'.[21] For the 'brilliant school', the piano was no more than an 'arena for cleverness and dexterity'.[22] Heine, meanwhile, referred to the 'victory of the mechanical over the spiritual', arguing that 'technical perfection . . . is what is now praised and exalted as the highest art'.[23] The status of virtuosity even became the subject of yet another *querelle*, as the forces of the *Revue et gazette musicale* were lined up against those of *La France musicale*. English critics joined in, with their reference to 'cartloads of rubbish by Messrs. Herz, Pixis, Chaulieu, Czerny, Hünten, and others of the gang . . . .',[24] and their protest that 'a school of piano forte playing has arisen, which consists almost entirely of feats of sleight-of-hand, and the sole object of which seems to be to play greatest possible number of notes in a given time'.[25] As *The Musical World* put it, the 'regular sonata has now disappeared, and its place is supplied by fantasies, capricci, airs with variations, pot-pourris etc, which serve too often as apologies for a hasty, loose, irregular and incoherent style of composition'.[26]

---

[20] See Patrick Brantlinger, *Bread and Circuses: Theories of Mass Culture and Social Decay* (Ithaca and London, 1983) for a contextualisation of this tendency.

[21] F.-J. Fétis, 'Nouvelles de Paris: Concerts spirituels', *La Revue musicale*, 1st ser., 3 [no. 11], [April] 1828, pp. 248–55, here 254.

[22] 'Thalberg et Liszt', *La Revue et gazette musicale*, 23 April 1837.

[23] Heinrich Heine, *Lutèce: Lettres sur la vie politique, artistique et sociale de la* France, vol. 19 of *Heines Werke, Säkularausgabe* (Berlin and Paris, 1977; orig. edn, 1855), p. 176.

[24] *The Musical Magazine*, June 1835. And in the same piece: 'New editions of Beethoven's Sonata and Bach's Fugues will, I hope, help to do away with the "Album des Pianistes du Premier Force" '.

[25] *The Musical World*, 15 July 1836.   [26] *Ibid.*, 15 April 1836.

Of course none of this was new. Indeed the chorus of the critics merely translated an age-old criticism of Italian opera – that vocal virtuosity was divorced from the word – to another plane, where instrumental virtuosity was divorced from meaning. Yet if the rhetoric was familiar, it acquired a new layer of meaning in the early nineteenth century. Underlying the critiques was a developing tension between virtuosity and the work, both of which had marked out their territory during the eighteenth century and stood poised for a dialectical relationship in the nineteenth. There is naturally a danger here in using today's categories to explain yesterday. Yet it is hard not to read such criticism as documenting a widening gulf between performance and composition. Virtuosity, after all, can be regarded as the natural outcome of the performer's quest for autonomy. It was the magnet, we might say, drawing the listener away from the qualities of the work towards the qualities of the performer. It highlighted technique rather than substance, the moment rather than the whole. In a similar way, the work-concept embodied the composer's quest for autonomy, preserving the work from contaminating contexts and contingencies, including the imperfections of its performances and the limitations of its material base. This strengthening forcefield between virtuosity and the work might be expressed as a tension between performance and text, between presentation and idea, between sensuous surface (or heard effect) and immanent knowledge, between, in a way, expression and form. And as the ambitions and pretensions of virtuoso and composer became mutually threatening, the ideological ground for that conflict of interests came into ever sharper focus.[27]

In this respect the twin ascendancies of the virtuoso and the work might be viewed as preparatory to what I have elsewhere described as two 'essential' meanings of Romanticism, themselves standing in a polarised relation.[28] Both were at root projects of the Enlightenment, but they came to full fruition in the early nineteenth century. It was above all under pressure of Romantic individualism that there was a change in the nature and role of virtuosity. The rise of the virtuoso, the perfect embodiment of *l'ego romantique* (usually attributed to composers), signified a commitment to individualism that was paralleled by the political ideology of Liberalism and by the investment in subjectivity within post-Kantian philosophical systems. And if the invention or reinvention of the individual was a potent enabling force in political and intellectual life, it was even more influential in the cultural domain; indeed it could almost be described as a primary motivation for the rise of aesthetics. Thus, virtuosity gained new power, status and dignity, and a new ideological underpinning (paradoxically resisting idealisation), through the offices of an ascendant individualism. It acquired an agenda of which it could be proud. And along with that came a new social status. As Heinrich W. Schwab points out, the exceptional gifts of the virtuoso gained new esteem for performers everywhere in the nineteenth century.[29] The strengthening

---

[27] One of the clearest articulations of this 'division between the Virtuoso and the Artist' is in Wagner's essay 'The Virtuoso and the Artist'. See *Richard Wagner's Prose Works*, ed. William Ashton Ellis (London, 1897), vol. 7, pp. 108–22.

[28] 'Romanticism', in Stanley Sadie and John Tyrrell (eds.), *The New Grove Dictionary of Music and Musicians*, 2nd edn (London, 2001), vol. 21, pp. 596–603.

[29] Heinrich W. Schwab, 'Formen der Virtuosenehrung und ihr Sozialgeschichtlicher Hintergrund' in Henrik Glahn, Søren Sørenson and Peter Ryom (eds.), *Book of the International Musicological Society Congress* (Copenhagen, 1972), vol. 2, p. 639.

of the work, on the other hand, signified a rather different dimension of Romanticism, suggestive of the autonomy of art, its unified character and its independence of the social world. The phrase 'ideology of organicism' (embracing idealisation) has been used to encapsulate something of this meaning. It describes the canonised musical work, congealed into a fixed configuration, its forms solidified until they might be equated with those of verbal or spatial works. The work, stable and unified, takes on something of the quality of a timeless truth; through its monadic character, it becomes a model of what the world might be.

It may be useful to attempt some categories of virtuosity, as a résumé of this history. There is the vocal virtuosity embodied in the practice of Baroque opera, but with certain continuities taking us through to Rossini. This was a performer category, though naturally composers served it. What it brings into focus above all is a certain duality between the work character and the event character of the genre. Then there are the composer-performer virtuosities of the eighteenth and early nineteenth centuries. These ranged from the violin schools of the Italian Baroque and the pianism of the Classical period, both addressed to relatively small, elitist audiences, to the post-Classical pianism of the 1820s, which reached out to a much wider public. This latter is, of course, the practice described in my first two chapters, and while its traditions continued into the 1830s and 1840s, they tended increasingly towards conformity and triviality.[30] In general the onset of the 1830s witnessed the beginnings of new directions. Post-Classical virtuosity began to give way to three further broad categories. The first, a composer-performer category, was neo-Baroque virtuosity, so labelled because it sought to recover an eighteenth-century equilibrium between virtuosity and work character; we might associate it with Moscheles, Mendelssohn, Chopin and Schumann (I will say more of this in chapter 4). The second, a performer category, was an emerging work-orientated virtuosity, understood as the technical mastery necessary to support an interpretation: a surrender, we might say, to the strengthening work-concept. And finally there was what I have already crudely labelled Romantic virtuosity. Here the performer staked a claim to the high ground of a liberal ideology. And this ideological element was crucial. It was here that the concept of virtuosity, allied with Romantic notions of the composer-performer as a free, in some sense otherworldly, spirit, achieved real dignity. For the Romantic virtuoso was no mere technician; nor was he a slave to the musical work. Liszt did indeed speak of the need to show the 'most profound respect for the masterpieces of great composers . . .'.[31] But he also argued that 'virtuosity is not a submissive handmaid to the composition'.[32] Reconciling these two statements into a single 'two-fold truth', in Dahlhaus's phrase, is the sense of a potency, a capacity to choose without the constraints of a limitation of technique, associated with the Romantic virtuoso. He stood for freedom, for Faustian man, for the individual in search of self-realisation – free, isolated, striving, desiring. Heroically overcoming his instrument,

---

[30] Schumann remarked: 'Of late the concert-going public has shown some resistance and ennui towards virtuosic compositions. . . .'. In 'Virtuosen', *Neue Zeitschrift für Musik*, 18 (1842), p. 169.

[31] *An Artist's Journey*, trans. and annotated Charles Suttoni (Chicago and London, 1989; orig. letters, 1835–41), p. 18.

[32] In his 1855 essay on Clara Schumann, in *Franz Liszt. Gesammelte Schriften*, ed. Lina Ramann (Leipzig, 1881–99), vol. 4 (1882), p. 193. Compare Wagner's reference to 'the intermediary of the artistic idea', in 'The Virtuoso and the Artist', *Prose Works*, vol. 7, p. 112.

he was a powerful symbol of transcendence. The type was represented most clearly by two men: Paganini and Liszt.

PAGANINI AND THE DREAM FACTORY; LISZT, L'ENCHANTEUR

It is unnecessary to record here the explosive impact of Paganini on the concert life of the early nineteenth century, to discuss the catalytic effect of his concert tours on pianistic virtuosity, or to list once more the many works composed by leading pianist-composers as a direct result of his influence. These matters are well documented and well known. However, it may be useful to consider some of the more general qualities of Romantic virtuosity associated with Paganini, before going on to look at some of these qualities, and others, in Liszt. One such defining quality has already been proposed. The Romantic virtuoso was above all an individual. 'I want to maintain my singularity', remarked Paganini,[33] and his repertory of novelties (some of them actually recovering much older, long-forgotten tricks of the trade) was developed to that end as well as to display his formidable technique. Not only was the Romantic virtuoso clearly differentiated from his rivals, his style of playing and stage manner distinctive and unique, imbued with subjectivity; he was also isolated (by his genius, which cannot be imitated) from the world at large, a solitary figure, with 'no brothers among men',[34] a 'being apart',[35] an 'exile from heaven',[36] though one whose solitude must be publicly observed, and even displayed. And as this suggests, his individuality was as much biographical as professional. His fame, in other words, rested not simply on a particular style of playing, but invoked no less a particular mode of living. A skein of legends was wrapped around him, and the resulting notoriety became an essential part of his appeal. Thus the public could follow Paganini's life with a mixture of repulsion and fascination. Even his diseased body was integral to his attraction.[37] The scandals and the mysteries helped. And it helped too that the life was larger than life. Again Liszt caught the point. 'People want to know the colour of your bedroom slippers, the cut of your dressing gown. . . . The newspapers, eager to profit from this pitiable curiosity, heap anecdote upon anecdote, falsehood upon falsehood. . . '.[38] This cult of the celebrity has a distinctly modern flavour.

For the developing image of the Romantic virtuoso in the early nineteenth century already approached that of a much later figure, the Nietzschean representation of Dionysian man, though it is arguably the Dionysus of *Twilight of the Idols* that is suggested rather than that of *The Birth of Tragedy*. The virtuoso was a man 'strong enough for freedom', and nothing pre-planned or pre-ordained could limit this freedom. Contemporary audiences were well aware of the disdain with which Paganini could treat the best-intentioned of collaborators, for the free man will not be subjugated or constrained. In his search for innovation, he will respect no convention, balk at no challenge, stop at no frontier. In this way the concert platform became an arena of risk and danger, an uncharted, unpredictable territory, and

---

[33] Quoted in Julius Max Schottky, *Paganinis Leben und Treiben als Künstler und als Mensch* (Prague, 1830), p. 278.
[34] *An Artist's Journey*, p. 15.   [35] *Le Moniteur universel*, 10 March 1831, p. 501.
[36] *An Artist's Journey*, p. 15.
[37] See Bernstein, *Virtuosity of the Nineteenth Century*, p. 12, for a comparison with images of Mozart's body.
[38] *An Artist's Journey*, p. 14.

in negotiating it the virtuoso had to take his chance. 'No living violinist dares to attempt as much as he does', wrote Karl Guhr, in one of the more detailed contemporary accounts of Paganini's playing.[39] The juggler risks another ball in the air, threatening not only the success of the enterprise, but also the pleasing nature of the pattern. Attendant on this was an acknowledgement that freedom, spontaneity and progress are barely compatible with any suggestion of limits or boundaries to knowledge and experience. The virtuoso could take us to the extreme limits of human potential. Like the acrobat, the sportsman, or the circus performer, he could stretch beyond what should be possible, affording us a glimpse of what human beings might be capable of – ever faster, ever further.

Paganini played mainly his own music, and he composed it with a view to displaying his technical mastery. Yet this very technical mastery could carry with it a sense of loss. When 'Rameau's nephew' complained of 'technical difficulty . . . replac[ing] beauty', he was effectively lamenting a loss of aesthetic quality, in which the performative hollowed out elements of work character.[40] This again was a recurrent theme of the critics, and it was already well rehearsed in the eighteenth century. The addition of difficulty, it is implied, involves the subtraction or erosion of expressiveness, though it has to be said that Paganini himself was generally exempt from this charge, at least in the critical opinion expressed during his own lifetime. Moreover the 'composing in' of difficulty – of virtuosity – could also be read as a virtue, helping to restore the etymology; indeed Jankélévitch refers to a 'beautiful difficulty' in his book on Ravel, and goes on to speak of the player 'complicat[ing] with pleasure the rules of the game . . .'.[41] The total command of technique also involved a sense of sacrifice; it was hard won, and that (ethical) quality was of its essence, suggestive of heroic resolution, a difficulty magnificently and bravely overcome (*di bravura*). Paganini's regime of practice became legendary in his lifetime. Hour after hour of work was the price of a technique nearing perfection, and that meant a technique not only capable of the most astonishing agility and precision, but one that could summon at will a range of colours that left commentators at a loss for words – a technique in short that drove yet deeper the wedge separating the virtuoso from the common man.

Romantic virtuosity demanded more than an ethos of individuality and freedom, however, and more too than a technical mastery driven by what Maurice Bourges called 'le démon du mecanisme'. It demanded also visibility. As Jankélévitch astutely remarked: 'There are no unrecognised virtuosi'.[42] Virtuosity needed to show itself – to present itself – in order to exist, and to that end it cultivated a visual dimension; it was charismatic, a spectacle to be observed and wondered at. Much of its power lay in its presentation, its appearance, the immediacy of its impact. The 'look' of the virtuoso was crucial, and that included the dramas and discontinuities of his bodily activity. For the adoration of an audience was part of the constitution of virtuosity. Accounts of Paganini's spectral appearance on the platform suggest a stage presence carefully calculated to intimidate, even to subjugate.

---

[39] Charles Guhr, *L'Art de jouer du violon de Paganini* (French trans: Paris, 1830), p. 5.

[40] Denis Diderot, '*Rameau's Nephew* (with *d'Alembert's Dream*)', trans. Leonard Tancock (Harmondsworth, 1966; orig. MS, *c.* 1761–*c.* 1779), p. 100.

[41] Vladimir Jankélévitch, *Maurice Ravel* (Paris, 1939), p. 84.

[42] Jankélévitch, *Liszt et la Rhapsodie*, p. 34.

Czerny's account of a 'perfect virtuoso', and of his power 'over the feelings and the hearts of his auditors' could easily be transposed to Paganini: 'in his own person, he appears to render probable and worthy of belief the celebrated fables of *Orpheus* and *Amphion*'.[43] And this dynamic, predicated on the power of the one over the many, reveals the other side of the *Übermensch*, not just a passive exemplary figure, but an active, controlling one. There could be an element of play in this – the Romantic virtuoso as magician or clown presenting his tricks like some ancient *jongleur*, captivating the audience with his sleight-of-hand. But there could also be a sense of profounder mystery, evoking all the connotations of a supernatural power, demonic or divine – the gift of virtuosity traded in a Faustian pact, or ceded to the chosen one as a rare mark of favour. The virtuoso, in other words, played to a more general mystification of art in the Romantic era, though only up to a point. To be a misunderstood genius has always proved more helpful to composers than to performers.[44]

The dynamic of virtuosity, then, is a two-way process. Audiences shape it almost as much as performers; they mould it to their own needs. And in this respect the public concert tapped into a rather fundamental human need, the need to admire and applaud, to experience extremes of emotion vicariously, through a kind of secret identification with epic motifs unavailable to us in the normal course of things. The great performer, no less than the great composer, could generate the catharsis that occurs when emotional release in an artificial world (a world of art) rebounds on to the real world, and could do so even when the musical materials lacked significance. A comparison with other media may be to the point. We weep at Hollywood's dénouement, as well as Tolstoy's, for the moment of recognition (*anagnorisis*) is arguably more dependent on our own need to recognise than Aristotle allowed. This is not of course to equate Tolstoy and Hollywood. Recognitions may be revelatory, tantamount to self-recognitions, where the poetic becomes temporarily real through the combined force of plot and character. Or they may be fleeting, ephemeral and illusory, born of wish-fulfilment, of a sense of identification with the screen idol whose persona all but obliterates plot and character. These are different qualities of aesthetic experience, and we may reasonably choose to valorise them, but it is hardly adequate to view the one as entirely significant and the other entirely trivial.

Undoubtedly there is something of the dream factory in the world of Romantic virtuosity. Indeed the emergence of that world in the early nineteenth century was rather like a dry run for some of the most characteristic features of a culture industry whose definitive formulation would await the mid-twentieth century. We can recognise already in the accounts of Paganini's concertising, for example, a type of listener familiar enough in today's world. I mean here the aficionado of this or that celebrity performer, the disciple who fetishises the performer and the performance at the expense of the composer, and in so doing feeds and catalyses a cult of virtuosity rather than a culture of the work. For Adorno, this category of listener was of course the worst type of 'dilettante', to use a term which came into its own in the seventeenth century, but whose pejorative connotations date, significantly, from the early nineteenth, when an avant-garde first began to oppose itself to popular culture and an

---

[43] Carl Czerny, *Letters on Thorough-Bass, with an Appendix on the Higher Branches of Musical Execution and Expression*, trans. J. A. Hamilton (London, n.d., orig. edn, *c.* 1840), p. 93.
[44] See Jankélévitch, *Liszt et la Rhapsodie*, p. 41.

ethos of professionalism began to hold sway. The performer fetishist, for Adorno, was yet another symptom of the widespread degeneration of listening consequent on the culture industry. This is history from the standpoint of the avant-garde, privileging text and idea, and implicitly celebrating the egotism of the composer. For Adorno there could indeed be no other history, and we can recognise the potency of his reading while also recognising its bias.

For it is reasonable to value the autonomy character attributed to performance by the rise of Romantic virtuosity, just as we value the autonomy character attributed to composition by the strengthening of a work-concept. We can invest something, in other words, in each of the torn halves. Performers, like composers, can make their claim on our reading of music history, and not merely as faithful servants of the text. Their qualities are in part redemptive. They can complete the incomplete, improve the mediocre, give expression to the expressionless, transform all that they touch through a focus on sensuous surface and heard effect – through what Sontag has called an 'erotics' of art. They can create a rounded, satisfying musical experience from works which may well be found wanting *qua* works, a case that was indeed made in relation to Paganini. And even when the music is significant, and the demands of the composer considerable, the qualities of virtuosity have some capacity to compete, not least because the performer, unlike the composer, has an opportunity to communicate directly with a real – as opposed to an 'ideal' – listener. Those qualities – freedom and subjectivity, spontaneity and chance, charisma and presence, a capacity to overcome, to attain the unattainable – can make their own statement, and in doing so they can draw us away from the qualities of the work; indeed they may even appropriate the work, turning it to ends that promote the medium rather than the message. As noted already, it is in this sense that we may speak of a dialectic between virtuosity and the musical work.

Liszt biographers are united in their view that his indebtedness to Paganini amounted to nothing less than an impasse cleared, a dam of creative energy released. That turning-point came in 1832, and it is fair to say that there were other catalysts, notably his friendship with Berlioz and his initial contacts with Chopin. Prior to this point Liszt was primarily a performer, but in the early 1830s he produced his first homage to Paganini, the *La Clochette* Fantasy (based on the finale of the B minor Concerto), as well as his homage to Lamartine, the original version of *Harmonies poètiques et religieuses*. His models, then, and his creative responses to them, indicate that from the start there were two impulses at work, that his embrace of the poetic rivalled his engagement with virtuosity. As noted in chapter 1, Michel Sogny adds an additional layer of interpretation, suggesting that 'creative admiration' was the key motivating force of Liszt's music from all periods, and viewing the Paganini influence in that light. Admiration, Descartes's 'première de toutes les passions', would take us in this reading beyond the formative modelling processes common to all young composers and would tap into a much more fundamental level of creativity, a form of identification with the object which, as it comes close to realisation (so that subject and object become virtually indistinguishable), releases the creativity of the subject. Like Byron, then, Liszt would 'live not in myself, but become a portion of that around me'. The self would be immersed in the sublimity of nature, in the exalted achievements of painters, poets and musicians, and in the process it would find its own creative voice, allowing these 'objects' to

79

be relived subjectively through music. There is a ring of authenticity to this reading which is fortunately not dependent on Sogny's attempts at posthumous psycho-analysis, where the 'fixation castratrice' of a youth from the Hungarian plains (rejected by the Parisian musical establishment) is confirmed through an 'interpretation' of the dream recounted by Liszt in his *Pages romantiques*.[45]

Sogny's interpretation is well exemplified by Liszt's own account of his response to Paganini. 'What a man, what a violin, what an artist! Heavens! what sufferings, what misery, what tortures in those four strings.' 'Here is a whole fortnight that my mind and fingers have been working like two lost spirits.'[46] What is clear from this is that Paganini's example not only released his own creative energy (by revealing to him the possibility of the impossible); it had the supplementary effect of immersing him again in the 'heroes' of world literature, painting and music. Note that 'mind and fingers' were both working. 'Homer, the Bible, Plato, Locke, Byron, Hugo, Lamartine, Chateaubriand, Beethoven, Bach, Hummel, Mozart, Weber are all around me, I study them, meditate on them, devour them with fury.' For Liszt, this was not simply a question of identifying with individuals, but rather of making contact (through those individuals) with the highest expressions of the human spirit. Characteristically this was achieved first and foremost through transcription, the ultimate mode of 'creative admiration', and there is a sense in which Liszt 'transcribed' poetry, painting, and even nature, just as he transcribed other music. His first inclination on hearing Paganini, then, was to produce (in 1832) the first stage of his Paganini triptych. And there is a powerful symbolism in this. Eighteenth-century virtuosity was in a sense encapsulated in Bach's re-workings of Vivaldi, and it is hard to avoid the suggestion that Liszt's reworkings of Paganini achieved something of the same for Romantic virtuosity. In both cases the mechanisms of translation could range from literal repetition (stretching keyboard technique through direct emulation of violin technique) to radical reinterpretation (paraphrasing violin technique in the terms of keyboard technique). But even the most remote reformulations arose from a spirit of imitation which has always played a central role in artistic creativity, and which acquired negative connotations during only the briefest period of Western art history.

Transcription was only the most blatant of Liszt's tributes to Paganini. At root, Paganini changed totally his understanding of the role and significance of virtuosity. It was something more than an agent, a 'mediator' (to use Wagner's deliberately pejorative term). Rather it was a powerful symbol of artistic perfection, engaging the total personality of the artist, 'not a secondary outgrowth, but an indispensable element of music'. Later, in his obituary of Paganini, he referred to a '*means*, not an *end*', but care is needed in interpreting such remarks.[47] The 'end' here is not, or not only, the realisation of a composer's intentions, where virtuosity would be viewed simply as a servant of the text. Rather Liszt saw the end as a capacity to express anything and everything through music, not least the vast spaces of the artist's 'vie intérieure'. Virtuosity was a means to *that* end; it was a way of ensuring that the limitations of the fingers should never prove an obstacle to the realisation of this grand

[45] Sogny, *L'Admiration Créatrice chez Liszt* (Paris, 1975), pp. 99–105.
[46] *Letters of Franz Liszt*, coll. and ed. La Mara, trans. Constance Bache, 2 vols. (London, 1894), vol. 1, pp. 8–9.
[47] 'Sur Paganini, à propos de sa mort', *La Revue et Gazette Musicale*, 7, 50 (1840), pp. 431–2.

ambition. In this way, God-like, the virtuoso mastered his own created world. Something of this potency also emerges in Liszt's essay on Clara Schumann, where it is clear that he sees the positive in virtuosity precisely in the ability to reach any goal, uninhibited by technical limitations. His impatience with technical skill for its own sake is made abundantly clear in his reference to Gusikow (in his 'xylophone' performances) as 'the musical juggler who plays an infinitely large number of notes in an infinitely short period of time . . . his talent, being misguided, has produced nothing but musical inanities to which the charlatans who write feature articles for the newspapers will ascribe incalculable value'.[48]

It was after the Vienna concerts of 1838 that Liszt embarked in all earnestness on the career of a travelling virtuoso, a career that focused both the liberating characteristics of virtuosity and its more threatening, dangerous potentials. Many of those qualities attributed to Paganini were very soon transferred to Liszt. For Amy Fay, he was 'Merlin-like', an 'old-time magician', a 'perfect wizard'; he was 'L'Enchanteur', presenting a tantalising vision of the unattainable, the 'promised land'.[49] For Schumann he was a 'demon exercising his powers', while, intriguingly, for Clara he invoked the other side of that noumenal coin; he was 'divine'; he could be 'compared to no other virtuoso. He is the only one of his Kind. He arouses fright and astonishment.'[50] Liszt was happy to collude in these perceptions, even down to borrowing from Paganini his awareness of the power of dress and physiognomy to exert their influence on an audience. However, he added something new to the image of the Romantic virtuoso. Later in life, he wrote about virtuosity in his essay on the Bohemian gypsy musicians. Here he argued that the virtuoso was not a mason, performing with conscientiousness and precision; he was not a passive instrument, reproducing an existing production; he was not a reader delivering a text. Rather he was the only one who could activate an entire world of feeling, for which the musical work was just the scenario. The virtuoso, with his capacity 'to endow the still lifeless form with an adamantine nature into which he may infuse life at his own given moment' was in that sense as much a creator as the composer. Just as an actor could not 'have "created" a dramatic role unless he had conceived it in a manner so peculiar to himself that, although another might imitate it, he could never appropriate it',[51] so the virtuoso 'engenders the music anew and in his turn. He gives it a palpable and perceptible existence, and by that act he establishes the claim of his art to be ranked with those called autonomous'.[52]

In looking specifically to the gypsy in music, Liszt identified putative racial-national qualities that allowed him to turn a reflecting mirror on to instrumental music generally, and on to the performative. The oral traditions of the gypsies were apparently a kind of non-narrative saga or epic of a people, with attendant connotations of the infancy of a history (Hegel's epic as 'originary myth'). Moreover, the special proximity of the gypsies to the

[48] *An Artist's Journey*, pp. 19–20. But see Heine's comments on Liszt's manipulation of his audience in *Lutèce*, pp. 223–4; also Susan Bernstein's remarks on presentation and authorship: *Virtuosity of the Nineteenth Century*, p. 7.

[49] Amy Fay, *Music Study in Germany* (London, 1886), pp. 187–201.

[50] For an account of Clara Schumann's meetings with Liszt in Vienna 1838, and of the subsequent deterioration both of their relationship and of her view of Liszt as a performer, see Nancy B. Reich, *Clara Schumann: The Artist and the Woman* (New York and London, 1985), pp. 209–16.

[51] *The Gypsy in Music*, trans. Edwin Evans, 2 vols. (London, [1926]), vol. 2, p. 267.

[52] *Ibid.*, p. 270.

raw material of existence – to Nature – rendered speech and abstract ideas less important to their needs than music-making, since the latter could express sentiment without proceeding to any direct application of it. Unlike Western, 'civilised' man, the gypsy allowed himself to be absorbed by Nature rather than attempting to master it. His was a 'poetic egoism', which could be satisfied by music alone. Like the ancient rhapsodes, he had a story to tell not only expressive of the spirit of his people, but of a more general love of God, country, cause and art. Interestingly, in the course of this discussion, Liszt introduced a further etymological twist to our understanding of the term virtuosity. It was indeed associated with the virtues; but both were ultimately derived from 'vir', with its cognate 'virility'. And here the word *bravura*, ubiquitous in the titles of the brilliant style, can be seen in a new, gendered, light, with a suggestion of machismo, of the exploits of medieval chivalry or folk heroism.[53] Like Mazeppa, the very masculine hero must in the end triumph over adversity, even if the triumph comes in death. The concert was a battlefield, with conquests to be made. Even the instrument was there for the slaying, as contemporary cartoonists were quick to notice.[54] Moreover the conquests could include women's hearts. Liszt was not just Merlin, the magician; he was Don Juan, the seducer, exerting his male power from the distance of the concert platform, and in ways that are rather familiar in today's popular culture.

This points to an essential difference in the reception of Paganini and Liszt. Where the former was perceived as remote and inaccessible, the latter reached down from Olympus to make immediate contact with his audience; his was a 'poetic virtuosity', to use Schumann's phrase, softened by its contacts with Berlioz and Chopin as well as Paganini. Moreover the differences between their two instruments carried significant connotative values in this respect. Paganini's violin was in a sense an extension of the man – of his arm; it was a (miraculous) part of him, so that man and instrument were together distanced from the audience. Liszt's piano, on the other hand, was an independent force, something to be mastered (another gendered term). It was 'played upon' by the hand, and this tactile quality was, and is, integral to the virtuosity of the (mechanical) piano. Like a hammer, the hand could pound the instrument into submission, engaging with it in a kind of furious combat; like a feather it could caress the keys (the *carezzando* touch), coaxing a response.[55] And the hand symbolised work; it was the agent of human skills. In that sense the velocity and precision of the virtuoso also tapped into ancient traditions of craft, the finely tuned workmanship of the artisan. Through the hand, the virtuoso demonstrated his superhuman skills, but at the same time his human sensitivities. His personality was transmitted through the hand to the instrument in a kind of expressive dialogue between man and machine, where the mechanical action of the one pointed up the free play of the other. The 'touch' of the virtuoso was the symbolic expression of this humanity.

---

[53] The gendering of virtuosity is, however, a two-way thing. When viewed pejoratively, it has often been associated with women. More subtly, the growing importance of interpretation could rather easily be linked with traditional (subservient) female roles.

[54] See Dana Gooley, 'Warhorses: Liszt, Weber's *Konzertstück*, and the Cult of Napoléon', *19th-Century Music*, 24, 1 (Summer 2000), pp. 62–88.

[55] Jonathan Bellman, 'Frédéric Chopin, Antoine de Kontski and the *carezzando* Touch', *Early Music*, 29, 3 (2001), pp. 398–407.

It was this sense of a humanity transformed by the divine spark, traditionally (as in some Classical theories of creativity) available to music and poetry rather than painting and sculpture, that marked Liszt off from Paganini in the public perception. Much more than Paganini, he could be viewed as the ideal of virtuosity, an artist in whom transcendental human achievements could be the more valued in that they were not explained away by myth and legend. The Romantic revolution created the Romantic hero, and one manifestation of that was the figure of the 'great artist', represented by Schiller as an individual in whom the finest of human qualities and attainments might be represented. For many, Liszt was just such a 'great artist'. He was viewed as a polymath whose special gifts and insights were manifest in visionary writings (their utopianism oddly out-of-tune with our own age) as well as visionary compositions, and whose magnetic performing presence was only the public dimension of a larger, more all-embracing creativity. Even the dramas of his biography, licensed by his genius, were of a different order from those of Paganini, less wrapped in mystery and rumour, more 'available' for the wish fulfilment of others. They were part and parcel of the 'great artist'. Of course even Romantic heros grow middle-aged. They become great pedagogues as well as great performers. They initiate traditions as well as breaking with them. They perpetuate themselves, even beyond death, by forming 'schools'. From the late 1840s Liszt effectively reinvented himself as a composer, teacher and prophet in Weimar. He continued performing of course, but the balance of interests here shifted more and more towards interpretation. His 'virtuoso years', the tours, the concerts, the endless parade of his own music before adoring audiences, were over. Virtuosity had never been the whole story, even while the virtuoso years lasted. And they lasted no more than a decade.

SURPLUS NOTES

During those virtuoso years, Liszt, like Paganini, conceived his musical works with his own public performance of them very much in mind, and that in part explains their numerous versions and variants. That composer and pianist are one and the same is no guarantee, of course, that the functions of origination and communication will be fused. For one thing, these divided functions may breach the supposed unity of personality.[56] And for another, the functions are themselves anything but pure. The composer arranges rather than originates meanings, and the performer communicates only when the listener consents. Nevertheless, where composer and performer are one there is a territorial overlap at the point where meaning or message is constituted, and this allows some possibility, though again no guarantee, that the performer will read the meaning that the composer intended, or something like it. The situation is naturally rather different where composer and performer are two persons. Here, the performer may render the text 'brilliant' by appropriating it in the service of virtuosity. But equally the composer may produce a text that prescribes a brilliant performance, most obviously in the kinds of test pieces that were composed in large numbers for the Paris conservatoire in the nineteenth century, but also in the case

---

[56] The age of recordings affords ample evidence of this, notably through recordings of their own music by Debussy, Bartók and Messiaen.

of a good deal of eighteenth- and early nineteenth-century opera, especially Italian. Here functional and aesthetic judgements may well come into conflict. The good test piece, we might argue, is one that performs its task well, allowing maximum scope for the demonstration of technical prowess. Yet we are less comfortable with this proposition when it is applied to the virtuoso aria, where the prescription of virtuosity has often seemed an unworthy aim. We may wonder at such puritanical judgements of virtuosity, but they are of ancient lineage, and even came to reflect (as Susan Bernstein hints[57]) certain national inclinations. Musical cultures, it seems, have demanded virtuosity and deplored it in equal measure.

For the composer to prescribe virtuosity is to weaken or obfuscate any sense of an idea represented, a story told, a meaning rendered. The gap between signified and signifier is at the very least narrowed. The telling is destined to exceed the tale. If we return for a moment to the idiomatic figures discussed in my last chapter, this point can be made a little more concrete. Not only do such figures exceed expression by inhibiting reference to conventional meanings (the meaning is in the performance rather than expressed through it); they further discourage the congealing of events into a form through the 'marking' of events for memory. Rather than render an idea or articulate a form, idiomatic figures, of their nature irreducible, proceed through addition. Our unease about virtuosity is partly due to this implicit challenge to expression and form, even – at root – to authority, and also to the kind of idealisation invited by work character. It offends our sense – our hope – that there must be something behind the music, that in a mysterious way, one we cannot fully understand, music can convey to us ideas of man and nature and morality. Virtuosity brusquely dismisses – pushes into the corners – any such pretension. It has an evanescent quality, contingent on a particular moment, a precise location (it 'takes place'),[58] an instrument, a performer, a style or 'manner' of performance, and all of these contribute to a sense of physical presence and immediacy that forces itself upon us, blocking out representation. Virtuosity presents, rather than represents. It encourages us to wonder at the act, rather than to commune with the work and its referents by way of the act.

If those (inexpressive) idiomatic figures point to anything, it is to the instrument itself, and in that sense they render the instrument an important source of meaning. Of this, too, we have tended to be suspicious, sensing that the idea should somehow transcend its medium. Here our puritanism echoes Plato, who regarded instruments as an excess, and it also calls to mind a long history of sacred music, in which instruments were intermittently branded artificial or mechanical, unlike the natural medium of the voice. Way back in 1622, as part of his supplication for an Oxford doctorate, Nathaniel Giles was asked if 'any artificial instrument [can] so fully and truly express music as the natural voice'.[59] Unlike vocal music, where the material base is part of our being, instrumental music deals with a material base that needs to be penetrated and transformed by 'collective human action',[60] to

[57] Bernstein, *Virtuosity of the Nineteenth Century*, p. 12.
[58] Some of the implications of this spatial dimension of performance are explored in doctoral research, as yet incomplete, by Danae Stefanou at Royal Holloway, University of London.
[59] John Hawkins, *A General History of the Science and Practice of Music* (London, 1853), p. 691.
[60] Ivo Supičič, *Music in Society: A Guide to the Sociology of Music* (New York, 1987), pp. 255–70.

be purposefully humanised and socialised, before it can become music. However, it can also resist that process, allowing the mechanical to stand in opposition not just to the natural but to the human, notably through a reification of instrumental technique. Here we may turn again to Weber's history of progressive rationality, by means of which instruments, together with tuning systems, were increasingly individualised and refined in response both to the technical resources available and to environmental contingencies.[61] Rationalised harmony, a product of rational tuning systems, is here opposed to the *vox*, an opposition already spelt out in Galilei, and in this sense instruments play their part in Weber's disenchantment of the world. 'Instrumental harmony' effects the 'disenchantment of song'.[62] Ivo Supičič has pointed out a further dialectical element in this history, which allows that the piano may be 'mechanical' when compared to the voice or violin, but that pianists might in turn be held up as rivals to the mechanism of the pianola.[63] Some of the criticism directed to virtuosity, then, stems from its identification with reified technique, with mechanism and with an (anti-aesthetic) objectivity. Unhappily it is beyond the scope of this study to explore an interesting sub-text of this, one in which a positive value is attributed to these very qualities, at least in certain quarters, in the context of an emergent Modernism.[64]

The opprobrium that has so often clung to virtuosity extends beyond the occlusion of reference and the surrender to mechanism. Virtuosity can also wear the stigma of the gratuitous. It is surplus or supplement, a surplus of technique over expression, detail over substance, even (implicitly) facility over quality. Susan Bernstein, understanding virtuosity in the broadest possible terms, expresses this critique in terms of the distance between a performance and the reality to which it relates, translating the inauthentic information purveyed by journalism, for example, into an excess over fact and interiority.[65] Where music is concerned, the suggestion might be that by composing in the difficulty (and difficulty may sometimes need to be differentiated from complexity in this context), the composer allows the work to be conceptualised as a simple idea, substance or structure overlaid or 'surfaced' by a fecundity of ancillary or decorative detail.[66] I will suggest that one effect of Liszt's recompositions of his early exercises was precisely to split apart structure and surface in this way. Yet this need not be viewed in adversely critical terms. After all, if we value music for its event character (as a performance), a separated surface need be neither empty nor shallow. There can of course be hints of circularity in attempts to define surface as 'supplement' and structure as 'simple', in that the one definition may determine the other. But the pre-existent models help validate a stratified model of the etudes, and norms of style give us a further

---

[61] He points out, for example, that the piano became the middle-class domestic instrument of northern rather than southern Europe: *The Rational and Social Foundations of Music*, trans. and ed. D. Martindale, J. Riedel and G. Neuwirth (Illinois, 1958; orig. edn, 1921), p. 124.

[62] For a robust interpretation of the 'struggle between instrumental and vocal forces grappling for totality', see Daniel Chua, *Absolute Music and the Construction of Meaning* (Cambridge, 1996).

[63] Supičič, *Music in Society*, p. 270.

[64] See, for example, Carolyn Abbate, 'Outside Ravel's Tomb', *Journal of the American Musicological Society*, vol 52, 3 (Fall 1999), pp. 465–530.

[65] Bernstein, *Virtuosity of the Nineteenth Century*, pp. 18–19.

[66] 'Too many notes', was Joseph II's verdict on Mozart's *Così fan tutte*, though it is likely that he referred more to the thickness of the orchestration than to the profusion of ornamental detail. This simple charge is the mantra of critical commentaries on virtuosity, not excluding Liszt.

supportive reference point. Within the style systems of early nineteenth-century pianism some of the unusual gestures, disjunct successions, or richly elaborated textures belonging to a brilliant surface are rather easily perceived as excessive to work character, at least where this is conventionally defined by formal, thematic or harmonic schemata. We should note, however, that it is a large step of interpretation to translate this excess into a judgement of appropriateness, and a giant step to read it as a judgement of propriety. To exceed may be to squander. But it may also be to transcend.

Liszt first used the term 'transcendental' in 1837–8 to refer to the first set of *Paganini Etudes*, composed around the same time as the *Grandes Etudes*. Among the several meanings the term might carry is a sense in which virtuosity might reach beyond (transcend) not just our normal expectations of human skills, but anything measurable or even imaginable within human experience. For Paganini and for the Liszt of the *Paganini Etudes* and the *Grandes Etudes*, the technical difficulties were designed to exclude not just the mediocre performer, but the best performers of the day, effectively and deliberately narrowing down the availability of the music – its use value – to a single location. Only Paganini, so it was intended, could play the *Caprices*; only Liszt the *Grandes Etudes*, as both Schumann and Berlioz explicitly remarked. 'Although another might imitate it, he could never appropriate it'. This is Romantic individualism with a vengeance, already light years distant from the conformity of post-Classical virtuosity. The very appearance of the music on the page – its notation – symbolised its impossibility, so that playing the unplayable could take on something of the quality of a magician's act. It is fortunately not my concern to identify the particulars of technique through which Liszt realised the 'transcendental virtuosity' of the etudes, beyond the obvious point that finger technique is of necessity supplemented by that of hand, wrist and arm, such that all registers of the keyboard may be kept in play (as Dana Gooley points out, this transforms rapid fingerwork into vertical gestures).[67] Liszt's own comments, like the enthusiastic pronouncements of his pupils and friends, are suggestive rather than analytical, and subsequent attempts at analysis, ranging from Deppe and Breithaupt through to Bertrand Ott in more recent times, all too often bear the mark of their own 'school' or theory.[68] What is abundantly clear is that no formulation of piano technique available in the 1830s was adequate to the demands made by Liszt in his *Grandes Etudes*. His immersion in technique resulted in what Busoni described as an 'immeasurable stride' forwards, a qualitative change, a shift to another level.[69] Contemporary critics were well aware of that stride. In 1839 one critic remarked how the fingers strained 'to attempt the impossibilities . . . recent studies impose upon the amateur as well as the concert player'.[70] Three years later another addressed the music of the 'new school', referring to the 'new form of accompanied melody . . . elaborated by Thalberg and Henselt and pushed to its extremes by Liszt', with its 'reveries, fantasies, morsels of crude harmony, tremendous passages, indiscriminately introduced to exhibit peculiar powers of the hand'.[71]

---

[67] Gooley, 'Warhorses', p. 76.

[68] See Reginald Gerig, 'On Liszt's Piano Technique', in Michael Saffle and James Deaville (eds.), *New Light on Liszt and his Music* (New York, 1991), pp. 253–69.

[69] Busoni, *The Essence of Music*, trans. Rosamund Ley (London, 1957), p. 158.

[70] *The Athenaeum*, 2 February 1839.   [71] *Ibid.*, 1 January 1842.

While these new technical challenges were generally evident in Liszt's works of the 1830s, from the *La Clochette* fantasy onwards, they culminated in the first versions of the *Paganini Etudes* and the *Grandes Etudes*. Such pieces were not entirely without rivals among piano etudes of the time. Several of Czerny's etudes from the *Schule das Virtuosität*, Op. 365 (No. 31, for instance) are technically combative, to say the least; likewise some of Kessler's Op. 20 (No. 19, for example), or several pieces from Kullak's *Octave School*. And then, unsurprisingly, there were the challenges posed by Thalberg, whose personal rivalry with Liszt is a matter of familiar record; few pianists of the time could run the gauntlet of the 25 *Grandes Etudes de Style et de Perfectionnement*, Op. 143.[72] Yet however technically demanding, such etudes usually remained securely within the traditional boundaries of the genre, where a technical problem is embodied in a figure and that figure is then worked cyclically throughout the piece. Liszt's etudes took a significant step beyond this. Not only were they more ambitious in scale and form, so that their technical difficulties were components of a larger narrative or drama. They also represented an advance in gestural character and sonority, marking a determinate stage of what George Barth has called the 'transformation of keyboard style' inaugurated by Beethoven.[73] It may be worth enlarging on Barth's observation. His major concern is to analyse some of the temporal changes that flowed from Beethoven's commitment to a legato pianism. In particular, he refers to Beethoven's renovative translation of a weakening rhetorical tradition into a new (or renewed) 'speaking style', characterised by long-breathed paragraphs that remain nonetheless highly articulated from within, their accents still 'expressive' rather than 'metrical'.[74] In a perceptive review, John Rink forges the link to Liszt, arguing that Beethoven's 'flexibility of tempo [directed] to . . . . profound emotional ends' was a harbinger of the 'temporal flux' so essential to Liszt's poetic language.[75] Liszt's temporal rubato was neither a mannerism nor an affectation, though it may well have helped promote these qualities in lesser pianists. Rather it indicated a performative orientation that is indispensable to the meaning of the music. A tempting comparison (to which I will return briefly in chapter 7) is with the 'intensional' complexity identified by Andrew Chester in some popular music, where multiple inflections of tone colour and timing by the performer enrich the individual moment and give it 'depth', as against an 'extensional' complexity, in which simple units are built into complex ones by the composer through combination and addition in space and time.[76]

Naturally Liszt's eloquence as a performer, 'speaking' or 'singing' the musical matter persuasively through his piano, is lost to us today. Yet his desire to record it for others is evident in the notations of the *Grandes Etudes*. It is easiest to see this in the etude that remains closest to the original exercise. Consider the phrasing and articulation of the opening melody of No. 9 in its original and recomposed forms (Ex. 23). Leaving aside the inconsistencies of

---

[72] That the publisher mistakenly labels No. 16 of Thalberg's set 'Preludio' speaks volumes about the interchangeability of titles within the practice.

[73] Barth, *The Pianist as Orator* (Ithaca and London, 1992).

[74] Barth investigates Czerny's role in the instigation of a 'modern' style of playing, discussing, among other things, the unhappy effects of the metronome.

[75] See John Rink, Review of Barth, *The Pianist as Orator*, in *Journal of the American Musicological Society*, 49, 1 (1996), pp. 155–61.

[76] Andrew Chester, 'Second Thoughts on a Rock Aesthetic: The Band', *New Left Review*, 62 (1970), pp. 78–9.

Example 23 *Etude en 12 exercices*, No. 9 bars 1–4
12 Grandes Etudes, No. 9 bars 18–26

Etude en 12 exercices, No. 9 bars 1–4

12 Grandes Etudes, No. 9 bars 18–26

the former (no autograph source is extant), we may note how in the latter Liszt breaks up the phrasing, 'composes in' the expressive accents, adds *tenuto* markings, and uses small notes for ornamental passages, in order to prescribe an ideal performative quality. More than that, he employs unique notations that attempt to capture some of those elusive modifications of tempo later examined by Hugo Riemann, who attempted to systematise them in relation to dynamics and phrase structures.[77] (Incidentally, an attempt to devise appropriate symbols for these new notations is recorded in the marginalia of the Stichvorlage for No. 1.) It is no doubt symptomatic of the strengthening work character associated with the *Transcendentals* that Liszt decided to remove these notations in the 1851 revision, though changing fashions may have played their part.[78] In any event the notations have an enduring fascination and value for us today, not least because they document something of Liszt's own practice as a pianist. As Example 23 suggests, the melodic idea of the ninth exercise, unchanged in its essentials, gained a quite new layer of meaning through surface performative strategies that, for Liszt, were part of the essential nature of the music. Of course, the melody was also recontextualised in the etude, gaining both a newly amplified, delicately shaded accompaniment layer, concerned above all to exploit the colours of the instrument, and an expanded formal setting that includes recitatives, developments and cadenzas. Among other things, the Classical textures of the exercise were transformed into more variegated sonorities, including the harp-like textures of the cadenza at the end of the introduction, the three-layer orchestration of the second theme, the wash of arpeggiated colour that accompanies the working of the first theme, and the darker colours, with the tessitura lowered by an octave, that distance the third theme from its surroundings in ways that were only hinted at in the exercise. It is easy to see from such textures how Liszt gained his reputation as a forerunner of impressionism in music. They amounted to nothing less than a revolution in sound. As Charles Rosen puts it: 'In his concentration on tone color Liszt may be seen as the most radical musician of his generation'.[79]

In this respect, there are parallels with the last of the etudes. Here the melody of the exercise is translated from simple to compound metre, and is supplemented by a left-hand 'echo' which in its turn necessitates further metrical modifications. However, in other respects the original melody remains intact, for the real transformation, and the *locus* of virtuosity in this etude, lies in the background accompaniment layer, if 'background' is indeed the *mot juste*. Where the exercise had combined melody and figure in ways that can easily be related to Classical, and even Baroque, models, the etude preserves the melody but translates the figure into something utterly different, a texture quintessentially of the Romantic piano (Ex. 24).[80]

---

[77] See in particular Hugo Riemann, *Musikalische Dynamik und Agogik* (Leipzig, 1884).

[78] Liszt's experiments in this direction, by no means exclusive to the *Transcendentals*, find an appropriate context in Parisian pianism of the 1830s, where there seemed to be a widespread concern to specify the performative. David Rowland has further remarked to me that the sequence of Liszt's refinements of notation and subsequent rejection of those refinements may find a parallel in Mozart.

[79] *The Romantic Generation* (London, 1995), p. 507.

[80] See the analysis of this transformation by Wilhelm Seidel, 'Über Figurationsmotive von Chopin und Liszt', in Glahn, Sørenson and Ryom (eds.), *Book of the International Musicological Society Congress* (Copenhagen, 1972), vol. 2, pp. 647–51. Seidel considers this example in the larger context of the evolution of figuration from eighteenth- to nineteenth-century keyboard music.

Example 24 *Etude en 12 exercices*, No. 12 bars 5–8
12 Grandes Etudes, No. 12 bars 14–17

Etude en 12 exercices, No. 12 bars 5–8

12 Grandes Etudes, No. 12 bars 14–17

It becomes in the recomposition a continuous tremolo figuration, whose evocative, shimmering sonority is designed to create an unbroken layer of sound against which the melody may unfold. Such sonorities were by no means unknown in the piano literature of the 1830s; compare the C major etude from Thalberg's Op. 26 set. But by allowing them to function as delicate backcloths to a 'canto', Liszt created an effect of remarkable poetic beauty, one which again looks to textures that would later be associated with Debussy and Ravel, and, more particularly, with Skryabin. For, as Skryabin would do well over half a century later, Liszt allows his iridescent backgrounds to gather cumulative complexity until they begin to advance somewhere close to front of stage, not just shading in the space around the melody but taking over from it the responsibility for articulating the larger structural crescendi that characterise the etude. As in the ninth etude, there is considerable expansion of the formal design, and there are also important changes to the tonal scheme, providing necessary developmental ballast for the enlargement and developing complexity of the background figurations. All this is important and will be discussed in due course. Yet at root the virtuosity of this etude – a steady, sustained, cumulative filling-out of texture-space through intricately worked figurations – is the more telling in that it is measured against the constant presence of an uncomplicated song.

Elsewhere in the cycle virtuosity is directed towards the forcefully articulated individual gesture, invoking a rhetoric of a rather different kind from the persuasive 'speaking style' of No. 9, but again one that might be traced to Beethoven. The gesture that opens the first etude is a case in point. If we compare the etude to its corresponding exercise we note a two-fold direction: an amplification of surface gesture and a corresponding reduction of structure, the combined effect of which is to weaken work character. The gestures are rendered emphatic, and thus susceptible to the potency of a performance, while the form is simplified. Or, to pursue the rhetorical analogy, the sense of a sustained, connected argument is diminished by the power and insistence of the individual utterance. Thus at the opening the original idiomatic figure, extended from three to five iterations to traverse the entire keyboard, is all but submerged; compare the introduction of the seventh etude, which extends the technique of the Op. 3 Impromptu in a very similar way (Ex. 25).[81] Moreover, there is a similar extension of the arpeggiations at the final cadence, where the divided hands of the early exercise are replaced by a sweeping right-hand figuration over left-hand chords. In such cases the finger equalisation Liszt learnt from Czerny was not so much abandoned, as supplemented with a hand, arm and body technique aptly characterised by François Clidat as 'three-dimensional'.[82] Elsewhere the revisions amount to a thickening of the texture by the addition of voices, as in bar 2 of both exercise and etude, and in the figuration preceding the penultimate cadence of the exercise. However, the key point is that far from expanding the structural foundations of the etude to support the more elaborate figurations, Liszt

---

[81] Of course the body of the seventh etude was newly composed for the *Grandes Etudes*, and we might note in passing here that in the heavily corrected extant autograph Liszt's first thoughts favoured an even denser texture. In other words, some of the revisions on the manuscript represent an early stage of just the kind of pruning that would later be completed in the *Transcendentals*.

[82] François Clidat, 'The Transcendental Studies: A Lisztian Pianist's Impressions', in Saffle and Deaville (eds.), *New Light on Liszt and his Music*, p. 306.

Example 25 *Etude en 12 exercices*, No. 1 bars 1–2
12 Grandes Etudes, No. 1 bars 1–2
Impromptu, Op. 3 bars 1–2
12 Grandes Etudes, No. 7 bars 1–2

Etude en 12 exercices, No. 1 bars 1–2

12 Grandes Etudes, No. 1 bars 1–2

Impromptu, Op. 3 bars 1–2

12 Grandes Etudes, No. 7 bars 1–2

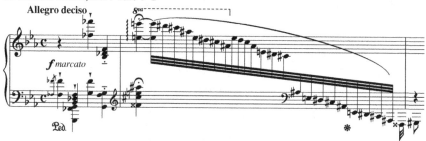

actually reduced those foundations by recomposing only the second half of the exercise. The effect of this was to reduce the form to a single cadential preparation, rather than a balanced chain of cadences. The work character of the exercise, predicated on conventional formal symmetries, has been replaced by a single anacrustic, performance-orientated gesture. In a word, a piece has been replaced by a flourish.

Despite their contrasted characters, the second and the fifth etudes are linked by surfaces that bring together technical difficulty and compositional complexity (in the sense of density of information). In each case it is this combination that defines the virtuosity of the etude, and is integral to its character, whether demonic (No. 2) or fantastic (No. 5). However, these surfaces, comprising both intricate reworkings of the original material and contrapuntal combinations of the reworked material with newly composed motives, are overlaid on thematic and formal structures that again follow the outline of the originals surprisingly closely, at least in expository sections. Thus, the bipartite design of the theme of the second exercise was retained by Liszt in the recomposition, though the transformation of both parts exemplifies the seemingly gratuitous technical difficulties that are not uncommon in these etudes. In the first part the octaves figuration is replaced by a technique of repeated notes in which every other note is doubled at the octave (Ex. 26a). In the second part the right-hand figuration is thickened with chord notes, and its cadential arpeggiation is translated into an even more forceful and flashy octave motive compressed into half the original duration. In this way the original figures are still identifiable, but are at the same time extended and amplified almost beyond recognition. The left-hand chordal accompaniment, meanwhile, is replaced by two strongly characterised gestures: a horn-call motive, introducing a *chasse* topic, and a low-register articulation of a repeated-note motive drawn from the original exercise (Ex. 26b). The concentration of motivic material here is considerable, and it is increased by the metrical displacement of the horn call in bar 13. All this is superimposed on a phrase structure largely 'given' by the exercise, at least for the initial exposition of the theme.

In the later stages of the etude the boundary between enriching complexity and confusing difficulty, already approached here, seems almost deliberately crossed. In a single bar three elements are locked together: a thickened version of the octave cadential motive, the horn call and the repeated-note motive. Later still, the same elements again collide, but with the first two now presented simultaneously with their own inversions (Ex. 26c). Likewise, the return of the opening theme in invertible counterpoint is reformulated in the etude as Example 26d, while the non-thematic figuration prior to the reprise is replaced by a series of chordal skips across the upper part of the keyboard. The overall, and desired, effect is of a relentless, cumulative, almost merciless, virtuosity coupled with an overload of information that reaches its climax after the reprise in a bravura coda of frightening difficulty, with wide chordal leaps in both hands, followed by rushing, accelerating octaves. The sheer strength of arms demanded by the more climactic moments of the etude, to say nothing of the technical accuracy required, emphasises the demonic (or heroic) quality of virtuosity deliberately cultivated by Liszt in this etude. Yet just as the original theme is an audible presence throughout, so the original formal design is there in skeletal form, and with its original tonal scheme. Once more we are encouraged to read the difficulty and

Example 26 (a) *Etude en 12 exercices*, No. 2 bars 1–3

                12 Grandes Etudes, No. 2 bars 6–8

      (b) *12 Grandes Etudes*, No. 2 bar 11

      (c) bar 40

      (d) bars 44–5

Etude en 12 exercices, No. 2 bars 1–3 (a)

12 Grandes Etudes, No. 2 bars 6–8

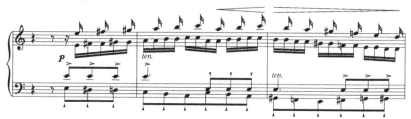

12 Grandes Etudes, No. 2 bar 11 (b)

bar 40 (c)

bars 44–5 (d)

Example 27 (a) *Etude en 12 exercices*, No. 5 bars 1–2
12 Grandes Etudes, No. 5 bars 17–18
(b) bars 82–3

Etude en 12 exercices, No. 5 bars 1–2   (a)

12 Grandes Etudes, No. 5 bars 17–18

bars 82–3   (b)

complexity as an accumulation of 'excessive' surface detail added to a relatively simple, 'given' structure; indeed the replacement of a two-subject exposition in the exercise by a monothematic scheme in the etude reinforces this stratification.

In the fifth etude there is a more radical revision of the formal conception, as well as the character, of the earlier exercise. Yet, as in the second etude, the principal theme is maintained in outline, and since its accompaniment is unchanged for the first strophe the filigree complexity of the surface variation (transforming the original contrapuntal figuration into an elaboration of a chromaticised decorative trill motive) it is again thrown into relief against a simple underlying pattern (Ex. 27a). In fact the periodisation of the theme, irregular in the exercise, is converted to a conventional eight-bar sentence with four-bar liquidation, reinforcing the separation of elaborated surface and orthodox structure. As in the second etude, we might regard this strophe as a character variation or transformation of an absent original, and even the second strophe develops its leaping left-hand accompaniment from a suggestion in the exercise. Of course the character of the virtuosity here is of an entirely different order from that of the second etude. The emphasis is on a variegated, airy sound-scape, a play of evanescent colours and textures, a world of musical fantasy in which events speed past us with a fleeting immediacy, elusive and intangible. The transformations of the original theme undoubtedly defined this character for Liszt in the first instance, but he went on to confirm it through the additional material in the etude, most of it presented in an extended introduction whose three main elements dominate the middle section and then combine in various ways with the main theme. As in the second etude, these superimposed layers of material contribute to the sense of a cumulative virtuosity, where, as at bars 52–5, two elements from the introduction are superimposed, or at bars 82–9, where two of the introductory elements, the main theme and the leaping accompaniment are all present in the texture (Ex. 27b). Again the sense of climax is created through density of information, and again the separation of surface complexity and structure is clear. Technically the demands are formidable, for lightness is all, and must be maintained across an astonishing range of chromatic double notes, wide leaps, broken-chord passages, sudden rhythmic surges, as-cending and descending sequential scale patterns, repeated staccato chords, hand crossings, and octaves; and all *leggiero*.

Compared to the tactile immediacy, the sleight-of-hand, of the fifth etude, the sixth presents a kaleidoscope of shifting colours marshalled by a steady amplification of texture, and with a tone that remains sombre and serious throughout, never harsh, full of light and shade. Here the virtuosity is directed above all towards an expansion of colouristic range, taking us from the dark hues and low tessitura of the opening to the delicate, harp-like filigree of the second strophe and the full-textured, sweeping arpeggios and heavy left-hand chording of the third, calling forth the whole tessitura of the instrument. In the later developmental sections in particular the tendency is towards an 'orchestration' of the piano, with fat chording and deep tremolos working to produce the fullest and richest sound possible. In the process, the transformation of the figuration and ground of the original exercise results in a more complete change of character than in any of the earlier etudes apart from the fourth. The metre is now triple, the tempo indication is changed from *molto agitato* to *largo patetico*, and the ground of the exercise maps on to the etude from the third rather than the first beat (Ex. 28a). The broken chord figuration has been replaced by broad arpeggiations, throwing the ground more clearly into relief and allowing a striking 'visual' virtuosity from the start by maintaining a *tacet* right hand for the whole of the first strophe (a feature that is naturally lost in recordings). The original figures, then, are not just amplified and extended, but modulated into background colours of ever greater textural intricacy (Exx. 28b and 28c). The strophes are tantamount to character variations, but they also preserve something of the traditional conception of a ground with 'divisions', and this again reinforces the sense of a simple underlying structure, whose steady processional tread remains omnipresent, 'surfaced' by ever more richly decorated figures. At the same time this ground alternates with a developmental, tension-building theme which has no direct antecedent in the earlier exercise, and whose interpolations and later transformations drive the music towards two climactic peaks of virtuosity, the octaves cadenza of bars 29–33, and the leaping chords of bars 54–7.

Composing the performance

Example 28 (a) *Etude en 12 exercices*, No. 6 bars 1–2
            12 Grandes Etudes, No. 6 bars 1–2
         (b) bar 13
         (c) bar 34

Etude en 12 exercices, No. 6 bars 1–2 (a)

12 Grandes Etudes, No. 6 bars 1–2

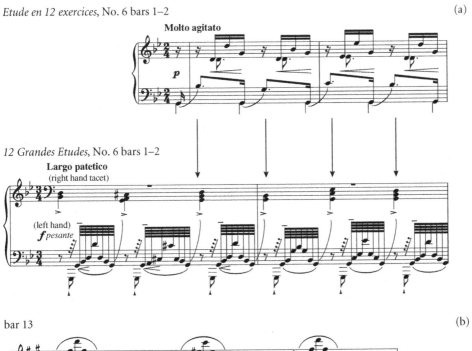

bar 13 (b)

bar 34 (c)

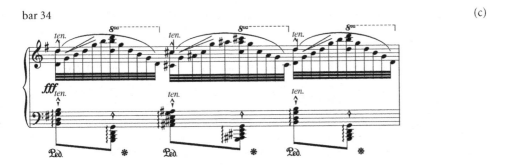

Exposition					Development		Reprise		Coda
bar 1	9	17	24		32		48	52	59
A	(x)	A	(y)		A		(x)	A	

Exposition					Development	Reprise			Coda
bar 1	27	32	60	86	135	196	224	254	277
A/B	(x)	A/B	A₁	B₁	A/B	A/B	A₁	B₁	

Figure 9 *Etude en 12 exercices*, No. 8; *12 Grandes Etudes*, No. 8. Formal designs

The rounded binary design of the sixth exercise is replaced in the etude by something closer to variation form, though this reading will be nuanced in later chapters. In contrast, the formal outline of the eighth exercise retains at least a skeletal presence in the etude, albeit with extensive 'stretching', the insertion of new material, and a clearer articulation of formal divisions. The effect, again, is to force apart the underlying structure and the bravura surface, rather as suggested in Figure 9. The transformation of the left-hand scales into a motive emerging through a figuration is especially intriguing in that it works from traditional finger virtuosity but stretches independent finger control to an unprecedented degree of technical difficulty, an easy prey to a muddled texture, and frankly all but impossible to achieve on a modern piano (Ex. 29a). Here the virtuosity, reducing but at the same time complicating the idiomatic figures of the exercise, arises from an intensification of the original affective character, just as the terse rhetorical scalar gestures are derived from the central part of the main theme of the exercise. Characteristically, Liszt stratifies the texture, allowing material to develop on several levels simultaneously. Thus, having separated out two components of the exercise at the beginning of the etude, he immediately reintegrates them on different strata, as in Example 29b. Likewise, in a rather different way, he allows two voices to shadow one another in the quasi-improvised central canto (Ex. 29c), with the added piquancy of cross-rhythmic groupings both within the right hand and between the hands. As in earlier etudes, the extremes of technical difficulty are reserved for the final stages, where they result partly from the collision and combination of the basic components of the piece, and partly from a gestural character in which familiar accompanimental patterns are extended technically to become fiercely difficult of execution and apotheotic in tone. The orgy of virtuosity preceding the reprise is a case in point. Like the sixth etude, moreover, the eighth 'orchestrates' its material through rapid scalic passages and tremolos that suggest a surplus over medium as well as structure.

It remains to characterise the contrasted virtuosities of the tenth and eleventh etudes. The translation of the opening figure of the tenth exercise into a chordal pattern with alternating hands (Ex. 30a) is symptomatic of the journey from a Classical toccata to a Romantic *tour de force*, from a finger technique to a hand technique, with all the attendant difficulties in preserving an evenness of line. This pattern is later developed as one of the principal motives of the etude, an energising figuration (complemented by a 'trill' figure across four octaves) that offsets the surrounding thematic substance (Ex. 30b); this in contrast to the exercise, where figuration was itself the main substance of the piece. We may note further the

Example 29 (a) *Etude en 12 exercices*, No. 8 bars 1–2
          12 Grandes Etudes, No. 8 bars 1–3
          (b) bars 7–8
          (c) bars 94–5

Etude en 12 exercices, No. 8 bars 1–2   (a)

12 Grandes Etudes, No. 8 bars 1–3

bars 7–8   (b)

bars 94–5   (c)

Example 30 (a) *Etude en 12 exercices*, No. 10 bars 1–2
 12 Grandes Etudes, No. 10 bars 1–2
 (b) bars 13–14
 (c) bars 62–3

Etude en 12 exercices, No. 10 bars 1–2 (a)

12 Grandes Etudes, No. 10 bars 1–2

bars 13–14 (b)

bars 62–3 (c)

differentiated textures involved in the transformations of the main thematic elements, and the technical difficulties involved, especially where there are contrapuntal collisions such as that in Example 30c. Such complexities contribute to the 'driven' character of this music: a furious virtuosity, *sempre marcatissimo feroce*. In contrast, the virtuosity of No. 11

Example 31 12 *Grandes Études*, No. 11 bars 8–9, 22–3, 97–8, 172–3

12 Grandes Etudes, No. 11

bars 8–9

bars 22–3

bars 97–8

bars 172–3

alternates the sumptuous with the half shades, Rachmaninoff with Fauré. Here the theme from the seventh exercise is 'orchestrated' in several different ways, as Example 31 indicates, including an arpeggiated strophe similar in texture to No. 11 from Chopin's Op. 10 etudes. For, as in No. 6 (and parts of No. 9), it is above all the colours of the instrument that are exploited in this etude, ranging from the bell-like sonorities of the opening, through the stratification of texture that characterises the 'refrain' and the 'quasi Arpa' accompaniment to the second theme on its first appearance, to the three-layered orchestration of its second appearance.

Through the *Grandes Etudes*, Liszt liberated the performer (initially himself) from the work, elevating presence and presentation, celebrating the body, the space, the occasion. The performer here is an orator, who gives life to the music through nuances and inflections that are indispensable to its being; Wagner captured something of this when he remarked to Liszt: 'It was often unimportant *what and whose* work you played'.[83] He is a painter, who draws on an expanding palette to add layer upon layer of colour to an original pencil sketch. He is a conjurer, who juggles precariously with an often unlikely collection of disparate musical ideas. A prejudice against this performative quality, perfectly embodied in the criticisms of Liszt by the Schumanns, went hand in hand with a developing conviction that the musical work must be a significant phenomenon rather than a mere source of sensuous pleasure, a separation that would have carried less meaning in the eighteenth century. 'Too many notes' threatened not just good taste, but ideas and significances. It is in this sense that Romantic virtuosity revealed a potential to critique the canon. In celebrating the ephemeral and elevating communication over making, it created its own ideal ontology, one which threatened the stable values of a middle-class culture with dangerous hints of the libidinal and the anarchic. 'Too many notes' could also threaten authority. Of course, the modern recording has problematised this ontology, suppressing oratory, display and ultimately freedom, and, paradoxically, subordinating the originality of the performer (by squeezing his or her interpretative space) to that of the composer. Yet this process was already under way before the age of the recording; witness the marginalisation of a virtuoso tradition of pianist-composers, centred on the art of transcription, in the late nineteenth and early twentieth centuries. A revisionist history of music might seek to do greater justice to such performers; it might want to value rather than apologise for virtuosity. Yet this is rather like arguing that there was no good reason that popular music should have threatened (rather than enriched) a tradition of Western art music. The fact is, it did. And in both cases, the point at issue is the triumph of a particular set of values. Virtuosity was marginalised by the rise and apparently uncheckable momentum of the German canon, predicated on a view of the musical work that coalesced historically and analytically around Beethoven's heroic style and its aftermath. And this is first and foremost an issue of cultural politics.

---

[83] *Franz Liszts Briefe*, ed. La Mara, 8 vols. (Leipzig, 1893–1905), vol. 4, p. 316.

Chapter Four

———

Making and remaking

MUTUAL DEDICATIONS

The strengthening work orientation of musical culture in the second half of the nineteenth century has been characterised by William Weber in the terms of an 'authoritarian canon'.[1] Recent commentators have been anxious to highlight this dimension of the Western canon, representing it as an instrument of exclusion, a means of legitimating and reinforcing the identities and values of those who exercise cultural power. The most blatant challenges have issued from Marxist, feminist and post-colonial approaches to art, where it is argued that class, gender and race have been factors in the inclusion of some figures and the marginalisation of others. But it is hard to deny that the construction of 'mainstream' traditions – as much to do with chauvinist politics as with art – has also coloured our view of certain national repertories, to say nothing of music from some of those 'peripheral' cultures gathered around the edges of Europe. Compared to such exclusions, especially when they are depicted in the aggressive primary colours of a politicised radical criticism, the sidelining of 'virtuoso music' from the mid-nineteenth century onwards may seem a matter of mezzotints. Yet it offers us at least part of the explanation not only for the comparative neglect of Alkan, Busoni and the virtuoso tradition generally, but also for a certain ambivalence in Liszt's status, even today. Defenders have taken up arms, anxious to demonstrate that Liszt was much more than a virtuoso, where they might rather have argued that it is no disgrace to be a virtuoso.[2] But the seal of whole-hearted approval is still withheld, even for works far removed from virtuosity, including of course his orchestral and choral music. Innovatory qualities are freely conceded, but reservations are expressed about the weight of the music, and about its episodic formal organisation. The defenders rush to a different battle, protesting that Liszt's forms are not merely episodic, where they might rather have suggested that it is all right to be episodic.[3] In the end the music, for all its

---

[1] William Weber, 'The History of Musical Canon', in Nicholas Cook and Mark Everist (eds.), *Rethinking Music* (Oxford and New York, 1999), pp. 336–55.

[2] See James Deaville, 'The Making of a Myth: Liszt, the Press, and Virtuosity', in M. Saffle and Deaville, *New Light on Liszt and his Music* (New York, 1991), pp. 181–96.

[3] This is a sub-text of some of Kenneth Hamilton's admirable writing on Liszt; see his *Liszt Sonata in B Minor* (Cambridge, 1996), chapter 2, and his chapter 'Liszt', in Kern Holoman (ed.), *The Nineteenth-Century Symphony* (New York, 1997), pp. 142–62.

centrality to programmes of Modernism explicitly labelled 'New German', has stubbornly resisted complete assimilation to the values of the great tradition.

And here again Chopin offers an intriguing comparison. He too was sidelined in many quarters during the nineteenth century, a salon composer rather than a concert virtuoso, but in any case a minor figure. Yet his present-day embrace by the canons of scholarship, as well as those of concert-goers the world over, seems unchallenged. His central place in the analytical literature, from Schenker onwards, makes the point. There are, I suspect, intrinsic reasons for this difference in status (I will elaborate in chapter 7), but there are also contingencies that predispose us to value the one more highly than the other. I have already remarked on their common starting-point in post-Classical concert music. Liszt's juvenilia (including Opp. 1, 2, 3, 4 and 6) all have their counterparts in Chopin's Warsaw-period music: in his variation sets, rondos and exercises.[4] Of their nature, these genres subordinate work character to the demands of a performance-centred practice. Yet as both composers moved towards a work orientation, they did so in very different ways. The briefest glance at their worklists is enough to indicate this in general outline. Where Chopin increasingly channelled his creativity into a cluster of narrowly defined genres largely for a single medium, Liszt allowed his ideas to spread out into multiple media, genres and forms, embracing the transcription and the paraphrase as well as the original composition. Where Chopin eschewed programmes, Liszt embraced them. Where Chopin endlessly refined and perfected a single version, Liszt channelled new thoughts into new versions. In making these points a little more specific with reference to Chopin's two sets of etudes, as well as to the *Etude en douze exercices* and the *Grandes Etudes*, I will suggest that the concept of *re*-working was of central importance to both composers, but that they understood something radically different by it, and that value-judgements are inherent in those differences.

Liszt's reputation was very largely made during the crucial decade separating his exercises and etudes. Indeed the two works neatly mark out the space between the prodigy and the Romantic virtuoso, if not yet the 'great artist'. Overcoming precocity poses its own no-torious problems, of course, and Liszt's journey to something like the self-knowledge of the mature artist was by no means a straightforward one. If we were to speak of interim stages, we might characterise them as a series of responses – some muted, some not so muted – to the greatness he perceived in others. Even in these early years, he expressed his 'creative admiration' in several capacities – as critic, performer, transcriber and composer. But it was above all through transcriptions and arrangements that he most naturally and readily ap-propriated the thoughts of others and made them his own, in a spirit not entirely removed from Stravinsky's self-confessed kleptomania. Thus his engagement with the twilight of Viennese Classicism was through transcriptions of Beethoven symphonies and transcrip-tions or arrangements of Schubert songs, characteristically filtering these into the one medium that was capable of embracing the epic and the epigrammatic. Already in the 1830s these transcriptions and arrangements were well under way. Likewise his response to a modern poetics of instrumental music was the *partitur* of Berlioz's *Symphonie fantastique*,

---

[4] See Chapter 2, note 10.

just as his response to a newly liberated Romantic virtuosity was a reworking for piano of several of the Paganini caprices. Again these were achievements of the 1830s.

The practices of transcription, arrangement and recomposition had their own histories when Liszt embarked on these projects. We might take as a notional beginning the keyboard intabulations of songs by Dufay and his contemporaries in the Buxheim organ book. Significantly, and paradoxically, these coincided with just that moment (the mid-fifteenth century) privileged by Reinhard Strohm for its 'invention of the masterwork' and by Rob Wegman for its transition from medieval 'making' into modern 'composing' – in other words with the rise of a musical work-concept.[5] It goes without saying that neither Strohm nor Wegman represents this as the neat replacement of an outmoded aesthetic with some new-found alternative. Like original compositions, arrangements and transcriptions (the terms are often used interchangeably, but the general tendency today is for 'transcription' to suggest a closer adherence to the original – a translation from one medium to another[6]) could reflect the making or the composing, and they have continued to carry this double trace right through to our own times. Even in the Dufay intabulations, we can distinguish between more-or-less literal transcriptions and idiomatically embellished recompositions. In later historical periods it becomes rather easier to fine-tune, and to differentiate between, a range of motives underlying the arrangement or recomposition, though it would be a mistake to imagine that categories are watertight, or that they are mutually exclusive. Thus the arrangement can 'make available' (enlarging or reducing) what is inaccessible, or further publicise what is popular; it can celebrate or pay tribute to the exemplary composer or the exemplary work; it can cultivate and preserve the idiom of an earlier age; it can interpret, critique or parody material in the public domain; it can use the offices of translation to highlight the idiomatic and the virtuosic; it can, quite simply, save composing time, especially where it is self-borrowing that is at issue.

The nineteenth-century arrangement recognised all these functions. But the genre was given particularity in this era by the emergence of piano virtuosity, and by the rise of domestic music-making in bourgeois circles. A neat synopsis of the development of the piano arrangement across the century can be made by comparing Liszt's Herculean transcriptions of the Beethoven symphonies with Czerny's earlier, more Classically conceived ones, and then comparing his technically challenging transcription of Mendelssohn's *Midsummer Night's Dream* with the later, more user-friendly and domesticated attempt by the Victorian salon composer Sidney Smith. Already in 1826 the critic of *Harmonicon* could write: 'Our age has been called proverbially the "arranging age"'.[7] He went on to remark that in the wrong hands, 'little else than mere abortions can be produced', but that through 'the power

---

[5] Reinhard Strohm, *The Rise of European Music 1380–1500* (Cambridge, 1993), pp. 412–88; Rob C. Wegman, 'From Maker to Composer: Improvisation and Musical Authorship in the Low Countries, 1450–1500', *Journal of the American Musicological Society*, 49 (1996), pp. 409–79.

[6] See Derrick Puffett, 'Transcription and Recomposition: The Strange Case of Zemlinsky's Maeterlinck Songs', in Craig Ayrey and Mark Everist (eds.), *Analytical Strategies and Musical Interpretation: Essays on Nineteenth- and Twentieth-Century Music* (Cambridge, 1996), pp. 72–119; also Millan Sachania, 'The Arrangements of Leopold Godowsky: An Aesthetic, Historical, and Analytical Study', diss., University of Cambridge (1997).

[7] *Harmonicon*, August 1826, p. 170.

of an enlightened artist' we encounter 'not a meagre translation, but an adaptation to a single instrument of the united powers of many, without its losing anything of its individual character'. In truth he was documenting the uneasy relationship that existed between the nineteenth-century arrangement and a prevailing Romantic ideology. Romanticism, after all, privileged the singular and the inimitable, qualities that seem on the face of it at some remove from the practice of transcribing. Thus the Romantic premium on originality brought into sharp focus ethical as well as ontological questions which had seemed less pressing (though they were indeed raised) during earlier periods. Not only was the status of the arrangement at issue in a medium-sensitive, work-orientated age; its propriety was also at stake. If there was a single, validating presence it was Bach, whose exemplary value for the nineteenth-century arrangement was immense. As Lawrence Dreyfus aptly expressed it, he transformed the inventions of others, 'interven[ing] against the received idea behind a style'.[8] This formed one pole of attraction for the nineteenth-century arranger, who was often more inclined to intervene – commenting, extending, developing, renewing – than to copy or translate. At the same time this tendency was countered by a no less powerful impulse to give due respect to an original, highly valued and 'untouchable' masterpiece.

To an extent the generic categories mediate between these two poles. Thus we may consider a spectrum of genres journeying from literal translation to free composition. In some readings this would take us from the transcription or *piano-partition* through the arrangement, paraphrase, and fantasy, to the variation set, though these categories can only be indicative and there is substantial overlap and shading of function between them. Thus the arrangement may involve free composition, just as the variation set may involve literal transcription. More importantly, the tension between the conflicting claims of fidelity and intervention could, and often did, form a vital part of the aesthetic property of nineteenth-century arrangement and recomposition. Liszt more than anyone steered a dangerous and exhilarating path between commentary and tribute, intensifying the original composer's work in a new medium, while exhibiting, as Charles Rosen suggests, 'a real sympathy and understanding of [his] idiosyncrasy'.[9] In this sense an arrangement might justly be compared to a performance, though the intervention involved in a performative interpretation usually leaves the notes themselves more or less intact. Busoni developed this point, and in doing so he usefully relativised the concept of transcription. Not only is the performance a kind of transcription; so too is the notated form of a work, which transcribes an unavailable original, a (Platonic) ideal form.[10] For Busoni, then, the distance between a work and a transcription is not a great one; nor should the one be valued more highly than the other. Even an existing piano work (Schoenberg's Op. 11 No. 2) could be legitimately 'transcribed' for the same medium, without – as he saw it – any breach of integrity.

[8] Laurence Dreyfus, *Bach and the Patterns of Invention* (Cambridge MA, 1996), p. 36.

[9] See Rosen, *The Romantic Generation* (London, 1995), pp. 512–17, for a general discussion of these issues.

[10] Ferrucio Busoni, *Sketch of a New Aesthetic of Music*, trans. Theodore Baker, in *Three Classics in the Aesthetics of Music* (New York, 1962; orig. edn, 1911), p. 85. See John Williamson, 'The Musical Artwork and its Materials in the Music and Aesthetics of Busoni', in Michael Talbot (ed.), *The Musical Work: Reality or Invention?* (Liverpool, 2000), pp. 187–204.

There may be a larger ethical point in all this. The ownership of ideas is more problematical than the ownership of objects, and this has arguably a particular relevance to musical works, since their ontology lies somewhere in the middle ground between ideas and objects. Busoni's point is that in the very act of writing down an idea we lose its original form. Moreover, it is in just this perceived space between idea and form that we might locate the recomposition. Liszt engaged in the recomposition of his own music throughout his creative life, and the *Transcendentals* are by no means his only mature reformulations of a youthful idea. In some cases, his recompositions may be largely a matter of refining the representation of an idea, and here Stephen Davies is no doubt right to make a rigid ontological distinction between the recomposition of one's own music and the arrangement of another's.[11] Yet in other cases the idea may either be represented entirely differently, or may itself be reshaped. And here, I suggest, the differences between these categories is by no means great. (It is worth noting, though, that the recomposition of one's own music implies a degree of self-reflection that is well attuned to the Romantic ideology; we are again reminded of Liszt's letter to his mother, requesting those copies of his early music.) Whether recomposing his own music or another's, Liszt's motivations, like the techniques of transformation he employed, were often just about identical: a channel for virtuosity, a tribute to the composer (!), an analysis of the idea.

For Liszt himself, the distinction was arguably of little moment. His signature could assign to its owner the translation, and in some cases the unmediated substance, of another's idea, with no plagiarism involved (the operatic fantasies). Or it could signify the translation of a single poetic idea into several musical forms (the Mephisto waltzes). Or it could represent a struggle through several attempts to achieve the clearest formulation of an epic idea (the Faust Symphony).[12] Or it could validate several versions of the same musical idea (the *Paganini Etudes*). This describes an 'open' compositional process, whose apparent permissiveness cuts against the grain of a strengthening German tradition centred on the notion of the *Werktreue*. To some extent this was the way of early nineteenth-century pianism, as indeed of early nineteenth-century opera. In both practices the work tends to include its variants, and in many cases even its versions; witness the difficulties facing later editors when they try to produce a definitive text of these repertories. And in both practices the balance between work character and event character shifted in favour of the former as the century unfolded. Liszt was by no means unresponsive to this development. He was careful to specify a 'seule version authentique' for the *Transcendentals*, for example, and more generally he arrived (with the *poème pianistique* and symphonic poem) at his own very particular and very influential understanding of a work-concept for the modern age. But his general practice – even in the later years – remained that of an inveterate reviser, liberally autographing the passing thought, the provisional statement, the alternative version.

Chopin too was an inveterate reviser, as the complexity of the manuscript sources indicates. Yet in his case it was the quest for an unattainable perfection that motivated his endless fine-tuning of the individual work. There are few rival versions in Chopin, for his inclination

[11] Stephen Davies, 'Transcription, Authenticity and Performance', *British Journal of Aesthetics*, 28 (1988), pp. 216–27.
[12] See László Somfai, 'Die musikalischen Gestaltwandlungen der Faust-Symphonie von Liszt', *Studia musicologica*, 2 (1962), pp. 87–137.

was to keep tinkering with the existing version, glossing even its published score.[13] Moreover he reworked his material in another sense. From the early 1830s he abandoned the popular genres of post-Classical pianism in favour of a select group of genres, many of them newly defined, and all of them deployed with a consistency that allows significance to be registered both through conformance and deviation.[14] Through this remarkable project of generic renovation, gathering many ideas into few forms, a process of reworking was inherent in the Chopin genres. It characterises in particular the four ballades, the four scherzos, the four impromptus, the two late fantasies, and also the two sets of etudes. One of Chopin's achievements in Op. 10 (dedicated, it will be remembered, to Liszt) was to reformulate, in terms peculiarly suited to the piano, the paradigmatic figuration and counterpoint of Bach. This opened the door to the innovatory pianism of his subsequent works, a pianism characterised above all else by the translation of Bach's equal-voiced counterpoint into a differentiated counterpoint moulded to the idiomatic nature of the piano. There is of course remarkable surface variety of texture and figuration in Op. 10, but as in Bach that variety belies a restricted repertory of basic patterns of invention. In using this term, I again pay tribute to Lawrence Dreyfus's challenging book, in which he demonstrates among other things how Bach creatively recycled and elaborated a restricted repertory of patterns of invention, adapting, altering and transforming the inventions of others. Much the same language describes Chopin's relationship to a post-Classical practice.

Now the basic figurations of Op. 10 were extended in several ways by the Op. 25 cycle. Exactly when Chopin started work on this set remains something of a mystery (for some reason commentators often opt for 1835), but we do know that the new etudes were completed in 1837, just before Liszt began work in earnest on the *Grandes Etudes* (again it will be remembered that Chopin renewed the association with Liszt through a dedication to Marie d'Agoult).[15] Not only does the later cycle work to the same generic blueprint as Op. 10; several of the etudes might be viewed as intensifications, elaborations – even in a way variations – of the patterns of invention, the forms and the affects found in the earlier work.[16] There is, in short, an element of reworking taking us from the patterns of Bach to the patterns of Op. 10 to the patterns of Op. 25. The effect of Op. 25, then, is to confirm and strengthen a tradition of inventions based on figurative consistency, where a limited repertory of figures is absorbed into a closed work-concept grounded in Baroque traditions. In the process the figures of post-Classical virtuosity were transmuted from a performance-orientated surplus to a work-orientated essence in what amounts to a conquest of virtuosity by the musical work. Historically, it seems to me that Chopin's major contribution here (aided and abetted by Moscheles, Mendelssohn and Schumann) was to recover or reinstate an essentially eighteenth-century equilibrium between virtuosity and work character. And the larger point

---

[13] The result is often a lengthy source chain, extending to multiple impressions of the (often divergent) first editions, and beyond that to autograph glosses on scores belonging to family and pupils; all immensely perplexing to the modern editor.

[14] See my article 'Chopin and Genre', *Music Analysis*, 8, 3 (1989), pp. 213–31.

[15] As far back as December 1833, Liszt wrote to Marie of Chopin, remarking that 'Son prochain nocturne vous sera dedié', in *Correspondance de Liszt et de la comtesse d'Agoult*, ed. Daniel Ollivier (Paris 1933–40), vol. 1, pp. 50–1.

[16] See Jim Samson, *The Music of Chopin* (London, 1985), pp. 71–3.

flowing from this is that Chopin's neo-Baroque virtuosity, for all its striking originality, could in the course of time be rather easily assimilated by an expanding canon of masterworks, the expression and validation of a bourgeois culture with universalist ambitions. Grounded in Bach (as Schenker demonstrated, even the underlying contrapuntal scaffolding of the mature music is not so different from Bach's), and committed to the idea of the *opus perfectum . . .*, Chopin was ripe for later appropriation, even in Schenker's breathtakingly chauvinistic terms: 'For the profundity with which nature has endowed him, Chopin belongs more to Germany than to Poland'.[17]

Not so Liszt. By dedicating Volume 2 of the Ricordi edition of his *Grandes Etudes* to Chopin, Liszt no doubt paid honest tribute to a fellow pianist-composer, as he did also to Czerny in Volume 1. At the same time the dedication served to mark out his separation from Chopin's neo-Baroque virtuosity no less than Czerny's post-Classical virtuosity. For Liszt's reworkings are of a different order altogether from Chopin's. As I have already noted, he enlarged the figures of his earlier exercises into performance-orientated events in which structure and surface are forced apart, and in which the reconstituted figures tend to function as ornament, gesture or colour, subordinated to larger melodic statements that are varied and transformed in what Dahlhaus described as an 'ever-changing array of masks and guises'.[18] The materials of the *Grandes Etudes* are in this sense unamenable either to figurative recycling or to thematic working. They are excessive in several senses, including the sense in which they threaten to exceed the work. Liszt's reworking, then, changed the earlier exercises utterly, redefining their genre where Chopin's Op. 25 had confirmed the genre of Op. 10. Thus any element that remains intact in the journey from exercises to etudes is in no sense an essence. It is by no means clear that we even have different configurations of an idea, for the idea (to use a loaded term, which will shortly be explored) has itself changed. Again the polarities are striking. The shared materials of the *Etude en douze exercices* and the *Grandes Etudes* serve to highlight the difference in aesthetic, whereas the different materials of the two Chopin cycles emphasise their shared aesthetic. Chopin's new composition is a recomposition; Liszt's recomposition is a new composition.

THE ORIGINAL TONE

In his numerous descriptions of the art of composition, Schoenberg's language tends to echo a familiar rhetorical division between the invention of an idea and a fitting way to present it.[19] Recomposition, one might reasonably assume, bypasses the first of these two stages. Liszt used similar language. To practise art means 'to create and use a form to express a feeling, an idea'.[20] Several things are caught up in this. For one, there is the issue of intention, of what is meant as distinct from what is said. For another, there is the implied separation of the idea and its presentation or form: the separation of what is said and from how it is said.

[17] See Ian Bent, 'Heinrich Schenker, Chopin and Domenico Scarlatti', *Music Analysis*, 5, 2–3 (1986), pp. 131–49.
[18] Carl Dahlhaus, *Nineteenth-Century Music*, trans. J. B. Robinson (Berkeley and Los Angeles, 1989), pp. 134–42.
[19] The title of his unfinished text on the musical idea expresses this distinction eloquently: *The Musical Idea and the Logic, Technique, and Art of its Presentation*, ed. Patricia Carpenter and Severine Neff (New York, 1995).
[20] *Franz Liszt. Gesammelte Schriften*, ed. Lina Ramann (Leipzig, 1881–99), vol. 4, pp. 140–1.

And hovering over both of these issues is the rather basic question of just what Schoenberg and Liszt understood by 'idea' in the first place. Working from these quotations alone, it seems that Liszt had in mind a more broadly conceived 'idea' than Schoenberg, perhaps one not even confined by the concrete materials of the art, since he describes it as akin to a 'feeling'. Indeed a key difference is precisely that for Liszt the idea was in part a poetic idea.[21] Yet elsewhere he is specific about the link between feeling and invention: 'In the end it comes principally to this – *what* the ideas are, and *how* they are carried out and worked up – and that leads us always back to the *feeling* and *invention*.'[22] That, like Schoenberg, he considered the idea to be welded to the composer's intentions is clear not only from the above quotation but from his discussion of Beethoven in *Lettres d'un Bachelier ès Musique*. Here he identifies an 'inner, intimate thought behind many of his great works', goes on to speak of the 'modifications of that thought',[23] and further suggests in the same context that the composer might help the listener by stating the 'fundamental idea of his composition'. (It is hard not to read behind this Marx's reference to the *Grundideen* that apparently motivated Beethoven's works.[24]) And in the same sentence Liszt again separates the idea from its presentation: 'Criticism is then free to censure or praise the more or less beautiful and adroit statement of that idea'; compare Schoenberg's 'logic . . . of its presentation'. For all that Liszt's conception of the idea is broader than Schoenberg's, then, there are basic similarities. And we should note too that although Schoenberg's language is nothing if not concrete (the idea is something one 'invents'), his own understanding of the concept developed and broadened over time. It will be worth tracing that development a little, not least because it drew into itself some of those qualities of the German tradition that conspired to marginalise Liszt.

That there should be a unique and original idea embodied in a composition is a precondition of a work-concept, and it is perhaps unsurprising that the terms *Idee* and *Gedanke* appeared with growing frequency in theoretical texts from the late eighteenth century onwards.[25] The work establishes its distinctiveness, its independence of genre and function, through an idea that is particular to it, and to it alone. Here we encounter an *auteur*-centred view of composition with a vengeance. For the idea, according to Schoenberg, is always new and, once invented, is indestructible. The first stage of his prescription ('inventing an idea') invokes origins, those mysterious starting-points evocatively characterised by Janáček as 'the most interesting [moments] in the history of composition – yet the darkest ones'.[26] Elsewhere in Schoenberg there is a suggestion that this stage is primarily a matter of 'heart',

[21] Katherine Kolb Reeve supplies a valuable context for this in her discussion of the 'musical effect', or, as Berlioz put it, the 'grandeur of the composer's ideas'. See 'Primal Scenes: Smithson, Pleyel, and Liszt in the Eyes of Berlioz', *19th-Century Music*, 18, 3 (1995), pp. 211–35.

[22] *Letters of Franz Liszt*, coll. and ed. La Mara, trans. Constance Bache, 2 vols. (London, 1894), vol. 1, pp. 273–4.

[23] *An Artist's Journey*, trans. and annotated Charles Suttoni (Chicago and London, 1989; orig. letters, 1835–41), p. 19.

[24] Adolf Bernhard Marx, 'Etwas über die Symphonie und Beethoven's Leistungen in diesem Fache', *Berliner allgemeine musikalische Zeitung*, 1, 19–21 (1824), pp. 165–8, 173–6, 181–4.

[25] See Carpenter and Neff's editorial 'Commentary' (pp. 1–74) in Arnold Schoenberg, *The Musical Idea*.

[26] Leos Janáček, *Janáček's Uncollected Essays on Music*, ed. and trans. Mirka Zemanová (London and New York, 1989), p. 74.

whereas the second stage (the fitting way to present it) is a matter of 'brain'.[27] And others have picked up on this Aristotelian distinction, or something like it. Saul Novack, for instance, refers to a 'mind-ear axis' operative in the creative process, where the two streams (we might characterise them as thinking about sound and intuiting in sound respectively) mingle and distract one another, but remain essentially distinct.[28] At the same time, it is perhaps unrealistic to assign an order of events.[29] Origins or starting-points, in other words, may be located at either end of Novack's axis. Strictly speaking, they are antecedents of the idea, enabling it rather than equivalent to it, and where recompositions are concerned they might be considered a given. Thus the starting-point for the *Grandes Etudes* was in a literal sense the *Etude en douze exercices*. However the starting-point for any individual etude – the birth of its idea – reached well beyond the object of transformation (the relevant exercise) to embrace something of the process of transformation.

Schoenberg thought of the musical idea as a concrete category. However, as Carpenter and Neff point out, his thinking about exactly how it was constituted evolved over time from 'the traditional meaning of musical idea as theme . . . toward an understanding of the idea as somehow standing for the wholeness of a work'.[30] The traditional meaning – a theme to be presented – was developed in theoretical traditions from Koch to Marx, but it also informed aesthetic positions such as Hanslick's, where the theme is identified (if anything can be) with the 'content' of a work.[31] Hanslick's understanding of the original, uniquely constituted theme containing within it the seeds of its own development ('The theme alone immediately reveals the mentality of the composer. . . . What is not, either actually or potentially, present in a theme cannot be later developed') bears directly on Schoenberg's notion of a self-generating developing variation.[32] And it emphasises that the privileging of a theme rich in developmental possibilities – the 'single bud' from which Hanslick's 'wealth of blossoms' will unfold – amounted to the privileging of a tradition of Viennese Classicism – Haydn through to Schoenberg – to which Liszt was only loosely connected. The principal 'themes' of the *Grandes Etudes* are by no means always identical to those of the corresponding exercises (in several cases a detail in the exercise is elevated in the etude; or the figuration of the exercise becomes the accompaniment to a quite new melody), so that even in this

---

[27] 'Heart and Brain in Music', in *Style and Idea: Selected Writings of Arnold Schoenberg*, ed. Leonard Stein, trans. Leo Black (London, 1975; orig. edn, 1946), pp. 53–76.

[28] Saul Novack, 'Aspects of the Creative Process in Music', *Current Musicology*, 36 (1983), pp. 137–50.

[29] In this context it may be worth invoking Kant's 'aesthetic ideas', distinct from concepts (not least because their teleology cannot be defined). In music, they arguably come close to Novack's 'thinking in sounds' and Schoenberg's 'thinking in tones and rhythms', and might be regarded as a mid-point between what I have described as thinking about sound and intuiting in sound. My own view is that the reciprocity of 'thinking about' and 'intuiting in' is as essential to performing and even to listening as to composition.

[30] Schoenberg, *The Musical Idea*, p. 18.

[31] Eduard Hanslick, *On the Musically Beautiful*, trans. and ed. Geoffrey Payzart (Indianapolis, 1996; orig. edn, 1854).

[32] See also less familiar formulations such as Hans Mersmann's 'substance' in his *Angewandte Musikästhetik* (Berlin, 1926). And linking Hanslick and Schoenberg more explicitly is Adorno's concept of consistency (*Stimmigkeit*) which seems close to Schoenberg's *Gedanke*, as representing the identity/unity of the idea of the work and its realisation as form/structure. One shadow falling on this cluster of formulations is Schelling's view of the 'idea' as an essence that somehow achieves an identity between subject and object.

very basic sense, the idea has changed. But in any case, to identify these themes – essentially they are either figurations or melodies – with 'idea' in the Brahmsian sense is not just to pick up the wrong analytical tool, but to hint that all other tools are bound to be inferior. We should heed Adorno, and 'allow the composition something in advance'.[33] As Dahlhaus pointed out, and I will pursue this in the next chapter, Liszt and Brahms 'sought ... different solution[s]' to the dilemma of post-Beethovenian form and thematic technique.[34]

Schoenberg's reflections on the musical idea were effectively commentaries on a German tradition of which he considered himself heir and custodian. In one sense they summarised those tendencies within the tradition that might be read as the prehistory of his own music, and that meant a narrowing of focus, a sidelining of developments extraneous to the narrative that transformed thematic working into dodecaphony. At an early stage of his thinking Schoenberg broadened his understanding of the idea so that he could first allow it to embrace the many potentialities of the theme, realised or not, and then dissociate it altogether from the theme as a surface appearance. 'Idea' remained a concrete category, but it now resided 'behind' or 'inside' the music. Even the *Grundgestalt*, the unifying thread of the work, was not strictly equatable with the idea, though it might be thought of as its model or embodiment in the world of material forms. Of course it is a good deal easier to trace the developing variation of a theme, advancing from the part towards the whole, as Schoenberg does convincingly for Brahms Op. 51 No. 2, than to reduce the putative traces of a remote *Gestalt* to their source, as he does unconvincingly for his own Op. 9.[35] But the key point is that this perceived interpenetration of the whole and its parts, where the idea both shapes and permeates the particular unfolding or becoming of the work, again privileges a German sonata-symphonic tradition. It is no doubt significant that the B minor Sonata is Liszt's most highly valued work, at least in scholarly circles, for it measures up to the criteria of an analytical canon supported by a covert ideological agenda and centred on the repertory that most neatly validates that agenda. Finding Hanslick's 'single bud' in the sonata could hardly be easier. To seek comparable integrative strategies in at least some of the *Grandes Etudes*, and to embody these strategies in a concealed originary idea pregnant with possibilities, is by no means unthinkable. But to do so would be to prise these works into Schoenberg's narrative and then to find them wanting; it would be to treat the self-sustaining characterful melody as though it were merely a potentiality. Coincidentally it would also be to demonstrate that on this level too the *Grandes Etudes* are by no means re-presentations of the ideas of the earlier exercises. To push it to absurdity: an analytical reduction of the etudes will not produce the exercises.

Schoenberg's final position on the musical idea removed it yet further from surface materials. Risking tautology, he identified it with the totality of the work, and more specifically with those dynamic forces that regulate its large-scale tension-release pattern. 'An *unrest* comes into being: a state of rest is placed in question through a contrast. From this unrest

---

[33] T. W. Adorno, 'On the Problem of Music Analysis', ed. and trans. Max Paddison, *Music Analysis*, 1, 2 (July 1982), p. 75.

[34] Carl Dahlhaus, 'Issues in Composition', in *Between Romanticism and Modernism*, trans. Mary Whittall (Berkeley, Los Angeles and London, 1974), p. 47.

[35] *Style and Idea*, pp. 429–31 and 222–3.

a motion proceeds.'[36] The idea, still a concrete category, is to be identified, it would seem, with an engagement between opposing eccentric and concentric forces, between an opening out and a closure, an intensification and a resolution. And somewhere at the heart of this dynamic, teleological process there is a point of equilibrium, a centre of gravity, we might say, which is particular to the work, and to no other work. It is this exclusivity, this singularity, that is common to each stage of Schoenberg's developing understanding of the musical idea, and that surely motivated his quest for the musical idea in the first place. The idea represents the unique thought of the composer, his 'vision', as Schoenberg expressed it, in language reminiscent of Plato's *eidos* (an intellectual 'seeing').[37] As soon as it is presented, however, the composer's thought inevitably enters the world of collective musical materials, and loses something of that singularity. No doubt this is why Schoenberg's quest for the musical idea drew him further and further from the surface of the music towards a more elusive, 'unavailable' background. His final position, while it is not identical to Liszt's use of the term (it lacks the poetic element), comes much closer to it, and it brought him to an understanding of the musical idea that might have applicability to Berlioz as well as to Beethoven, to Liszt as well as to Brahms, to Debussy as well as to Schoenberg himself.

It has been argued that the technical history of music demonstrates the increasing penetration of the musical idea into the realms of material and systems.[38] That process, involving a dynamic relationship between the demands of an ever more intense and exclusive subjectivity and the impositions of ever more rationalised, unyielding systems, begs to be modelled in some way, and one might do so tentatively along the following lines. The musical idea, either in Liszt's sense or in the broadest of Schoenberg's senses, is understood as the thought of the composer, born either of intuition or of reflection. Once formed, it is a concrete category, in the sense that it is shaped in sound, even if – firmly embedded in subjectivity – it remains intangible and just about indescribable. Again, precisely because of its deeply subjective roots, it is also, at least notionally, ahistorical (Schoenberg described it as 'timeless'). The process of making it known or tangible, of drawing it into the world, involves a mediation of the self and nature, from which the self has long since become separated. By 'nature' here we might understand an abstract, ahistorical category (not unlike Busoni's 'musical cosmos') which can only become available to the composer when it has been partitioned into tonal (in the widest sense) and compositional systems.[39] Although these systems are human products, and historically in flux (again we might invoke Weber's progressive rationality as one interpretation of their evolution), they take on an a priori quality as 'second nature'; they stand for nature. Moreover they constitute an abstract category, even when they are arrived

---

[36] Schoenberg, *The Musical Idea*, p. 20.

[37] Compare Wagner on the dramatic composer: 'He has an "idea" ("*Einfall*"), a so-called musical "Motiv"... Does it please X, Y, or displease Z? What's that to him? It is *his* motiv, legally delivered to and settled on him by that marvellous shape in that wonderful fit of absorption', *Richard Wagner's Prose Works*, ed. William Ashton Ellis (London, 1897), vol. 6, p. 170.

[38] See Alexander Goehr, 'Poetics of my Music', in *Finding the Key: Selected Writings of Alexander Goehr*, ed. Derrick Puffett (London, 1998), pp. 58–76.

[39] It is far beyond the scope of this short section to engage with the relation between music theory and nature. For a cluster of historical and theoretical perspectives, see Suzannah Clark and Alexander Rehding (eds.), *Music Theory and Natural Order from the Renaissance to the Early Twentieth Century* (Cambridge, 2001).

at inductively from actual music. The idea then negotiates with these systems through the medium of musical materials, a concrete and historical category: really a repertory of commonalities, as we noted in chapter 2, ranging from formal and generic schemata of various kinds to figures, motives, harmonies. It goes without saying that both these intermediary systems are arrived at partly though a social dialectic, though it is not possible to explore this here. This working model of creativity presents us with ahistorical and inaccessible poles (self and nature) mediated by history and community (musical materials and partitioning systems). Thus:

Idea	concrete-ahistorical
Material	concrete-historical
Partitioning systems	abstract-historical
Nature	abstract-ahistorical

While this model is undoubtedly both over-schematic and over-reductive, it offers a useful framework for discussing collective styles, authorial styles, and recompositions. In the terms of the model, we might suggest that in Liszt's *Etude en douze exercices* there is some measure of conformity between the musical idea and the materials through which it is made tangible. This after all would describe a collective style, here post-Classical pianism, in which the singular ideas of many composers – their 'thoughts' – are expressed through common materials and common systems. (At the same time the individual ideas have themselves some capacity to reshape the collective materials.) Thus, as indicated in chapter 2, figures gesture to each other from work to work; they echo each other, enlarge each other's meaning, and in doing so break up the integrity of individual texts. A subset of such a collective style is an authorial style, or idio-style. Here ideas form a family, since they express a single self, and they leave traces of their singular origin as they move into the world of forms. Yet even in an authorial style the idea itself remains intangible, compromised in the forming, in a manner potently dramatised by Schoenberg in *Moses and Aron*. To seek intentionality here is effectively to seek the idea prior to its forming, 'to capture the idea quite naked before it strays into the conceptual field like some heavyfooted cow', as Lawrence Durrell graphically puts it.[40] This is an impossible game, since what is meant is partly lost in the saying, and in the (collective) forms of saying. To locate an authorial voice, on the other hand (and this is not at all the same as an intention), is to identify a particular relation between idea and materials. This is a difficult game, since the idea can only leave trace elements in the world of forms; hence the opacity of Schoenberg's several attempts to define it. The authorial voice might be recognised, then, in the traces of ideas, sometimes informally identified with so-called 'fingerprints' of style, and in the elements of non-identity between those traces and the collective materials they inhabit and at the same time transform. We might find something of the authorial voice in Liszt's *Grandes Etudes*, for example, in their surplus to (non-identity with) the forms and figurations of virtuoso pianism in the 1830s. Or in

---

[40] Lawrence Durrell, *Nunquam* (London, 1970), p. 15.

the 'markedness' of their formal and tonal gestures relative to the schemata of a Classical inheritance.

A subset of the authorial voice is the recomposition of an earlier work. Here ideas are not just linked through family resemblance; they overlap in substance and might even be identical. A recomposition, after all, raises at least the possibility that what survives the process of transformation might just be an essence, rather like that 'ultimate, decisive element' that Walter Benjamin seeks amidst the translated versions of a text.[41] In the case of the *Grandes Etudes* this seems distinctly implausible in all but a couple of cases. It is only in the very limited sense of a thematic substance, and even then only in some cases, that we may speak of the etudes as reformulating the ideas of the earlier exercises. Certain things remain, of course. Themes are amplified or reduced, details drawn out and made prominent, figurations enlarged. But everywhere the roles are changed and the contexts are new, so that shared elements are neither traceable to a common unifying thread nor readily identifiable with an idea that remains intact through different presentations. If anything we might regard the later versions as critical – even analytical – commentaries on the earlier. Just as Liszt transformed utterly the (sometimes undistinguished) ideas embodied in Chopin's songs in his paraphrase, so he transformed the ideas embodied in his own early exercises. To rearrange the echoes in the hope of revealing an original tone is thus a kind of wishful thinking. It is not a question of the idea reliving in a new impulsion. The idea itself has changed. More than that, the nexus of musical materials through which it must find a voice has also changed, not least in response to the challenges of Liszt's own music of the 1830s. This extended beyond an immeasurable enlargement of keyboard technique to include methods of characterising, varying and transforming the substance of a musical work, involving a repertory of textural, thematic and harmonic devices. After all, as the range of possibilities available to the composer is widened, so too that widened range makes ever greater demands on him.

The very fact that Liszt returned to the modest achievements of his youthful exercises as the basis for a work of such ambition is enough to demonstrate that the idea itself – in the traditional, narrow sense of the term – was less germane to his conception of the *Grandes Etudes* than its treatment. It demonstrates too that a unification of part and whole through thematic substance was not a pressing need or concern. It was through the fusion of a transcendental virtuosity and an act of transformation that he brought these pieces into being, and it is arguably in just that fusion that we might begin to approach the idea or thought behind them. Exactly as in one of his operatic fantasies, the idea, we might say, is to transform the idea. Moreover that transformation was directed not only towards virtuosity but towards the characteristic, towards the animation and definition of a unique poetic character, with a capacity to move us through its 'effects'. In this sense each etude is rather like a character variation of the original exercise; it is a variation on an absent theme. Naturally the *Grandes Etudes* stand alone. But they also exist symbiotically with their models, in a manner by no means unknown in the rest of Liszt's output. In more than

---

[41] Walter Benjamin, *Gesammelte Schriften*, ed. Rolf Tiedemann and Hermann Schweppenhäser (Frankfurt am Main, 1980–), vol. 4, p. 18.

Example 32 (a) *12 Grandes Etudes*, No. 2 bars 1–5
(b) bars 14–16
(c) bars 90–3

12 Grandes Etudes, No. 2 bars 1–5   (a)

bars 14–16   (b)

bars 90–3   (c)

the obvious sense of the term, the exercises are the true intertexts for the etudes, allowing significance to reside in the play of echoes, of memories and correspondences, of recognitions and differences. Even the uniqueness of the themes of the etudes has less to do with their potential for later development than with their capacity to embody a poetic idea or feeling as a self-sufficiency; as Wagner expressed it, the theme is 'at bottom incomparable and for that reason presented to the world only in variation form'.[42] The act of transformation from exercise to etude was self-evidently a one-way traffic. However, the listener today can

---

[42] *The Diary of Richard Wagner, 1865–1882: The Brown Book*, ed. Joachim Bergfeld, trans. George Bird (London, 1980), p. 72.

purchase a return ticket, hearing in the one what it will become and in the other what it was. The idea is inaccessible. But we may perhaps hear its echoes, reverberating in the chasm that separates etudes and exercises. It emanates from neither work, but from the space between both, from the play of echoes.

THE PLAY OF ECHOES

One strategy adopted by Liszt in these recompositions is to draw forward a hidden feature of the original, even to the point where it may become the principal theme or motive of the etude, vying for precedence with the transformed original theme or at least entering into dialogue with it. In the second etude, for instance, the opening repeated-note motive is extracted from the accompaniment to the main theme of the earlier exercise, and its relation to the scherzo of Beethoven's Fifth Symphony is certainly not coincidental, establishing at the outset a distinctive character for the etude (Ex. 32a). Following this brief introduction, the Beethoven motive then appears as an accompaniment to the main theme, as in the exercise, but now underlined with accents (Ex. 26a); and as the piece unfolds the motive cuts into the structure laid out by the exercise, prising apart the original formal components with new developmental material as well as penetrating the components themselves. Thus the chromatic space between the A minor and C major sections of the original exercise is now filled in by a tension-building sequential paragraph working three separate elements: the Beethoven motive, the first part of the theme (that is, the part that coincides rhythmically with 'Beethoven') and the cadential gesture from the second part of the theme (Ex. 32b). The C major resolution at bar 27 marks the point analogous to bar 9 of the exercise, but the subsequent material departs radically from the original. The second theme itself is not 'new' as in the exercise, but rather a variant of the first theme (with some links to the first etude), so that the effect is not so much a presentation of two balanced components, as a single ground from which the remorseless, cumulative energy can be generated. Moreover, the second part of the theme is omitted and replaced by a further developmental paragraph which follows the outline of the introduction, but now embodies that concentration of motive working discussed in the last chapter (e.g. Ex. 26c).

The formal uncertainties of the earlier exercise are only partially resolved here. The re-worked introduction leads into a restatement of the opening in invertible counterpoint, and this might again be taken to support the notion of a midway division of the form. However, there can be no doubt of the rhetorical power of the harmonic preparation for the 'true' reprise – the return of the second part of the theme – and the effect is all the more powerful for the omission of that same material from the earlier C major section. A chart of the main formal outlines of the two versions will help clarify their mutual relationship (Fig. 10). In a nutshell, what Liszt has done is to map powerfully developmental episodes, in which the Beethoven motive is prominent, on to the original design, while at the same time strengthening the form by consolidating the first part of the theme in the earlier stages and holding back the repeat of the second part of the theme for the reprise. The idea, as I said, is in the transformation. An exercise of (dubious) Classical balance has been transformed here into a character piece whose driving intensity of expression results partly from its

A₁	A₂		B	A₂	A₃	C	A₂	C
A min			C maj		A min			

X	A₁	A₂	Dev (X/A)	B₁	Dev (X/A)	A₃	Dev	A₂	Dev (X)	X
	A min			C maj		A min				

Figure 10 *Etude en 12 exercices*, No. 2; *12 Grandes Etudes*, No. 2. Formal designs

Example 33 *12 Grandes Etudes*, No. 3 bars 1–4

12 Grandes Etudes, No. 3 bars 1–4

cumulative virtuosity and partly from the growing determination of the Beethoven motive to dominate everything else, including the original theme of the exercise. These two impulses work together to build the tension preparatory to a coda of white-heat virtuosity, the more powerful for the rhythmic foreshortening of the motive in bars 83–91. The term 'demonic', already overworked in this study, as elsewhere in the Liszt literature, seems inescapable. And Beethoven has the final word (Ex. 32c).

I noted in chapter 2 that the rising three-note motive that initiates the main theme of No. 2 is prominent again, in prime and inverted forms, in Nos. 3 and 4. Interestingly, Liszt's reworkings of the third and fourth of the exercises also have certain similarities, though the effect is to push their poetic characters further apart. In both cases he translated the material of the exercise into an accompaniment for a newly composed melody, and conceived the form partly as a series of variations. As in the second etude, then, the centre of gravity shifted decisively in the recomposition, though in a contrary direction. Rather than a subordinate idea becoming primary, the primary idea became subordinate. For the third etude (the fourth will be considered in chapter 7) this is perhaps to overstate the case, since the accompaniment not only retains its melodic character but emerges once more as the primary element as the music unfolds. The ⁶⁄₈ metre does of course strengthen the associations with a pastoral topic, as does the slower tempo and the superimposed melody, itself growing out of the top-voice progressions of the exercise. But beneath this placid surface there is a play of metre and rhythm that was already embryonic in the early exercise, and to some extent works in counterpoint to the exercise, if we are holding it in our memory. Thus, it is hard not to hear hemiola effects in the superimposition of a melody in compound rhythm on an accompaniment that was originally in duple rhythm, or to pick up on rhythmically displaced echoes within the accompaniment itself (as in bars 7–8). Moreover, right from the start the two voices of the original exercise are telescoped by Liszt into a left-hand pattern whose change of metre only becomes apparent to the ear at the third bar, as a glance at Example 33 will indicate. And even the larger phrase rhythm has something of this same fluidity, as the three-bar groupings first expand to four-bar and then two-bar groupings for the bridge to the next strophe.

Most commentators describe this etude as a theme and variations. Yet such blanket categories can be as misleading as helpful. The first three strophes (bars 1–36) consist of three statements of the new melody. Yet the melody is not so much varied as repeated in changing tonal and textural contexts, an approach that would prove important in Russian music later in the century but was already fully developed by Liszt in the 1830s. He himself remarked that 'there is nothing wrong with repetition', and his use of it in this etude and elsewhere occupies a borderland somewhere between the character variation of the early Romantics and the more fully developed thematic transformation of his own full maturity.[43] Thus we have a restatement of the melody in the left hand followed by a further restatement in the new tonal setting of Db major at bar 25. Following this the new melody disappears, and we come to realise that its true function was as a countermelody to the 'accompaniment'. The work might then be understood as a blend of variations and ternary, with the accompaniment material as the true 'theme', subject to later transformation, while the three statements of the countermelody make up the first part of a three-part design. The middle section presents an animated transformation of the theme in the tonic, with something of the character of a developmental strophe, working the bridge material from bars 11–12 together with a particle of the theme to build a major climax that culminates in an apotheotic restatement of the theme at bar 65. This is a remarkable passage. It has something of the appearance of a thematic reprise, but the harmony is strongly implicative. A dominant seventh on F 'resolves' on to a powerfully impassioned new theme (albeit with its rising three-note motive transparently derived from the countermelody) in A major, creating, with the earlier Db major, a symmetrical relation to the tonic. The succeeding strophe returns to the tonic for a further transformation and motivic development of the theme (*presto agitato assai*) in Schumannesque syncopation. Liszt then returns to the mood, and fragmentarily to the melody, of the opening, with the significant marking *dolce pastorale*. It may be regarded either as a truncated closure of the ternary design (effectively a coda) or as a final strophe of the variations. We may note how the left-hand theme is stripped down to the descending-third motive, while the fragments of the right-hand melody evaporate.

What is the role of the early exercise in all this? It provides the theme of the variations, hints at the pastoral topic, and provides the seeds from which the new countermelody grows. The restatement in Db might even be seen as analogous to the restatement in Bb major-minor in the exercise, and the transformation in the middle section might be related to the contrasted material at bar 48 of the earlier piece. But in the course of focusing the pastoral character, unifying the melodic material and 'shaping' the music into an arch-like design, Liszt reduced the original material to a more basic melody, rejecting several of the other materials in the original exercise (see the analytical commentary on pp. 57–8). There are parallels here with the fifth etude, where again the profusion of ideas in the original exercise (see pp. 59–60) is severely reduced in the recomposition, though something of the unpredictable succession of contrasted elements in the exercise is retained. As in the second

---

[43] *Gesammelte Schriften*, vol. 1, p. 103.

Example 34 (a) *Etude en 12 exercices*, No. 5 bars 1–2
12 *Grandes Etudes*, No. 5 bars 1–3
(b) bars 7–9
(c) bar 61

Etude en 12 exercices, No. 5 bars 1–2 (a)

12 Grandes Etudes, No. 5 bars 1–3

bars 7–9 (b)

bar 61 (c)

etude, Liszt precedes the recomposition of the main theme with an introduction, this time a sequence of discontinuous, fragmentary materials which signals the mix of fantasy and modernity in the etude as a whole. The first of these materials transforms and splits apart the opening of the exercise (*a* in Ex. 34a), before giving way to two intercutting elements (*b* and *c* in Ex. 34b), of which *c* might be compared to the Beethoven motive in the second etude in that it alternates with, combines with, and eventually dominates the theme from the original exercise. The elliptical, prefatory gestures of this introduction, disjunct and almost inchoate in character, are suggestive not just of a general mood of fantasy, but more specifically of the musical genre 'fantasy', which traditionally began with an improvisatory introduction. The gestures here are motivically focused and bear directly on the formal argument of the etude, but at the same time they signal that the centre of gravity has shifted somewhat from motive and design towards texture and sonority.

Continuities are established at bar 17 with two sixteen-bar presentations of the original theme, now magically transformed into a characteristic melody, as in Example 27a. Following this double strophe, *b* and *c* from the introduction take over the musical argument (bar 41), and *a* also returns at bar 52. Bar 41 clearly marks a division in the form, initiating a sort of middle section that is increasingly dominated by the thematic motive *c* in play with the textural motives *a* and *b*. The technique is developmental, in that it works these motives by conventional sequence with diminutions, but it is also transformational, in that *c* is given in varied forms. It is also at this point that the harmony begins to wander from the relative security of the double strophe. There is surface chromaticism, often symmetrically ordered, but there is also a sequential pattern taking us through a fifths cycle to a structural downbeat at bar 61, where motive *c* is exposed in chromatic form with simultaneous inversion in V of F♯ minor (Ex. 34c), before working through enharmonically to a return of the main theme, or a version of it, in A major (and modulating) at bar 71. The shape of the piece until this point has been an alternation of discontinuous motives (thematic and textural) with a continuous melody in the rough design A B A. From bar 71 onwards Liszt proceeds to bring these elements together in a variety of ways, some of them described in chapter 3 (e.g. Ex. 27b). This is the point at which the intensity curve of the music rises most sharply and we approach a climactic passage which is essentially new thematically, but retains the rhythmic shape and accompaniment pattern of the main theme (bar 90). This is the fulcrum of the piece, and from it the tension recedes to a closure on B♭ initiating the final section, in which motive *c* is the dominant element, though all other elements remain in play. The recession is not complete, however, for the music swells again, before more explicit reference to the introductory material brings it to a close. In summary, then, Liszt's strategy in this etude is to allow a handful of fragmentary motives to comment on the transformed theme from the original exercise, to alternate and combine with the theme, to invade its territory and eventually to take it over. The play of echoes has a new impulsion, all but severed from the original tone, and leaving audible only the remnants of its conventionally articulated work character.

The revisions to the fifth and sixth exercises have the effect of pulling the relatively neutral affective characters of the originals in almost opposite directions. This conforms to a general tendency of the *Grandes Etudes*, when performed as a cycle, to mark out sharply contrasted

Example 35 (a) *12 Grandes Etudes*, No. 6 bars 5–8
(b) bars 8–10

12 Grandes Etudes, No. 6 bars 5–8 (a)

bars 8–10 (b)

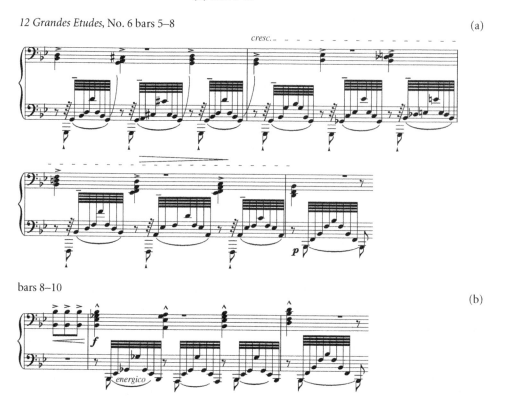

characters between successive etudes. The transformation of the ground of the sixth exercise into the theme of the sixth etude immediately signals this change of character by referring rather explicitly to the opening of the *Dies Irae* chant, beloved of the Romantic generation.[44] Moreover, the Neapolitan inflection to the supertonic, together with the low tessitura, further darkens the complexion of the music. As Example 28a indicates, the *Dies Irae* reference is enabled by the addition of two extra beats to the beginning of the ground, and this at the same time allows five bars of $\frac{2}{4}$ metre to translate into four bars of $\frac{3}{4}$, though both harmony and theme conspire to present this as three groups of four beats. This play of hemiolas is given a further twist on repetition, to produce three groups of two beats followed by the group of three that takes the music through to B♭ major (Ex. 35a). It is only with the ensuing material, which expands the opening three notes of the etude into a 'new' motive (inverting the final interval to emphasise the major third link, as in Ex. 35b), that the underlying $\frac{3}{4}$ metre is finally clarified, though at this point the motive is almost immediately cut short by the

---

[44] See Jaroslav Jiránek, 'Franz Liszts Beitrag zur Musiksprache der Romantiker', in *Studia Musicologica*, 28 (1986), pp. 137–51, especially p. 142.

second strophe of the variations. It functions here as a hint of things to come, particularly through the mediant tendency of its harmony. Thus, strophe 1 moves from G minor to B♭ major, the new motive from B♭ major to D major, and strophe 2 from B minor to D major. Exactly as in the earlier etudes, Liszt's strategy is to allow the new material to gain in importance throughout the etude, and following the second strophe it builds, by way of a succession of mediant harmonies, to a powerful climax culminating in a double-octave cadenza.

The new material, it should be noted, is a sequentially treated motive rather than a self-contained melody, and in that sense, despite their very different characters, it again parallels the comparable ideas in the second and fifth etudes. The climax at bar 29 prepares the way for the third strophe in G major, the only major-mode presentation of the principal theme. And from this point a transformation of the new motive carries all before it, generating two paragraphs of increasingly 'massive' character before dying away in a series of receding echoes before the final cadential flourish. The overall formal conception, then, has something in common with some of Chopin's nocturnes, presenting a characteristic theme with variations, whose length remains a constant, in alternation with a developmental motive, which is not tied to any fixed duration. Where the former is tonally and texturally stable, offering three contrasted character variations in the form of changing harmonic and colouristic backgrounds (we might describe them as funereal, ethereal and apotheotic respectively), the latter is goal-directed and modulatory, so that the overall effect is neither a traditional double variations nor yet a fusion of variations and sonata form. Exactly as in etudes 2 and 5, the narrative of the piece is partly determined by the tendency of material extraneous to the original exercise (or subordinate within it) increasingly to dominate and eventually to submerge the original material.

At the opening of the eighth etude Liszt performs one of his most ingenious operations on the original materials by separating out and at the same time transforming the two elements that make up the beginning of the exercise. As already noted (chapter 3), the left hand is transformed into a figuration incorporating a motive, of which the latter is neither present nor even hinted at in the exercise. This intercuts with the original right-hand idea, now transformed into a *chasse* theme (Ex. 29a), and the two elements are then combined, as in Example 29b. The narrative that subsequently unfolds presents more clearly than in any of the preceding etudes a sequence of thematic transformations of both these ideas, anticipating a standard structuring device of Liszt's maturity. Thus the right-hand *chasse* theme, originally marked *presto strepitoso*, becomes a jaunty trot in the relative major and then a triumphant gallop in the tonic major (Ex. 36a). More radically, the terse left-hand motive from the opening is transformed into a lyrical, expansive canto in the middle section, with the rhythm of the *chasse* maintaining a vestigial presence, as in Example 36b, and this canto is given in turn its own 'lament' form (bar 102), its own apotheosis (bar 117) and its own tonal synthesis (bar 255). The latter of course raises the whole question of sonata form, which is a more obvious presence in this etude than in any of its predecessors, just as it was already a somewhat emaciated presence in the early exercise. Indeed, as Figure 9 indicated, it is possible to map the overall structure of the etude on to that of the exercise, at least in a basic way.

Example 36 (a) *12 Grandes Etudes*, No. 8 bars 60–3; bars 224–7
(b) bars 86–9

12 Grandes Etudes, No. 8 (a)

bars 60–3

bars 224–7

bars 86–9

It may be helpful to spell this out a little more fully. The main theme of the etude retains the tripartite structure of the original main theme, and even its middle section bears some relation to its counterpart in the exercise, as noted in chapter 3. Interestingly, the move to E major in the exercise is replaced as a secondary tonal area by the more orthodox tonal relative, Eb major, associated first with a transformation of the *chasse* theme (corresponding to the E major statement of the theme in the exercise) and then with a transformation of the opening motive into a kind of 'second subject'. This latter has no real counterpart in the exercise, but its subsequent working corresponds more or less to the original development section. Moreover, when the opening motive returns in something like its original form (bar 151), its subsequent development and its juxtaposition with elements of the *chasse* theme – a series characterised by symmetrically ordered harmonies and formidable technical difficulty – culminates in a transitional passage that corresponds closely to the exercise, and ultimately in the reprise of the opening theme. The reprise is of course much more ambitious in the etude. Not only does it follow the original form of the theme with an apotheosis in the major;

it also brings back the 'second subject' in the tonic major in an obvious reference to sonata thinking. It goes without saying that the etude greatly enlarges the scale of the exercise, partly through passages of sequential development (as from bar 135). It also intensifies its affective character, amplifies its technical resources, and enriches its formal organisation through an alliance between thematic transformation and sonata form. Yet for all that, the 'idea' underlying the eighth etude is not so very remote from that of the original exercise. And this is even more true of the ninth, which follows its prototype in general character, in thematic material and even to some extent in formal design.

The basic five sections of the ninth exercise (*a b a c a*) are all present in the etude, but Liszt greatly expands the form with additional inserted material, and, as elsewhere in the collection, this material functions rather in the nature of a commentary on the materials of the exercise. Effectively he gives the original exercise an enhancing surround, and at the same time allows it to spread out into an ambitious extended structure infused with elements of sonata thinking. Helen Hall has pointed to some of the motivic links that bind the newly composed introduction, an extended 'improvisation' culminating in a cadenza, to the main canto, and she further illustrates how Liszt compresses his thematic material as the cadenza approaches, privileging the moment when the theme finally realises the fragmentary suggestions of the introduction.[45] This technique really sublimates a familiar device of popular pianism, where the lengthy introductions to fantasies and variation sets would tease the audience with promises of a familiar melody. The two subsequent insertions are between *b* and *a* and between *c* and *a* of the original design, and in each case the inserted material again culminates in a cadenza in a manner highly characteristic of Liszt; for the cadenza in his music is not just a decorated cadence, but a means of dissolving the melody, often at the point of its maximum flowering. These two sections are developmental in character, based on the introduction (though ultimately derived from the principal melody), and the second of them actually draws on some of the transitional material present in the exercise, as Example 37 indicates. However, a more significant change comes after the final statement of *a*. In the later stages of this statement, Liszt opens the form by allowing a developmental passage based on *a* to build a major climax, which then subsides on to a restatement of *c* in the tonic and a final coda. There is thus an element of tonal synthesis, as a second group (*c*), originally in Db major, is drawn into the orbit of the tonic in the manner of a sonata-form reprise. This might be represented diagrammatically as in Figure 11. This of course tells us little about the shape of the music. It is not least through the nature and range of their intensity curves that the differences between exercise and etude are registered.

The tenth etude, meanwhile, exposes what is arguably one of the most remarkable transformations of all, as the repeated notes of bar 3 acquire upper and lower chromatic auxiliaries (Ex. 38a) and are then expanded into a new theme (*B*), a kind of 'first subject'. Affinities with the ninth of Chopin's Op. 10 etudes (in the same key) have often attracted comment.

---

45 Helen Hall, 'The Evolution of Liszt's Compositional Style as Reflected in the Three Versions of the Transcendental Etudes', diss., University of Victoria (1983), pp. 71–2.

Example 37 *Etude en 12 exercices*, No. 9 bars 17–18
12 Grandes Etudes, No. 9 bars 66–8

Etude en 12 exercices, No. 9 bar 17–18

12 Grandes Etudes, No. 9 bars 66–8

a	b	a	c	a
Ab	f	Ab	Db	Ab

x	a	b	x	a	c	x	a'	c	x
Ab	f			Ab	Db		Ab	Ab	Ab

Figure 11 *Etude en 12 exercices*, No. 9
12 Grandes Etudes, No. 9. Formal designs

Example 38 (a) *Etude en 12 exercices*, No. 10 bar 3
                 12 Grandes Etudes, No. 10 bar 3
           (b) bars 23–4
           (c) bars 179–80; 209–11

Etude en 12 exercices, No. 10 bar 3   (a)

12 Grandes Etudes, No. 10 bar 3

bars 23–4   (b)

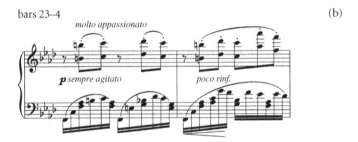

bars 179–80   (c)

bars 209–11

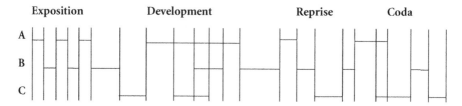

Figure 12 *12 Grandes Etudes*, No. 10. Formal design

The translation of the opening figuration into a motive which preserves something of the character of the original exercise (*A*) has already been described (Ex. 30b). This motive is employed in dialogue with the first subject, and later as part of its accompaniment, when the first subject appears in more expansive form at bar 23 (Ex. 38b). The result is a remarkably tight construction. Motive and theme intercut and combine, as the theme – on its second appearance – drives the music towards a 'second subject' (*C*), emerging from the first, but with its own separate identity, and harmonised as ♭VI –V– I in E♭ minor. The etude is essentially built from transformations of these three elements – the figurative motive, the Chopin theme and the second subject – and in a structure that again looks towards sonata form. Thus, following the second subject, there is an extended development section, in which the figurative motive (now extended by a consequent to create a six-bar unit, the whole of which is repeated) leads into a sequential working of the second subject, and from there to a densely interwoven counterpoint of all three basic elements, reminiscent of some of the contrapuntal play of the second etude (Ex. 30c). The final stage of this development section works the first subject, compressing its constituents and employing octave displacements to build a massive climax immediately preceding the reprise at bar 106. Here the first subject returns in its fuller form, and this time the second subject is adjusted tonally, approaching the tonic by way of ♭VI of ♭VI (A minor–D♭ major–F minor). The beginning of the development section is then repeated to bar 179, at which point there is a two-stage coda based on radical transformations of the second subject, now in a $\frac{3}{4}$ metre, and first subject respectively (Ex. 38c). The mapping of the three thematic elements on to this broad, sonata-like structure is best shown in a chart of intercutting elements, as in Figure 12. As in several of the earlier etudes, the point of the recomposition is to bring new material into dialogue with the material explicitly derived from the exercise. Here it is the driving figuration that stands for the exercise, and the two thematic components that are new. And once again the 'new' material overwhelms the old.

The decision to transpose the original seventh exercise and to present its recomposition as the eleventh of the etudes is the strongest of all arguments for Liszt's view of the *Grandes Etudes* as a self-contained cycle of mutually compatible pieces, which is not at all to say that he would never have performed them separately. The emotional and structural density of the eleventh etude – a massive 'slow movement' – effectively strengthens the sense of an end-weighted cycle, in which the etudes in the second half of the cycle, the last five, are the most ambitious. It is tempting once more to invoke Chopin (to whom, it will be remembered, these five were dedicated in the Ricordi edition), since his Op. 25 etudes are end-weighted in just this way, the last three together forming a powerfully expressive climax to the cycle as a whole. Liszt creates an imposing architecture here by adding two new thematic elements to the theme from the seventh exercise. The first of these emerges from a redirection of the original 'tail' to the theme, as indicated in Example 39a. It also forms the basis of the atmospheric, harmonically cloudy, introduction, and in its fully realised form it functions as a refrain, mediating between the original theme and the 'second subject', and characteristically used either to build or to release tension. Again, as this language suggests, analogies with sonata form are not entirely inappropriate. Thus, following the introduction we have two presentations of a 'first subject', the rescored theme from the seventh exercise. The first of these has a new and important three-note accompaniment, while the second takes over the syncopated pattern of the original (see Ex. 39b). The first complete presentation of the modulating refrain theme then takes us to the dominant of E major (the tonal cycle here will be discussed in chapter 5), the key of the second subject and the secondary tonal area of the etude.

That second subject is one of Liszt's most inspired melodies, beautifully and effortlessly sustaining its long-breathed melodic arcs across a mosaic of mainly four-bar units on a model and variant pattern, as in Figure 13. It yields to the modulating refrain theme (*trionfante*), which has acquired by now an additional 'echo' motive, and this in its turn is subject to motive working in the first part of an extended development section. The first subject is also worked sequentially in this section, and the refrain theme is developed in association with the three-note accompaniment to the first subject (the figure with which the etude both begins and ends). The goal of this dramatic development is the apotheosis of the second subject (*grandioso*) that takes place in the tonic at bar 128. This is the tonal reprise, the high point of the etude emotionally and structurally, and following it all three themes are given a tonic presentation in the manner of a sonata-form synthesis. Thus, following the majestic reprise of the second subject the refrain theme returns at bar 150, this time steadily lowering the temperature and preparing the way for a further brief reference to the second subject (*calmato*), which in turn forms a bridge to the two closing references to the first subject, the theme of the exercise. Overall this etude transforms the original exercise both by giving it new background settings, appropriately atmospheric in character, and by embedding it in an ambitious, expansive formal design.

In the last of the etudes, Liszt replaced the opening gesture of the exercise with a recitative-like introduction, where the first phrase of the melody is twisted chromatically to introduce a parenthesis suggesting A major (Ex. 40), before sliding through further chromatic voice leading to the tonic, and to the main theme in its new metrical and textural guise (see Ex. 24a). This follows the outline of the original remarkably closely, though with additional 'echoes' of the melodic lines, until the change of key at bar 37. At this point there is a divergence between exercise and etude. The etude moves not to the dominant, as in the exercise, but to E major, a tritone distant, picking up in the process some of those tonal threads from the introduction. This replacement of the dominant with the tritone is significant, reinforcing the symmetrical ordering of harmonic space that is increasingly common in the later Liszt. Moreover, the intensification of material here really amounts to a new middle section, in

Example 39 (a) *Etude en 12 exercices*, No. 7 bars 7–8
12 *Grandes Etudes*, No. 11 bars 37–9
(b) *Etude en 12 exercices*, No. 7 bars 1–2
12 *Grandes Etudes*, No. 11 bars 22–3

Etude en 12 exercices, No. 7 bars 7–8 (a)

12 *Grandes Etudes*, No. 11 bars 37–9

Etude en 12 exercices, No. 7 bars 1–2 (b)

12 *Grandes Etudes*, No. 11 bars 22–3

4 + 4 + 4 + 9

2 + 2   2 + 2   2 + 2   4 + 2 + 3

a-a'   b-b'   c-c'   d-d'

Figure 13 *12 Grandes Etudes*,
No. 11, bars 41–61. Phrase structure

Example 40 *Etude en 12 exercices*, No. 12 bars 5–6
12 Grandes Etudes, No. 12 bars 1–6

Etude en 12 exercices, No. 12 bars 5–6

12 Grandes Etudes, No. 12 bars 1–6

which the descending scale from the melody is developed sequentially in a rhythmic stretto that steadily accumulates tension in preparation for the climactic return of the theme in the tonic at bar 49. This clearly marks a major structural downbeat, and might initially be read as a full tonal and thematic reprise. However, the tension immediately subsides through a brief working of a version of the second limb of the melody, and this closes on a structural dominant at bar 62. At this point the introduction returns, interrupting the course of events by diverting the music from the expected tonic resolution by way of another tonal parenthesis, this time centred on E♭ minor. Finally, at bar 74, the 'real' reprise arrives in an elaborated form, before giving way to a closing section based on yet another version of the second limb of the melody. As noted in chapter 3, the recomposition here is partly about an expansion of formal and tonal organisation. But primarily it is about transforming a melody by transforming its setting.

    How, then, might we summarise some of the methods of recomposition adopted by Liszt? Basically, four things happen. Figuration is amplified, themes are characterised, forms are expanded, and narratives are created. The first of these marks the shift from post-Classical to Romantic virtuosity, and is common to just about all the etudes. The second translates

Classical to Romantic melody, and is especially evident in those etudes where an original theme is stripped of accessory elements and given a new, self-sustaining poetic character, as in Nos. 3, 5 and 6, or where it is wrapped in a new, enhancing accompaniment, as in Nos. 9 and 12. This bears on the third point, formal expansion, not least because the cultivation of characteristic themes promotes variation-transformation procedures rather than the rounded binary designs of the early exercises. These procedures 'stretch' the form, especially when combined with large-scale ternary designs, or, as in some of the later etudes, with sonata thinking. In other respects, the expansion is achieved by adding introductions and codas, transitions and developments, and new thematic material. I will develop this just a little. There are five newly composed introductions (six if we include No. 7), all in their different ways foreshadowing the substance of the piece. Two are opening flourishes (Nos. 2 and 7), two establish the mood or atmosphere of the etude (Nos. 5 and 11), and two are recitatives, improvisatory in character (Nos. 9 and 12). 'Coda' may not always be the appropriate term to describe Liszt's closing sections, but in any case their functions were twofold: to dissolve thematic elements in a spirit of reminiscence (Nos. 3, 5, 9, 11 and 12), or to draw them together in a bravura gesture of synthesis (Nos. 2, 6, 7, 8 and 10). Finally, transitions and developments, characteristically built from chromatic sequences with extensions and diminutions of a kind familiar from Classical practice and often associated with new thematic material, are inserted into the structure of most of the etudes, prising apart the forms of the original exercises. My fourth point will be developed in a later chapter. But in brief, Liszt creates narratives either through thematic transformation, as in Nos. 8 and 11, or through the use of new material to comment on, and in several cases to dominate, the ideas drawn from the original exercise, as in Nos. 2, 5, 6 and 10.

I referred earlier to the 'chasm' separating exercises and etudes. Would the innocent ear even detect that they were by the same composer? Some of the early exercises (Nos. 8, 9 and 12, in particular) might indeed be mistaken for something they could never have been: pencil sketches for the full-colour portraits. But this is not a potent point. We are ever anxious to hear the distinctive voice of maturity struggling to be heard amidst the conformities of juvenilia. Again I invoke Chopin, whose idio-style, we are sometimes led to believe, emerged *ex nihilo*, already fully formed; whereas if we truly listen, the striking feature of Chopin's earliest music – the early polonaises, for example – is surely how unlike Chopin most of it really is, and how similar to Hummel and Weber. The same holds for Liszt. The step from exercises to etudes was a step from conformity to originality. Moreover the originality of the etudes had little to do with their thematic basis in the exercises. It would be going too far to suggest that the choice of model was entirely arbitrary; certain materials are less amenable to recomposition than others, as the fate of the eleventh exercise confirms. But just as a successful improvisation can make the most of a randomly chosen theme, so the etudes register their uniqueness through Liszt's treatment of the model, not his choice of it. One part of this story is about Romantic virtuosity, of course, and about the idealised performance aesthetic it stood for. This was not just a matter of the formidable technical difficulties of the etudes, their accumulation of surface complexities on a slender structural base. A performance orientation, honed on the event and its effect, will relish the beauty and poetry of the thematic substance – its character – rather more than its potential for dissection and argument, its capacity to relate the part to the whole. It will also favour extremes of intensity ('effects'), allowing collisions, conflicts and climaxes to succeed each other with a kind of incontinent abandon; in some of these etudes, we surge from climax to climax as on a heady roller-coaster ride. There was, however, another part of the story: the quest for a compositional ideal, for a uniquely constituted musical work, well-formed, whole, and worthy of contemplation. Both impulses were at work in 1837, albeit in an uneasy alliance. But when Liszt revised the *Grandes Etudes* in 1851 there could be little doubt about which had the upper hand.

Chapter Five

———

Forms and reforms

Liszt's withdrawal from public pianism in the late 1840s to a post at the Weimar court might be taken as symptomatic of a more general shift in values: from virtuosity to interpretation, from the 'perfect musical performance' to the 'perfect performance of music', from the performance to the work. Weimar was indeed an appropriate context for this change of mission.[1] Detlef Altenburg has commented perceptively on the two Classicisms that informed Liszt's Modernist agenda there: the Viennese Classicism that culminated in Beethoven and Schubert and the Weimar Classicism that came to fruition in Goethe and Schiller.[2] Liszt was under no illusions about how he fared in relation to Beethoven, but he did nonetheless see his own music, especially from the Weimar years, as drawing the obvious conclusions from Beethoven's legacy. At the same time he entertained high hopes of achieving a working relationship with the Grand Duke Carl Alexander that might prove as fruitful for the arts in general as that between Goethe and the Grand Duke Karl-August.[3] The 'Altenburg', his residence for most of this period, was a powerhouse of radical, reformist thinking about music and the arts throughout the 1850s, even if the ideas themselves (as distinct from the rhetoric surrounding them) were not always so very new. At the Altenburg Liszt held court. Surrounded by his circle and visited by leading lights of the cultural world, he was high priest to the new music, destined to become (with Wagner and Berlioz) a key player in the *Neue deutsches Schule* 'announced' by Franz Brendel in 1859.[4] Liszt had always taken

---

[1] In a letter to Mosonyi, Liszt referred to the need to 'expiate my virtuoso reputation with the disapproval my compositions have excited'. See 'Two Unpublished Liszt Letters to Mosonyi', in Benjamin Suchoff (ed.), *Béla Bartók Essays* (London, 1976), p. 486.

[2] Detlef Altenburg, 'Franz Liszt and the Legacy of the Classical Era', *19th-Century Music*, 18, 1 (Summer 1994), pp. 46–63, and his edited volume, *Liszt und die Weimarer Klassik* (Laaber, 1997). See also Hans Rudolf Jung, 'Das Wirken Johann Nepomuk Hummels und Franz Liszts in Weimar', in Serge Gut (ed.), *Liszt-Studien 2: Kongress-Bericht Eisenstadt 1978* (Munich and Salzburg, 1981), pp. 78–89; Wolfram Huschke, *Musik im klassischen und nachklassischen Weimar* (Weimar, 1982); and Gerhard J. Winkler, 'Liszt's "Weimar Mythology"', in Michael Saffle (ed.), *Liszt and his World* (New York, 1998), pp. 61–73.

[3] Already in January 1844 he had written to Marie d'Agoult: 'Weimar under the Grand Duke August was a new Athens. Let us now think of building the new Weimar. Let us openly and boldly renew the traditions of Carl August.' See Adrian Williams (ed.), *Franz Liszt: Selected Letters* (Oxford, 1998), p. 206.

[4] The term was used by Brendel in his speech celebrating the twenty-fifth anniversary of *Neue Zeitschrift für Musik*. Under Brendel's editorship, *NZfM* was the voice of the 'New German School'. See also Weitzmann's earlier remarks in his article 'Franz Liszt in Berlin', *NZfM*, 26 (14 December 1855), p. 264.

composition seriously. But prior to Weimar he was a pianist-composer, and his music was geared to his appearances on the concert platforms of Europe's cultural capitals. From the late 1840s he was to be a composer in a fuller, more self-conscious sense, reaching beyond the piano, writing for posterity, cutting a path to the future, and adopting in the process some of the posturing that would later be associated with Modernism in music. At the same time, like Schumann, whose mission in *Neue Zeitschrift für Musik* was in part 'to acknowledge the past and to draw attention to the fact that new artistic beauties can be strengthened by the past', Liszt was keen to demonstrate that the new meshed with the old. In the polemics of the 1850s, he emphasised that the proponents of programme music had close affinities with the great masters, that they, no less than the symphonists, were rooted in tradition. The 'Weimar years' were in this sense associated as much with the consolidation of his Classical heritage as with his manifesto for a music of the future.

On settling in Weimar, Liszt tidied his work desk. He grappled with new projects, of course, including the piano concertos and the first versions of the early symphonic poems, through which he 'discovered' the orchestra, and a group of several major works for solo piano, among them the *Trois Etudes de concert, Consolations,* Scherzo and March, second Ballade and B minor Sonata. But he also reviewed his earlier compositions, and went on to revise several of them in a spirit somewhere between salvage and renovation. These included the *Morceau de Salon, Etude de perfectionnement* (1840), which became *Ab Irato* in 1852; the early *Harmonies poétiques et religieuses* (1833–4), redesigned as the fourth piece of the later cycle with that title, also in 1852; seven pieces from the *Album d'un Voyageur* (1834–5), which found their way into the first book of *Années de pèlerinage,* drafted at various times between 1848 and 1855; and of course the *Paganini Etudes* and the *Grandes Etudes.* In a letter to Czerny in April 1852, Liszt wrote: 'I have gone through a rather severe work of revisions, and have remodelled entirely several of my old works (amongst others the Studies which are dedicated to you, and of which I will send you a copy of the definitive edition in a few weeks)'.[5] For most of these revisions the intention was not a complete rethinking of the work, a reformulation of its 'idea'. It was literally to revise, to re-present the idea, and for that reason the revisions can serve as an instructive measure of the distance travelled by Liszt over rather more than a decade of his creative life. He himself made it clear that he regarded the results not as alternative versions, but as improvements and replacements. Thus, of the *Album d'un Voyageur* pieces, he remarked that they were 'considerably corrected, increased, and transformed … I have been continuing writing in proportion as ideas came to me, and I fancy I have arrived at last at that point where the style is adequate to the thought'.[6] Elsewhere he remarked, 'I consider it very profitable to correct one's mistakes as far as possible, and to make use of the experiences one gains by the editions of the works themselves. I, for my part, have striven to do this; and, if I have not succeeded, it at least testifies to my earnest endeavour.'[7] Later, in a letter to Franz Brendel of 7 September 1863, he referred to the 'corrections, eliminations and additions' he made to his arrangements of the

---

[5] *Letters of Franz Liszt,* coll. and ed. La Mara, trans. Constance Bache, 2 vols. (London, 1894), vol. 1, p. 130.
[6] *Ibid.,* pp. 130–1.
[7] In a letter to Alfred Dorffel, 17 January 1855. See La Mara (ed.), *Letters of Franz Liszt* , vol. 1, pp. 229–32.

Beethoven symphonies, adding that 'as we grow old we deliberate more and are less readily satisfied. . . .'.[8]

On the revisions to the *Grandes Etudes*, he was even more specific:

After a complete agreement with [Haslinger] I set to work and produced a third edition of my 12 Studies (very materially improved and transformed) and begged Messrs Härtel to publish it with the note 'seule édition authentique, revue par l'auteur, etc'. Consequently I recognise only the Härtel edition of the 12 Studies as the sole legitimate one, which I also clearly express by a note in the Catalogue, and I therefore wish that the Catalogue should make no mention of the earlier ones.'[9]

Liszt even secured legal rights to the Haslinger plates of the early versions. Of course we are not obliged to agree with his assessment of the different versions of any of these pieces. Liszt had moved on. He was composing in a new climate, had turned his back on an earlier aesthetic, and was anxious to ensure that his major works of yesterday conformed to his thinking of today.[10] We, on the other hand, can give a fair hearing to each stage of his evolving musical personality and to its products. Humphrey Searle has argued, for instance, that the changes made to the early version of *Harmonies poétiques et religieuses* destroyed the spontaneous, improvisatory quality that gave the piece much of its character in the first place.[11] No doubt something was gained in formal and textural clarity; but there was also something lost. Likewise Leslie Howard, in a note on his recording, comments that in the case of No. 7 from the *Transcendentals*, Liszt 'got it wrong: the early version is better'. Busoni, moreover, was of the same view, arguing that the early version of the etude had 'broader characteristics and more uniformity'.[12] Nothing could be more wrongheaded than to take the composer at his word and allow the *Transcendentals* to subsume the *Grandes Etudes*, as the editors of the *Neue Liszt Ausgabe* (unlike Busoni in the earlier Complete Edition) have unhappily done. The two works were products of two different environments and aesthetics. For all that they are versions of the same, each makes its own statement.[13]

The revisions to the *Grandes Etudes* can be dated rather precisely. The final page of the Stichvorlage for the *Transcendentals* (destined for Breitkopf & Härtel) was signed and dated by the composer 'Eilsen 2 avril 1851'. He had travelled to Bad Eilsen in November 1850 to join the Princess Carolyn Sayn-Wittgenstein, who was ill and often confined to bed during this period. Liszt returned to Weimar on 20 January 1851, but in mid-February he returned to the spa. It seems that he began work on the revision on 8 February in Weimar, and continued to

---

[8] *Ibid.*, vol. 2, p. 62.   [9] *Ibid.*, vol. 1, p. 230.
[10] Later in life he referred to the danger of 'allowing oneself to be decided by [the public's] humours – and to this danger every executive artist is especially exposed'; see La Mara (ed.), *Letters of Franz Liszt*, vol. 1, pp. 310–11.
[11] Humphrey Searle, *The Music of Liszt*, rev. edn (New York, 1966), pp. 12 and 25.
[12] Busoni, *The Essence of Music*, trans. Rosamund Ley (London, 1957), p. 161.
[13] See Jürgen Hunkemöller on the merits of the two versions: 'Perfektion und Perspektivenwechsel: Studien zu den drei Fassungen der "Etudes d'exécution transcendante" von Franz Liszt', *Archiv für Musikwissenschaft*, 51 (1994), pp. 294–313, especially p. 306. At the time of writing the editors of the *Neue Liszt Ausgabe* propose to rectify the omission of the *Grandes Etudes*.

work on it during this second stay at Bad Eilsen.[14] The couple then returned to Weimar on 3 April, the day after Liszt completed the revision. Three guiding principles seem to have been in his mind as he reshaped the etudes in Bad Eilsen. First, as with the revisions to the *Paganini Etudes*, Liszt was anxious to tone down what he then took to be gratuitous virtuosity. In part this was a matter of simple pragmatism, but it also reflected a shift in motivation, as Liszt thought of the work increasingly as an object to be contemplated at leisure rather than designed for a particular performance. Some of the more extreme difficulties of the *Grandes Etudes* were excised; the textures were in numerous instances thinned out in support of greater clarity; and some of the 'piled-up' density of information was reduced. Paradoxically the effect of taking out some of the notes in this way – removing the clutter – was to make the music yet more brilliant in effect. As Busoni remarked: 'first he learned how to fill out and later learned how to leave out'.[15] Knowingly or not, he was following Schumann's advice to the letter. In his review of the *Grandes Etudes*, Schumann argued that Liszt could have been a remarkable composer, but that he would have had 'to initiate the reverse process with his compositions – that of simplification rather than of complication'.[16] Secondly, the revisions recorded Liszt's growing concern for formal coherence and for the 'weight of the past'. In the early Weimar years the several strands of his thinking about thematic and formal organisation began to come together in novel and interesting ways, and there are indications of this in the changes made to the *Grandes Etudes*. And finally, the revisions in several cases supported the poetic dimension Liszt introduced to the music by adding titles to ten of the etudes. The first two of these shaping principles will be examined in this chapter. The third will be the concern of chapter 6.

The Stichvorlage itself is a fascinating document, currently lodged with the extensive collection of Liszt materials in the Goethe- und Schiller-Archiv in Weimar. As indicated briefly in chapter 1, it consists of the Haslinger edition of the *Grandes Etudes*, with revisions effected by several methods and at several levels on the published score. For three of the etudes (Nos. 4, 10 and 12) the printed text was replaced by an entirely new manuscript, though in Nos. 4 and 12 there are paste-overs with brief sections of printed text from the Haslinger edition. In other etudes (notably No. 6) the printed text was retained, but manuscript pages with revised text were stitched on to several of the pages. Elsewhere, and most commonly, the printed text was retained but manuscript paste-overs were used for the major corrections, while minor corrections were effected either by using a blade to scratch out notes, or by making tessellations and additions in brown crayon, black ink or maroon ink (engraver's markings are in grey pencil). Although the practice was by no means consistent across the etudes as a whole, it is possible to deduce something of the temporal sequence of corrections from the colour of crayon or ink. It seems that Liszt's tendency here was to revise in layers. To begin with, he made significant textual changes either with paste-overs or in brown crayon. Then, at least in some cases, he returned to the text to make further changes either in black ink or occasionally pencil. And finally he used maroon ink to make more detailed

[14] See his letter to Carolyn of 8 February, in Williams (ed.), *Franz Liszt: Selected Letters*, p. 301.
[15] Busoni, *The Essence of Music*, p. 158.
[16] Schumann, *On Music and Musicians*, trans. P. Rosenfeld, ed. K. Wolff (London, 1946), p. 148.

changes to dynamics, pedalling and expression marks. Since this forms a kind of archetype of the revision process, deviations – for example, maroon ink to effect a major change – can sometimes be indicative of a 'last minute' decision. The first three etudes will serve as examples of the probable mechanics of the revision process.

The first etude was revised only in presentational aspects and has no paste-overs. While it must remain conjectural, the following seems a likely sequence of events. Liszt made the initial changes in brown crayon, including the added title 'Preludio', the added e″ in bar 1, the cancellation of *accelererando molto* in bar 6 and of *marcatissimo* in bar 9, and the reduction of the left-hand chords to bare octaves in bars 14 and 15. At a later stage he used a pencil, notably to make the significant alteration to the chord in bar 12. The effect here is striking; there is a loss of motivic consistency (the A♭–G of the bass line in the 1837 version is picked up in subsequent bars), but a hint of the third-related harmonies favoured elsewhere in the cycle. At the same time Liszt clarified the revisions to bars 14–15 by inserting the new formulation in the margin, also in pencil. At a third stage he used maroon ink to add *e accellerando* [sic] in bar 7, to replace *a piacere* with *rit* in bar 12, and to add the articulation (accent and slur) to the revised form of bar 14 (the version in the margin). The changes to the left-hand chording in the final two bars (and the filling out of the right-hand chords) were also in maroon ink, suggesting that they too were made at this late stage. Finally, on another occasion (possibly while looking through the entire work) Liszt may have noticed that he had neglected to add the articulation to the revised form of bar 15, since this has been done in brown crayon. Most of these changes work to sharpen the bravura effect of the etude, by delaying the accelerando, giving greater direction to the left-hand progression in bars 12 and 13, hardening the attack on the appoggiaturas in bars 14 and 15 (the earlier spread chord is difficult to bring off), and allowing for a more climactic peroration in the final two bars. Characteristically, this third version of the piece is marginally easier to play, but more brilliant in effect than the second version.

In the second etude, the major changes were effected by means of paste-overs and brown crayon, while more detailed performance indications are again in maroon ink. Thus, most of the new notation symbols were deleted in brown crayon (the additional *tenuto* marking that replaces the double line at bar 2 in the published version is not in the Stichvorlage), along with cancelled bars, changes to chords (for example, the removal of d″ from bar 55 of version 2) and several of the crescendo and decrescendo markings. More detailed dynamics and pedalling indications, including those on the paste-overs, are in maroon ink. The simplified presentation of the theme (bars 6–13) is the first of the paste-overs, drafted in black ink but with annotations in maroon. Example 41 presents all three forms of the theme. As Leslie Howard suggests, one factor in the revision may have been changes in the construction of pianos around the mid-century. In any event, it is worth noting that Liszt's journey was not always in a single direction. For the 'bridge' between the two parts of the theme, version 3 moves yet further from the form of the original exercise than version 2. For the second part of the theme, on the other hand, it returns to a form closer to the exercise, notably through the decision to remove the 'horn-call' motive, thus reducing much of the density of the texture (there are also hints of the Beethoven motive in the strumming chords that replaced the horn call). This is also one of the motivations for the major revisions – the second, and

Example 41 *Etude en 12 exercices*, No. 2 bars 1–2
12 Grandes Etudes, No. 2 bars 6–7
Transcendentals, No. 2 bars 6–7

Etude en 12 exercices, No. 2 bars 1–2

12 Grandes Etudes, No. 2 bars 6–7

Transcendentals, No. 2 bars 6–7

most extended, of the paste-overs – to the C major section and its subsequent development (bars 26–48 of version 2), though there are formal issues here that will be discussed later. The third paste-over is the restatement of the second part of the theme (bars 69–71). Finally, the acrobatic chordal leaps of bars 76–7 of version 2 (*con bravura*) are replaced in a short paste-over by more manageable passages (*marcatissimo*) in version 3, and again the technical simplification makes a more powerful sound possible.[17]

The initial changes of substance in the third etude were made either with a paste-over or with brown crayon. Thus, brown crayon was used to replace *tranquillo* with *placido* at the beginning, to cancel bars made redundant by paste-overs, and to add missing slurs. The rhythmic simplifications in the left hand (bars 47 and 49) are also in brown; likewise the replacement of a tonic pedal with a dominant for the *dolce pastorale* section at the end of the piece, and the upstem on the f″ in bar 3 of that section. At what may have been a second stage of revision black ink was used for the adjustment to the first bar (where the tonic pedal is sounded from the beginning) and the removal of the doubled notes in bar 9, as

17 See Hunkemöller, 'Perfektion und Perspektivenwechsel', p. 305.

also the *una corda* indication and the arpeggiations. As elsewhere, dynamics, pedalling and performance indications are in maroon, including on the paste-overs. The new notation signs were also deleted in maroon, and Liszt added a general instruction to the engraver to omit these throughout. The two major changes to this etude occur in its later stages. First, Liszt recast the climactic passage at bar 65, using a paste-over to replace bars 65–81. For the second part of this passage, the revision is largely a matter of simplifying the lay-out, but for the first part the revision is more substantive, using a fuller texture to carry the climax and a syncopated left-hand chording to maintain the momentum prior to the impassioned transformation of the melody at bar 71. By far the most telling change, though, was the deletion of the *Presto agitato assai* section of version 2 (bars 82–103). The possible reasons for this will be discussed later, but it should be noted here that it was not part of Liszt's original thinking. First he attempted to simplify the passage, scratching out chord notes to leave bare octaves (this change can only be seen beneath the paste-over); then he returned to the original by pasting over the revision; and only then did he delete the entire passage in brown crayon. At the end of the last page, Liszt wrote: 'für die 4te Etude "Mazeppa" Vide Das Manuscript'.

For the rest, we may consider only some salient points. Revisions to the fifth etude were designed primarily to simplify execution. Thus the changes to bars 7–16 (the first paste-over) simplify both the descending *leggierissimo* figure, by telescoping the left-hand counterpoint into skipping thirds, and the principal motive, whose formulation in version 2 is distinctly difficult to realise effectively (Ex. 42). Again Liszt tried to make these changes on the printed text initially, as we can see from corrections beneath the paste-over; only then did he add the paste-over (note the extra bar at the end of the introduction). Similarly the reduction of the texture at bars 25–8, where chord notes were scratched out with a blade on the Stichvorlage and a brief paste-over was added, are aimed at clarity, with the overall effect highlighting melody rather than accompaniment. As with the other etudes, the order of revisions can sometimes be deduced by colour, as in bars 38–40, where all changes were made in crayon apart from those to the left hand in bar 39, which are in maroon ink and may therefore have been added at a later stage. Subsequent changes to the text either sharpen the articulation of the motive through registral separation (as in bars 40 and 42) or remove it altogether to lighten the texture (as in bars 51–4) and perhaps relieve what Liszt came to feel was an excessively monomotivic quality (pedalling and slurring are also changed to this end). Although for practical reasons a large part of this revision was effected by means of paste-overs, the structure of the etude is little influenced by the changes, though as I will note later there is one telling exception to this. In general, the aim and effect of the revisions was to enhance the sense of lightness and velocity.

At the beginning of the revision to the sixth etude Liszt was above all concerned to clarify the texture, thinning the chords and reducing the arpeggiation from 8-groups to 6-groups (though, interestingly, he kept 8-groups in the right hand from bar 13). He also simplified the execution at the expense of visual effect for the opening strophe, by dividing the material between the two hands, where in version 2 the right hand is tacet until bar 8. The entire section is a paste-over, with the change of tempo indication (*Lento* for *Largo patetico*) and other expression marks added in maroon ink (subsequently the reduction to the arpeggiation

Example 42 *12 Grandes Etudes*, No. 5 bars 7–9
Feux-follets bars 7–9

12 Grandes Etudes, No. 5 bars 7–9

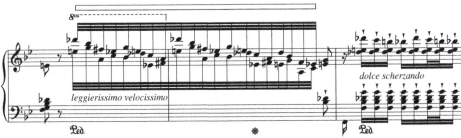

Feux-follets bars 7–9

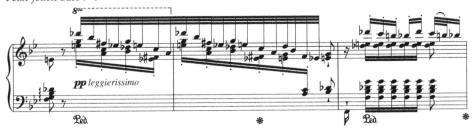

is achieved by simple cancellations). At the same time this simplification of texture and harmony is countered by elements of orchestration, such as the 'brass-choir' filling-in of the three-note anacrusis of the new theme (as at bar 8), and by some complexification of material, as in the approach to the third strophe in G major, an extended manuscript stitched rather than pasted on to the page. Since the general tendency of the revisions is towards textural simplification in this third version, it will be worth asking later in this chapter why in this case, and in some others, the music is at certain points actually intensified and enlarged. Moreover it is striking that Liszt made analogous changes in the approach to the climactic variation of the seventh etude, whose formal conception is not dissimilar. This, however, was part of a more substantial raft of revisions for No. 7, including a reworking of the introduction (another stitched-on manuscript) and of the closing stages of the etude. And since these changes have significant implications for the formal organisation of both the sixth and seventh etudes, they will be discussed in more detail in the next section. It may be noted here, though, that there are several minor changes in No. 7, including changes to pedalling, and reformulations of cadential figures.

Interestingly, the formulations of the opening idea of the eighth etude, and of the later transformation of that idea in the central canto, are both simplified in version 3, with small paste-overs used in every case (the rhythmic simplification of the canto is especially notable). Most changes to the text are in brown crayon in this etude (including dynamics on the paste-overs), but there is also a layer of black, affecting in particular detailed changes to the chording (as in the parallel bars 3 and 6 of version 2; or the change to the left-hand chords in bar 66). The major recasting of the middle section is achieved through a paste-over for

Example 43 12 *Grandes Etudes*, No. 9 bars 20–1
Ricordanza bars 20–1

12 Grandes Etudes, No. 9 bars 20–1

Ricordanza bars 20–1

bars 33–62 of version 3, covering page 72 and the first half of page 77 of the Stichvorlage (pages 73–6 are cancelled). The reformulations of two later passages (bars 232–41 and bars 261–74 of version 2) are also effected by paste-over, though the rewriting of the final bars is in black ink at the bottom of the page. In contrast to the eighth, the ninth etude retains its formal shape in the 1851 version, though there are many changes of presentation, including a recasting of the main melodic line, as in Example 43. This is done by paste-overs for the first and third of the three strophes, and by a verbal instruction in the second. In view of the discussion in chapter 3, it is certainly intriguing that Liszt decided to 'finesse' the melody further in this version, breaking the continuity with *sospiro*-like rests before each accented appoggiatura, while at the same time reducing the accompaniment layer. The combined effect of this is to focus attention yet further on the expressive character of the melodic line. Moreover, the preoccupation with performer eloquence in this etude extends to the addition of fingerings at several points (in maroon ink), to the introduction of chordal arpeggiations, and to an instruction to print some of the decorative writing in small notes. In the final stages of the third strophe of the melody (bars 88–95 of version 3) Liszt reversed the usual direction of his revisions by thickening the texture and broadening the phrase structure, in the process intensifying the major climax of the work.

Since the tenth and twelfth of the etudes are largely in manuscript (page 4 of the twelfth is a stitched-on printed page), it remains to discuss the Stichvorlage for the eleventh. The recomposed introduction is a paste-over, enhancing the 'bells' of the accompaniment, but at the same time adding an extra two bars that work through more fully the E major implication of the opening harmonies. Changes to the main theme – simplification of the chording, and the addition of arpeggiations – are made directly on the text or in the margins in black ink, while dynamics and phrasing are added in maroon. The sense of flow here is increased by the change in the accompaniment pattern from three crotchets to a minim and crotchet (see also the closing bars of the piece), and this is reinforced by Liszt's cancellation of the *tenuto* marking on the last crotchet of bar 12 (in maroon ink). The redrafting of bars 14–21 of version 2 is a paste-over, and it is worth noting here that the bell-like (Debussyan) sonorities are underlined by Liszt's thickening of the chords in bars 19–21. There is a further paste-over for the parallel passage at bar 28, incorporating the new transition into the 'refrain' theme at bar 38 of version 3. The added ties in the left-hand accompaniment were added in brown crayon, but the additional notes in the right hand at bars 50 and 52 of version 3 may well have been an afterthought, since (unusually) they are in maroon ink, and were probably inserted when Liszt was adding expression marks, dynamics and slurring.

The next few pages are intriguing, not to say puzzling. The rescored second subject (with its new accompaniment 'quasi Arpa') is on a stitched-on manuscript page. For the refrain that immediately follows this second subject Liszt continued the practice of adding ties to the accompaniment pattern of version 2. He then cancelled the entire page (the one with the refrain), but in the manuscript that replaced it (another stitched-on page) he still retained the original accompaniment. Moreover, the ensuing passage, immediately preceding the greatly enlarged reprise of the second subject (bar 90), has a left-hand formulation significantly different from that in the final form. In other words, the whole of this section is really an intermediate stage between versions 2 and 3 (see Ex. 44), and we can only assume that Liszt made the final revision at proof stage. The beginning of the second-subject reprise is also totally transformed in version 3, and very much more powerful in effect. For a start, the pedal point is a dominant rather than tonic. Moreover, by spacing the pedal over several octaves, Liszt not only simplified the ungainly right hand of version 2; he also enhanced the bell-like sonorities and at the same time displaced the theme rhythmically in a novel and effective way. All of this necessitated a further paste-over. Finally, it seems likely that the replacement of bars 145–6 of version 2 with an alternative formulation was another last-minute decision, since it is presented on the only paste-over written entirely in maroon ink. At the bottom of the last page of the twelfth etude, Liszt wrote 'Eilsen 2 avril 1851'.

THE SELF AND THE FORMS

It was apparent long before Liszt arrived in Weimar that his mission as an artist – and this is appropriate language; indeed it is his own language[18] – was one of social engagement and intervention, embracing, as he put it, a 'grande synthèse religieuse et philosophique'. Weimar attracted not least because it offered him a testing ground for his belief in the socially regenerative powers of music, a belief that owed something to his early association with the Saint-Simonians and with Felicité Lammenais. More than that, his reformist sermon embodied a sense of specifically Christian mission that not only set it apart from Wagner but

---

[18] 'We believe that a great religious and social MISSION is imposed on artists', in 'De la situation des artistes et de leur condition dans la société', *Gazette Musicale*, 15 November 1835, p. 333.

Example 44 *12 Grandes Etudes*, No. 11 bars 72–3
Stichvorlage for *Harmonies du Soir* bars 90–1
Harmonies du Soir bars 90–1

12 Grandes Etudes, No. 11 bars 72–3

Stichvorlage for *Harmonies du Soir* bars 90–1

Harmonies du Soir bars 90–1

seemed at odds with most other forms of proto-Modernist critique in the later nineteenth century. It is within this broader context of moral and social meliorism that we need to view his ambitions for a renovation of just about all aspects of musical life – performance, patronage, education and criticism – and it is in turn within the context of those ambitions that we may situate his renovative agenda for musical composition, for a (humanitarian) music of the future. It is true that his Weimar aesthetic seemed to nod occasionally towards the more widely subscribed aestheticism characteristic of the post-1848 years, but at root Liszt's stated objective at Weimar remained much as it had always been: to improve the world through music.[19] If there was to be a retreat from this broad-brush reformism, it

---

[19] This is in any case not quite the contradiction it appears. At least in some of its most characteristic manifestations, Aestheticism proposed not that art should be removed from the world but that the world's history and nature

would come very much later. All the same, it probably has to be conceded that it was only really at the foreground level of an aesthetics of composition that Liszt's thinking achieved anything like specificity. And here, as John Williamson reminds us, it was German Idealism, however mediated, that informed his position.[20] The several strands of his thinking about compositional progress were drawn together during the Weimar years, not least through the catalytic agency of Franz Brendel, whose indebtedness to Hegel is everywhere apparent.

Hegel's legacy was admittedly doubled-edged, and it has to be said that Liszt's own enthusiasm for him was distinctly muted. It is no surprise that artists were disinclined to embrace the full implications of a philosophy of history that was – to put it mildly – less than sanguine about the future of art. Yet that same philosophy, selectively applied to art, could privilege the contemporary by identifying history as progress. Likewise Hegel could value the abstract nature of (textless) music, its expression of subjective inwardness, while at the same time lamenting its incapacity to deal with 'the specificity and the particularity of external existence'. Liszt and Brendel took on board Hegel's notions of progress and even some aspects of his classification of the arts to develop an aesthetic of music in alliance with the poetic. Hanslick, on the other hand, turned to Hegel's formalism to develop an aesthetic of absolute music. In the end it was Hanslick's position that came to be read as the late nineteenth-century embodiment of an Idealist aesthetics, even if, in some quarters at least, the category 'absolute music' proved elastic enough to accommodate Bach at one extreme and Wagner (though never Liszt) at the other. The debate was by no means straightforward, and some of its twists and turns will be discussed in the next chapter. But for now we may note that the polarised positions articulated by Brendel and Hanslick looked to a common source in Hegel, just as the associated compositional praxes – 'New Germans' and the symphonists – looked to a common source in Beethoven. More that that, composers and critics alike used strikingly similar organicist and historicist arguments to bolster their opposed positions. It is inadequate, then, to read the polemic as a tidy opposition of programme music and the symphony. For Liszt, true progress could only be achieved through a correct understanding of the past, and that meant especially Beethoven. Wagner made the point in his essay on the symphonic poems, claiming that Liszt was 'the first to place the worth and significance of the works of his forerunners in their fullest light', and going on to specify Beethoven as the principal forerunner.[21] It was in Weimar that Liszt made clear his belief that a new form was 'an advance on earlier forms' only if one could track its origins and 'discern the gradations through which [the] form was gradually produced'.[22]

might be read most clearly through its art. This is certainly true of Ruskin, and even to some extent in Pater (for example, in the last part of his essay on style).

[20] John Williamson, 'Progress, Modernity and the Concept of an Avant-garde', in Jim Samson (ed.), *The Cambridge History of Nineteenth-Century Music* (Cambridge, 2002), pp. 287–317.

[21] Richard Wagner, 'On Franz Liszt's Symphonic Poems', in *Richard Wagner's Prose Works*, trans. William Ashton Ellis, 8 vols. (London, 1892–9), vol. 3, p. 241. See also Liszt's well-known account of the Beethoven legacy and the problem of form in his letter to Wilhelm von Lenz of December 1852, in *Letters of Franz Liszt*, coll. and ed. La Mara, trans. Constance Bache, 2 vols. (London, 1894), vol. 1, pp. 151–2.

[22] Franz Liszt, *Sämtliche Schriften*, ed. Detlef Altenburg (Leipzig, 1989–), vol. 5, pp. 34–5. The reflexivity embodied in this thought identifies Liszt's understanding of the 'new' as a function of modernity.

Accordingly his concern in Weimar was not just to channel his thoughts on the poetic into a new genre. He was no less concerned to develop a new conception of form, while ensuring at the same time that such a conception would be firmly rooted in the past, that it would be true to its origins. In a way, this returns us to our discussion of idea and form in the previous chapter. I suggested there that the developing interest in the musical idea in the nineteenth century was linked to a strengthening, *auteur*-based work-concept. I want to argue here that it was further motivated by a shift in musical syntax, as the tonal regulation of greatly expanded musical forms gave some ground to their thematic integration. Dahlhaus has commented on two different responses to the challenge of idea and form in the post-Beethoven era, and in particular to the challenge of reconciling the brevity of the idea with the monumentality of the form.[23] Following Schoenberg, he distinguished between the developing variation of Brahms and the sequential repetition of Liszt and Wagner, though he was careful not to present these as mutually exclusive options. Moreover, underlying both these responses, and this is Dahlhaus's real insight, is a conception of form that is driven by theme; in a word, one in which the form presents 'the history of a musical theme'. This conception, standing at the intersection of Classical formal and tonal principles on the one hand and a modern thematic narrative on the other, was motivated by two tendencies in thematic process, both again traceable to Beethoven. On one hand there was a drive towards the unification of thematic material, and on the other towards its individuation. It was by bringing these two together through the technique of thematic transformation and allowing the resulting narratives to redesign traditional archetypes of form, that Liszt felt he could advance logically from the Beethoven model.

Where thematic development promotes goal-directed structures by breaking a whole into dependent parts (which both remember and anticipate that whole), thematic transformation has no such teleology. Rather it creates new wholes from an original whole. And this relates it closely to a more general individuation of thematic ideas in the Romantic era, where the self-standing theme is presumed to have a distinctive poetic character, an embodied meaning, an expressive uniqueness (as heightened speech or fragmented song), an 'essential sustaining substance'.[24] Dahlhaus's point is that in the post-Beethoven era this thematic substance was a starting-point for form-building; that the form 'presented itself primarily (though by no means exclusively) as a consequence drawn from thematic ideas, not as a system of formal relations'. Elsewhere he describes a tension between what he calls 'architectural' and 'logical' form, the prescribed plan *contra* the destiny of the idea,[25] with the further implication that the form will no longer be shaped primarily by harmony, that the closed periods and 'nested' tonal structures of the Classical style will make room for more open-ended and

---

[23] Carl Dahlhaus, 'Issues in Composition', in *Between Romanticism and Modernism: Four Studies in the Music of the Later Nineteenth Century*, trans. Mary Whittall (Berkeley, Los Angeles and London, 1980; orig. edn, 1974), pp. 40–78.

[24] See chapter 12 of Robert Hatten, *Musical Meaning in Beethoven* for further discussion, including the proposal that the thematic is by definition strategically marked. See also Dahlhaus's comment on the 'speech-like' quality of Liszt's programme music, *Nineteenth-Century Music*, trans. J. B. Robinson (Berkeley and Los Angeles, 1989), p. 242.

[25] *Nineteenth-Century Music*, p. 255. See also Kofi Agawu, 'Formal Perspectives on the Symphonies', in Michael Musgrave (ed.), *The Cambridge Companion to Brahms* (Cambridge, 1999), p. 134.

processive modulating sequences. Dahlhaus's formulation needs a little shading. It is true that thematic narratives generated form in the nineteenth century, but they did so against the background of Classical formal archetypes, deforming these archetypes in the process (just as modulating sequences by no means exclude the possibility of larger tonal plans). Moreover this is true of both models of thematicism identified by Dahlhaus; it is as true of Brahms, in other words, as of Liszt. The close motive working in Brahms, resulting at times in textures that are well-nigh totally thematic, is mapped on to sonata structures and modifies those structures in ways that Reger and Schoenberg would later extend, reaching a culminating point of sorts in the first of Schoenberg's Three Piano Pieces, Op. 11. Likewise the thematic transformations and variations of Liszt meld with basic principles of sonata form in ways that have analogues in Chopin and Berlioz and would in due course leave their mark on the music of Russian composers and of Smetana.

If we are to differentiate 'transformation' from 'development', then we might usefully associate it with 'variation', and specifically with the kind of character variations, expressive of changing moods and emotions, famously distinguished by A. B. Marx from the divisions or embellishments of the Classical genre. One of the achievements of late Classicism, often noted by commentators, was an interpenetration of the apparently contradictory principles of variation form (based on repetition) and sonata form (based on development). Again Beethoven was the key figure, notably in the great variation movements of his later years, which take on directional qualities through dramas of tonal contrast and through large-scale patterns of tension and release (though they can also express transcendence through stasis, slow tempos, hymn-like textures and diminutional variations). This formal synthesis was not lost on the immediate post-Beethoven generation, and they learnt something too from the parallel tendency in Schubert to infuse sonata structures with the techniques of variation (with hints of transformation). Indeed the conception of form crystallised by Liszt during the Weimar years, where 'characteristic' themes evolve through processes (and this is a key word) of variation and transformation against an emaciated sonata-form background, picked up on a range of cognate procedures developed by the Romantic generation from models in Beethoven and Schubert. They may also have drawn occasionally, and here some of Liszt's refrain structures come to mind, on Schubert's tendency to rethink rondo form, notably in slow movements.[26] In general, the post-Beethoven era was much concerned with blending formal archetypes and with recontextualising Classical formal functions. It was this that enabled Liszt to speak of an 'ideal' peculiar to his age, an ideal towards which composers such as Schumann, Berlioz and Chopin aspired in their very different ways, including the character variations built in to several of Schumann's formal designs, the thematic transformations in Berlioz, and the deformations of sonata form through thematic narratives in Chopin.

The latter parallel is worth developing. Both Chopin and Liszt favoured 'emergent structures'. There was of course nothing new in tonally inductive, equivocal introductions that only gradually homed in on a tonic. They were a commonplace of Viennese Classicism.

---

[26] The eleventh etude comes to mind here. I am indebted to David Maw for drawing my attention to this aspect of Schubert's formal process.

However, as Robert P. Morgan reminds us, Beethoven prepared the way for an extension of this principle of gradual clarification to larger structural levels.[27] Then, in the music of the Romantic generation, and especially in Chopin and Liszt, this becomes a typical plan, with sonata-based structures culminating in a gesture of apotheosis rather than synthesis.[28] It is easy to see how this type of structure relates to Dahlhaus's theme-based 'logical' rather than design-based 'architectural' model of form. The concept of a thematic narrative allied to an intensity curve, in which the notion of climax or fulcrum is crucial, cuts against or may even dissolve the concept of a form built of Classically articulated periods and designs. And it need hardly be said that the former, which would receive its clearest theoretical for-mulation in Ernst Kurth, is expressive of a larger Romantic tendency to stress the teleology of 'becoming', itself embodied in the notion of climax.[29] This forms part of the sub-text of Liszt's call for the composition of sonatas rather than virtuoso pieces during his early days in Weimar. Of course he was appealing in the main for greater dignity in pianism. But he was also looking to ways of reconciling modern thematic composition with the 'weight of the past', and that meant, by and large, reconciling Romantic conceptions of form – intensity curves, narratives – with the Classical sonata principle. In a way it involved a synthesis of the technique of the miniature, often shaped as a single impulse of departure and return, and the sonata. One can see something of this in the revisions to the *Grandes Etudes*. One impulse at work here was quite simply the quest for greater formal clarity, where Liszt would adapt or reduce the original material to approach something akin to a sense of Classical balance. But in other cases an original, often diffuse, architectural ground plan was transformed into an evolving structure that focused its energies on a single point of tonal and thematic reprise, functioning as the climax, fulcrum or 'expressive goal' of the piece.[30] In practice this tended to mean stripping away material, often developmental material, that impeded the sense of a single large-scale intensity curve.

The more substantial changes to the second etude are symptomatic of the first of these impulses, of Liszt's return to what I called a sense of Classical balance, even in some ways a re-turn to the formal principle (and work character) suggested, though inadequately realised, by the original exercise. The crucial difference from the second version is the rethinking of the C major material. Rather than the monothematicism of the second version, Liszt here presents a 'new', if derived, theme (as in the exercise), replacing through-composed development with a genuine contrast of mood and tonal quality. This is effectively a trans-formation or character variation of the original theme, and accordingly it not only has a quite different (lighter) tone, but replaces the closely related C major with a more remote, albeit weakly defined, C minor.[31] It is, in short, a foil for the surrounding A minor material, and it is worth noting that the character of the Beethoven motive (baldly exposed at the

[27] Robert P. Morgan, 'Coda as Culmination: The First Movement of the *Eroica* Symphony', in Christopher Hatch and David W. Bernstein (eds.), *Artistic Theory and the Exploration of the Past* (Chicago, 1993), p. 358.

[28] *Ibid*. See also Leonard B. Meyer, *Style and Music: Theory, History and Ideology* (Philadelphia, 1989), p. 198, and Charles Rosen, *Sonata Forms* (New York, 1988), p. 393.

[29] See Ernst Kurth, *Selected Writings*, ed. Lee A. Rothfarb (Cambridge, 1991), p. 12.

[30] The term 'expressive goal' is used by John Rink in *Chopin: The Piano Concertos* (Cambridge, 1997), p. 64.

[31] See Hunkemöller, 'Perfektion und Perspektivenwechsel' for a discussion of the sonata-form basis of this etude.

opening of the section) is also transformed in this section. Moreover, Liszt replaces the highly concentrated reworking of the introduction from the second version with a much simpler formulation in which the opening theme (rather than the horn call) has a voice alongside the Beethoven motive, and continues unbroken towards the non-thematic preparation for the reprise. Really the outcome is a quite different formal conception, one that, paradoxically, is both more closely integrated and has greater internal contrast. By removing the horn-call motive, Liszt not only simplified the texture of the etude; he also concentrated its motivic activity around the main theme and the Beethoven motive, together with their transformations. One by-product of this is that the third version, unlike the second, derives all its material from the early exercise; even the replacement for the horn-call accompaniment is linked to the Beethoven motive. Again, *pace* Liszt, one can make a case for both the second and third versions of this etude. The second highlights the 'demonic' character through an alliance of cumulative virtuosity, increasing complexity and density of motivic information and a through-composed, goal-directed teleology. The third preserves much of this character, but offsets it with thematic transformation and tonal contrast, lessening the density of information and allowing for a play of more traditionally contrasted components.

In the revisions to the third etude Liszt changed the formal conception of the work significantly by removing the developmental *Presto agitato assai* section entirely. I will suggest in the next chapter that there were programmatic issues involved here. But there were also formal considerations. Apart from altering the proportions of the piece, this change had the effect of weakening the sense of successive strophes and strengthening the sense of a unitary arch-like design with an obvious fulcrum. It is certainly no coincidence that the other major revision concerned precisely that fulcrum. Its reorchestration is illustrated in Example 45. And while the revision may seem relatively minor, it is actually very telling. In the 1837 version there is a real sense of thematic arrival and definition at bar 65, whereas in the revision there is greater continuity promoted both by the voicing of the right hand and by the rhythmically activated supporting chords in the left hand. A moment of articulation is replaced by a more continuous process of tension and release that 'composes through' the climax. Moreover this intensity curve can be extended in both directions from this fulcrum to embrace the entire span of the etude within a single, relatively uniform process, characteristically reaching its point of maximum intensity closer to the end than the beginning. The symmetrical thirds-related tonal scheme then falls neatly into place around the fulcrum, whereas in the second version the A major theme was followed by a further developmental strophe in F major. Two trivial, but indicative, further revisions might be cited. First, the replacement of the performance direction *con passione* for the A major theme to *appassionata assai*, together with the lower dynamic, is designed to ensure that its positioning in relation to the fulcrum is not in doubt. And second, Liszt now transfers the dominant pedal from the *Presto agitato assai* section of the second version to the beginning of the final strophe or coda of the third version. It would be quite wrong to suggest that Liszt has lost touch with variation form here. But the variations, rather as in the early exercise, are now more clearly blended with a large-scale ternary design and with an arc-like impulse of tension and release, resulting in a 'one-part form', to use Schenker's language.

Example 45 12 *Grandes Etudes*, No. 3 bars 63–6
Paysage bars 63–6

12 *Grandes Etudes*, No. 3 bars 63–6

Paysage bars 63–6

As noted above, Liszt's revisions to the fifth etude affected only relatively minor aspects of its construction and were directed in the main towards clarity of texture and ease of execution. The formal design of the piece, in other words, was not essentially changed in the revision, with an elliptical introduction providing new material that alternates with, blends with, and eventually dominates, the two presentations of the strophe derived from the earlier exercise. At the same time there are telling changes in the later stages which accord with those made to the third etude. Essentially Liszt reduced the intensity of the secondary climax from bar 53 in his third version, replacing the climactic sequence based on *c* with a further iteration of *a* (see Ex. 46). This has the effect of reducing instability and assuring a more continuous downward curve of intensity following the fulcrum of the piece. Moreover, the revisions to the last few bars (effectively the deletion of one bar and the addition of four bars of arpeggiation) strengthen further this sense of closure and balance. For all the difference in affect, the parallel with the third etude, both in the positioning of the fulcrum and in the subsequent revisions, is striking. Clearly Liszt's aim in both cases was to create a coherent shape for the piece as a whole, one in which everything falls into place around a central climactic point. And in this respect his revisions to the sixth and seventh etudes are significant. The key change in the sixth concerns the approach to the G major strophe. Here Liszt steepened the intensity curve by simultaneously compressing the material (bar 28 from the second version is omitted, and the succeeding five bars are reduced to four) and enlarging it (compare the versions in Ex. 47). The intention was clearly to characterise the G major strophe even more obviously as an apotheosis of the theme (and therefore of the earlier exercise). The overall effect is to create a kind of 'terraced' structure, and even the successive statements of the alternating developmental material, each more intense than its predecessor, contributes to this quality.

Example 46 12 *Grandes Etudes*, No. 5 bars 106–9
Feux-follets bars 107–11

12 *Grandes Etudes*, No. 5 bars 106–9

Feux-follets bars 107–11

It will be remembered that the seventh etude was newly composed for the *Grandes Etudes*, and thus exists in only two versions, which will be examined in tandem here. They are importantly different in formal conception. The introduction begins similarly in both versions, but its continuation (from bar 9) was significantly revised in 1851. The 1837 version develops the opening figure by sequence and diminution to describe ascending chromatic steps in the bass, arguably already looking to the main theme (Ex. 48a). This culminates in a series of repeated octaves against which a new motive (*a* in Ex. 48b) unfolds in a symmetrically

Example 47 12 *Grandes Etudes*, No. 6 bars 28–33
Vision bars 28–31

12 Grandes Etudes, No. 6 bars 28–33

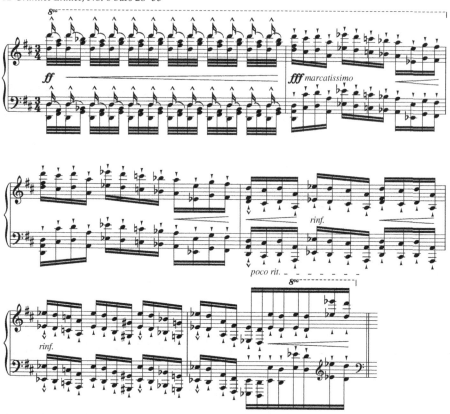

Vision bars 28–31

ordered sequence at the minor third. The break in the symmetry then allows a resolution of the chromatic descent on to the Bbs of the main theme, presented here without the three-note anacrustic figure. This kind of tonal induction, where a play of symmetries is halted by tonal imperatives, was influential in Russian music and later in Debussy, and it will be discussed in the final section of this chapter. In 1851 Liszt abandoned the opening figure after bars 1–8, but followed a compressed form of the original tonal sequence from bar 9 through to bar 12. From this point his concern was clearly to achieve some measure of integration between the material of the introduction and that of the theme. Motive *a* is still present, but its rhythmic formulation already suggests the theme, and the three-note anacrusis is planted in advance of its thematic appearance in bar 19. The final chord of the introduction now functions conventionally as an augmented sixth resolving to the Eb major of the main theme.

The march theme itself is the basis of a subsequent series of variations or transformations, though unlike the fifth and sixth etudes, the seventh presents its main theme not as a periodic structure subject to elaboration but as a motivic shape subject to rhythmic variation and melodic extension.[32] This open-ended character is emphasised on the first two presentations by a pronounced interruptive quality, where a developing volume and intensity is caught short and held in check. Thus in the first version the march is interrupted at bar 36, and then again at bar 54, where the introductory material returns. It is worth looking at the revision at these two points. At the first, where the third-related harmonic progression is drawn back to the tonic by way of a bVI–V progression, the gesture is transformed in the revision into a brief recollection of the introduction (Ex. 48c), though the bass motive from the original version (*x* in Ex. 48c) is retained. Interestingly, Liszt suggests a minor rather than a major V at bar 26 of the second version. At the second, the return of the introduction in the first version is replaced by a further variation of the march in an unstable F minor. The sequential shift to E minor at bar 49 realigns the revised version to the 1837 version, though the explicit references to the introduction (both in the accompaniment, and as an interruption) are removed. This makes for an intriguing situation when the two versions reach agreement with the subsequent shift to Bb minor/Db major. Here references to the introduction in the revised version appear *in medias res*, whereas they emerged naturally from preceding material in the earlier version. It is likely that greater continuity in the gradual unfolding of the form was Liszt's principal motivation for the revision. Rather than intercutting introduction and theme, he allowed successive statements of the theme to accumulate energy, while insinuating elements of the introduction into the accompaniment.

The rather 'unrelieved' quality associated with this procession of sequential statements of the march theme is mitigated by melodic and accompanimental variations, but also by reharmonisations of the repeated-note motive, which can function either as a tonic or a dominant note in relation to the underlying harmony. This contributes to the sense of tonal instability that is finally resolved by the shift to Db major at bar 70 of the first version, bar 63 of the second. This represents a tonally stable plateau which functions as a further variation or transformation of the theme but at the same time takes on something of the character

---

[32] This reading of the form will be nuanced, and even qualified, in chapter 6.

Example 48 (a) *12 Grandes Etudes*, No. 7 bars 9–12
(b) bars 15–16
(c) *Eroica* bars 27–9
(d) *Eroica*. Tonal frames.

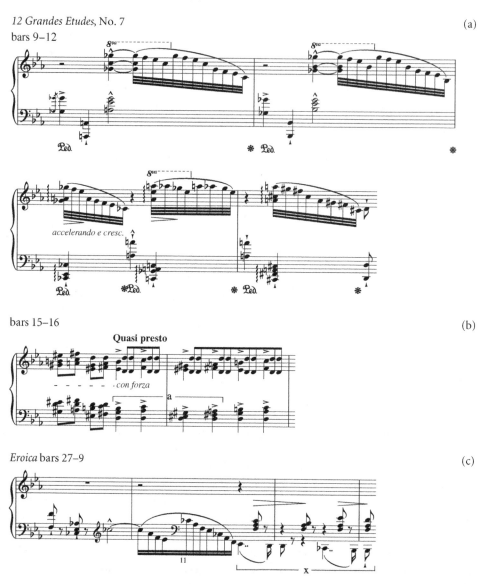

12 Grandes Etudes, No. 7
bars 9–12

(a)

bars 15–16

(b)

Eroica bars 27–9

(c)

of the contrasted tonal area of a sonata-form movement. Both versions of the etude are in accord at this point, but they diverge significantly in the later stages of this variation. The first version elaborates the second limb of the first variation as part of a dominant preparation for the climactic variation in the tonic at bar 86. The second, on the other hand, follows

Example 48 (*cont.*)

Eroica. Tonal frames. (d)

its version of the first variation by extending the reference to the bass motive (*x* in Ex. 48c)
into a more extended reprise of the second part of the introduction, with its characteristic
dotted-note figure. This creates a more extended and tension-building preparation for the
return of the climactic variation. In other words, it strengthens the sense of a tonal reprise as
in a sonata-form movement, while at the same time highlighting the climactic variation as
the apotheosis of the theme and the pinnacle of the form, the highest plateau, as it were. The
return of the introduction prior to this reprise, incidentally, is common in Liszt, and is also

a feature of late Chopin (the Fourth Ballade and Polonaise-Fantasy), and more generally of the Fantasy as a genre. It is strengthened here by the removal of those earlier interpolations of introductory material in the 1837 version.

As in the fifth and sixth etudes, Liszt gave considerable attention in the revision to the most appropriate way to release the tension following this, the major climax of the piece. In the 1837 version, the octaves variation is succeeded by yet another climactic variation, through which the intensity continues to increase in preparation for the return of the second part of the introduction. This is the repeated-note figure from Example 48b (omitted in the revision), and it is by way of this figure that the tension is gradually allowed to subside in preparation for a final variation or coda. In the 1851 version Liszt eliminated much of this material, so that the octaves variation could emerge all the more strongly as the true climax of the work. Thus, the entire variation at bar 98 of the 1837 version was deleted, and so was the repeated-note figure from the introduction; indeed the decision to remove this was more-or-less made for Liszt when he excluded the material from his revised introduction. The result of all this is that the coda, or final variation, now follows on directly from the octaves variation. There is evidence in the coda of Liszt's concern to achieve a closer integration of material than in the 1837 version, particularly when we relate the coda to the introduction. In the revised form of the introduction, Liszt strengthens the play of E major and E♭ major by representing the tonalities motivically through the three-note anacrusis, and he reinforces this in the coda by adding a version of the motive suggestive of both keys in the bass (Ex. 48d). The revision, then, creates a tighter structure and a more goal-directed one; there is again a more obvious progression to the main climax of the piece, associated with a sonata-like moment of tonal reprise, and a more obvious recession from that climax. Yet once more we should resist too easy a dismissal of the earlier version. Here we lack the sense of a close-knit argument and a single arch-like shape. Instead we are hurled breathlessly from climax to climax. However, that offers its own rewards, of a different order altogether from those of the final version. In a word, we are invited to succumb to the excitements of an event, rather than to reflect on the qualities of a work.

If we consider the forms and revisions of the sixth and seventh etudes, we can trace a developing sequence from variation form through to variation form tinged with elements of sonata form. In the eighth etude that sequence is extended in that sonata form is here a much more obvious background presence, while the variations of the sixth and seventh etudes are replaced by more blatant thematic transformations. These shadings of formal process are arguably more realistic descriptions than the rigid classifications offered by Schütz, who distinguishes cleanly between strophic variation forms such as 3, 4, 6 and 12, 'through-composed' etudes such as 2, 5, 7, 8 and 10, and *Lied* forms such as 9 and 11.[33] The sonata-form outlines of the eighth etude are present in both the second and third versions, notably through the background 'interruption' of the structure coinciding with a structural dominant (bar 135 of version 2; bar 134 of version 3). But there were, nonetheless, substantial

---

[33] Schütz, 'Form, Satz- und Klaviertechnik in den drei Fassungen der *Grossen Etüden* von Franz Liszt', in Zsoltán Gárdonyi and Siegfried Mauser (eds.), *Virtuosität und Avantgarde: Untersuchungen zum Klavierwerk Franz Liszts* (Mainz, 1988), pp. 71–115.

modifications made in the 1851 revision, and along lines that are already familiar from the other revisions discussed in this chapter. The essential point is that the moment of tonal and thematic reprise is given heightened formal significance as the fulcrum across which the rest of the piece is balanced. And, as in the seventh etude, this meant eliminating a substantial body of music, in this case both before and after the moment of reprise. Essentially the two versions are in formal agreement to the point at which the extended preparation for the reprise has been under way for some ten bars. At this point the 1851 version cuts more or less directly to bar 150 of the earlier version. More crucially, it omits the entire section from bar 161 to bar 224. This omitted section includes some of the wildest music of the 1837 version, in which the various motives play in juxtaposition and superimposition, spilling over into symmetrically organised figurations and leaping chord passages that eventually prepare the reprise of the main theme. It further includes the reprise of the theme, which in the earlier version builds further tension as it approaches the second group in the tonic major (it will be remembered that this consists of transformations of the two ideas presented at the outset of the piece). Replacing all of this material in the 1851 version is a short transitional passage which leads directly to the reprise of the second group. The major difference here rests in the treatment of the reprise. In 1837 it functioned Classically, restating all the original material before building towards an apotheosis of the two main themes (as discussed in chapter 4). In 1851 it actually corresponds to that apotheosis. As in the seventh etude, then, the effect is to replace an undulating intensity curve with a single upward surge to the climax or fulcrum of the piece, at which point we have a transformation of each theme in turn.

The ninth etude was not changed in any essential formal respects in 1851. However, the tenth was so comprehensively altered that Liszt rewrote the entire piece in manuscript. Admittedly many of these changes concerned the presentation of the basic material. The effect of the revision of the Chopin theme in its first iteration (Ex. 49a) is to simplify the technique while at the same time clarifying and giving depth to the melody. Likewise the figuration motive is simplified to produce a more brilliant effect, as is the new accompaniment pattern to the E♭ minor strophe. The first major change to the formal conception of the etude comes after this strophe at bar 61 of the 1837 version. The development section of the earlier version is greatly truncated and altered, avoiding the contrapuntal density of the original (e.g. Ex. 40c) and also much of its bravura writing, and instead working the Chopin theme in various ways, including a quite new stretto-like ostinato variation that anticipates the Beethovenian coda. At the same time the two sections have similar starting-points, and they retain several points of contact throughout. Both versions reach agreement with the reprise of the Chopin theme. Apart from presentational differences, they then remain in accord through to the *Presto feroce* in triple metre of the first version. Those presentational differences are often telling, however, and again the direction of the revision is towards greater clarity of theme and texture. The triple-metre transformation of the second subject (bar 179 of version 1) is omitted entirely from the 1851 version, so that the two versions come together again only with the final transformation of the Chopin theme. Even here, the revised form radically modifies the original, as Example 49b indicates, with important rhythmic, motivic and (later) harmonic changes. What is striking in the revision as a whole is that once again it concerns the material either side of the reprise: the reduction and recomposition

Example 49 (a) *12 Grandes Etudes*, No. 10 bars 6–7
Transcendentals, No. 10 bars 6–7
(b) *12 Grandes Etudes*, No. 10 bars 209–12
Transcendentals, No. 10 bars 160–1

12 Grandes Etudes, No. 10 bars 6–7 (a)

Transcendentals, No. 10 bars 6–7

12 Grandes Etudes, No. 10 bars 209–12 (b)

Transcendentals, No. 10 bars 160–1

of the development section, and the omission of the first stage of the original two-stage coda.

There are some analogies here with the revision of No. 11. Here the two versions are in agreement (at least in terms of formal organisation) right through to the refrain following the E major canto. But at that point an entire extended section of developmental material from the first version is omitted in the revision. As noted in chapter 4, this material is based mainly on the refrain theme, the first subject and the three-note motive with which the 1837 version (but not the revision) begins and ends. The decision to omit this section (some thirty-three bars) leaves Liszt with very little space between the E major version of the second subject and its apotheosis in the tonic, effectively the reprise. And this in turn subtly modifies our perception of the form. It is above all in the earlier version that the influence of sonata form is clearly registered, even if the cut of the thematic material is very different from that characteristic of an actual sonata. As in several extended works by Chopin, the piece is rather easily heard as a sonata-form design in which the thematic order is reversed in the reprise, and this is reinforced by the extended dominant preparation for the return of the tonic. In the revision, without the extended development section and without the structural dominant preparing the reprise, we might well hear a type of refrain or rondo form, in which the two principal themes are mediated by what I called in chapter 4 the 'refrain' theme. It may be that the closest parallel here is with the revision to the third etude, where again the more agitated, developmental material, this time following rather than preceding the reprise, was excised in the revision. Common to both etudes is their conception as unified mood pieces or character pieces, and it is possible that Liszt saw the introduction of developmental material, of argument, as extraneous to their character. This may also have influenced his decision to remove the recitative-like introduction to the twelfth etude in the revision, as also the return of that material towards the end of the piece. Without these sections there is nothing to disturb the obsessively rotating melody and the endlessly fluttering accompaniment patterns; nothing, in short to disturb the atmosphere of the music. For 'atmosphere', we might be tempted to read 'programme'.

TONALITIES

This description of Liszt's formal processes has recognised both the deformation of Classical models and the establishment of alternative models, which we may characterise broadly as evolving rather than closed. A working generalisation about the forms might hold that they emerge very largely from an ordering and interaction of self-sustaining themes, that this play of themes is in its turn motivated by a select repertory of dramatic plots, and that the plots are registered against a background of Classical formal archetypes. Some of James Hepokoski's deformation families are distinctly relevant here, and especially the strophic/sonata hybrids that characterise some of the later etudes (Nos. 9–11).[34] Yet the plots underlying this music are not straightforwardly aligned to such categories. In one such plot a characteristic motive is played off against a melody (the main theme of the earlier exercise) before invading it, combining with it, and eventually dominating it. In another, an introduction clouded in tonal and thematic obscurity, yet foreshadowing in a fragmentary way the basic constituents of the piece, yields to an expository definition of key and theme, and from there, by way of a dynamic, evolutionary progression, to an apotheosis or summation of the main thematic elements. In yet another, the music takes on the character of a march or procession, leading us from distant beginnings towards a proximate climactic point before dissolving or receding again. Such descriptions are suggestive of struggle and victory, darkness and light, growth

---

[34] James Hepokoski, *Sibelius Symphony No. 5* (Cambridge, 1993), especially pp. 5–7. In addition to strophic/sonata hybrids, we might invoke the 'introduction–coda frame', to which sonata activity is subordinated.

and decline, all of which support the kinds of 'expressive genre' identified by Robert Hatten, notably the 'tragic to transcendent' or 'lamento e trionfo' genre. As such they might well invoke concepts of narrativity, and might further tempt us to explore the resonance of Liszt's programmatic titles. But I will keep such issues at bay for the present, and recall instead that common to all these plots – at least in the final form of the etudes – is a careful graphing of the intensity curve of the music relative to the background formal design; indeed the 1851 revisions were partly motivated by this imperative. In general this tends to mean that the main climax of the music – the fulcrum, as I have described it in this chapter – will often correspond to a key moment of tonal and thematic reprise, and it is above all in this sense that new thinking may align itself with old, that deformations may merge with renovations, and that an authorial voice may assert itself against a collective background. The composer claims his materials, but is keen to establish their pedigree.

I want to suggest in the present section that there is a parallel in this respect between Liszt's relationship to Classical forms and his relationship to Classical tonality. The point at issue here is his allegiance to, and at the same time his expansion and modification of, diatonic tonal functions in the etudes. And here we need to bear in mind not just that Liszt's tonal practice was itself an evolving one, but that the etudes bear the imprint of three distinct stages of that evolution, of which each stage reflects back on the previous stage. Thus in 1837 he was still circumscribed by the Classical tonal practice of 1826, and although he expanded it immeasurably and in indicative directions, there is still a sense in which the earlier harmonies constrained what he could do. Thus the *Grandes Etudes* are less advanced harmonically than some other works of the late 1830s; or, and more interestingly, they present us with a disjunction between passages based on the earlier exercises and passages that are newly composed. In practice this can mean a juxtaposition of diatonic and chromatic space, which inevitably begs the question of an overall structural integration. Likewise in 1851 he was constrained by the harmonic practice of 1837. And this is significant, for in the early 1850s there is good evidence of a more qualitative change in Liszt's harmonic thinking, where an increasing complexity of chromatic diminutions led to fundamentally chromatic rather than diatonic harmonic patterns. For these reasons, we might expect to find in the etudes harmonic tendencies that are as yet only tentatively realised, and that would come to full fruition only in some of his later compositions. There is of course an extensive theoretical literature dealing with these issues, both in general terms and in relation to Liszt, and much of it will be invoked in the discussion which follows, albeit it in a necessarily generalised and synthetic way.

There are certain rather obvious ways in which nineteenth-century tonal practices were firmly rooted in Classical traditions. One respectable argument, embodied in the thought of Schenker, would have it that what really changed in the nineteenth century was the weighting between existing components of musical syntax rather than the components themselves, and that there was accordingly no obvious dividing-line between Classical and Romantic harmony.[35] Under the expressive imperative of the Romantic generation there was

---

[35] See David Allen Damschroder, 'The Structural Foundations of "The Music of the Future"; A Schenkerian Study of Liszt's Weimar Repertoire', diss., Yale University (1981).

a subtle but marked shift in the balance between the diatonic and chromatic elements of a tonal structure, operating both at the level of the musical phrase ('stretching' the underlying cadence, which shapes the phrase), and, through far-reaching modulation schemes, at the level of the work as a whole. Yet this shift in balance, so the argument would run, left intact a background structure grounded in a diatonic model of tonality, and governed by a strong tonic–dominant polarity; at least it did so through to some of the more 'advanced' idioms of the late nineteenth century. Once more Beethoven's heroic style formed the most potent model of a dynamic and organic tonal practice controlled by the tonic–dominant relation, and it functioned as such throughout the century, for Liszt as for many others. It may be that casual claims about Liszt's evasion of dominant harmony undersell the extent to which such conventional diatonic backgrounds continue to function in his music, at least until the very late works.[36] What perhaps needs to be scrutinised carefully is the level at which V actually functions. As a foreground presence it is ubiquitous, and often without explicit tonal significance; on the middleground – the level at which thematic articulations tend to be registered tonally – it is often conspicuous by its absence; as a background structuring device, on the other hand, it operates Classically as an agent of tonicisation, though, as Zdenek Skoumal suggests, some blurring of function may occur here.[37]

The first of the *Transcendentals* is no doubt unrepresentative of the cycle as a whole, but its underlying harmonic structure – (IV)–V–I – could hardly spell out more clearly a continuing allegiance to diatonic function. Elsewhere the tendency, predictably enough (given the model in Liszt's youthful *Etude*), is for expository statements to exhibit diatonically determinate features, and for key structural moments to achieve tonal articulation by way of a traditional structural dominant. In the second etude, for example, both parts of the main theme (bars 6–15) are shaped by conventional tonic–dominant harmony, while the reprise is prepared by an extended dominant pedal at the background level. It would be rather easy to graph the voice leading here over a I–♭VI–V–I harmonic foundation. Even in the third etude, where third-related modulations are conspicuous, it would be misleading to suggest that these entirely replace more familiar backgrounds, given the submediant orientation of the D♭ major section (Ex. 50a) and the approach to A major by way of an extended, conventionally 'punning', augmented-sixth harmony, suggestive of a displaced subdominant modulation (Ex. 50b). In other words the thirds cycle disguises a background tendency towards the subdominant. Likewise in the fifth etude, where the principal theme is again given a conventionally diatonic setting, the tonally elusive chromatic symmetries occupying much of the foreground are anchored by a dominant pedal, at least for some of the time, though the background structure of this etude does exhibit some unusual tonal characteristics. And again in the sixth, despite the prevalence of third-related tonal progressions, an underlying tonic–dominant relation underpins the entire structure, as Example 51 illustrates. It is perhaps unnecessary to exemplify this point further, beyond demonstrating that the tonal background is more often than not aligned to Classical formal

---

[36] See, for example, Richard Taruskin, 'Chernomor to Kashchei: Harmonic Sorcery; or, Stravinsky's "Angle"', *Journal of the American Musicological Society*, 38, 1 (1985), p. 125.

[37] Zdenek Skoumal, 'Liszt's Androgynous Harmony', *Music Analysis*, 13, 1 (March 1994), pp. 51–72.

Example 50 (a) *Paysage* bars 31–6,
(b) 65–71

bars 31–6

bars 65–71

divisions. Thus, in the eighth etude a conventional tonal scheme in the exposition (a first group in the tonic through a second group in the relative major to a closure on the dominant, marking the familiar 'interruption' of the background structure in Schenkerian terms) gives way to a brief modulating section before the reprise of the second group in the tonic. Significantly, such conventional tonal structures are clearer in the 1837 version than in the revision, as we noted in relation to the eleventh etude. Here the tonal organisation of the earlier version (including the extended dominant preparation of the tonal reprise) supports the greater proximity to sonata form.

This is not the whole story, of course. There are many passages in these etudes which do not lend themselves to straightforward tonal analysis of this kind, passages where voice-leading and motivic working take place within dissonant sonorities, and where the underlying harmony appears, at the very least, diatonically indeterminate. A decade after Liszt revised the etudes, the composer and critic Felix Draeseke, himself a member of the Liszt circle, characterised what he called 'the modern tonal system' by its 'suspension of diatonic writing', which in turn led to 'the freest treatment of harmony'.[38] Draeseke could have been referring to just such passages in the etudes. But again we might note that they are usually embedded within diatonic contexts, and might well be understood as literal 'suspensions' of a

---

[38] Quoted by William Kinderman in his introduction to William Kinderman and Harold Krebs (eds.), *The Second Practice of Nineteenth-Century Tonality* (Lincoln, Nbr., and London, 1996), p. 2. The division between conservative and progressive theorists is discussed in Robert W. Wason, 'Progressive Harmonic Theory in the Mid-19th Century', *Journal of Musicological Research*, 8 (1988), pp. 55–90. See too Keith T. Johns, 'The Music of the Future and the Berlin Critics: Franz Liszt Returns to the Singakademie, December 1855', *Journal of the American Liszt Society*, 23 (1988), pp. 19–29. Relevant to this discussion is the theory competition organised by *Neue Zeitschrift für Musik* in 1859 in an explicit attempt to find theoretical validation for the new music.

Example 51 *Vision* bars 1–32. Harmonic outline

Example 52 *Transcendentals*, No. 2 bars 15–30. Harmonic outline

predominantly diatonic unfolding, more extensive and elaborate perhaps than comparable passages in so-called Viennese Classicism but not in principle different. Characteristically they are introductions, transitions or development sections. Much hinges here on whether we can reasonably understand such chromatic and/or dissonant foregrounds as surface prolongations of an implicit diatonic background,[39] as distinct from prolongations of a dissonant sonority,[40] or indeed part of an altogether different framework of organisation.[41] Consider a chromatic passage such as bars 15–30 of the second etude. Its tonal function is to fill the chromatic space between A minor and C minor, and it achieves this through modulating sequences in progressive diminution, as indicated by the sketch in Example 52; they might well be viewed rather as an extension of the characteristically Schubertian 'half-step shift'.[42] Apart from the translation of a predicted major mode into a minor, these harmonies span I and III in a conventional way, but it is easy to envisage contexts in which the cyclical or symmetrical potential of the sequences might be exploited. In a passage such as bars 20–8 of the sixth etude, whose triad progression is summarised in Example 53, we are taken further in that direction. We might of course read the harmonies here as a prolongation of V, but to confine the reading to this level is to ignore the integral relation between the thirds cycles and the larger tonal plan of the piece. And on other occasions, as an harmonic outline of the introduction to the seventh etude suggests (Ex. 54), non-diatonic sonorities and

[39] James Baker, 'The Limits of Tonality in the Late Music of Franz Liszt', *Journal of Music Theory*, 34, 2 (1990), pp. 145–73. For a relevant discussion of the late works, see also Bernard C. Lemoine, 'Tonal Organization in Selected Late Piano Works of Liszt, in Serge Gut (ed.), *Liszt-Studien 2*, pp. 123–31.

[40] A classic text here, including discussion of Liszt, is Robert P. Morgan, 'Dissonant Prolongations: Theoretical and Compositional Precedents', *Journal of Music Theory*, 20, 1 (1976), pp. 49–91.

[41] See, for example, Allen Forte, 'Liszt's Experimental Idiom and Music of the Early Twentieth Century', *19th-Century Music*, 10, 3 (1987), pp. 209–28.

[42] See Charles Rosen, 'Schubert's Inflections of Sonata Form', in Christopher Gibbs (ed.), *The Cambridge Companion to Schubert* (Cambridge, 1997), pp. 174–92.

Example 53 *Vision* bars 20–8. Triad progression

Vision bars 20–8. Triad progression

Example 54 *Eroica* bars 1–20. Harmonic outline

Eroica bars 1–20. Harmonic outline

Example 55 *Harmonies du Soir* bars 1–10. Harmonic outline

Harmonies du Soir bars 1–10. Harmonic outline

motivic working are just too strongly characterised at the foreground level to be explained away by the underlying E major frame. The opening of the eleventh etude is comparable (Ex. 55), outlining a tonal stratum at odds with the tonic (the orthography partly conceals this), though with some potential to link up with the E major second subject.

These and comparable passages (Ramon Satyendra refers to 'contextual' as opposed to 'traditional' tonal structures) might well be described simply as deviations from, or colorations of, an earlier diatonic practice.[43] Yet this is only part of the picture. At the very least it begs the question of structural integration to separate out diatonic and chromatic structures in this way. We should at least consider the implications of Draeseke's 'modern tonal system', which are that a good deal of late Romantic harmony can no longer be adequately understood in terms of root-progressions, however distended, that shape the phrase, but rather invokes an emergent 'organic chromaticism', to use Henri Pousseur's phrase.[44] Here chromatic voice-leading is released from any obligation to reach and secure a tonic (or even a dominant), and becomes in itself a principle of progression, with tonicisations possible, partly through tonal mixture, on any degree of the chromatic scale. Moreover, as Satyendra suggests, the more complicated the harmony the simpler may be the linear, semitonally motivated progressions.[45] (While it need not concern us here, such semitonal relationships in late Liszt can operate at deep levels of structure, where displacement counterpoint really does begin to supplant harmonic syntax.[46]) This chromatic, rather than diatonic, tonal

[43] Ramon Satyendra, 'Chromatic Tonality and Semitonal Relationships in Liszt's Late Style', diss., University of Chicago (1992), p. 6.
[44] Henri Pousseur, 'Webern's Organic Chromaticism', *Die Reihe*, vol. 2 (Eng. edn, London, 1958), pp. 51–60.
[45] Satyendra, 'Chromatic Tonality and Semitonal Relationships', pp. 167 ff.
[46] *Ibid.*, p. 154.

Example 56 *Paysage* bars 71–4

Paysage bars 71–8

Example 57 *Feux-follets*. Tonal scheme

Feux-follets. Tonal scheme

system has been discussed at length by Patrick McCreless, who invokes Gregory Proctor's concept of 'transposition operation', used principally for 'real' or exact, rather than diatonically adjusted, transposition by major and minor thirds and major seconds, and applies it to transposition by semitone.[47] Liszt employs such transposition both at Proctor's major third, as in parts of the third and sixth etudes, and at McCreless's semitone, as in parts of the second and eighth, and in the A major section of the third etude (Ex. 56). Moreover such semitonal shifts can also operate over larger structural spans, as in the A major reprise of the fifth etude in the context of a B♭ major tonic, though this is approached (significantly) by way of F♯ minor (Ex. 57).[48] McCreless's larger point is that in the late nineteenth century there evolved a 'harmonically based chromatic tonal space', a *background* from which diatonic prolongations may emerge in the *foreground*, just as tonicisations may be established without integral reference to a single overriding tonic.[49] The A major in the fifth etude is a case in point. Likewise the tonicisation of D♭ at bar 63 in the seventh etude has a logic in relation to previous voice-leading, but appears at a seemingly arbitrary point in the chromatic-enharmonic field.

A chromatic tonal space may be organised according to underlying harmonic principles, and some proposals as to the nature of that organisation will shortly be explored. However it may also be ordered thematically or modally. If we glance again at Example 52, we may

[47] Patrick McCreless, 'An Evolutionary Perspective on Nineteenth-Century Semitonal Relations', in Kinderman and Krebs (eds.), *The Second Practice of Nineteenth-Century Tonality*, pp. 87–113. Proctor's study is 'Technical Bases of Nineteenth-Century Chromatic Tonality: A Study in Chromaticism', diss., Princeton University (1978). See also Richard Bass, 'From Gretchen to Tristan: The Changing Role of Harmonic Sequences in the Nineteenth Century', *19th Century Music*, 19, 3 (Spring 1996), pp. 263–85.

[48] Compare the reprise in Chopin's *Impromptu* in F♯ major, Op. 36.

[49] Much of this theory has antecedents in Kurth. See also Paul J. Revitt, 'Franz Liszt's Harmonizations of Linear Chromaticism', *Journal of the American Liszt Society*, 13 (1983), pp. 25–52.

Example 58 *Transcendentals*, No. 2. Scale types

Transcendentals, No. 2. Scale types

note how a chromatic element is thematised at a key structural point (x), so that it is a syntactic rather than a derived feature (links with the first etude strengthen this). Moreover it locks into the figure in the introduction to create an octatonic collection, and is in a sense 'completed' by the chromatic figure in the coda (Ex. 58). Modal chromaticism, on the other hand, arises from the transformational capacity of semitonal part movement, which may result in what Ramon Satyendra has called 'inflected repetitions' (he distinguishes here between 'real sequence' and semitone-related transformation), or in what some Bartók scholars have described as 'mistuning'.[50] A few examples may suffice (Ex. 59): a transitional moment from the third etude (a), an expressive transformation from the eighth (b), and passages from the ninth (c) and twelfth (d). Again these are not crucial organising principles in the *Transcendentals*, apart from No. 4 (see Ex. 70). But they are the seeds of a device that would become more common in the later Liszt, where inflected repetitions are part of a process of incremental transformation, taking place gradually across an extended time span. Effectively they create modal differentiations, sectional forms (Satyendra refers to 'weakly-bound formal units') and sonority variations that would all become part of the armoury of Russian composers in the nineteenth century and that would in due course feed into the music of Debussy and Ravel.[51]

Before considering the harmonic ordering of chromatic space, and how this interacts with the diatonic backgrounds of Liszt's etudes, it may be helpful to invoke an early-nineteenth century model that rivalled that of Beethoven's heroic style. The point has often been made that Schubert proposed very different ways of conceiving extended cyclic works, avoiding dynamic goal-directed narratives in favour of more leisurely scenic routes, where essentially similar melodic-motivic materials ('breathing the same life', as Schumann put it) are allowed to drift freely through third-related regions in a gradual, spacious, and in a sense anti-heroic, teleology. In particular, James Webster has referred to Schubert's 'insecurity' about the dominant, though recent commentators have preferred to view this more positively as, for example, a preference for circles of thirds, both in the small-scale structure and as larger

---

[50] 'Chromatic Tonality and Semitonal Relationships', pp. 40–50. The reference to Bartók scholarship is primarily to János Kárpáti, especially his *Bartók's String Quartets* (Budapest, 1967), where the phenomenon of mistuning, first discussed by Szabolcsi, is explored.

[51] See Lajos Zeke, ' "Successive Polymodality" or Different Modes Based on the Same Final in Liszt's Works', *Studia Musicologica*, 28 (1986), pp. 173–86. Also E. Seidel, 'Über den Zusammenhang zwischen der sogenannten Teufelsmühle und dem 2. Modus mit begrenzter Transponierbarkeit in Liszts Harmonik', in Gut (ed.), *Liszt-Studien 2*, pp. 172–206; Lajos Bárdos, 'Modale Harmonien in den Werken von Franz Liszt', in Klára Hamburger (ed.), *Franz Liszt: Beitrage von ungarischgen Autoren* (Budapest, 1978), pp. 133–67; and 'Ferenc Liszt, the Innovator', *Studia Musicologica*, 17 (1975), pp. 3–38.

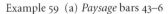

Example 59 (a) *Paysage* bars 43–6
(b) *Wilde Jagd* bars 85–8, 101–4
(c) *Ricordanza* bars 31–2
(d) *Chasse-Neiges* bar 71

Paysage bars 43–6 (a)

Wilde Jagd bars 85–8 (b)

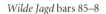

bars 101–4

Ricordanza bars 31–2 (c)

Chasse-Neiges bar 71 (d)

modulatory schemes, a preference that was later shared by Liszt.[52] In this respect we might invoke Chopin's extended works, which also favour third-related tonal regions, but which are usually powerfully goal-directed, delaying (often to the last possible moment) rather than avoiding the structural V; in other words the fifth retains a primary controlling function. In Schubert, on the other hand, the inherent tension of the tonic–dominant relationship often makes room for a more even-handed tonal allocation, and in a context where the range of key relations has been greatly expanded by his acceptance of both modes as 'equally valid representations of the tonic'.[53] It is not my concern here to debate the structural role of modal mixture of this kind in Schubert; it has been understood both in relation to diatonic systems and hexatonic/diatonic systems.[54] But there are undoubtedly close parallels to be drawn with Liszt's harmonic practice, not least in those issues of inflected repetition and sonority variation discussed earlier. Indeed it is perhaps not too simplistic to locate Liszt somewhere between Schubert and Chopin in this regard. Like Schubert, he worked with relatively static tonal platforms often ordered by thirds cycles, while dramatic power is focused upon moments of transition.[55] Like Chopin, he allowed a sense of goal direction to govern his overall structure, so that the moment of tonal and thematic reprise is more apotheosis than synthesis.

There is some suggestion in all this that Schubert may offer a prototype of what Kinderman and Krebs have called a 'second practice' of nineteenth-century tonality, a practice that came into its own in the later nineteenth century. Of the several strands to this so-called 'second practice', I will discuss here associative tonality, hexatonic systems and chromatic symmetries. Certainly it is easy to see how we can get from McCreless's 'chromatic tonal space', where tonicisations are established against a chromatic background, to Robert Bailey's 'associative tonality', usually understood in terms of a 'double-tonic complex' or 'tonal pairing'.[56] The sense here is that two coexisting rather than contrasted keys, usually third-related, are associated at the highest level of structure, and thus function as a kind of controlling double tonic. While this may on occasion seem over-formalised, it does represent a basic insight, as a response to the diminished structural value of the dominant in a good deal of late nineteenth-century music. To understand the etudes in these terms, however, would in most cases be an over-interpretation, given that those few middle-ground structures that do seem to propose real alternatives to a tonic–dominant polarity suggest circles of thirds rather than tonal pairings. There are, on the other hand, some tentative suggestions of such pairings in the seventh etude, and again in the eleventh. In the seventh, Liszt allows his coda to juxtapose Eb major and F♯ minor, thus picking up both the Gb major inflection to the tonic on the first, third-related presentation of the march theme, and (more remotely) the Db major of the second 'complete' strophe (Ex. 60). In the eleventh the underlying tonal

---

[52] James Webster, 'Schubert's Sonata Form and Brahms's First Maturity', *19th-Century Music*, 2 (1978), p. 35.

[53] *Ibid.*, p. 19.

[54] See David Beach, 'Schubert's Experiments with Sonata Form: Formal-Tonal Design versus Underlying Structure', *Music Theory Spectrum*, 15, 1 (1993), pp. 1–18, and 'Harmony and Linear Progression in Schubert's Music', *Journal of Music Theory*, 38 (1994), pp. 1–20; compare Suzannah Clark, 'From Nature to Logic in Schubert's Instrumental Music', diss., Princeton University (1997).

[55] The point is well made in Rosen, 'Schubert's Inflections of Sonata Form'.

[56] See, especially, 'The Structure of the "Ring" and Its Evolution', *19th-Century Music*, 1 (1977), pp. 48–61.

Example 60 *Vision*. Associative tonality

Vision. Associative tonality

Example 61 *Harmonies du Soir* bars 135–43. Harmonic outline

Harmonies du Soir bars 135–43. Harmonic outline

relationship is between the Db major of the first theme and the E major of the second. However, from the start E major is a presence, not only in the introduction, but in some of the harmonic twists and turns of the first theme and in the 'refrain'. On the other hand, the Db tonic is not in doubt throughout the reprise, and it is only in the coda that Liszt again colours the first theme lightly with a wash from the sharper end of the harmonic spectrum (Ex. 61); compare Example 55. We may contrast these examples with the second etude, where the minor third relation (A minor–C minor) is treated as a more conventional tonal opposition.

A more productive line of enquiry might seem to be the circle of major thirds, as opposed to fifths, a structuring device associated especially with Schubert but also present in Beethoven. This tonal practice has been rationalised by Richard Cohn as part of a 'hexatonic system' that interacts with the diatonic system (not least through the Schubertian 'half-step shift' alluded to earlier), opening up the possibility that the harmony might be appropriately understood within an alternative tonal system rather than as a deviation from earlier practice.[57] Cohn identifies four hexatonic systems which are in turn related to, if not products of, a voice-leading ideal in which adjacent harmonies are related to one another on the basis of the number of pitch-classes that they share and on the 'efficiency' of the voice leading between them. Moreover, such efficient, or in Cohn's language, 'maximally smooth' voice leading will of its nature draw together modal mixture and the circle of thirds.[58] It needs to be stressed that this system stands in opposition to diatonic hierarchies, and that its explanatory value is at its greatest where the musical materials are diatonically indeterminate. Nonetheless, it is part of Cohn's neo-Riemannian theoretical premise that diatonic and hexatonic space may interact in several ways; put simply, the journey round the circle of thirds may be terminated at various points and in various ways to align with more conventional fifth-related harmonies. And while this may raise theoretical questions more generally, it is at first thought a tempting model for Liszt's etudes, given their appropriation of diatonically

[57] Richard Cohn, 'Maximally Smooth Cycles, Hexatonic Systems, and the Analysis of Late-Romantic Triadic Progressions', *Music Analysis*, 15, 1 (1996), pp. 9–40.

[58] See also Peter Rummenholler, 'Die verfremdete Kadenz. Zur Harmonik Franz Liszts', *Zeitschrift für Musiktheorie*, 9 (1978), pp. 4–16; and Zoltán Gárdonyi, 'Neue Tonleiter-und Sequenztypen in Liszts Fruhwerken (Zur Frage der "Lisztchen Sequenzen")', *Studia Musicologica*, 11 (1969), pp. 169–99.

Example 62 *Paysage*. Thirds cycles

Paysage. Thirds cycles

Example 63 (a) *Transcendentals*, No. 2. Arpeggiation
(b) *Chasse-Neiges*. Arpeggiation

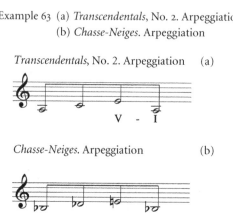

secure models in the form of the early exercises. It is of course true that the third relation is prominent in the tonal organisation of the etudes, and that modal mixture is common. Consider the initial tonal contrasts: A minor–C minor in No. 2, F major–D♭ major in No. 3, B♭ Major–F♯ minor in No. 5, G minor–B minor in No. 6, C minor–E♭ major in No.8, A♭ major–F minor in No. 9, D♭ major–E major in No. 11, B♭ minor–D♭ major in No. 12. It is also true that the circle of thirds operates in the detail. But it is only really the third and sixth etudes that hint at a more structural circle of thirds, as suggested in Examples 51 and 62, and even here, aside from the diatonic basis of the tonal platforms themselves, there are diatonic implications in the larger tonal direction that run counter to the circle of thirds, favouring a subdominant direction in No. 3 and a dominant in No. 6.[59]

The other third-related schemes are more readily explained in different ways. As noted earlier, Nos. 7 and 11 may be understood in terms of a rudimentary tonal pairing. In Nos. 8 and 9 Liszt presents conventional tonal relatives within a minor-mode tonic, and the subsequent unfolding is in every way conformant to Classical models. In No. 2 the third-relation is part of a larger-scale tonic arpeggiation (Ex. 63a), while in No. 12 it initiates an arpeggiation of a different order altogether, resulting in the central tritonal relation of B♭ minor–E major (Ex. 63b). It has been plausibly suggested that tonic arpeggiations such as those in Example 63a, characteristic of Liszt's early and middle-period music, might be regarded as an incipient form of the 'equal relations' found in his later works.[60] This strengthens our sense that the etudes embrace a wide range of practices, from diatonic schemes,

[59] See the discussion of No. 6 in Schütz, 'Form, Satz- und Klaviertechnik'.
[60] Howard Cinnamon, 'Tonic Arpeggiation and Successive Equal Third Relations as Elements of Tonal Evolution in the Music of Franz Liszt', *Music Theory Spectrum*, 8 (1986), pp. 1–24.

Example 64 *Transcendentals*, No. 2. Introduction

Transcendentals, No. 2. Introduction

through expanded diatonicism based on (Schubertian) tonic arpeggiations to something approaching hexatonic systems. On the other hand, the arpeggiation in Example 63b suggests a simpler, more reductive principle of chromatic symmetry that embraces octatonic as well as hexatonic systems, and that informs harmonic detail as well as larger tonal schemes. This in turn has deep roots in the chromaticism of a Classical tonal practice, where prolongations of a structural harmony are often ordered by symmetry, notably based on the semitone or on the minor third.

It was Busoni who first drew attention to the principle of symmetry underlying so many of Liszt's keyboard figurations, and it seems that such symmetry became increasingly integral to the harmonic structure of his later music. One way of reading the history of nineteenth-century harmony generally is through the increasing prominence of chromatic symmetries – whether disposed as chords, scales or underlying structural patterns – and their strengthening capacity to act as a counterweight to diatonic hierarchies. They can include configurations based on the tritone, diminished seventh, whole-tone scale and octatonic scale, on the augmented triad and hexatonic scale, and on other so-called 'distance models', notably the French sixth. Such structures were of course theorised to some degree in the nineteenth century (see note 38), but they have been subject to much closer scrutiny by those later theorists who have been concerned with the pre-history of early twentieth-century tonalities, notably the tonalities of Debussy, Bartók, Stravinsky and Messiaen. For obvious reasons Bartók scholars in particular have been interested in the Lisztian inheritance. By way of an excursus, I should mention that very different traditions of theory and pedagogy bear on the analyses of chromatic symmetries in German-Hungarian Bartók scholarship (Lendvai building on Riemann) and in the American college circle (Antokoletz building on Perle).[61] Some sense of these different scholarly traditions is also apparent in the accounts of harmonic symmetries in Liszt; compare, for example, Thomas Hitzlberger's interpretation of passages in the third, fourth and sixth of the *Transcendentals* with the approach of most of the North American theorists cited in this chapter.[62] Common to both traditions, however, is the sense of a duality, dialogue or intersection between symmetries (octatonic or hexatonic space) and hierarchies (diatonic space). Again the parallels with some technical

[61] See, for example Ernö Lendvai, *The Workshop of Bartók and Kodály* (Budapest, 1983); Elliott Antokoletz, *The Music of Béla Bartók* (Berkeley and Los Angeles, 1984); George Perle, *Twelve-Tone Tonality* (Berkeley and Los Angeles, 1977). An interesting precedent for the systematic theorising of symmetries is the work of Bernhard Ziehn, well known to Busoni; see in particular *Canonic Studies*, ed. Ronald Stevenson (New York, 1977; orig. edn, 1912).

[62] Thomas Hitzlberger, 'Zwischen Tonalität und Rationalität: Anmerkungen zur Sequenz- und Figurationstechnik Liszts', in Gárdonyi and Mauser (eds.), *Virtuosität und Avantgarde*, pp. 32–59. To be fair neo-Riemannian studies have gained new impetus in recent North American theory; witness Richard Cohn, who himself refers to Lendvai's work.

Example 65 (a) *Feux-follets*. Harmonic patterns in the introduction
(b) *Feux-follets* bars 42–5; Debussy, *L'Isle Joyeuse* bars 52–9

Feux-follets. Harmonic patterns in the introduction   (a)

Feux-follets bars 42–5   (b)

Debussy, *L'Isle Joyeuse* bars 52–9

Example 66 *Harmonies du Soir*. Harmonic patterns

developments in Russian music, and the pre-echoes of early twentieth-century tonalities, are rather obvious.

In his later music it is the symmetry of the augmented triad and the related hexatonic scale that are especially prominent in Liszt.[63] As noted earlier, the third and sixth of the etudes order some of their tonal and harmonic events symmetrically by way of the augmented triad (Exx. 51 and 62). However, in the cycle as a whole it is the symmetry of the diminished seventh that is predominant, together with its subset, the tritone and its superset the octatonic scale. I have already illustrated how in the twelfth etude the tritone interval generates two diatonic spaces (Ex. 63b), just as in the third the augmented triad generates three (Ex. 62). In the second etude tritonal symmetries are rather a means of chromatic structuring, though at several levels of structure. The opening 'Beethoven' motive is disposed as interlocking tritones: Beethoven by way of Paganini, one might say (Ex. 64). Later, in the *Prestissimo* bridge to the reprise (bar 57) a more complex symmetrical structure 'fills in' the tritonal outline, superimposing on its dominant harmony a Neapolitan scalar pattern. This interplay of chromatic symmetries and diatonic hierarchies is of course an extension of Classical procedure, notably in Weber (*Der Freischütz*) and in Beethoven.[64] But whereas in Beethoven the former remain clearly subsidiary to the latter, some of the Liszt etudes, notably the fifth, work towards a more equitable relationship.

We may consider, for example, the play on the three diminished-seventh harmonies superimposed on a dominant pedal in the introduction to No. 5 (Ex. 65a). This sets the tone for the juxtapositions of symmetries and hierarchies that are characteristic of this etude, anticipating in many ways the harmonic practice of Debussy. Indeed it is tempting to relate the rapid juxtapositions of diminished-seventh sonorities and triads in bars 42–5 to the juxtaposition of whole-tone sonorities and triads in Debussy's *L'Isle Joyeuse* (Ex. 65b). Likewise, in the introduction to No. 7, it is the diminished-seventh harmony that glues the passage and at the same time shapes its tonal indeterminacies, so that there is nothing remotely inevitable about the return of an implied E major, and with it a parenthetical Neapolitan 'frame' (Ex. 54). Elsewhere in the cycle there are hints that the symmetry of the diminished seventh might be inflated to larger tonal levels, creating in effect partial minor-thirds cycles. In the eleventh etude, for example, the presentations of the refrain theme map the diminished triad G–E–Db, which – on a more immediate level – prepares the tonal and thematic reprise (Ex. 66).

---

[63] See two essays by Larry Todd: 'The "Unwelcome Guest" Regaled: Franz Liszt and the Augmented Triad', *19th-Century Music*, 12, 2 (Fall 1988), pp. 93–115, and 'Franz Liszt, Carl Friedrich Weitzmann, and the Augmented Triad', in Kinderman and Krebs (eds.), *The Second Practice of Nineteenth-Century Tonality*, pp. 153–77.

[64] See Christopher Wintle, 'Kontra-Schenker: *Largo e Mesto* from Beethoven's Op. 10 no. 3', *Music Analysis*, 4 (1985), pp. 145–82.

By way of conclusion, it may be worth pointing up two intriguing aspects of all this. One has already been touched on. The reductive, generalising nature of theory comes up against certain difficulties when we are dealing with recompositions, given that in a recomposition elements from temporally separated compositional periods coexist. I leave this issue – essentially about the integration and mixing of systems – hanging in the air, and move to the second, very different topic. This concerns the two larger themes addressed in this chapter, form and tonality. It seems that the tendency of work on formal process is to travel from theory towards analysis, and analysis in turn enables us to offer evaluative judgements about individual etudes. Work on harmony and tonality, on the other hand, tends to travel in the other direction, and that almost inevitably neutralises questions of value. In most of the theoretical literature I have cited in the final section of this chapter, the aesthetic does not really raise its head. This, no doubt, is in the nature of music theory as a subdiscipline. But the question of value is not a trivial one, and I will want to address it more fully in the final chapter of the book.

Chapter Six

▬

Suggestion and symbol

FROM TOPICS TO TITLES

One significant indicator of an early nineteenth-century expressive aesthetic is the expanded range of expression marks utilised by composers in their instrumental works, as though they sought to make as specific as possible the poetic content of a work in the absence of title or programme. Thus, the *Grandes Etudes* parade the following, among many others: *energico vibrante, tumultuoso, radolcendo, lamentevole, delirando, disperato, incalzando,* and *presto feroce*. Significantly, most of these markings were removed by Liszt when the etudes were revised in 1851, no doubt partly to signal that the emotional temperature of the music had been lowered by just a notch in the interests of formal coherence, but also because something of the signifying role of expression marks could now be assumed by the newly assigned titles. Another instance of this is the removal of the term *patetico*, with its semi-programmatic resonance, from the openings of both the fourth and the sixth etudes, once the titles had been assigned. Thus, *Allegro patetico* became *Allegro* in *Mazeppa*, and *Largo patetico* became *Lento* in *Vision*. What all this raises is the vexed question of the status of titles in Liszt's etudes, and in his music generally. For one thing, the titles assigned to most of the etudes are rather non-specific, indicative of generalised moods and settings rather than particular narrative or pictorial themes. And for another, his attitude to the assignation of specific titles to specific pieces was, as I will shortly demonstrate, somewhat permissive.

In some of the *Grandes Etudes* the expression marks already seem to point towards a referential meaning or topic. *Dolce pastorale* in the coda of the third etude is one such case, already looking to the *Paysage* of the *Transcendentals*. *Mit Verzückung* for the triumphant G major strophe of the sixth etude is also suggestive, hinting at an elevated, quasi-religious sentiment that preempts the title *Vision*. More intriguingly, the Schlesinger (but not the Haslinger) first edition of the eighth etude has the title *Pan daemonium* in parenthesis, hinting at the dark forces (the *chasseur noir*) associated with the *Wilde Jagd*, though we cannot be sure that this emanated from Liszt. And finally, at the beginning of the eleventh etude, Liszt marked the bass pedal notes *Glocken*, which were already, we might suppose, a component of those *Harmonies du Soir*; again it is significant that this marking was removed in 1851 once the title had been assigned. The titles may not have been in Liszt's mind in 1837, then, but several of the general topics and affects were almost certainly glimmering. The first title to be assigned was for the fourth etude in its intermediate (1840) version, where it was designated *Mazeppa* after Victor Hugo, and given a dedication to Hugo. Then, in 1851, titles were added to a further nine etudes, leaving the second and tenth as the only ones that might be regarded (by default) as straightforward etudes, though I shall qualify this shortly. There is, however, an intriguing twist to the story of dates and titles. As noted in chapter 1, Liszt dated the orchestration draft of the symphonic poem *Mazeppa* precisely, writing 'Eilsen 1re Semanie [*sic*] de 1851'. Now the orchestration draft occupies pages 1–33 of the draft-book, and on page 34, immediately following it, Liszt wrote the title *Wilde Jagd – Scherzo* at the top of the page. The music for that piece then occupies pages 34–74, and at the end Liszt again signed and dated the piece, this time Eilsen, 2de Semaine de Janvier 1851. Surprisingly, however, the music here is not the eighth of the *Transcendentals*, which he had not yet begun revising, but the Scherzo and March. In other words, even after he had drafted the symphonic poem *Mazeppa*, he was considering using the title *Wilde Jagd* for a quite different piece, and had no difficulty at all in transferring the title to the eighth etude.

What, then, are we to make of the individual titles assigned to the *Transcendentals* in 1851? In general Niecks is probably right to describe them as 'fanciful afterthoughts',[1] but this is not to say that they had no bearing on the revisions. And much more to the point, listening strategies will be influenced by a programmatic component, irrespective of the stage at which it was introduced. And not only listening strategies, for, as Mark Tanner has argued, performers can be influenced by programmes, even by hidden programmes.[2] The first title, 'Preludio', is of course functional rather than poetic. Initially it is tempting to view it as a kind of survival from the title on the Stichvorlage of the first of the *Grandes Etudes*, which has 'Préludes' scribbled in Liszt's hand. The plural here is intriguing. It could have been a slip of the pen. But given that Marie d'Agoult referred to the entire collection as 'Préludes' in her letter of October 1837 (see p. 10) and that Liszt referred to his performance of a 'prélude-étude' in Italy, it seems possible that the title on the Stichvorlage referred to the collection as a whole, and that it was only later changed to *Etudes*. Since he had earlier announced his intention to write a set of *Grandes Etudes*, the likelihood is that Liszt was not unduly concerned about the differential nuances between 'preludes' and 'etudes'. In any event we may note that although prelude-like characteristics already attended the early exercise in 1826, the title is actually much more appropriate to the first of the etudes (in either of its two versions) than to the first of the exercises. In other words, the revision of the exercise, by eliminating the formal reprise and the double structural downbeat, comes closer to the genre characteristics of its final title, which I described in chapter 2 as an 'elaborated cadence'.

In a similar way, the tentative pastoral suggestions of the third exercise were made more specific in the *Grandes Etudes* and confirmed by the title *Paysage* in the *Transcendentals*. This is naturally a highly generalised term, but it may be worth noting that there is a poem so titled in Hugo's *Odes et ballades*, with an inscription from Horace.[3] The Muse calls the poet from

---

[1] Frederick Niecks, *Programme Music in the Last Four Centuries: A Contribution to the History of Musical Expression* (London and New York, [1907]), p. 294.

[2] Mark Tanner, 'The Power of Performance as an Alternative Analytical Discourse: The Liszt Sonata in B Minor', *19th-Century Music*, 24, 2 (2000), pp. 173–92.

[3] The poem was composed in 1823, and can be found in Victor Hugo, *Oeuvres Complètes*, gen. ed. Jean Massin (Paris, 1967), vol. 2 no. 1, pp. 518–19.

'd'un monde étroite l'impure turbulence' to 'un frais vallon, ton paisible royaume, ou, parmi l'églantier, ou le glaïeul, tu penses voir parfois, errant comme un fantôme, ces magiques palais qui naissent sous le chaume, dans les beaux contes de l'aïeul'. Hugo's Horatian reference reminds us that the pastoral topos had an ancient lineage, playing into a wider dialectic of history and nature, and even – it has been suggested – into a dialectic of the simple and the complex, where the one is rendered through (by way of) the other.[4] It is unnecessary to attempt an historical trawl through versions of pastoral here, beyond saying that the tendency of the eighteenth century had been to hollow it out or parody it, and that of the early nineteenth century to reinvent it in pantheistic terms, often freighted with something of the Kantian 'sublime'. There is, it need hardly be said, little hint of sublimity in those post-Classical pastoral pieces whose ubiquity was noted in chapter 2. As far as we can generalise here, such pieces took their origins either in the (emaciated) conventions of late eighteenth-century depictions of pastoral, notably in opera and oratorio, or in stylisations of folk music. In the early nineteenth century, on the other hand, a more elevated conception of nature, either as universal mother and comforter or as a destructive, irrational and indifferent force, became integral to the imaginative culture of the Romantic generation, just as an unprecedented dignity and new-found ideological significance attached itself to folk music. Yet, aesthetic ambition aside, there are continuities in the depiction of pastoral across this historical divide, most obviously in the use of folkloristic elements, but also in the musical gestures used in programmatic portrayals of nature. As one early nineteenth-century reviewer remarked of a *Rondo Pastoral* by Frederick Kulau, 'the time we need hardly say is six-eight'.[5] Likewise a major mode, stepwise melos (often in parallel thirds), regular pulsation and rocking accompaniment pattern were common genre markers, as were bell-like pedal notes, predominantly quiet dynamics and expression marks such as *placido* and *tranquillo*.[6]

More crucially, as Robert Hatten points out (though he goes on to qualify the observation), such pastoral signifiers were more about the evocation of a mood or the premising of a topic, than about the grounding of a plot archetype, and for that reason the 'affective' translated into the 'characteristic' relatively smoothly.[7] The pastoral intonation suggested, above all, a prevailing unity of mood or a single semantic meaning, even if the 'passing storm' as a temporary disruption of the mood became itself a convention of the genre.[8] Moreover, this consistency of mood, taken together with the tendency of the pastoral to 'undercut' a climax (noted by Hatten), is of some significance if we look again at the revisions to the third etude. It will be remembered that the major change made by Liszt in 1851 was the deletion of the *presto agitato assai* material from the 1837 version. This material is no 'passing storm', it

---

[4] William Empson, *Some Versions of Pastoral* (New York, 1974).

[5] *The Harmonicon* (1833), p. 61. See also Koch's *Musikalisches Lexicon* of 1802 (facsimile edn, Hildesheim, Olms 1964, column 1142) for the § basis and other defining features of the pastorale.

[6] See Hermann Jung, *Die Pastorale: Studien zur Geschichte einer musikalischen Topos* (Bern and Munich, 1980), for a detailed account of the history and varieties of the pastoral in music.

[7] Robert Hatten, *Musical Meaning in Beethoven: Markedness, Correlation, and Interpretation* (Bloomington and Indianapolis, 1994), p. 92.

[8] See, for example, the finale of Steibelt's popular Third Piano Concerto; also Knecht's 'Portrait musical de la Nature'.

should be observed, but an impassioned development of the principal theme, building to the main climax of the piece through sequential working of its opening phrase. As noted in the last chapter, the removal of this material has the effect of subordinating our sense of successive varied strophes to the dynamic of a single curve of tension and release. We might add here that it further focuses our attention on theme (subject to variation) rather than development, and thus promotes a unity of mood entirely appropriate to the programmatic image; even the questioning motive of bar 11, which is briefly worked and expanded at bar 47, does little to dispel this. In this sense, formal and poetic imperatives may have worked together to motivate and dictate the revision. Moreover, the deletion of the *presto* served to foreground and 'place' the human presence in this landscape, that impassioned A major section whose declamatory rests speak to us with an expressive urgency that is by no means typical of the general character of the piece. The pacification of this material, and its absorption by the *dolce pastorale* of the coda, is neatly symbolised by the unmistakable bells signified by Liszt's dominant pedals in the closing stages of the piece (cf. *Harmonies du soir*).

One may easily imagine Liszt playing through his early exercises in Geneva, trying them at different tempi and at different dynamic levels in an attempt to define a characteristic intonation for each of them. By slowing down the third exercise he would have sensed its full pastoral potential, and the change of metre would have followed from that. Conversely, by speeding up and lightening the fifth, he would have recognised an incipient quick-silver scherzo-like character, barely suggested by the original. The light-fingered recomposition of the theme would then have sharpened the definition of that character, and the newly composed fluttering figurations and fragmentary motives would have confirmed it. Yet if this is a scherzo, it is a scherzo of a rather specific tone, with echoes of *Oberon*[9] and *A Midsummer Night's Dream*, of 'Queen Mab' and the 'Dance of Will-o'-the-Wisps';[10] these rather than anything in Beethoven, or for that matter anything in Schumann, for all the temptation to invoke the 'Papillon' from *Carnaval*. As these intertexts suggest, it is a world of fantasy that is evoked here, shading (through variation and transformation) into elements of the playful, the elusive, even the grotesque. The chromatic symmetries, notably based on the diminished seventh and octatonic scale, are themselves programmatic of fantasy in the mid-nineteenth century. We have of course no way of knowing at what stage the programmatic title first suggested itself to Liszt (if one were to speculate on any single source, the *Will-o'-the-Wisp* from Goethe's *Faust* would be the most likely candidate), but the likelihood is that it was not in his mind in 1837. Almost certainly he sought a programmatic 'fit' for an existing character piece in 1851, though, as James Bryant Conway has suggested, some details of the revision may well have been dictated by the title.[11] In any event, the fit is a close one. By transforming the original theme into an expansion of a trill motive, Liszt arrived (no doubt unwittingly) at an almost pantomimic representation of the

---

[9] Parts of the overture and the opening chorus.
[10] The first draft of *The Damnation of Faust* dates from 1846.
[11] James Bryant Conway, 'Musical Sources for the Liszt *Etudes d'exécution transcendante*: A Study in the Evolution of Liszt's Compositional and Keyboard Techniques', diss., University of Arizona (1969), p. 57.

feux-follets, no less 'literal' than Musorgsky's writing theme from *Boris Godunov*, and inscribing a similar, if greatly accelerated, pattern. Likewise, the newly composed 'motto' theme allowed for a more individualised portrait, in rather the same way as in Debussy's *Poissons d'or*.[12]

The reference to Debussy invites further comment. It is of course a commonplace of music history to identify Liszt's piano writing as an important influence on impressionism, to use again an over-used but somehow indispensable term. Certainly *Feux-follets* gives us plenty of scope for tracing such lines of influence, not least through its double-note textures and frequent three-layered stratification of the keyboard. However, it is perhaps more important to note that this kind of poietic intertextuality represents only one level, and a rather restricted one, on which such cross-referencing can usefully operate. An aesthesic intertextuality is by definition more-or-less unlimited in range and ahistorical in character, and it leaves open the possibility of 'reverse' influence, where a chronologically later intertext may enlarge the meaning, or even reconfigure the structure, of an earlier one. Thus, for today's listener it may be rather hard not to hear Liszt's *Feux-follets* through the prism of a genre that came into its own in Debussy and Ravel, was reinvented by Bartók in his so-called 'night music', and had a resonance in Ives (the second movement of the 'Concord' Sonata) and even in Lutosławski (the second movement of the Concerto for Orchestra). By no means all of this music relies on a title to act as a pointer to relevant imagery; the associative-symbolic qualities of texture, theme and motive are often quite enough. That said, where a title is present, it will be perverse to ignore it. Whether or not it was a generative component of the compositional process, it remains part of the aesthetic property of the work. So when Liszt decided to call the fifth etude *Feux-follets*, he transformed it into a nature portrait, and thus into a species of pastoral. It is an animised universe of half lights and phantasmagoria he evokes here – of magic forests and fire-devils, of spectral dancing images, personified as those masters of the deceptive, the mercurial and the illusory, Will-o'-the-Wisp and Jack o' Lantern, but hinting too at cognates with musical pedigree such as the 'unearthly' Erl-king.

Liszt's early sketchbooks are rife with literary references, together with pregnant titles and semi-coherent scribblings. Occasionally these jottings hint at the topics and titles of the *Transcendentals*, though nothing very concrete can be adduced from such hints, other than the suggestion that certain themes preoccupied him fairly consistently from the beginning of his creative maturity. Thus, as I will demonstrate in the next chapter, the title *Mazeppa* crops up on several occasions, while in the early sketchbook D-WRgs N6 both *Vision* and *Eroica* can be found, though in contexts that are quite unrelated to the music of the *Transcendentals*. *Vision* appears at the end of a Schiller quotation that Liszt originally intended to use for the preface to *Harmonies poétiques et religieuses* (it is superimposed on a sketch of that piece, with a Goethean *Salva* at the head of the page),[13] and it is intriguing that in the same sketchbook there is a brief working of the first four notes of the *Dies Irae*

---

[12] We should note the double meaning of *feux-follets* here, as fire-flies and as the deceptive play of light (phosphorescence) on marshlands, personified as Will-o'-the-Wisp or Jack o'Lantern.

[13] The Schiller quotation is found in chapter 5 of Hugo's early novel *Han d'Island* (Victor Hugo, *Oeuvres complètes*, vol. 2 no. 1, p. 113).

chant (on which of course *Totentanz* is based).[14] It will be remembered that in 1837 Liszt reworked the sixth exercise to incorporate the *Dies Irae* motive into its ground, or 'cantus firmus'. This, together with the marking *Largo patetico*, the title *Vision* and the low tessitura, encouraged Márta Grabócz to translate the heavy tread of the music into a funeral march (the anomaly of a slow triple metre is only apparent here, as the tread is in crotchets rather than minims), though few of the other, more obvious markers of this genre are present.[15] Peter Raabe went further, following Busoni in his speculation that the piece was composed in memory of Napoleon.[16] On the other hand, neither Grabócz nor Raabe points out that one of Hugo's odes (of March 1821) has the title *Vision*, especially interesting in light of the quotation from *Han d'Island*, and that its apocalyptic imagery (partly drawn from Chateaubriand and Milton) seems well placed to inspire (or, strictly speaking, to mirror) a fantasy on *Dies Irae*.[17] Even without the Hugo referent, the title 'vision' might suggest a sacred trope, an idealised scene (or series of tableaux) conjured up by the imagination, and this is confirmed by the hymn-like chordal texture, the slow harmonic rhythm, monumental-tragic in character, and the harp-like arpeggiations of the second strophe (Hugo's 'Ange de la France'?).

Such parallelism can be suggestive, and it is strengthened by the transformation of the second theme in the later stages of the piece, hinting, or so we might suppose, at Hugo's 'voix inexorable'. But all this should be kept within sensible bounds. Even if Hugo's *Vision* really was the one Liszt had in mind, he chose not to make the reference specific. Moreover, he added the title after the music was in essence composed, so that it was almost certainly designed as no more than an orientating factor in communication, though one cannot rule out completely the possibility that Liszt had some of the titles of the Transcendentals in mind in 1837. There is of course a continuity created in *Vision* by the insistent tread of its apparently duple-metre theme (for the opening ground) and its triple-metre 'refrain', but for all the undoubted extra-musical resonance, it is hard to mould this continuity into anything like a narrative. If anything, it lends itself more to a reading which sequences psychological modalities, to borrow a term from Eero Tarasti, each of them prefaced by a transforming element which itself then grows throughout the piece until it can function as a final valediction. I will return to the expressive genre of *Vision* in the next section, but it will be worth pointing out here that Liszt's revision of the text in 1851 had the effect of underlining this sequence, in that it strengthened the sense of a climactic character variation (or 'heroic-transcendent' modality) at the apex of the structure.

However generalised the titles of the *Transcendentals*, they inevitably trigger a rich play of connotative meanings behind the scenes. 'What vast subjects...', cries Niecks, 'are indicated by single words'.[18] Thus an *Eroica* in E♭ major cannot but invoke Beethoven, and beyond

[14] See Anna H. Harwell Celenza, 'Death Transfigured: The Origins and Evolution of Franz Liszt's *Totentanz*', in Jim Samson and Bennett Zon (eds.), *Nineteenth-Century Music: Selected Proceedings of the Tenth International Conference on Nineteenth-Century Music* (Aldershot, 2002), pp. 125–54.

[15] Márta Grabócz, *Morphologie des Oeuvres pour Piano de Liszt* (Paris, 1996), p. 129.

[16] Peter Raabe, *Liszts Schaffen* (Tutzing, 1968; orig. edn, 1931), p. 23; Busoni, *The Essence of Music*, trans. Rosamund Ley (London, 1957), p. 162.

[17] *Oeuvres Complètes*, vol. 1 no. 2, pp. 811–14.   [18] Niecks, *Programme Music*, p. 3.

that either Promethean myth, or Napoleonic history, or a heady amalgam of the two.[19] To make anything more concrete of such connotations would be foolhardy, given that even Beethoven's *Eroica* has endured multiple contradictory readings of its 'content', from the earliest critics through to Solomon, Floros and Schleuning.[20] But at least we might note Liszt's enduring preoccupation with the world of the modern epic, with its reanimation of the ancient heroes, and above all with its status as an encyclopaedia of parables for the Romantic artist. In the nineteenth century, the hero was above all marked by difference; he was not simply a larger-than-life version of the rest of us, but someone isolated by his capacities. The more he rose above his fellow-men intellectually and morally, the more he differed from them. Liszt bought into this understanding of the hero, both as a virtuoso and a composer, but only up to a point, and that point, we should note, fell far short of Wagnerian inventions. As Michael Tanner has suggested, the Wagnerian hero exists in exalted solitude, the result of some primeval mistake, 'free' but willed, longing to redeem or be redeemed.[21] The hero, in short, acts out on stage something of the composer's own transmutation of a hands-on social meliorism into a largely impotent philosophical pessimism. In contrast, the Lisztian hero is a Byronic actor and doer, by no means weighed down by Fate, far from powerless in a forsaken world, anything but stoically accepting. Even Liszt's own call for a 'humanitarian' music was a call to arms worthy of the ancient heroes. A better future will be worth fighting for.

Something of the stridency of *Eroica* seems to speak of that affinity with heroes of the old type, for all that Busoni hears it as 'more defiant than heroic'.[22] The heroic equates here with the post-revolutionary march genre, which, as Ratner reminds us, has its natural habitats in the parade ground and the battlefield, with connotations of 'authority, of the cavalier and the manly virtues', of a world in which the military topos is associated with nobility of spirit.[23] (The popularity of battle pieces, including battle symphonies, in the late eighteenth and early nineteenth centuries was noted in chapter 2.) Adolf Bernhard Marx spelt out the musical markers in some detail – the unmistakable dotted rhythm on the weak beats of a quick $\frac{4}{4}$ tempo, the ancillary triplets figure – and all are present in *Eroica*, together with the repeated note 'signal' theme, the hints of military fanfares and the enlargement of the theme in an apotheotic *guerriero* restatement.[24] Interestingly, the musical links with Beethoven's *Eroica* are minimal – not much more than the characteristic key and some triad-outlining melodic shapes. If we seek a more revealing intertext, it might be with Henselt's etude with the same title from his Op. 5 collection, especially as that collection also contains an *Elfenreigen* (Dance of the Fairies) and a *Hexentanz* (Witches' Dance), topics that resonate with the fifth and eighth of Liszt's etudes respectively.[25] Of course, as I pointed out in relation to *Feux-follets*, an 'aesthesic' intertextuality opens the door to all kinds of suggestive readings. It has to be

[19] See Dana Gooley, 'Warhorses: Liszt, Weber's *Konzertstück*, and the Cult of Napoléon', *19th-Century Music*, 24, 1 (Summer 2000), pp. 62–88.
[20] See the reception history in Thomas Sipe, *Beethoven: 'Eroica' Symphony* (Cambridge, 1998).
[21] Michael Tanner, *Wagner* (Princeton, 1996).   [22] *The Essence of Music*, p. 162.
[23] Leonard Ratner, *Classic Music: Expression, Form, and Style* (New York, 1980), p. 16.
[24] *Die Lehre von der musikalischen Komposition*, 2nd enlarged edn (Leipzig, 1841), part 3, p. 56.
[25] Though we should note Liszt's reservations about Henselt's etudes; see *Letters of Franz Liszt*, coll. and ed. La Mara, trans. Constance Bache, 2 vols. (London, 1894), vol. 1, p. 24.

said that our present age is often uncomfortable with the assertiveness of this music, and may even fail to hear some of the uncertainties that undercut that assertiveness. There is no doubt a cruel irony in the likelihood that for many listeners today the most tempting of all intertexts for *Eroica*, especially irresistible in the coda of the piece, is that tribute to an anti-hero of our time: Henry Mancini's theme music for *The Pink Panther*.

The *Wilde Jagd* in question is again hard to pin down precisely. More than likely the title was drawn from Weber's *Freischütz*, well known to Liszt, where the wild hunt is conjured up by Semiel following one of the seven castings of magic bullets. The 'Pan daemonium' subtitle of 1837 does at least point in that general direction, but the 'wild ride' was in any case part and parcel of the Gothic imagination of early Romanticism, associating the mystery and romance of woodland scenes with more menacing, sinister and supernatural qualities. Bürger's ballad *Wilde Jäger* (based on an old German legend) tells of the defiant sacrilege of the wild Count of the Rhine, whose penalty for hunting on the Sabbath is to be hunted for ever through hell.[26] In a way it offers us a picturesque version of Promethean, and Faustian, themes. Schumann conjured it up with more decorum than may seem appropriate in *Wilde Reiter* from his *Album for the Young*, but its musical resonances extended much further afield. Raymond Monelle, in an interesting exploration of equestrian topics, casts the net wide, referring to the headlong dash of the Erlking, to the valkyries and other versions of the witches' ride to the battlefield to transport dead warriors to Valhalla, as well as to Mendelssohn's Goethe-inspired *Die erste Walpurgisnacht*. Berlioz, no admirer of Mendelssohn, was impressed by the *Hexenspuk* from that work, and his own 'witches' sabbath', together with demonic adventures by Meyerbeer and Mercadante, may well have fed Liszt's musical imagination, which in turn may have fed Musorgsky's, Skryabin's and Ravel's.[27]

It has often been noted that Liszt had a characteristic 'demonic' idiom, just as he had a characteristic 'chorale' idiom. The chromaticism of the former (in which the tritone both distorts diatonic functions and enables symmetrical structures), together with its extremes of dynamics and its fragmentary textures, stands in an antithetical relation to the diatonic stability, quiet dynamics and textural simplicity of the latter. *Wilde Jagd* might well be grouped with the 'demonic' works, though as Leslie Howard rightly suggests the untitled 1837 version meets the programmatic description rather better than its 1851 revision. Ironically, this is the one etude where we know for certain that Liszt did not have the precise title in mind in 1837, though he almost certainly had a clear sense of the general topic at that time. This is suggested not only by the 'Pan daemonium', but by details of gesture, harmony and genre already present in the earlier version. As to gesture, the 'headlong dash' is achieved by a rhythmic play on an equestrian motive, with subsequent dislocations that are almost worthy of Stravinsky (Ex. 67); and we may add to that the rushing scales typically associated with tempests of the earth and of the mind. As to harmony, much of this opening section highlights the tritone, whose diabolical associations were conventional, and it may be worth adding that the opposition of tritone and perfect fifth establishes an harmonic world that

---

[26] This in turn formed the model for Walter Scott's *The Wild Huntsman*, and was later the inspiration for Hugo's poem *Le Chasseur Noir* (from *Les Châtiments* of 1853).

[27] Monelle, *The Sense of Music: Semiotic Essays* (Princeton and Oxford, 2000), pp. 45–65.

Example 67 *Wilde Jagd* bars 1–15

Wilde Jagd bars 1–15

would later be developed by Skryabin, often within a similar semantic field. As to genre, we may note that although *Wilde Jagd* resembles a sonata-form movement in both its later versions, the cut of its themes is closer to a scherzo than a sonata, albeit a scherzo very different in type from *Feux-follets*. (It will be recalled in this connection that the Scherzo and March was originally labelled *Wilde Jagd – Scherzo*; Liszt clearly regarded the duple metre as compatible with the genre.) Here it is tempting to take another brief sideways glance at Chopin, whose first Scherzo, composed around 1835, not only redefined the genre as an ambitious single-movement structure, but associated it with a demonic idiom, which is then tellingly juxtaposed with a chorale idiom.[28] The scherzo character of *Wilde Jagd* is reinforced, moreover, by the folk-like, bucolic second theme, whose transformation of the equestrian motive produces something of the effect of a 'trio', even if subsequent events belie this reading.

While most of the titles of the *Transcendentals* depict an idealised object, state or event that exists somewhere beyond the selves of composer and listener (though with which either self may naturally find some identification), *Ricordanza* hints at self-portrait, at subjectivity and self-reflection, and it is appropriate that this title should have been applied to the etude that more than any other takes its inspiration from the human voice, both singing and speaking. The 'singing style', characterised by appoggiaturas, melodic arcs and refined embellishments, is common to all three versions of the ninth etude, but it was given additional poignancy in 1851 by Liszt's reformulation of the melody, as in Example 43, and additional expressive power by the impassioned climactic redrafting of the end of the final strophe. When he chose the title, Liszt probably had in mind little more than a confirmation of that world of tender sentiment, nostalgia and reverie already signalled by the early exercise, a world whose origins in *Empfindsamkeit* are rather clear (Busoni referred to 'a bundle of faded love letters'[29]). However, the insertion of four improvisatory commentaries, characterised by recitative, filigree pianism and motivic development, in the two later versions allowed them to reflect on the early exercise in a manner that might even be thought to offer a rather more specific justification for the title *Ricordanza*.[30] Thus the introduction, marked *improvisato*, is a quest for melody, a quest in which stability proves to be temporary and illusory, rapidly transmuting into unmetred rhapsody (a kind of 'speaking') or colouristic figuration. Rather as in the introductions to operatic fantasies, the melody comes in and out of focus, discernible even in the figurations, but obstinately refusing to coalesce into a recognisable whole. In contrast, the attempts of the two central interpolations to work a motive from the melody in the Classical manner ultimately lead to a kind of liquidation or dissolution of both melodic substance and emotional intensity into cadenza-like figurations. And finally, in the most blatant gesture of *ricordanza*, the coda fleetingly recalls the opening motive in a series of contracted repetitions.

The last two etudes return to a pastoral imagery that is at times explicitly iconic. The bells at the beginning of *Harmonies du soir*, already so designated in 1837, are transparently part of the evening soundscape. A determinedly programmatic interpretation would allow them to echo through harmonic opacities that, read by way of the title, might convey something of the haziness of the evening air. The resonating harmonies of both the original exercise theme and the subsidiary modulating theme would then extend this sound image

---

[28] Interestingly, Chopin's Third Scherzo of 1839 reinforces the demonic idiom and is about as close to Liszt as he ever comes.

[29] *The Essence of Music*, p. 162.

[30] To read into its evolving melodic shapes a technical expression of 'recollection' (see Helen Hall, 'The Evolution of Liszt's Compositional Style as Reflected in the Three Versions of the Transcendental Etudes', diss., University of Victoria [1983], p. 35) is to take a step too far.

of tintinnabulation, and it is intriguing that in 1851 Liszt uncharacteristically thickened the texture at bars 21–3, confirming in the process the prevalence of bell-like sonorities. As so often, human passions emerge to the foreground of this pastoral scene, here through the E major 'song', *accompagnamento quasi Arpa*, one of Liszt's most affecting melodies, and later the basis of one of his most powerful and transcendent apotheotic transformations. Unlike *Harmonies du soir*, the title *Chasse-Neige* is remarkably specific, and there are two senses in which Liszt's revision of 1851 might be thought to have responded to it. First, the addition of chromatic-scalar accompaniments in the later stages of the piece, growing ever more insistent until the melody is all but submerged by them, is evocative of the whirlwinds of drifting snow, though naturally the power of this passage extends well beyond its pictorialism. And second, the deletion of the introduction and of the later passage in which the introduction returns, serves to strengthen the sense of an obsessively bleak and uniform snowscape, metaphorically suggestive: a 'sublime and steady fall of snow which gradually buries landscape and people'.[31]

It is hard to say why Liszt decided not to add titles to the second and tenth of the etudes. Earlier I suggested that they might be regarded, by default, as the only straightforward etudes. Yet their placement within the 1851 series undermines any claims they might stake to the status of 'absolute music', and invites us to attempt poetic readings even without the orientation offered by a title. It is perhaps no coincidence that these are the two etudes in which the intertexts (with Beethoven and Chopin respectively) are so explicit as to suggest a programmatic intention. The second etude, then, might be read as a dialogue between the capriccio theme of the exercise and the 'fate' motive from Beethoven to which it is obliged to submit. This is one layer of interpretation. But we may add to it another layer, grounded in the tendency in later reception to describe the second as the 'Paganini etude', partly because of its violinistic figurations, but also because of the perceived 'demonic' character of its *moto perpetuo* virtuosity and tritonal motive (Busoni referred to 'Paganini devilries'). Such associations are reinforced not only by the ubiquity of the diminished-seventh harmonies, but also by the revision of the tonal structure in 1851 to allow a *Freischütz*-like pairing of A minor and C minor. As to the tenth etude, the mapping of Liszt's melody on to Chopin's has already been mentioned, and may be illustrated here (Ex. 68a). We might note, however, that even Chopin's method of creating rhetorical emphasis through repeated notes is taken over by Liszt, as Example 68b indicates. Read in these terms, 'Chopin' is in dialogue with the toccata-like material derived from the exercise, emerging from that material first tentatively, then more fully, with interruptions, impassioned extensions and transformations, and with a final triumphant peroration.

SEEKING THE PLOT

Referring to a developing tradition of Beethoven interpretation, Liszt commented in 1855 on 'the need to see the guiding ideas of great instrumental works precisely designated'.[32] Of

---

[31] Busoni, *The Essence of Music*, p. 162.

[32] In his essay, 'Berlioz und seine 'Harold-Symphonie', *Gesammelte Schriften*, ed. Lina Ramann (Leipzig, 1881–99), vol. 4, pp. 24–5.

Example 68 (a) Chopin, *12 Etudes*, Op. 10, No. 9 bars 1–2
Liszt, *Transcendentals*, No. 10 bars 22–3
(b) Chopin, *12 Etudes*, Op. 10, No. 9 bars 33–4
Liszt, *Transcendentals*, No. 10 bars 122–5

Chopin. *12 Etudes*, Op. 10, No. 9 bars 1–2 (a)

Liszt. *Transcendentals*, No. 10 bars 22–3

Chopin. *12 Etudes*, Op. 10, No. 9 bars 33–4 (b)

Liszt. *Transcendentals*, No. 10 bars 122–5

course, titles such as 'paysage', 'vision' and 'eroica' can scarcely function as precise designates. At most, they narrow the range of possible interpretations available to the listener, offering little more than suggestive points of orientation. Yet even these are enough to register that the 'idea' behind the etudes in their final form may have become, or may have crystallised, a 'poetic idea'. Attributing a poetic meaning to an existing piece was of course already common practice in the early nineteenth century, especially in Beethoven criticism, and Liszt, like Berlioz, was quite prepared to extend the practice to his own music. If there is an apparent anomaly here, Schumann addressed it specifically in a review of music by Sterndale Bennett in 1838: 'In what way the Sketches [by Bennett] came into existence, whether from within outward, or the reverse, is of no consequence and difficult to decide. For the most part, composers do not know that themselves: one piece is made in one way, another in another. Often an outside picture leads further; again, often a tone-series calls forth a picture.'[33] Elsewhere Schumann described his own experience in relation to one of the *Fantasiestücke* Op. 12 of 1837, in which he subsequently 'found' the story of Hero and Leander. This resonates with Liszt's approach. For Liszt, the aim of the title was not to tell the story of the music, but to offer a way of focusing and clarifying its emotional or poetic content through designates with which the listener will be familiar. For this reason he had no qualms about assigning the programme or title *post hoc*, selecting it because of its conformity to one of the relatively small handful of highly generalised archetypes (of plot and expression) that underlie much of his music.

In recent years there have been numerous attempts to develop Leonard Ratner's topic theory into a more comprehensive theory of interpretation.[34] This usually means establishing an interactive relationship between topic recognition, where we determine correlations through iconism or intertextuality, and genre or plot identification, where we 'read' compositional strategies, often by invoking what Robert Hatten calls 'markedness'. The first of these without the second takes us close to fairly simple (and venerable) theories of expression. The second without the first shades into more recent, plot-based understandings of music and narrative. The general assumption is that by allowing the two perspectives to interact, we enable a rich interpretation, one that allows for a contextualisation of topics rather than their straightforward identification. In the case of Liszt's etudes the first stage (Hatten calls it 'correlation') is perhaps best approached by way of the characteristic theme or melody.[35] And here the etudes might slot into Dahlhaus's much larger 'history of the musical theme', a history that reached a determinate stage in Wagner, where melodies are indeed the personification of ideas. It is unnecessary to rehearse again the characterisation of themes in the *Transcendentals*, achieved through an intertextuality that probes layer upon layer of sedimented historical meaning. There are pastoral meditations, playful fantasies and

---

[33] For the broader context of this remark, see the discussion in Niecks, *Programme Music*, pp. 188–9.

[34] See, for example, Kofi Agawu, *Playing with Signs: A Semiotic Interpretation of Classic Music* (Princeton and Oxford, 1991); Robert Hatten, *Musical Meaning in Beethoven*; Márta Grabócz, *Morphologie des Oeuvres pour Piano de Liszt*; Raymond Monelle, *The Sense of Music*; Jean-Jacques Nattiez, *Music and Discourse: Towards a Semiology of Music*, trans. Carolyn Abbate (Princeton, 1990); and Eero Tarasti, *A Theory of Musical Semiotics* (Bloomington, 1994).

[35] See Hermann Jung (*Die Pastorale*) on this question, i.e. replacing the rhetorical with the 'characteristic' and the 'poetic'. Also Janet Levy, 'Texture as a Sign', *Journal of the American Musicological Society*, 35, 3 (1982), pp. 482–531.

sombre incantations; there are heroic marches, anguished laments and nostalgic arias; there are impassioned pleas, lyrical reflections and restless questionings; and running through all this there are portentous introductions, passing asides and elaborate commentaries. These are the building blocks (the topics) from which an interpretation might be constructed by examining the work-specific strategic choices made by the composer (the plot).

Commentators engaged in a quest for musical narrative, such as Fred Everett Maus and Anthony Newcomb, have suggested that we can 'follow the story' of a work by identifying its marked elements (usually defined as such by their deviations from conventional schemata).[36] They argue that, for example, modifications of an implied succession, interpreted in relation to that implied succession, may generate the events of a narrative, and that the narrative in its turn may well be motivated by an underlying 'plot archetype', by no means congruent with a formal archetype such as sonata form. However, such wordless narratives are not dependent on a semantic content, and it is not at all self-evident that the addition of a narrating 'virtual agent' makes for a radical departure from more conventional analytical readings of a formal process. It is by adding a semiotic dimension that Tarasti, Grabócz, Hatten and others have arrived at something more closely resembling a critical hermeneutics, in that the marked elements are linked to a putative semantic content that enables an interpretation of the technical. Ian Bent has traced something of the prehistory of this kind of investigation in nineteenth-century criticism, and it is to the point that he singles out Franz Brendel's 'critique of music criticism', in his first essay as the new editor of *Neue Zeitschrift für Musik*.[37] Brendel's call is for a 'third viewpoint', in which 'technical adjudication' and 'psychological description' might be married. Not only would these be the preconditions for the third viewpoint; that viewpoint would have to 'absorb . . . and transcend them'. It might reasonably be argued that this requirement had already been met in certain areas of music criticism in the early nineteenth century, not least in a strand of Liszt's own writing that culminated in the preface to the *Album d'un Voyageur*. However, Brendel's manifesto was important not least because it was a manifesto, and one that has been echoed at several subsequent stages in the histories of both criticism and scholarship. The recent evolution of Anglo-American musicology replays Brendel's themes. But they can also be heard to resonate in semiotic approaches to music, several of which have been developed in continental as well as American scholarship.

I am inclined to be cautious of this perspective, but it will be worth exploring it nonetheless, since Liszt's titles positively invite us to do so. That it may become an easy prey to wishful thinking, especially where the technical foundation for a programmatic reading is less than secure, is surely demonstrated by Márta Grabócz's analysis of *Vision*.[38] Grabócz identifies four variations of the main theme of the etude, of which the first has 'un rhythme lent, caractéristique de la marche funèbre', while the second, through its modality, register and

[36] Fred Everett Maus, 'Music as Drama', *Music Theory Spectrum*, 10 (1988), pp. 56–73; also Anthony Newcomb, 'Once More "Between Absolute Music and Programme Music"', *19th-Century Music*, 7 (1984), pp. 233–50, and 'Schumann and Late Eighteenth-Century Narrative Strategies', *19th-Century Music*, 11 (1986), pp. 164–74. For a more recent study, see Vera Micznik, 'Music and Narrative Revisited: Degrees of Narrativity in Beethoven and Mahler', *Journal of the Royal Musical Association*, 126, 2 (2001), pp. 193–249.

[37] In the 'General Introduction' to Ian Bent (ed.), *Music Analysis in the Nineteenth Century, Volume 2: Hermeneutic Approaches* (Cambridge, 1994), pp. 1–27.

[38] *Morphologie des Oeuvres pour Piano de Liszt*, pp. 129–31.

harp-like accompaniment has 'le caractère ou intonation plus clairs', revealing perhaps 'le côte pathétique du thème'. She then describes a passage of sequential modulations at the major third interval, which leads to the third variation in the major, 'evoquant l'intonation "eroico" ou "triumphando"', and from there to the final variation, which she regards as 'une version chromatique, dissonante parfois avec accompagnement bitonal, autrement dit encline au ton macabresque . . .', and coda. The difficulty here is that Grabócz's 'fourth variation' is in reality nothing of the kind, but rather a development or consequent of the derived secondary idea, whose significance has not been fully grasped in her analysis. As I argued earlier, this idea is initially plotted after the first statement of the theme, extended after the second (this is Grabócz's modulating passage), and allowed to dominate the musical argument after the third, triumphant, statement. It is instructive to see how so many curious interpretative misreadings can flow from a simple error such as this. A conventional V–I harmonic succession becomes 'bitonal'; a broad, affirmative, expansive peroration becomes 'macabre'.

It may be interesting to examine *Eroica* from a similar perspective, in the impertinent belief that I might do a little better. I noted earlier that the basic topic, as clarified by the Beethovenian-Promethean title, is embodied in the march theme of the etude. I also noted (in chapter 5) that in purely formal terms, this theme forms the basis of a set of character variations, albeit rather freely conceived and influenced by the sonata principle. A poetic interpretation of the etude might draw the topic and the formal process together in ways that may qualify the heroic affect, or at least suggest that it has to be fought for, and may at the same time qualify the conception of the piece as a variation form. The introduction presents registral, dynamic and gestural contrasts that all contribute to an effect of impassioned urgency and excited anticipation. This is heightened by the semitonal top-voice ascent of bars 1–9, by the formal diminutions of bars 9–11, and by the implicative harmony, in which diminished and dominant sevenths look to an E major tonality, though as the march theme begins, the final dominant seventh is retrospectively recognised as an augmented sixth in E♭, 'marking' the arrival of the tonic. The initial version of the march theme itself might be characterised as subdued but resolute, emerging as from a distance but with its purposeful, directional quality reinforced by sequential repetitions through a rising-third interval. Any sense of stability it promotes soon proves illusory, however, as the theme is prematurely arrested by an attempt at the introductory flourish followed by a falling second ('lament') motive (*x* in Ex. 48c), in which energy and optimism are quickly dissipated. This interruption is formally 'marked', and it enables us to read the entire passage as an unsuccessful attempt to establish the theme, which arrives in its 'true' form at bar 32. Yet even this stable, and more fully orchestrated, version of the theme is aborted by the unexpected harmonic opening to a C major chord (formally and tonally 'marked') at bar 42, followed by a no less sudden implosion of momentum through the textural contraction of bars 42–3.

The ensuing passage was described in chapter 5 in terms of further variations of the march, and this conforms to the consensus view in published commentaries that *Eroica* is a variation set. However, a poetic reading might encourage us to draw a further distinction between different presentations of the theme. What enabled me to describe bar 32 as a 'true' form of the theme was not just that it has a more developed melodic profile, but that its repeated notes are now harmonised as tonics, and its harmonic setting is now diatonic. Read back from that, the earlier version (where the repeated notes are harmonised as dominants, and the harmonic sequence is third-related) is recognised as incomplete and unstable. And this also describes the material between bars 44 and 62, where the repeated notes are again dominants, and where the technique is developmental, albeit unfolding in two distinct stages. The first of these stages proceeds by modulating sequence, and with destabilising harmonic and phrase-structural qualities; the second draws together elements of the theme and the introduction. It is really only with the clarification of the 'marked' (because distant) tonal area of Db major at bar 63 that we have a second full presentation of the theme, more animated and elaborately accompanied than the first, but again with the repeated notes harmonised as tonics and the setting diatonic. Yet here too the momentum is rudely checked, as Liszt uses a moment of conformity with the earliest presentation of the theme to repeat and extend the 'lament' motive, related though inversion to the opening anacrusis figure, and then to bring back the final section of the introduction. This, however, is subtly modified to achieve closer integration with the theme, both motivically (the three-note anacrusis) and harmonically (preparing the Eb major of the 'reprise', rather than the original E major). At this point we have the third full statement of the theme in the tonic, the most fully scored, virtuosic and extended of all, and the only unambiguously 'heroic' presentation (*con bravura*). However even this apotheosis of the theme breaks off abruptly with a diminished-seventh question mark, leaving the coda to return to the earliest formulation (bar 103), complete with the three-note anacrusis. With the reference to the introduction at bar 112, the dominant seventh in E major this time functions as such, allowing a Neapolitan inflection to the final cadence.

Really the formal design of *Eroica* is best thought of as three separated, increasingly emphatic strophes, embedded in more fragmentary, unstable material. In the strophes the march theme is given in extended form and with its repeated notes harmonised as tonics. In the surrounding material the theme is worked sequentially and the repeated notes are harmonised as dominants. The narrative that unfolds depends at every stage on processes of disjunction and interruption, and it might be sketched somewhat as follows. From the start there is a disjunction between the expressive (implicitly subjective) quality of the introduction and the measured (implicitly communal) quality of the march. This disjunction is programmatic of the piece as a whole. Thus the tentative first steps of the (collective) march are interrupted by the brief return of the introduction and by the expressive (individual) 'lament' figure. The first 'stable' presentation of the march follows, essaying the heroic affect, but it 'collapses' at bars 42–3, and the ensuing material represents an initially uncertain, but increasingly insistent, attempt to re-establish it. The second, more elaborated, presentation of the march theme follows, but that too is subverted by the intrusion of subjectivity, in the form of an extension of the 'lament' motive, together with elements of the introduction. The third presentation of the march, marked here by its congruity with the tonal reprise, is clearly the goal of the piece. It represents the clearest and fullest expression of the 'heroic' intonation signalled by the title. Yet here too the march breaks off in mid-stride, and the coda is left to remember wisps of the theme in its original, 'tentative' form, with the anacrusis presented in both prime and (anti-heroic) inverted forms. Again the 'voice of the individual' (the closing reference to the introduction) intrudes, and the final cadence is an end that emulates a beginning.

Such an interpretation accepts the heroic affect implied by the title, but inflects it through a reading of the formal context. It is reasonable to ask how, if at all, the approach differs from the imaginative fancies of a nineteenth-century critic. One point worth noting is the abundance of scare-quotes in my account of *Eroica*, signalling the hypothetical status of the reading and at the same time revealing my own insecurities about it. The nineteenth-century critic, in contrast, was happy to present an autobiographical statement on the premise that the critic's job was not to formulate theories but to convey his experience of a work directly to the reader. Beyond that, my interpretation makes some claim to be grounded in crotchets and quavers both through topic affiliation and formal-stylistic analysis. It is from this technical base that an expressive genre or plot archetype might be articulated, in which the increasingly insistent quest for a collectively expressed heroic affect is no less insistently subverted by individual doubt and uncertainty. Naturally, it would be rather easy to devise comparable narratives for the other etudes. In the case of *Wilde Jagd*, the controlling topic, together with a range of programmatic images, is already specified by the title. However, any narrative we might construct would need to reveal other facets of the cursed huntsman and his wild ride, albeit only in the most general terms. Thus, there is the folkloristic 'trio', an episode of pleasure in the chase, rustic in character, that is progressively drawn into the 'demonic' orbit of the piece, the orbit of the Black Horseman or the 'Sable Hunter' in the programmatic terms of Bürger's ballad. And there is an expressive, 'human' face (a 'second subject' in sonata-form terms: the Fair Horseman?, the plight of the Herdsman?) that can invoke pathos (*languendo*) and passion (*molto appassionato*). It too yields to the prevailing atmosphere (a developmental link to the reprise of the main theme, whose stretto effects at this point might suggest the 'rout profane'), then reasserts itself, but is in the end subordinated to the cursed ride. In *Harmonies du soir*, we might likewise devise a plot based on the mediation of the pastoral setting (the main theme) and the human presence (the E major second subject), where the principal mediating element is the modulating refrain. Here our narrative would take account of the several characters assumed by all three components of the piece, where the tone of the refrain responds to the preceding, or anticipates the succeeding, statements of the other two themes, culminating in the quiet transcendence of the final statement of the pastoral theme.

It is scarcely necessary to go through the etudes individually along these lines. In each of them a signal is sent out by the title, and that enables, indeed invites, a reading of the musical events in the light of a programme, however loosely conceived. The topics embodied in characteristic themes are focused by the programme, and formal functions (introduction, presentation, transition-development, variation-transformation, reprise, coda) acquire metaphorical meanings (become plots) in relation to those topics. It should be added that just as a poetic idea may influence how we read a musical form, so too a musical form can influence our reading of a poetic idea. Indeed, since Liszt's plot archetypes, or expressive genres, are restricted in number, it is by no means surprising that the programme may be subordinated to them, especially as the programmes are deliberately generalised in nature. As Dahlhaus points out, the aim is seldom if ever an isomorphic relationship, but rather a mutual interaction between two types of material, technical and poetic.[39] This inter-action, mediating in some ways between the two polarised perspectives I brought to bear on the early exercises (in chapter 2), belongs within the province of an historical hermeneutics. Its starting-point is bound to be a present-day perception, but its tendency is towards a re-covery of nineteenth-century expressive meanings, and that may even include a dimension of authorial intention. That said, there can be no single interpretation. Nor did Liszt really intend such a thing, for all his optimistic reference to 'precisely designated' ideas. His aim was to orientate the listener in the right general direction. A programmatic title is, after all, just one step beyond a genre title. It establishes, and fine-tunes, a listening strategy within which numerous interpretations will be possible. Indeed the only thing that may seem at first glance surprising in all of this is that the matter should have become the basis of such a fierce polemic in the 1850s.

ON TO ONTOLOGY

Almost exactly a year before Liszt assigned titles to the *Transcendentals* the critic of *The Athenaeum* argued that 'music runs some danger of being pushed across the boundaries which separate it from Poetry and Picture'.[40] This was symptomatic of a growing nervousness among traditionally minded critics about music and programmes around the mid-century. It is worth asking why this should have been so. After all, programme music was nothing new. It had a lengthy history prior to 1800. However, in the two decades or so preceding the *Transcendentals* there was not only a dramatic increase in the output of programmatic pieces but also, and more crucially, a greater aesthetic ambition associated with their composition, at least in some quarters. At the same time the issue of music and the poetic became a key item on the agenda of music criticism.[41] In his discussion of Beethoven criticism in the Leipzig *Allgemeine Musikalische Zeitung*, Robin Wallace noted alternative critical responses to the Idealist agenda set by philosophical aesthetics: Hoffmann's belief that music without a text 'can transcend ordinary human life' and Wendt's belief that a text 'humanizes music and makes it more accessible'.[42] In part these alternatives echoed an eighteenth-century debate about priority between vocal and instrumental music, and in this respect Wendt's was the more conservative position. However, by freighting the debate with the language and concepts of an Idealist aesthetics both critics took it on to another level, anticipating the polemic of the 1850s; and here it was Hoffmann whose position would come to be viewed as the more conservative. The argument was really centred around two categories, musical unity and the musically poetic. And it is worth noting at the outset that these categories, often taken as defining the opposition between absolute and programme music, were regarded as

---

[39] Carl Dahlhaus, *Esthetics of Music*, trans. William Austin (Cambridge, 1982; orig. edn, 1967), p. 59.

[40] *The Athenaeum*, 19 January 1850.

[41] Dahlhaus reminds us that the term 'poetic' tended to mean simply 'artistic' in the early nineteenth century (*Analysis and Value Judgement*, trans. Siegmund Levarie [New York, 1983; orig. edn, 1970], p. 16). This was Schumann's meaning, and it was only in the later nineteenth century, notably in Liszt, that the meaning was enlarged.

[42] Robin Wallace, *Beethoven's Critics: Aesthetic Dilemmas and Resolutions during the Composer's Lifetime* (Cambridge, 1986), p. 29.

centrally important to both positions. On one side, the poetic was thought to be embodied in the musical work, whose unity allowed it to stand for an idealised world (for what the world might become). On the other side, the poetic was itself a shaping force, contributing to a new and higher unity, a fusion of sister arts.

It is not an exaggeration to say that it was the developing aesthetic of absolute music, associated above all with Beethoven reception, that made an issue of programme music. As instrumental music was increasingly freighted with expressive ambition, it forced a separation and even an opposition. Either its expressive qualities privileged it and sealed it off from the pollutions of context, or they opened a pathway to a higher synthesis with the poetic. That Beethoven himself seemed to look in both directions at various times is certainly to the point. But more telling is the extent to which his music became the prime location for the debate. Thus, for Adolf Bernhard Marx the formal organisation of Beethoven's music, much though he was inclined to analyse it, was no empty play of symmetries, but was rather linked to an enabling poetic content, itself motivating the *Grundideen* or fundamental ideas of the music. To understand the major works of Beethoven, he insisted in the pages of the Berlin *Allgemeine Musikalische Zeitung*, is to grasp those ideas. Compare this with Berlioz: 'in Beethoven and Weber, poetic thought is ubiquitous and cannot be overlooked. . . . This music needs no words to make its expression specific; . . . . we are raised towards a higher ideal region, sensing that the sublime life dreamed of by poets is becoming real. . . .'. Or with Schumann, whose agenda for the proselytising *Neue Zeitschrift für Musik* included the rehabilitation of what he called the 'poetic principle', and hence the establishment of a 'fresh, poetic future'. At the same time there is a difference between finding the concealed programme in Beethoven, and prescribing the overtly programmatic for others. Marx was prepared to advocate programmatic or 'characteristic' music as a genre of the future, a genre motivated less by the illustrative acumen of music than by the impulse towards a synthesis of the arts. Schumann, on the other hand, fell some way short of this position. Despite his own use of programmatic titles and his enthusiasm for poetic readings of the instrumental music of others, he was alive to the possibility that actual (as distinct from imagined) programmes may detract from, rather than enhance, the poetic idea.

His reservations were given their clearest expression in his 1835 defence of the *Symphonie fantastique*, in which he derided Berlioz's programme as degenerate, and argued that it trivialised the music.[43] Interestingly, he homed in on an issue in the perception of 'multi-media' (as we might call it today) that would later be identified as a problem by Hanslick. 'Once the eye has been directed to something, the ear loses its capacity for independent judgement'. That this need not be represented as an adverse criticism is clear from a highly significant elaboration: 'Often when the musical imagination is at work, an idea acts upon it unbeknownst. Often the ear is influenced by the eye – and that ever-alert organ, amidst the world of noises and musical sounds, holds constant certain visual profiles which can transform themselves and develop into audible contours as the music takes shape'. Indeed this might even be viewed as a necessary precondition for the further step

---

[43] The English translation of this text in Ian Bent's *Musical Analysis in the Nineteenth Century* (vol. 2, pp. 161–94) is revelatory.

taken by Liszt, who regarded the poeticising of absolute music as a pathway to the musically poetic. Liszt's contribution to the Beethoven debate in his essay on *Harold in Italy* makes the nature of this further step explicit. The quotation at the beginning of my last section can bear repetition and expansion. 'The attempts, becoming more and more frequent during the past 15 years or so, to comment on Beethoven's symphonies, quartets, and sonatas, and to explain and fix in poetic and philosophical treatments the impressions they give us, the pictures they awaken in us – these attempts show how great is the need to see the guiding ideas of great instrumental works precisely designated'.[44] Before that, in his preface to the *Album d'un Voyageur*, he had already presented his rationale for the *poème pianistique*. Here, in the *Harold* essay, published in *Neue Zeitschrift für Musik* exactly twenty years after Schumann's essay on the *Symphonie fantastique*, he developed this into a much more ambitious agenda for the symphonic poem. Far from trivialising the music, the programme dignifies it. Indeed, given the challenge of the modern epic (Goethe, Byron, Mickiewicz), where the actions of heroes make way for the inner dramas of the soul, the function of the programme 'becomes indispensable, and its entrance into the highest spheres of art appears justified'; it is 'as inevitable as the declamatory style in opera'. The 'poetic solution' for instrumental music is an idea whose time has come, for 'both arts [poetry and music], more than ever before, feel themselves mutually attracted and are striving for inner union'. Those (professional) musicians who hanker after the old forms have no understanding of 'the thirst after the eternal, the dream of the ideal, the search for the poetically beautiful in every form'. In truth, the modern (vocational) musician has a deeper respect for the past, for 'to honour these patriarchs one must regard the forms they used as exhausted and look on imitations of them as mere copies of slight value'. We need 'new forms for new ideas'.

Liszt had his co-writers in the *Harold* essay, aside of course from the Princess Carolyn; and aside, too, from Wagner, Brendel and the 'circle'. Both Dahlhaus and Eggebrecht have argued that the (somewhat contrary) aesthetics of Kant and Herder were central to his conception of the symphonic poem. Likewise, Liszt himself invoked Hegel on more than one occasion, while the voices of the Weimar past (Schiller as well as Herder) echo through the text of the essay. Ideas about the nature and status of music relative to poetry were well rehearsed in late eighteenth- and early nineteenth-century philosophical aesthetics, and they provoked a lively response from critics and composers in the first half of the nineteenth century. But in the 1850s these ideas became grist to the mill of a narrower, fiercer polemic, often involving some wholesale misunderstandings and some unlikely syntheses. Thus, in the early part of the essay Liszt argues, with Herder, for the privileged status of music as 'the embodied and intelligible essence of feeling', but falls some way short of assigning to it a Schopenhauerian identity with metaphysics. Rather he implicitly recognises, with Kant, that it is not 'thought-provoking', and that this creates a necessary dependency. The function of the programme which meets that dependency is described in terms that again remind us of Kant's description of aesthetic understanding, though narrowing and specifying Kant's more general meaning. Effectively the programme is a control on the perception of the listener, a way of first stimulating, but then orientating and constraining, the 'free play' of

---

[44] *Gesammelte Schriften*, vol. 4, pp. 24–5.

the imagination, and thus allowing it to come into harmony with understanding. Liszt's ideal, and it is hard not to hear Schiller's *Aesthetic Letters* in some of this, is that through the use of a programme the beautiful might pave the way from sensation to thought, and in so doing might bring harmony to the individual and from there to society as a whole. There are, moreover, obvious parallels with Wagner in Liszt's fusion of an Hegelian understanding of the ripeness of the historical moment ('new forms for new ideas') with a Kantian view of the relation between genius and convention ('genius gives the rule to art'). As in Wagner, too, there is a tortuous reasoning by which music, an instrument of our liberation from language-based understanding, achieves the status of a higher poetic (superseding language) only through association with a text.

It is historically tidy that Schumann and Liszt presented their opposed views on the programme through essays on two Berlioz symphonies. (Their comments on each other's music preserves this symmetry, in that each thought the other a flawed genius, but for opposite reasons.) The Berlioz works undoubtedly raised the stakes in the battle for the poetic, simply by virtue of their scale and medium. Pictorial titles were common currency in popular concert music, for the piano of course, but also – though to a lesser extent – for the orchestra. But by building ambitious programme symphonies on the acknowledged tradition of Beethoven and Weber overtures, Berlioz posed a special challenge to the symphony, turning the polemic into a controversy over progress and modernity. Epic forms of instrumental music, his symphonies proclaimed, should be programmatic. This added up to an identity crisis for instrumental music, a crisis already partly diagnosed by Schumann but one to which Liszt tried actively to respond. His ambition was nothing less than a modern parallel to the 'antique epos', and to that end he drew on what he called the modern 'philosophical epopoeias' (to which Weimar Classicism had an input) as well as on ancient myth in building his vast cycle of extended overtures, or, as he dubbed them in 1854, 'symphonic poems'. Essential to their character was a programme rooted in world literature and known legend, a familiar, high-status topic on which the music could discourse. The constitution of the genre is not really addressed in the *Harold* essay, beyond its putative union, as distinct from combination, of music and image. But in practice what Liszt calls a union, like much-discussed unions of words and music, is more justly labelled a dialogue. A musical argument colours our view of a poetic topic; a poetic topic influences our reading of the musical argument. As to musical processes, the symphonic poem is invariably in a single movement, often carving a double-function form from a blend of existing formal archetypes; it underlines the more dramatic moments of the plot with vivid, pictorial orchestrations; and it allows its poeticised themes and materials to generate a network of repetitions, transformations and developments that respond to both formal and programmatic imperatives. As Liszt put it in an often quoted sentence: 'In programme music . . . the return, change, modification, and modulation of the motives are conditioned by their relation to a poetic idea'.[45] How far this happens in practice is another matter; put bluntly, it does in some works, and not in others.

The *Harold* essay was Liszt's contribution to a decade's polemical debate, inaugurated by Wagner in 1849, extended by Brendel and Hanslick, and brought to a terminus of sorts

---

[45] *Gesammelte Schriften*, vol. 4, p. 69.

in the 'announcement' of a New German School in 1859.[46] Indeed, although it was long in the planning, the essay emerged hard on the heels of Hanslick's classic presentation of an aesthetic of absolute music.[47] And it was itself followed shortly after by Wagner's open letter in support of Liszt's symphonic poems, which needless-to-say is more about himself than Liszt (just as, to be fair, Liszt's essay is more about *him*self than Berlioz).[48] What Wagner admires is the flexibility of Liszt's forms and the creative counterpoint they establish with traditional archetypes, and again he proposes a lineage from Beethoven. Yet elsewhere Wagner was less forthright. In his later essay 'On the Application of Music to the Drama', he argued that although programmatic instrumental music brought much that was new in harmony and in theatrical and pictorial effects, it carried with it alarming tendencies towards 'downright melodrama music', from which redemption would be possible only 'by openly and undisguisedly turning that line itself towards the drama'.[49] This was of course a self-validating analysis. But it was also prescient. Not only was the history of the symphonic poem a short one, and by no means trouble-free; its agenda – the fusion of a unique musical process with a clearly indicated poetic concept – never really proved to be a vote-winner, at least not in the heroic terms conceived by Liszt. Indeed, as I shall argue briefly in the next chapter, Wagner was precisely on target when he suggested that programmes could all too often encourage musical characterisations that risked ridicule when their signifieds were *in absentia*, but made perfect sense when they were enacted on stage.

It is precisely this point that invites speculation about ontology. Although he argued that a musical work, unlike a literary work or painting, consisted only in a single stratum made up of sounds, the Polish philosopher Roman Ingarden admitted several 'non-sounding elements' superimposed on the sound formation. These elements, secondary to the sounding element or 'base' in that they are not essential to all kinds of music, are nonetheless integral to the work of music as an aesthetic object. They include constructs such as movement and form, as well as emotional qualities and representational themes. These latter 'lead us away from themselves and make us think of a more or less distinct object'. If this is an imagined (as opposed to a real) object, it remains within the world of art but inhabits the sphere of the 'quasi-musical' (rather than 'extra-musical').[50] This sphere nevertheless belongs to the work, resulting in what Ingarden calls a 'higher-level totality' made up of the musical work and the imagined objects. Ingarden did not have Liszt or his *Harold* essay in mind here, but his account of the ontology provides Liszt's visionary manifesto with a hard-edged analytical rationale. He could almost have been writing Liszt's agenda. 'The constructs provided in a

---

[46] See James Deaville, 'The Controversy Surrounding Liszt's Conception of Programme Music', in Jim Samson and Bennett Zon (eds.), *Nineteenth-Century Music*, pp. 98–124.

[47] Eduard Hanslick, *On the Musically Beautiful*, trans. and ed. Geoffrey Payzart (Indianapolis, 1996; orig. edn, 1854). Dahlhaus reminds us that the term 'Absolute Music' was coined by Wagner: *The Idea of Absolute Music*, trans. Roger Lustig (Chicago and London, 1989; orig. edn, 1978), p. 18.

[48] This was published in the spring of 1857 in *Neue Zeitschrift für Musik*. It is printed in volume 3 of *Richard Wagner's Prose Works*, ed. William Ashton Ellis (London, 1897), pp. 235–54.

[49] *Ibid.*, vol. 6, pp. 173–91; these quotations on pp. 179 and 182.

[50] Roman Ingarden, *The Work of Music and the Problem of its Identity*, trans. A. Czerniawski, ed. J. G. Harrell (Berkeley and Los Angeles, 1986; orig. edn, 1928). See also Daniel Chua, *Absolute Music and the Construction of Meaning* (Cambridge, 1996), p. 4: 'What, after all, is an "extra-musical" object? It is obviously not Music, but neither is it non-music'.

piece of programme music . . . may be called quasi-musical objects because they do belong to that type of musical composition but are not themselves "musical" . . . But they are not extra-musical . . .'. At the same time Ingarden freely acknowledged the grey areas in all of this (the 'quasi-musical'). 'How these themes can nevertheless represent something . . . separate from them . . . is a complex problem and would demand separate treatment'.[51] And it may be that his uncertainties about the ontological status of programme music can be directed back on to Liszt's self-consciously original and modernising agenda. In other words, we might argue that the 'quasi-musical' is troublesome only when it *becomes* an agenda. The pictorial, non-literary titles attached to so many of Liszt's piano works – and that includes *Paysage, Feux-follets, Vision, Ricordanza, Harmonies du Soir* and *Chasses-Neiges* – are really in the tradition of the nineteenth-century *poème pianistique*. They are to be sure part of the aesthetic property of the piece, but they are unlikely to prompt claims for an inner union or a higher fusion with the music. *Mazeppa* is a different matter altogether. An heroic legend is given status as an historical ballad by Byron, and that in turn is given metaphorical significance for the modern artist in a lyric by Hugo. The title may indeed have been a 'fanciful afterthought', but its subject-matter is both specific enough and challenging enough to forge the materials of a modern epic. It is a programme worthy of a symphonic poem.

[51] Ingarden, *The Work of Music*, pp. 107 and 108.

Chapter Seven

▬

Mazeppa times 7

'IL TOMBE ENFIN! . . . ET SE RELÈVE ROI!'

The translation of the fourth of the 1826 exercises into the most tempestuous of the *Grandes Etudes*, the gladiator of the cycle, invites a little speculation about just what was in Liszt's mind. The early piece, whose links to Cramer have been noted (Ex. 2), is among the least consequential of the exercises in the *Etude en douze exercices*. It is a simple study in hand-crossing, with a texturally contrasted consequent, cast in a straightforward binary form rounded by a short coda. It was suggested in chapter 2 that we might read into its figure some hint of a *chasse* motive, or rather that we might easily imagine how Liszt allowed that figure to suggest an equestrian topic when he recomposed the piece in 1837. All the same, we may be inclined to ask not just how he came to think of the figure as an accompaniment for that big, broad, intemperate tune, but also why the figure is presented in an ever more compressed form through successive strophes, in what appears to be such a graphic representation of the frenzied ride of our Cossack hero. In other words, did Liszt conceive this piece as a bravura etude to which he later appended a peculiarly fitting programmatic title, as he surely did with the other etudes? Or was Victor Hugo's poem already lurking in his thoughts when he recomposed the piece in 1837? (August Stradel reminds us that it was in 1837 that Liszt transcribed Schubert's *Erlkönig*, whose archetypal plot – '*Das dahinrasende Ross, Gewitter und Sturm*' – is suggestive.[1]) There is no way of resolving this question definitively. But it will be interesting to reflect on it as we consider the dating of the third version of the piece, in which the title *Mazeppa* was used for the first time. This self-standing piece, dedicated to Hugo, differs from the Haslinger edition of the fourth of the *Grandes Etudes* at three points only. There is a brief five-bar introduction, onomatopoetic in character, a revision of the final stages of the fourth strophe (in the central lyrical section), and an altered ending that rather clearly corresponds to the 'fall' in Hugo's poem.

Peter Raabe was the first to propose 1840 as the date of composition for the third version of *Mazeppa*, and that date has been followed by many commentators since his catalogue was first produced.[2] Shortly I will argue that the date should stand, but Raabe provided

[1] Stradel, a Liszt pupil, made several contributions to the Liszt centenary issues of *Neue Zeitschrift für Musik* in 1911. The Schubert reference comes in the second part of his two-part article 'Liszts Mazeppa-Werke', 43 (October 1911), p. 597. It is also worth pointing out that in addition to requesting a copy of the early exercises in a letter to his mother from Geneva in 1835, Liszt also asked for Hugo's *Les Orientales*, from which *Mazeppa* is taken.

[2] Raabe, *Liszts Schaffen* (Tutzing, 1968; orig. edn, 1931).

no evidence for it, and it is not entirely surprising that it has been challenged by more recent Lisztians, notably Ernst Burger, who favours 1847, the date of its publication as a separate piece by Schlesinger (it was issued shortly after by Haslinger in Vienna).[3] After all, there is on the face of it no good reason to suppose that there would have been a space of seven years between composition and publication; this was by no means typical. And more pertinently, there is evidence that Liszt was considering using the title *Mazeppa* for other pieces right up to the early months of 1847. Indeed it is almost as though this were a title in search of a piece.[4] In the early Revolutionary Symphony sketchbook (D-WRgs N6), used between 1829 and 1832, he added the title to a fragment of piano music, marked *con furore* and with a four-flat key signature; it amounts to four systems of music, of which the last two and a half were cancelled. Then, in the later *Tasso* sketchbook (N5) there is a fragment in G minor also labelled *Mazeppa*, and among some further sketch pages (gathered as Z18 in Weimar, though certainly originally part of N5) there is another version of the same G minor fragment. And in yet another sketch from Z18, which we can assign (from its reference to Kiev) to February/March of 1847, there is a further draft of a piece in B♭ minor, again labelled *Mazeppa*.[5] In other words, assuming that the titles were indeed intended to apply to the music in these cases, it seems that as late as 1847 Liszt either drafted redundant material for the symphonic poem (the second theme of the finale is a distinct possibility) or considered using the title *Mazeppa* for a piece other than No. 4 of the *Grandes Etudes*.

The former seems the more likely, since in the end the documentary evidence does indeed support something close to Raabe's original date for the intermediate version of *Mazeppa*, at least for the new title and the added introduction. Not only is there is an extant *Gedenkblatt* dated 4 February 1841 with the title *Preludio*, containing the introductory eleven chords appended to the opening of the intermediate version of *Mazeppa*.[6] There is also a letter from Liszt to Schlesinger, dated 1839 from internal evidence (at the latest 1840), making specific reference to this *preludio*.[7] The letter reads as follows:

Decidedly, my dear Maurice, it will be better not to announce any other than the following pieces: the ETUDES – HUGUENOTS – JUIVE – and VALSE MILANCOLIQUE – only let them be advertised better than they were last Sunday, that is to say in more prominent type. One confuses the public by announcing so many pieces of which several can obviously not be available at this time. Send me your Music paper so I can write the PRELUDE to Mazeppa. You will receive the

---

[3] Ernst Burger, *Franz Liszt: A Chronicle of his Life in Pictures and Documents*, trans. Stewart Spencer (Princeton, 1989), p. 167.

[4] The title *Mazeppa* was used by several composers of concert music in the early nineteenth century, notably Quidant for his *Grande Etude-Galop de Concert*, and Loewe in his 'tone poem' after Byron (an *Allegro feroce* in § time). It was also appended to one of Moscheles's Op. 70 Etudes in some later editions.

[5] For the detailed contents of N5, see Rena Charnin Mueller, 'Liszt's Tasso Sketchbook: Studies in Sources and Chronology', *Studia Musicologica*, 28 (1986), pp. 273–94.

[6] The Gedenkblatt is to be found in Bayreuth, in the Richard Wagner Archiv (D-BHrwa Hs 121 A/2). I am grateful to Adrienne Kaczmarczyk for drawing my attention to this source. In fact the Schlesinger edition prints this *preludio* in a facsimile of the autograph, and only in the Haslinger edition is it engraved.

[7] The letter was published with its facsimile and in translation by Albi Rosenthal: 'Franz Liszt and his Publishers', *Liszt-Saeculum*, 2, 38 (1986), pp. 4–6. Rosenthal wrongly associates the *preludio* with the first of the *Transcendentals*.

ADELAIDE at the end of the week; don't advertise it for another eight days. T[out] a v[ous] F. Liszt.

So it seems that Liszt described the fourth etude as *Mazeppa*, and added the brief introduction, either in 1839 – the very year the *Grandes Etudes* were issued – or 1840. The delay in publication until 1847 remains for the moment unexplained; indeed the decision to publish the piece separately is in itself a little curious. Now, in the absence of concrete evidence we cannot assume that Liszt was responding to Hugo when he recomposed the early exercise in 1837. The etude can be viewed quite simply as a characteristic blend of variation and ternary forms, a set of variations that incorporates a central section based on a transformation of the melody. The parallel with Hugo's poem might then have occurred to Liszt shortly afterwards, motivating the reissue of the etude as a separate programme piece, with the musical text tweaked slightly in the direction of the poem. This is all plausible. Yet it is striking that of all Liszt's programmatic pieces, the *Mazeppa* works have been considered among the most 'literal'. Niecks described the symphonic poem as 'perhaps the most daring piece of tone-painting in existence. It consists almost entirely of the picturing of the outward'.[8] And while there was undoubtedly a major expansion of material and resources in the orchestral work, its basic conception remains firmly rooted in that 1837 etude. In other words, it is hard to expel the lingering suspicion that in 1837 the Hugo poem was already in Liszt's mind. Whatever the truth of that, it is clear that Hugo figured in Liszt's life and reading in the 1830s; they were already acquainted in 1827, when Liszt was a mere sixteen-year-old, and they met frequently in social and musical circles, as Arnaud Laster has documented.[9] Hugo had a deep interest in music, with a taste for Gluck and Mozart, and, of the 'moderns', for Weber, Spontini and, above all, Beethoven.[10] Laster has suggested that it was in no small measure through his contacts with Liszt that Hugo was initiated into his lifelong appreciation of Beethoven. For both men, Beethoven was 'le plus grand musicien', and it is striking that Hugo went on to associate Beethoven and Shakespeare somewhat in the manner of a later 'New German' – and especially a Wagnerian – criticism. It is evident, then, that Liszt could readily find support in Hugo for his view of Beethoven as the major exponent of a modern, 'poetic' music. Indeed Hugo's tidy definition, 'La musique, c'est du bruit qui pense', takes on particular significance when we recall Liszt's remark, in a letter to Marie d'Agoult, that for the poet Beethoven was 'le plus grand penseur de cet art si rêveur'.[11] It is mainly through the *Mazeppa* works that the names of Liszt and Hugo have become

---

[8] Frederick Niecks, *Programme Music in the Last Four Centuries: A Contribution to the History of Musical Expression* (London and New York, [1907]), p. 302. This a familiar perception. Shortly after Niecks published his book, Theodor Bolte referred to the work as 'ein ausgesrochenes und wirksames Programm-Musikstück', in 'Liszt als Orchesterkomponist', *Neue Zeitschrift für Musik*, 42 (October 1911), pp. 573–6.

[9] Arnaud Laster, 'Victor Hugo, la Musique et les Musiciens', in Victor Hugo, *Oeuvres Complètes*, gen. ed. Jean Massin (Paris, 1967–71), vol. 5 no. 1, pp. i–xix. See also Norbert Miller, 'Elévation bei Victor Hugo und Franz Liszt: Über die Schwierigkeiten einer Verwandlung von lyrischen in symphonische Dichtungen', *Jahrbuch des Staatlichen Instituts für Musikforschung Preussischer Kulturbesitz* (Berlin, 1975), pp. 131–59.

[10] Interestingly, he had the greatest admiration for Paganini, but less for his virtuosity than his interpretative insights.

[11] Quoted, and contextualised, in Laster, 'Victor Hugo, la Musique et les Musiciens'.

associated. However, Liszt also set Hugo's poetry on several occasions, not least in a group of six songs published in 1844 (four of them later revised for an 1860 collection), and, as I noted earlier, he may even have borrowed the titles for *Paysage* and *Vision* from Hugo. It was also to his poetry that Liszt turned for the first of his 'overtures' (later, symphonic poems), *Ce qu'on entend sur la montagne*. Richard Pohl suggested that he had already planned a piece based on this poem, so resonant with Lisztian themes, in the early 1830s. But the symphonic poem as we now know it was conceived in the late 1840s (sketches were shown to Princess Sayn-Wittgenstein in 1847), even if it was substantially revised over the ensuing decade.[12] The *Bergsymphonie* was indeed the first of the orchestral works to be drafted. But I will later suggest that the original plan to write an 'overture' on *Mazeppa* may have pre-dated it. The story of the seventeenth-century Cossack hero Ivan Mazeppa was well known in Parisian circles in the early nineteenth century, partly from Book 4 of Voltaire's *Histoire de Charles XII*, but especially from Byron's ballad of 1819, itself drawing on the references in Voltaire.[13] In the Byron Mazeppa's extraordinary tale is told in recollection, as the old man recounts his youthful exploit to Charles on the battlefield 'after dread Pultowa's day'. In this way we learn of that most remarkable of rides, where Mazeppa is lashed to a wild horse by an outraged husband. 'Away! – Away!', and they begin their headlong gallop from Poland into the Ukraine, under a burning sun, over fields and heaths and through woods, then across a broad river, and, thus refreshed, again through woods, soon to be followed by packs of hungry wolves, to encounter other wild horses, who are put to flight by the strange sight; then, after three days, the collapse and death of the horse, with Mazeppa trapped there, trying to scare off the circling vultures by moving his fingers; finally deliverance by the Ukrainian Cossacks, as his fetters are untied; and in the more distant future, his elevation as a Cossack chief, 'wearing the pelisse of the ancient hetmans', as Hugo later put it.[14] Hugo's very much shorter poem, composed in May 1828 as part of the remarkable collection *Les Orientales*,[15] occupies itself with the ride itself (corresponding to section IX of the Byron), but in the second of its two sections it goes on to elaborate an allegory of the suffering artist, with the horse as the driving force of genius ('Génie, ardent coursier'), undergoing a kind of death and resurrection. It requires little imagination to see how such a tale, in which the artist heroically surmounts all obstacles to create a work that will enable him to triumph in

[12] For an account of the complicated source chain, see Keith Johns, *The Symphonic Poems of Franz Liszt*, rev. and ed. Michael Saffle (New York, 1996), pp. 139–40.

[13] For the Voltaire, see *Oeuvres Complètes de Voltaire* (new edition based on the Beughot edition [Paris, 1878], vol. 16, pp. 236–50). This was in a sense contemporary military history (written *c.* 1728–30), much of it based on first-hand accounts. The key players in the drama are Charles XII of Sweden and Peter the Great of Russia, and the story of Mazeppa (representing in a way the dilemma of the Ukraine, squeezed by Poland and Russia) is a short episode within it.

[14] Much later in life, Liszt recalled how he was charmed by this line ('des vieux hetmans il ciendra la pelisse'); see *The Letters of Franz Liszt to Olga von Meyendorff, 1871–1886*, trans. William R. Tyler, with introduction and notes by Edward N. Waters (Washington DC, 1979), p. 75.

[15] *Oeuvres Complètes*, vol. 3 no. 1, pp. 589–92. Hugo's poem was certainly indebted to the Byron, but it was also inspired by Louis Boulanger's painting, *Le Supplice de Mazeppa. Le Départ*, and was indeed dedicated to Boulanger. For a fuller discussion, see C. W. Thomson, *Victor Hugo and the Graphic Arts (1820–1833)* (Geneva, 1970), pp. 112–13.

Example 69 *12 Grandes Etudes*, No. 3 bars 4–7
12 Grandes Etudes, No. 4 bars 1–2

12 Grandes Etudes, No. 3 bars 4–7

12 Grandes Etudes, No. 4 bars 1–2

posterity, would have positively invited an act of self-identification on Liszt's part. 'Enfin le terme arrive . . . il court, il vole, il tombe, Et se relève roi!'

To explain the fourth of the *Grandes Etudes* through an association with this poem would be pure speculation. But we are entitled to speculate, or at least (more cautiously) to comment on those qualities of the music that might have encouraged Liszt to add the programmatic title a few years later. Already in the third etude he had used the figure from the original exercise as an accompaniment to a new melody, rather than elaborating or 'orchestrating' the figure itself. This may have suggested a similar procedure for the fourth, especially as in both cases the melody takes its impetus from a simple inversion of the original (Ex. 69). Liszt maintained the essential texture of the exercise in his accompaniment for the fourth etude, but changed its metrical and harmonic schemes to serve the new melody, which is without doubt the principal shaping element (unlike the third etude, where the melody recedes in importance). Of course, the conception of the piece, and in particular the relation between melody and accompaniment, is by no means conveyed by this description. Likewise, to describe the melody as loosely based on Classical principles of periodic construction is to convey nothing of its broad, sweeping character, resolute iambic rhythm and rolling circular motion, all contributing to its *Ur*-quality, a propulsive, relentless, undeviating energy. Moreover, the momentum generated by this long-breathed melody is intensified by the tight, unbending motoric drive of the accompaniment, which pushes the melody onwards determinedly from beneath. Liszt may not have had Hugo's horse and its hapless rider in mind, but no musical configuration could have more justly actualised the central image of

Example 70 *12 Grandes Etudes*, No. 4. Inflected repetitions

12 Grandes Etudes, No. 4. Inflected repetitions
Strophes

the poem. The subsequent strophes are usually described as variations,[16] but might better be considered modified repetitions or even thematic transformations. In brief, strophe 2 inflects the consequent chromatically, hinting briefly at A♭ major, and adds a new element at bar 33. Strophes 3 and 4 make up a contrasted central section in B♭ major, with thematic transformations drawing on elements of the first two strophes. Strophes 5 and 6 then have the character of a transformed reprise, in which the $\frac{6}{4}$ metre changes to $\frac{6}{8}$ and then to $\frac{2}{4}$. The chromatic inflection in strophe 6 reverses the direction of that in strophe 2, this time pointing momentarily towards A major, and the return of that extension to strophe 2 brings the piece to a close. The cycle of inflected repetitions may be represented as in Example 70 (strophe 5 follows the pattern in strophe 1).

The most crucial distinction between these strophes lies not so much in their varied melodic or harmonic profiles, however, as in the progressive compression of their accompaniment patterns. Example 71 indicates the sequence. And again Hugo's poem proves tempting. If the basic configuration of the etude captures the central poetic image to perfection, then its subsequent unfolding as a structural *accelerando*, propelled by the ever more feverish accompaniment patterns of the outer sections, seems to convey its narrative with no less authenticity. Of course, within this musico-poetic image and narrative certain things belong to the music rather than the poetry. For example, the central section is hard to account for in terms of Hugo's poem (though it could be fitted quite nicely to Byron's!), even if one commentator persuades himself of a link with the fifth verse.[17] Likewise, the bravura, cadenza-like passages that separate several of the strophes, possibly triggered by

[16] See, for example, Carl Dahlhaus, *Analysis and Value Judgement*, trans. Siegmund Levarie (New York, 1983; orig. edn, 1970), p. 76.

[17] James Bryant Conway, 'Musical Sources for the Liszt 'Etudes d'exécution transcendante: A Study in the Evolution of Liszt's Compositional and Keyboard Techniques', diss., University of Arizona (1969), p. 41.

Example 71 12 *Grandes Etudes*, No. 4 bars 1, 25, 56, 73, 106, 127

12 Grandes Etudes, No. 4

bar 1

bar 25

bar 56

bar 73

bar 106

bar 127

the consequent from the original exercise, have a largely structural function. But as soon as Liszt has authorised the poetic association in the third version of the piece, we have no trouble in accommodating such musical features, and can even allow them to influence our poetic understanding. Mazeppa, alone in the plains, drifts into a kind of reflective, semi-conscious reverie, very possibly recalling the fatal beauty which brought about his ordeal (the cantabile strophes); he rebuilds his energies between one obstacle and the next (the linking episodes). And so forth. Certainly the newly composed material in this version leaves us in little doubt. The prelude graphically 'whips' the horse into motion ('Un cri part . . .'), and the altered ending depicts the fall, together with Mazeppa's plaintive cry, and (briefly) his subsequent triumph.

When Liszt made his final revision in 1851, he used the opportunity to think again about the programmatic version of *Mazeppa*, recasting it in a more ambitious form. He had by then already composed the first draft of the symphonic poem. That at least was the order of composition on paper. At any rate, the prelude of the piano work combines material from the 1840 version and the symphonic poem. It is expanded not only through a 'stretching' and arpeggiation of the opening chords, and a revision of their registral placement, but by the addition of a *cadenza ad libitum* in octaves, based on the prelude to the symphonic poem. This builds a head of tension that strengthens the sense of arrival, or rather departure, at bar 7, where the reckless journey begins. Here, and elsewhere in this etude, Liszt's practice runs counter to the usual tendency of the final revision to simplify and reduce, in that he enlarges the dimensions of the earlier versions considerably. The changes to the first strophe are no less significant. As Example 72 indicates, the metre is now $\frac{2}{4}$, and the initial accompaniment figure is changed radically, not only in rhythm, but also in pitch, with the momentum of the music now greatly increased by the accented dissonances produced by the recomposed figure. In the course of this modification the etude detaches itself from the pitch structures of the original exercise, though it returns to the crossing-over of thirds, abandoned in versions 2 and 3. Here again the programme dictates, subordinating the accompaniment to the melody by simplifying the accompaniment pattern and reducing the space between melody notes. It is as though strophe 1 here aligns with strophe 5 of the original. Subsequent strophes also modify the rhythm and pitch structure of the accompaniment patterns of the earlier versions, as a comparison between Examples 71 and 72 indicates. But the principle of a progressive compression of materials in the outer sections is maintained, and the depiction of an increasingly demented, uncontrollable, fast and furious ride to retribution is all the more realistic.

The central section and the bridges either side of it are also entirely recast in the fourth of the piano versions of the etude. Here the impulse seems to have been formal rather than programmatic. The key point is that strophes 3 and 4 are translated into a real 'slow movement', their tonal differentiation from the outer sections (again a third-related scheme) supplemented by contrasts of texture and character. In the earlier versions, Liszt's marking for the B♭ major section was actually *un poco animato il tempo*, and in the very few performances which respect that marking the momentum of the music barely slackens. In the fourth version it is *lo stesso tempo*, and the contrast is heightened by a recomposition of the preceding bridge, so that there is less room to 'let down' the intensity. Strophe 3 is then given a much

Example 72 *Mazeppa* bars 7, 31, 63, 82, 117, 139

less fussy accompaniment (Ex. 72), allowing the melody to sing out, where in the earlier versions it competed with other layers; even details such as the change from d to d♭ in bar 69 enhance the sense of a slow movement, and incidentally refer across to the change of mode in the symphonic poem. And strophe 4 is similarly reconfigured, and at the same time chromatically enriched (Ex. 72). The later stages of strophe 4, immediately preceding the reprise, were clearly regarded as critical by Liszt, and the differences between versions require a little spelling out, especially as the two first editions of version 2 (No. 4 of the *Grandes Etudes*) are divergent. The Haslinger edition allows the music to subside from the C minor climax of strophe 4 by working a fragment of the melody before building the tension again in a chromatic ascent to the octaves cadenza preceding the reprise. The Schlesinger edition, on the other hand, continues to build from the climax, developing its cadential phrase in an ascending sequence that leads straight into the octaves cadenza, and this is the form also followed by version 3, the self-standing *Mazeppa*. Version 4 enlarges the passage by avoiding the C minor cadence altogether, and building through to a major climax in which chromatically descending $^6_4$ chords are emancipated from an accompanimental to an essential role, at which point they align themselves to the chromatic ascent from the Haslinger edition of version 2. This modification is entirely in line with the changes made to other etudes at this stage, in that its effect is to increase the sense of anacrusis to the reprise, and thus to privilege the reprise as the apex or fulcrum of the structure.

In general, then, the revisions were dictated partly by the programme, and partly by the same need for clarity of texture and form that we noted in connection with the other eleven etudes. On the other hand, where the ending of the etude is concerned, it is rather clear that Liszt's extension of the material in versions 2 and 3 was a direct response to Hugo's poem. As in version 3, the 'fall' is represented graphically by descending diminished-seventh chords, followed by a dramatic silence. But in the fourth version Mazeppa's cry is expanded into a very much fuller, more poignant, recitative, echoed by a contemplative, chorale-like phrase and punctuated by *secco* chords. This is rather obviously a depiction of Mazeppa helpless on the ground, as he struggles to release himself and then to drag himself across the ground ('ce condamné qui hurle et qui se traîne ce cadavre vivant...'). And following it Liszt gives us a full eleven bars of triumphant peroration ('la fanfare éclatante'), representing the hero's subsequent return as the ruler of the Cossack tribes. This greatly extends the chordal flourish of the earlier versions, though it still falls a long way short of the full-scale martial finale he composed for the symphonic poem. At the end of the piece Liszt leaves us in no doubt about his meaning, appending to the musical text the final words of Hugo's poem: ' "Il tombe enfin! ... et se relève Roi!" (Victor Hugo)'.

BEYOND BLACK AND WHITE

It seems that shortly after composing the third version of the etude, where for the first time he associated this music with Hugo's poem, Liszt gave some thought to an orchestral 'overture' with the title *Mazeppa*. In the so-called 'Lichnowsky' sketchbook (D-WRgs N8), used by Liszt between 1841 and 1845, there is a reference to '3 Ouvertures: Corsaire, Mazeppa, Sardanapale', though at this stage it was no more than an intention; there are as yet no musical sketches (Liszt was giving thought to an opera on *Sardanapale* in the early Weimar years). The overture was eventually drafted as a *particella*, a rough score laid out in anything between two and six systems, with general indications of scoring provided by the composer, and this source, part of the 'Mazeppa' draftbook (D-WRgs N2), is extant. As noted earlier, this was completed in January 1851, though there is no clear evidence of the precise period of drafting. Most of Liszt's early overtures were written in this form, and were then usually handed on to August Conradi or Joachim Raff, who orchestrated them more fully. The so-called 'Esquisse pour Mazeppa' held in the Bibliothèque Nationale, Paris (F-Pc Ms. 155) is a manuscript draft in the hand of Joachim Raff with copious annotations by Liszt,[18] including *Korrekturblätter*. It was certainly based on the *particella*, and it differs in many respects from the final version of the piece. For the early symphonic poems Liszt's usual practice was to correct the first version (often a Conradi score) in the light of early rehearsals and performances and then to give this corrected score to Raff, who would produce a definitive version in close collaboration with the composer. Accordingly, there is a further manuscript of *Mazeppa* in Raff's hand (D-WRgs A6), with minor corrections and additions by Liszt, which functioned as the Stichvorlage for the work and was almost certainly produced just before publication in 1854. There is, then, a three-stage source chain prior to the published score: the *particella*, the draft by Raff–Liszt, and the Stichvorlage in Raff's hand. The work was first performed in Weimar on 19 April 1854, and over the ensuing decade or so it had performances in Sondershausen, Vienna, St Petersburg, Leipzig, Magdeburg, Prague and Löwenberg.[19]

As the early source history suggests, there is more than a grain of truth in the traditional view that Liszt had a lot to learn about writing for the orchestra when he began his series of 'overtures' in Weimar. Of course he had extensive experience of making piano scores and transcriptions of orchestral works, notably of Beethoven and Berlioz. And, as many commentators have noted, such experience undoubtedly influenced his writing for the piano, including the etudes. This goes beyond the many implicit, and often conventional, references to orchestral instruments in the *Grandes Etudes* and *Transcendentals* (horn calls, trumpet fanfares, 'pastoral' cellos and flutes, bells, rushing scalar strings, brass choir, harp) to embrace the 'orchestral' scoring of some of their more climactic moments. Often this is achieved through *tremolo* writing which is less than subtle pianistically, but it can also involve the sort of sleight-of-hand that allows all registers of the keyboard to remain active, in a passing simulacrum of the orchestral *tutti*. Imitating the orchestra is one thing; composing for it another. And it is clear that Liszt was far from confident when it came to scoring his own orchestral music, at least during the early years at Weimar. On the other hand he quickly mastered the basics of the craft, and very soon found himself resisting the proposals of his associates. Bartók went much too far in describing an 'absolutely individual orchestral technique',[20] though it is true that there are remarkably individual moments, but

---

[18] For a general description of this manuscript, see Michael Saffle, 'Liszt Music Manuscripts in Paris', in *Liszt and his World* (New York, 1998), p. 120.

[19] Johns, *The Symphonic Poems of Franz Liszt*, pp. 84–6.

[20] Béla Bartók, 'Liszt Problems', in Suchoff (ed.), *Béla Bartók Essays* (London, 1976), p. 504. Compare Rosen: 'His orchestration is, in most cases, dreadful' (*The Romantic Generation* [London, 1995], p. 541).

competence at least was quickly within his grasp. He was, after all, embarking on a major change of orientation, nothing less than a transition from pianist-composer to composer. Interestingly, Chopin responded to a similar imperative at around the same time, though he was unable to see it through. But where Chopin looked towards chamber music, Liszt turned to the orchestra, and (later) the oratorio. His first attempts at independent orchestral works represent, then, a powerfully symbolic moment in his coming-of-age as a composer.

Although the concert overture was already treated as an independent genre in the mid-nineteenth century, several of Liszt's early orchestral 'overtures' retained some vestige of an original generic function, in that they were indeed intended to introduce something: a ceremony, a cantata, an opera. This is true of *Tasso*, *Prometheus* and *Orpheus*, though not of the *Bergsymphonie*, *Héroïde funèbre* or *Mazeppa*. It was really only in 1854 that he abandoned the title 'overture', released the music of all these pieces from a preludial role, and brought their poetic content to the fore by adding a preface. It was at this point that he came up with the term 'symphonic poem', and in some cases the revisions of the mid-1850s reflected, at least in part, the change of title and genre. In the case of *Mazeppa*, which was conceived from the start as an independent programme piece, the changes made in 1854 were motivated by purely musical considerations. By this stage Liszt had clarified his thinking on the nature of the genre and on what he took to be its historical significance. Something of this will be discussed in the final section of this chapter. But it will first be useful to locate the divergences between the orchestral and the fourth piano versions, and at the same time to trace the evolution of the former through its main compositional stages, identified below as *A* (*particella*), *B* (Raff-Liszt draft), *C* (Raff-Liszt Stichvorlage) and *D* (published score). This could form a major study in itself, but at least the main points can be outlined in a comparative section-by-section study of the different versions. Unless otherwise stated, bar numbers refer to *D*.

Introduction. The sequence of chords at the beginning of the piano etude is replaced in the symphonic poem by a single chord, which then launches the rushing anacrustic figuration on strings. As Niecks puts it, we begin with a shrill cry and then the wild horse is off. It is worth noting that this figuration first appears in the orchestral draft and is only later transferred to the piano version, though this version lacks both the important ascending scalar motive at bar 4 of *D*, and its inversion at bar 20. In the symphonic poem the introduction is bipartite, with an interim structural downbeat at bar 20, where the figuration ends and the energy levels are cranked up by the new sequential motive. Not all of this is present in the earlier versions. At the beginning, *A* and *B* have a sustained wind chord (semibreve), only later translated to a quaver in *C*. *A* has the rushing string figuration (albeit with several corrections) as in *D*, but not the rising scalar motives from bars 4–5 *et seq.* These were added in *B*, but clearly as an afterthought. The inversion of this motive introduced at bar 20 is present in both *A* and *B*, but the accompaniment sonority in the upper strings is very much simpler. The whole texture is filled out, and the rhythmicised horn motive added, only in *C*.

Strophes 1 and 2. Strophe 1 of the symphonic poem proceeds as in the piano version, with the big tune in trombones. However, the accompaniment pattern is radically changed. (One might indeed extend Exx. 71 and 72 to relate an interesting narrative of the many different accompaniments in successive versions of *Mazeppa*, as the pattern from the original exercise recedes, and the programme – embodied in the melody – takes over.) The interlude between these two strophes is extended in the symphonic poem, incorporating a version of the motive at bar 4 as well as a unison strings version of the transition used in the piano piece. In the symphonic poem Liszt considerably extends strophe 2 by working part of the main theme in F♯ minor. This, together with a repetition of the transition motive, leads (by way of an enharmonic pun) to B♭ minor for the 'slow movement', completing the circle of major thirds. In A the scoring indications are primitive and are not followed in either B or C. Moreover the accompaniment to the main theme in both A and B is a string-crossing pattern, changed to repeated notes in C, at least for the first part of the strophe (at bar 44 of C the original string-crossing accompaniment is used). The transition in A is an arpeggiated figure, and this is retained in B, to be replaced by a chromatic scalar figure in C. The unison strings figure is also extended by three bars in C. In strophe 2 the accompaniment figure in A and B is again rather different (more pianistic) and the final stages of the strophe are more compressed than in C. The transition (from the change of key signature at bar 84) is also greatly expanded in C, notably through the insertion yet again of the unison strings figure, now in F♯ minor. Even more significant is the omission of the fourteen-bar preludial passage (bars 108–21 of D) from both A and B.

Strophes 3 and 4. The change of mode from B♭ major to B♭ minor is the most telling transformation from piano to orchestral versions here, though B♭ major (which is the key signature throughout) is briefly restored at the end of strophe 3. An expanded form of the unison string figure then acts as a transition between the two central strophes, with strophe 4 now appearing in B minor. In the symphonic poem strophe 4 then leads into an extended development section, working two fragments from the main theme and culminating in an E major transformation of the theme in the form of a climactic peroration, immediately prior to the reprise. This entire section from strophe 4 to the reprise is a massive expansion of the material in the piano piece, its sequential journey through different tonal plateaus strongly suggestive of the different stages of the wild ride. It is striking how much more crude are the earlier versions of this slow movement and development section, especially in their orchestration, as suggested in A and realised in B. Formally, the first key difference is the transition between the two strophes, which in A and B is a short passage of some eight bars, entirely lacking the unison string transition. The approach to the E major climax is different in all three manuscript versions, proceeding in the direction of a gradual refinement where B already suggests the formulation in C and D. But most striking of all is the return of the introductory rushing string figuration in both A and B in preparation for the reprise, replaced in C by a dramatic pause and ruthlessly hammered cadential chords.

Strophes 5 and 6. The orchestral version follows the piano piece reasonably closely here, except for an expanded transition between the two strophes, again culminating in the unison string figure. The other major difference is in the final stage of strophe 6, in preparation for a considerably expanded version of the programmatic 'fall', signalled by a fatalistic tread on timps. Here the opening of the principal melody (representing a broken Mazeppa) is added to the fragments of recitative. The essential differences in the earlier versions, aside from orchestration, are again a shorter, simpler transition (the unison string figure is lacking in both A and B) and a less elaborated representation of the 'fall'.

Finale. At this point an entirely new section is added in the symphonic poem, introduced by trumpet fanfares representing the arrival of the Cossacks. It is based on two themes, a triumphant march in D major, which reworks material from Liszt's earlier *Arbeitetchor* (1849), and a pastiche oriental theme in D minor (Liszt changes the scoring of this passage in *C* by doubling the theme on second violins). This theme, with its modal inflection, ornamentation and triangle accompaniment, both echoes the 'Turkish' music of a Classical repertory and strikingly anticipates a soundworld characteristic of Russian composers such as Balakirev and Borodin. Following a developmental working of this oriental melody there is a transformation of the march, with both themes intertwined with the trumpet fanfare; indeed as the main climax approaches all three elements are present in the texture. The *dénouement* is the *grandioso* return of the Mazeppa theme in the closing moments of the work, a powerfully synthetic gesture that is not present in either of the earlier versions. Interestingly, the original ending was extended by the composer in *C*. Liszt went so far as to suggest to Wilhelm Wieprecht that this march finale might lend itself to an arrangement for military band ('It must *begin* with the ⅜ chord [*sic*], perhaps after a couple of introductory bars *roll* on the drum – without any *distinct* tone').[21]

It is clear even from this brief summary that the first of the Raff–Liszt manuscripts is in essence an orchestration of the *particella*, following its broad formal outlines and many of its pointers for instrumentation reasonably closely. Indeed the one was almost certainly drafted hard on the heels of the other. The second of the manuscripts, on the other hand, represents a rather major reworking of the material, clearly stemming from Liszt though in Raff's hand. Liszt's corrections on this manuscript are of a relatively minor nature, including additional dynamic indications, reformulations of the scoring (notably in the E major section and in the final march) and some rethinking of the substance (at bar 150, for example, and in the very final bars). The distance between the first of Raff's manuscripts and the Stichvorlage is indeed a persuasive testament to Liszt's rapid acquisition of new skills in the early 1850s. Nor is this simply a matter of a greatly refined orchestral palette, instantly apparent from a glance at the two manuscripts. It also has a bearing on the form and proportions of the work.

In rethinking the proportions of *Mazeppa*, Liszt was motivated by his growing realisation that there needed to be a greater difference in scale between the piano etude and the symphonic poem than the original drafts allowed. The basic outline of the work remained the same in its final form, of course, with its six strophes preserved. However, the transition passages were extended, and at the same time made more cohesive, partly by inserting the unison string figure between strophes 2 and 3, and again between strophes 3 and 4. The development section was also extended, the approach to the reprise rendered at once more dramatic and more programmatically coherent (the return of the opening figuration in the earlier versions is difficult to account for programmatically), and the 'fall' given a more graphic and expressive quality. Most telling of all was the decision to bring back the Mazeppa theme at the end of the finale, a gesture of cyclical return that is at the same time a potent representation of the triumphant elevation of Mazeppa as a Cossack Chief. The result is a

---

[21] *Letters of Franz Liszt*, coll. and ed. La Mara, trans. Constance Bache, 2 vols. (London, 1894), vol. 1, p. 278.

work whose later stages can be rather easily related to *Tasso* (as Arthur Hahn suggests, in a study that offers a line-by-line account of the programme, relating the music to Hugo's poem at almost every point)[22] through its archetypal sequence of lament and triumph.

It remains to consider briefly the later arrangements for two pianos and for four hands. It seems that Liszt originally planned to make the four-hand arrangements of the symphonic poems in 1855–6, and made a start with *Tasso*. However, he 'soon gave up this project . . . on account of the unadvisable mutilation and defacement by the working into and through one another of the four-hand parts, and submitted to doing without tone and colour and *orchestral light and shade*, but at any rate fixing an abstract rendering of the musical contents, which would be clear to the ear, by the two-piano arrangement'.[23] Accordingly he made the two-piano arrangement in 1855, and only much later (1874) attempted a version for four hands. It goes without saying that as arrangements both are masterpieces, with the two-piano version the more effective of the two. But what is really most interesting about them is how limitations of medium are turned to creative account by Liszt, so that the music assumes at times a significantly different character. Our narrative of the accompaniments could be extended yet further here, for example, since the Mazeppa theme is given yet another textural backcloth in these settings. Moreover, in the case of the later four-hand arrangement there is even a rethinking of the dimensions of the central section of the work, with the bridging material preceding the B♭ minor strophe reduced by thirteen bars (the recomposition begins from bar 104), and a parallel abridgement preceding the B minor strophe. I can think of no reason particular to the medium that might have dictated this change, which was in all likelihood a modest rethinking of the form of the work at this late stage. Elsewhere the differences are to do with the redistribution of voices and the redesigning of textures. But at times, and especially in the interludes and transitions, Liszt introduces new elements, born of the constraints of the medium. In the final stages of the introduction of the two-piano version, for example, he replaces the flute scalar figure of the original (bar 20 ff.) with an arpeggiated 'rocket' figure, entirely different in layout, though similar in effect. In other words, like all Liszt's transcriptions, these are more than just transcriptions, and might reasonably be thought of as additional versions.

TESTS OF TIME

The story of *Mazeppa* has modest beginnings. A simple exercise, conventionally crafted, adopts the manners and materials of a wider repertory. Through its idiomatic figures, it documents the wider practice of pianism; it exemplifies a genre. Looming behind it – making it possible – is a larger world of pedagogues, publishers, salons and concerts. And of course the public. The exercise is conformist in orientation, hardly really a work, in the sense of a unique, self-standing, expressive utterance transcending the moment of its creation. Its transformation into a *Grande Etude* in 1837 opens the figures out to a quite other and larger ambition. Designed for Liszt to perform, the etude celebrates the sheer joy of display,

---

[22] Arthur Hahn, *Franz Liszt: Symphonische Dichtungen* (Leipzig, 1920), p. 99.
[23] La Mara (ed.), *Letters of Franz Liszt*, vol. 1, p. 273.

the pride of mastery, the relish of power. It salutes the potency of the instrument and the authority of technique, both of them triumphs of rationality and mechanism. It channels our attention towards a single point, the action of the performer. Form and expression are weighted down – suppressed – by a gestural surface matted with technical difficulties. Event character is paramount. In the 1840 version, the addition of a programmatic title effects yet another transformation, and one that is hardly proportionate to the modest textual changes. This version is self-standing, a programmatic character piece in which the focus has shifted from the hero at the keyboard to the hero of the programme. Even the technical difficulties appear to recede as they gain poetic justification, for the programme itself embodies an ethical premise of virtuosity: that success should be hard-won. Then, in the 1851 revision, *Mazeppa* is once more part of a cycle of etudes. Here the performative yields not just to the programmatic but to the formative, to compositional qualities that might judge it well composed, to shape and articulation, coherence and differentiation. The etude is designed to withstand scrutiny. It allows an accommodation of virtuosity and work character, where the latter embodies a symbiosis of programme and form. Precisely that symbiosis might be regarded as the ideal of the symphonic poem as a genre, and it is in the symphonic poem *Mazeppa* that the materials originating in Liszt's little exercise reach their most ambitious formulation. To paraphrase Goethe, they may not imitate the frenzied ride, but they excite in us through their artistic qualities something of the feeling of that ride. Here the musical work triumphs over the claims of genre and performance, though not perhaps of history. For victories may be pyrrhic.

Writing in 1906, Niecks remarked that Liszt's symphonic poems had been before the public for about half a century, but had still not become popular.[24] His brief reception history pits Ramann against Hanslick, Weingartner against Riemann. The adversely critical voices sing a now-familiar song, telling of incoherent, rhapsodic, loosely constructed forms, of bombastic, flowery and sentimental content. The counter arguments are no less forcefully made, and there are those (Saint-Saëns, Kretzschmar, Ambros, Lobe) who sit on the fence, acknowledging the creative power of this music while pointing to its technical and formal limitations. It is by no means obvious that the jury has yet returned, a full century after Niecks pronounced it 'out'. Even the most informal inspection of recording catalogues and concert programmes suggests that, despite their centrality to Liszt's entire creative enterprise, the symphonic poems are still regarded as marginal to the symphonic canon. They have not been forgotten, but they are by no means as popular as those of Richard Strauss, nor as regularly played and recorded as a select group of symphonic poems from the Russian and Czech schools of the late nineteenth century. Nor did they inaugurate a music of the future. The history of the symphonic poem turned out in the end to be a brief chapter, while the symphony, gloriously misrepresented by Franz Brendel as a prehistory of the symphonic poem, is still with us.[25] In all of this we confront directly the vexed issue of quality and value in Liszt, not only in the symphonic poems, but in his music generally.

---

[24] *Programme Music in the last Four Centuries*, p. 316.
[25] In the revised (1862) edition of his history. The description 'prehistory of the symphonic poem' is Dahlhaus's. See *Esthetics of Music*, trans. William Austin (Cambridge, 1982; orig. edn, 1967), p. 63.

It is difficult to steer a course here between a relativism that would in the end reduce to personal preference and an absolutism that borders on theology. The most innocent of starting-points might be to consider functional judgements, where the value of the aim is not in question. There can be little doubt about how the fourth of the *Grandes Etudes* will fare if we judge it purely and simply as 'virtuoso music', by which I mean music whose primary aim is to prescribe virtuosity. This is by no means a cut-and-dried category, and is perhaps better thought of as an orientation than a genre. But at least we can claim that it assigns to the performer a major responsibility for actualising the musical meaning; our interest is as much in how he is playing as in what he is playing. For a work-orientated criticism, this condition will naturally be found wanting; hence Schumann's cautionary word about the *Grandes Etudes*: 'Great results can only be produced by great causes, and a public cannot be brought to enthusiasm for nothing'.[26] But virtuosity is, after all, about doing, not making. As noted earlier, its tendency is to sacrifice reference to mechanism and structure to surface. 'Virtuoso music', then, stands or falls on the success of an event, and that in turn is contingent on the technique and charisma of the performer. Moreover, since the event is not repeatable, the gestures which prescribe its musical effects can carry their own justification. The score may contain hidden meanings, worthy of contemplation, but its primary role is to programme an effective performance. It is tempting to glance across at some of today's popular music. Here too much of the emotion and meaning is injected by the persuasive performer, often through an intensional complexity that imbues the individual moment with weight, significance, and even depth. It is fairly obvious that scores in these repertories, where they exist at all, provide minimal information. On a fairly simple groundplan, the performer works his or her magic, inflecting the melody through tonal and ornamental variation and investing repetitions with constantly changing significance. The analogy should not be pushed too far, but it is perfectly reasonable to suggest that as work character came to assume more importance within the Western tradition, the performative was marginalised, finding a more congenial home in the world of popular culture.

As a 'warhorse' the fourth etude passes muster. Like at least one other warhorse, however, it is not entirely what it might seem. It smuggles in a larger ambition to meet the claims not just of a performance culture welded to the immediate and the sensational (in a literal meaning) but of a compositional culture premised on the atemporal and the thoughtful (also in a literal meaning). Performer and composer may have been one and the same, but they were not necessarily in harmony. The performance event, after all, can validate features of 'virtuoso music' that might well prove troubling in later contemplation. Even at the simplest level of articulating an accompanied melody, the opening of the fourth etude illustrates this tension (Ex. 71). In live performance the visible technical difficulties of maintaining the pattern of the exercise as an accompaniment to the melody can make for an exciting effect. However, their tendency is to inhibit the momentum of the melody, so that it is very difficult to preserve the sense of a high-tempo energy, even in the most agile hands. The success of the event is to a crucial extent performer-dependent. If we compare this with the 1851 revision (Ex. 72), we have a graphic illustration of the swerve from performer to composer. Here the

---

[26] Robert Schumann, *On Music and Musicians*, trans. P. Rosenfeld, ed. K. Wolff (London, 1946), p. 152.

melody is given its head, driven by an accompaniment that has been strategically distributed to facilitate unimpeded execution. And similar comparisons might be made for the third and fourth strophes – the middle section of the etude – where the concentration of detail in the 1837 accompaniment (Ex. 71), demanding the most skilful control of hierarchical levels on the part of the performer, is reduced to a simple monolithic pattern in 1851 (Ex. 72). In both instances the revision allows the separate elements of the texture to come into sharper relief. Moreover, this impulse towards greater clarity is perceptible in the formal revisions too. As I noted earlier, the 1851 version strengthens the formal differentiation between the outer sections of the etude and the middle section, and recasts the later stages of that section to enable a greater sense of climactic preparation for the reprise. In general the formal outlines are clearer and the virtuosity is more structural in the later version. In a word, there is a greater focus on self-reflective work character, where meanings are presumed to be less dependent on performance contexts.

For all this concern for work character, the genre title 'etude' and the supplementary specification 'of transcendental execution' still invite us to regard the 1851 version of the fourth etude as 'virtuoso music'. On the other hand, the programmatic title immediately distracts us from this categorisation, and points us in a rather different direction. How, we may now ask, does *Mazeppa* fare as an example of programme music? No doubt it should be obvious that to evaluate a programme piece as though it were a sonata is an elementary error. Yet it is an error commonly made; witness the recitation, familiar from Schumann onwards, about programme music 'standing up' (or not) in purely musical terms. As noted in the last chapter, the content of a programmatic work is encapsulated in the dialogue and interplay between programme and form, understanding form in the broadest possible sense to signify a non-referential configuration. There seems no just cause, then, to take it to task for failing to achieve something that was never in its sights. How we listen is perhaps another matter. Yet even those of us who find it hard to focus on the words of a Schubert song are prone to admit that they are an essential component of the piece, and would remain so, even if the composer had added them to existing music. Where programme music is concerned, the dialogue may of course be a bit one-sided, especially where the title is generalised, as in *Paysage* or *Vision*. In such cases the music works hard to flesh out a rather undernourished programmatic image. But even if one-sided, there is still a dialogue. And in *Mazeppa* the programme feeds generously into the work, with both a narrative thread and a suggestive analogy between that narrative and artistic creativity.

I have already noted that there are three points at which Liszt changed the text of the fourth *Grande Etude* after its first publication: the new introduction, the representation of the 'fall', and the end of the fourth strophe prior to the reprise. Moreover, at all three points he made further substantive changes in the *Transcendentals* and in the symphonic poem. The first two changes were programmatic, and were made in 1840. We may compare the three introductions added by Liszt to the *Grande Etude*. In 'purely' musical terms, the brisk anticipatory gesture in the 1840 version weakens the powerful opening (*in medias res*) of the 1837 version, but has the obvious and immediate poetic justification of graphically inaugurating the ride. The greatly extended cumulative introduction to the symphonic poem, with its own thematic argument, is also explicitly programmatic, but here the ride itself is already underway prior to the Mazeppa theme. The fourth of the *Transcendentals* fuses these two, adding some of the figuration from the symphonic poem to the opening chords from the 1840 version, but again postponing the ride until the appearance of the Mazeppa theme. Here the opening, with its powerfully anacrustic figuration, is musically stronger than in 1837 but less satisfactory from a programmatic standpoint than in 1840. In contrast, the 'fall' and the subsequent triumph are represented in a perfunctory way in 1840 but enlarged and specified in 1851, even to the point where it is only the programme that saves the final cadence from bombast. It is in the finale of the symphonic poem, however, that the programme really comes to the fore, in the 'fall' itself, in the fanfares that announce the approaching Cossacks, in the double characterisation of them as martial (war-like) and exotic, and in the graphic reappearance of Mazeppa in triumph at the end. The third change is formal rather than programmatic. In the Schlesinger edition of the *Grandes Etudes* and in the self-standing *Mazeppa* Liszt allows the fourth strophe to open out into a brief developmental passage in order to strengthen the subsequent reprise. However the effect of this is all but annulled by its placement *after* the climax of the strophe. In the 1851 version he resolves this difficulty by removing the climax, and directing the head of tension towards the reprise. In the symphonic poem he goes further, translating the second half of the strophe into a full-scale development section, of which the reprise is a conventionally necessary outcome.

In looking at the larger design of the symphonic poem, we can hardly avoid addressing some of the standard criticisms of Liszt's instrumental music: an excessive dependence on repetition, a preference for weakly bound formal units, and in general a looseness of construction embodied in the term 'episodic'. It will be worth invoking Schubert again. Relative to Classical models, Schubert's extended forms can also appear diffuse and even distended, but a top-down hierarchical structure still seems to bind them together, albeit along rather different lines from Beethoven. Right from the first of his symphonic poems, *Ce qu'on entend sur la montagne*, and even in its early drafts, it is clear that Liszt was attempting something very different.[27] That he was capable of a taut structure is evidenced by several non-programmatic works, and especially by the B minor Sonata, but in the bigger single-movement programme pieces he allowed narratives of thematic transformation to intersect with still-active formal archetypes (often employing 'double' structural functions), loosening the form and opening it out to the poetic impulse.[28] Both thematic narrative and form contribute to the dramatic plot, which is often gathered around key climactic points or expressive goals, and the plot in its turn is understood in light of the programme. It is interesting to compare the two Hugo-inspired works, the *Bergsymphonie* and *Mazeppa*, in this respect. The former spreads a plethora of related motives across a 'stretched' sonata-allegro form in which the expressive goals are two presentations of a powerful (if subdued),

---

[27] Although the initial version was composed 1848–9, the piece was reworked several times before publication in 1857; see the source history in Johns, *The Symphonic Poems of Franz Liszt*, pp. 139–40.

[28] See Carl Dahlhaus, 'Liszts Bergsymphonie und die Idee der symphonischen Dichtung', *Jahrbuch des Staatlichen Institut für Musikforschung* (1975), pp. 96–130; and 'Liszts Idee des Symphonischen', in Serge Gut (ed.), *Liszt-Studien 2: Kongress-Bericht Eisenstadt 1978* (Munich and Salzburg, 1981), pp. 36–42. See also Joachim Bergfeld, *Die formale Strucktur der Symphonische Dichtungen Franz Liszt* (Eisenach, 1931).

synthesising chorale theme. Yet for all the analytical rigour of the motivic web, the sequence of events appears discursive, since it is determined as much by semantic – programmatic and expressive – exigencies as by any formal requisition.[29] Nor should this be regarded as an adverse criticism. *Mazeppa*, on the other hand, is unified to a fault, with successive varied repetitions of a single theme driving the music across a compressed, undifferentiated sonata-form background to its Nemesis; I leave aside the march, which is really a joined-on finale. In *Mazeppa* the poetic element seeks to justify the lack of differentiation relative to the formal archetype; in the *Bergsymphonie* it seeks to justify an excess of differentiation.

The thematic narratives in both works rely on a poeticisation or characterisation of their basic building blocks. Here cross-referencing within the entire cycle of symphonic poems helps focus topoi such as the elementalised nature motives, the 'ethereal' strings and harp, and the chorales of the *Bergsymphonie*, as well as the equestrian, martial and oriental themes of *Mazeppa*.[30] The quest for a characteristic theme, whether or not it is explicitly programmatic, was of course an essential component of Liszt's understanding of the poetic. A self-sustaining theme of this kind would ideally have the power to move us deeply. Yet while this quest was integral to programme music, it could prove a high-risk strategy, prone to an exaggerated display of sentiment. Or at least so it might seem to the listener who persists in ignoring the programmatic dimension of the piece. It could encourage, in other words, the over-emphatic, the sentimental, the extravagant, the theatrical, the affected, the sensational, even the hysterical. Such qualities are rather easily accommodated by us in the opera house, but they are liable to be reduced to 'effects' – or, worse still, to kitsch – on the concert platform, where a validating programmatic component struggles to remain in our consciousness. This was really what Wagner meant when he referred to 'melodrama music', and suggested that any such tendencies would be more appropriately placed at the service of the drama.[31] In other words, programme music, like virtuoso music, runs some risk of being heard as a parade of effects, and the more so if our critical vantage point is unsympathetic to the genre and its ambitions. It may seem hard in today's world to restore the terms of a functional judgement for either category without in the end reducing the music to an historical document.

This is another way of saying that both the virtuoso tradition and the symphonic poem were discredited in the era of Modernism, and have not really been rehabilitated. The rise of the recording industry, and the related decline of a recital culture, proved inimical to virtuosity and friendly to the work-concept; moreover, academic musicology fell into line, persistently focusing on the work as a text and ignoring its status in performance. Likewise, programmes and the poetic had a hard time in the twentieth century, proving no match for the twin ascendancies of a symphonic canon and an avant-garde, to say nothing of the

---

[29] For a comprehensive study of motivic working in the *Bergsymphonie*, see Alfred Heuss 'Eine motivisch-thematische Studie über Liszts symphonische Dichtung "Ce qu'on entend sur la montagne"', *Zeitschrift der Internationalen Musikgesellschaft*, 13 (1911–12), pp. 10–21. See also the study of formal design, motives and tonality, together with an attempt to relate these to Hugo's poem, in Rey M. Longyear, 'Structural Issues in Liszt's Symphonic Poems', in Michael Saffle (ed.), *Liszt and his World*, pp. 247–70.

[30] See the relevant discussion in Johns, *The Symphonic Poems of Franz Liszt*, pp. 17–45.

[31] See Chapter 6, note 49.

formalism and positivism of musicology. There are some indications that new directions in scholarship, and perhaps even in compositional praxis, might allow for a more receptive climate in the future: the reinvention of virtuosity, without its heroic dimension, in some late-Modernist repertories (Berio, Carter, Ferneyhough[32]); the new performer freedoms embraced by others; and the developing interest in performance in recent musicology, tantamount to reclaiming music as a performing art (so-called 'performance studies' have been all but institutionalised in the academy). Then there is the wider challenge to music and musicology of a postmodern culture, where the austerities and exclusions of Modernism and formalism have yielded to the contextual and the cross-disciplinary; scholars look for putative narratives in sonatas and symphonies, while composers make them explicit through titles, and even programmes. Where Liszt reception is concerned, all this ought to be good news. Yet it is perhaps a little too soon to uncork the champagne. If we are to risk a generalisation based on the most informal assessments of popularity, it seems that modern audiences are sympathetic towards epic pretensions only when they are allied to so-called 'absolute' music (the symphony), and, conversely, that they are at ease with programme music – unembarrassed by it – only when its ambitions are modest: in a word, when it is pictorial and illustrative rather than epic in character. The heroic affect, innocent of irony, may have been attuned to an Idealist age, but it has seemed less amenable to modern sensibilities, whether in the guise of virtuoso music or programme music. Of course, all that could change.

In 1970, some time before the brouhaha about 'new' musicologies, Carl Dahlhaus used the symphonic poem *Mazeppa* as one of the case studies in his book *Analysis and Value Judgement*.[33] One can argue both about the analysis and the value-judgement. Dahlhaus mystifies Liszt's decision to translate the B♭ major of the middle section to B♭ minor, and then to transpose this to a less remote B minor, and he stretches the credulity of theorist and listener alike by suggesting that the inflected repetitions in strophes 2 and 6 offer 'a distant analogy to the changed tonality in a new key area of a sonata form'. Even his reading of the form is questionable; his Variation 4 is in reality the climax of a development section that had been expanding through successive versions of the piece since 1837; in other words, it is not a separate strophe, but an extension of Variation 3 (my strophe 4 in the earlier discussion). And to argue that this climax should have coincided with the reprise – their separation is an 'aesthetic-formal flaw' – is to take an oddly prescriptive view of formal process within a genre that encouraged, in Dahlhaus's own language, 'differentiated forms emanating from the interweaving of diverse principles'. On the other hand, one can admire the historical sympathy that enabled Dahlhaus to expose a deep-rooted problem in Liszt's reputation, both in the nineteenth century and the twentieth. His argument can be summarised in two theses: that in the nineteenth century neither the New Germans nor the formalists gave Liszt's 'differentiated forms' their due (for the one group they were 'merely a function of content', while for the other they were 'formless'); and that there was

---

[32] Ferneyhough, too, has his 'Transcendental Etudes', transposing something of Liszt's enterprise to a later century (rather than replicating it, as Liapunov did in his attempt to complete Liszt's cycle with an additional twelve etudes).

[33] See Dahlhaus, *Analysis and Value Judgement*, pp. 75–9.

a comparable aporia in the twentieth century between the 'admiring technical interest' of theorists and the 'aesthetic mistrust' of critics. This is thoughtful, and the second thesis may well have described the state of affairs in German scholarship and criticism in 1970. I am not certain that it holds today, though if I am right this merely reinforces Dahlhaus's larger point about the historical constitution of taste. Liszt has been much investigated by theorists and analysts since 1970 (see footnotes 35–64 to chapter 5), but by and large this work is unpolluted by questions of value; indeed the more technically sophisticated its descriptions, the less inclined it seems to pass judgement. On the other hand, as noted earlier, it is by no means implausible that the development of a more critically orientated musicology since 1970, at least in Anglo-American scholarship, may prove receptive to Liszt's quest for the poetic. That would effectively reverse Dahlhaus's characterisation of theoretical and critical perspectives; I leave out of the reckoning here the kind of rehabilitation that amounts to Liszt fetishism.

That Dahlhaus felt able to speak of 'aesthetic-formal flaws' and 'semi-failures' indicates that he allowed some room for aesthetic judgement beyond the historical contingencies he invoked. The possibility that we might preserve some element of unmediated Kantian aesthetic judgement is indeed a tantalising one, given the 'overcoming' of aesthetics proposed by Hegel in the nineteenth century (because art disclosed the world inefficiently), and by Heidegger in the twentieth (because it disclosed the world all too efficiently); given too the widespread reduction of the aesthetic to the cognitive or the political in present-day critical theory, or alternatively to the ethical among more conservative critics. We may ask, then, two things. What are the contingent factors that conspired to marginalise or problematise Liszt? And, in light of these factors, are we still able to speak of aesthetic success or failure? To answer the first question we need to revisit our historical narrative of the piano and its repertory, and then briefly to sketch a similar narrative for the orchestra.[34] Earlier I described a journey from the real to the ideal piano, from performance to work, from salon to recital. The piano recital, gaining in institutional strength through the second half of the nineteenth century (as it was harnessed to the consolidation of middle-class interests), became the ceremony of the atemporal work. That the recital was increasingly centred on an *un*pianistic exemplary repertory, Bach and Beethoven, is somehow fitting, for it was to be one of the principal sites of the conquest of virtuosity and the performative by an aesthetic of absolute music in the late nineteenth and early twentieth centuries. By then, the practice of pianism had congealed into recital programmes whose structure was recognisably that of today, with hierarchies of value plain to see: a new testament, an old testament, an improving literature, including some of a dangerously Modernist persuasion, and finally, as though to set the canon in relief, occasional concessions to the more frothy or sentimental novellas of popular taste.

By definition, canons exclude. They exclude repertory, but they also exclude categories. Thus the success of the work was achieved at the expense of the performer. Improvisation and virtuosity were among the casualties, but in more general terms the capacity of the

---

[34] A comparable narrative could be constructed for sacred music, and again Liszt's placement and standing would be ambiguous.

performer to generate musical meaning outside the orbit of putative compositional intentions was steadily drained from pianistic practice, and from most of the Western tradition. This may seem an odd claim in light of performance traditions in the first quarter of the twentieth century, where a 'virtuoso tradition', however much it had receded compositionally, fought its corner on the concert platform. 'It's not a question of what's written', proclaimed Paderewski. 'It's a question of musical effect.'[35] It is true that the individuality of the interpreter was all-important in the practice at this time, and that notorious licence was taken with the musical text. Yet even Paderewski's blunt affirmation of a position argued rather more subtly by Busoni needs to be evaluated carefully. At root it still commits to the idea embodied in the composer's work, but argues that the clarification of that idea may well need some attunement of the imperfect configuration of notational symbols. In any case this philosophy of performance was soon to become the way of the past, pushed to the margins by a growing industry of records and recordings, and, as Kenneth Hamilton suggests, at some cost to 'interest, spontaneity and sheer panache'.[36] As I noted earlier, the performative as an active constituent of musical meaning does still have a place in today's world, but that place is above all to be found in the realm of popular culture; here it remains alive and well.

If we stand back from this broad historical narrative, and evaluate Liszt's place within it, we would be hard pushed to argue that he was a marginalised figure. Not only was he a pioneer of the piano recital, at least in its mid-nineteenth-century form; his playing and teaching in later life, or so we are led to believe, moved more and more in the direction of fidelity to the score, at least where the composer was deemed to merit this. Compositionally, too, he fell in step. His revisions in the early Weimar years, including the transformation of the *Grandes Etudes* into the *Transcendentals*, were designed to 'make available' his virtuoso pieces to an increasingly work-orientated practice, while his development of the *poème pianistique*, whose aesthetic was crystallised in the preface to the *Album d'un Voyageur*, helped establish a renovative work-concept for later nineteenth-century pianism. For all that, his earlier career, and a substantial body of the music composed during his virtuoso years (even in its later revised form), ensured that his reputation as 'merely' a pianist-composer proved hard to shake off. That meant a tendency to push the etudes towards 'virtuoso music', and the poetic works towards 'salon music'. Somehow Liszt fell between the cracks of solid, secure classifications in late nineteenth- and early twentieth-century reception. If we are to attribute this to contingent rather than immanent factors, they might well be the hardening edges of categories of style and taste at the time. At risk of leaping too far, I suggest that three categories of music – Classical, avant-garde and commercial – were firming up and separating out, and that there was less and less leakage between them. Liszt's piano music often straddles these categories, and for this reason it risks offering something to everyone, but leaving no one fully satisfied. All that said, his place in recital programmes throughout the twentieth century and into the twenty-first was and is secure. If we have reservations about his piano music, they are not born of any lack of familiarity.

---

[35] Quoted (and sourced) in Adam Zamoyski, *Paderewski* (London, 1982), p. 95.
[36] Kenneth Hamilton, 'The Virtuoso Tradition', in David Rowland (ed.), *The Cambridge Companion to the Piano* (Cambridge, 1998), p. 74.

The story is rather different for the orchestral music, and especially for the symphonic poems, whose aesthetic is distinct from that of the *poème pianistique*. In 1824 A. B. Marx used the pages of the *Berliner allgemeine musikalische Zeitung* to describe 'an alliance ... in the realm of music, proceeding from Germany as its middle point'. He was referring here to Beethoven and the ascendancy of a German symphonic tradition, but also (implicitly) to the metaphysical aspiration of 'absolute music', embodied in a discourse of autonomy that highlighted a deep-rooted conjunction of ideas and feeling. Yet although an aesthetic of absolute music, of its nature purporting to transcend history, was a product of the Enlightenment and early Romanticism, it acquired its regulative authority only in the second half of the nineteenth century and beyond. It remained closely associated with the Beethoven orchestra, but as it blossomed into a larger symphonic canon it was increasingly linked to developing ideas of German identity and nationhood. In writing of the *Symphonie fantastique*: 'So much for the programme. He can keep it as far as we Germans are concerned', Schumann was already (perhaps unwittingly) placing a marker for that link. And even Franz Brendel, for all his later commitment to the revitalising power of the symphonic poem, complained in his *History* of trivial tone-painting in orchestral music (as he complained of virtuosity in piano music), comparing it unfavourably with Beethoven's spiritual qualities, the embodiment of *deutsche Innerlichkeit*. It proved extraordinarily hard to 'place' Liszt's enterprise as an orchestral composer within this national canon of symphonic music, firmed up in festivals, concert life and publishing enterprises. Undoubtedly his aim was an ambitious one – precisely to recapture something of the innovatory profundity of Beethoven's forms through the medium of the symphonic poem – and in pursuing it he gained the full support of Brendel. Not only did this represent a commitment to work character; it amounted to nothing less than an attempt to formulate an epopoeia for orchestral music, just as the Wagnerian music drama tried to do something similar for opera.

Les Préludes apart, the symphonic poems were not euphorically received on their early performances.[37] There may have been straightforward practical reasons for this in the case of early try-outs in Weimar (as the early versions of *Mazeppa* indicate, the orchestrations were often more primitive and the formal organisation less cohesive than in the later revisions). But there was surely more to it than this. That the time was ripe for meeting-points between absolute and poetic music is not in question, and in that sense Liszt's project carried with it a certain historical authenticity, no less than Wagner's. However, the reception of the new genres of both Liszt and Wagner tells a curious story in this respect, especially where the epic is concerned. The *poème pianistique* found a comfortable solution, avoiding epic ambitions in a quest for 'le sens intime et poétique des choses'. The symphonic poem, on the other hand, gained acceptance only when it relinquished the epic pretensions of the symphony; specifically, it came into its own as an agent of fantasy, colour and narrative, at times politicised as non-German nationalism, notably in Russia, France and the Czech lands. Conversely, the music drama instated, or reinstated, an epic dimension to opera, a genre which for long enough had been regarded as at least as close to popular entertainment as to high art. Indeed it is arguably in Wagner that Liszt's epopoeia, fusing music and the

---

[37] For a detailed reception history, see Johns, *The Symphonic Poems of Franz Liszt*, pp. 83–138.

poetic to achieve a higher art, came at least somewhere close to successful realisation. The surrender of symphonic poem to music drama is even acted out in the later history of the genres. From its inception in Weimar Idealism, the symphonic poem wandered far and wide, and its eventual homecoming in Strauss registered something of the realist impulse encountered on those journeys, before Strauss himself abandoned it in favour of music drama and opera.

These historical narratives of piano and orchestra, both culminating in an association of absolute music and modernity, and in a commitment to what has become known as the work-concept, may offer some explanation for the ambivalent standing of Liszt's piano music and for his positioning at the uncomfortable edge of our orchestral canon. With Dahlhaus as co-author, we may argue that although both the standing and the positioning have changed, often radically, since the mid-nineteenth century, for taste is an historical category, they have somehow remained ambivalent and peripheral (there are many kinds of uncertainty, and many points on the edge). Of course we may choose a different co-author. In his two commentaries on Liszt, Béla Bartók is less concerned with contingencies, more engaged by disinterested aesthetic qualities. Yet here too we are reminded that some problems just might not go away. Bartók's argument – and it seems to presuppose some notional universals in musical taste – is that Liszt's prolixity and eclecticism, his over-susceptibility to all emotions, trivial and sublime, rare and banal, threatens the unity of the music. 'There is perhaps not one of the greater works which sustains from beginning to end that perfection that we so much admire in the works of those we call the great classics.'[38] This chimes with the verdict of a third, more recent, co-author. Charles Rosen, in an inspired phrase, speaks of 'disreputable greatness', remarking on the masterly treatments of a 'sometimes undistinguished' musical content, 'reflecting a poetic content either inflated or all too commonplace'.[39] It needs to be stressed that Rosen, like Bartók and Dahlhaus, offers his criticisms from a basically supportive standpoint.

The easy thing to do would be to deconstruct the values that allow Rosen to speak of 'vulgarity', Bartók of 'empty pomp', or Dahlhaus of 'semi-failures'; indeed to some degree my earlier discussion does just that, or makes a start on it. Yet it may be more worthwhile to acknowledge that these judgements have been made by what Jerrold Levinson has called 'properly backgrounded listeners', and to probe the criteria which have produced them. To paraphrase Stein Haugom Olsen (who makes no reference to Levinson's category), it is perfectly reasonable to allow that aesthetic judgements may be legitimated by a socially constituted practice (that of appreciating Western art music), without reducing them to mere community consensus.[40] The practice, Olsen argues, will have its own concepts and rules, allowing judgements to be based on rational arguments, and it may (though need not) cut across many social communities. One can of course try to position oneself outside the practice. I will return to that possibility at the end, for it may have special significance for Liszt. But equally one can recognise that even within the practice concepts and rules change, and that those changes will naturally influence our judgements. Hence the notorious difficulty

---

[38] Suchoff (ed.), *Béla Bartók Essays*, p. 503.   [39] *The Romantic Generation*, p. 491.
[40] Stein Haugom Olsen, 'The Canon and Artistic Failure', *British Journal of Aesthetics*, 41, 3 (July 2001), pp. 261–78.

we have as contemplating subjects in establishing anything like a just critical distance from the contemplated object, and the more so when it emanates from the discredited projects of a proximate past, such as virtuoso music and programme music. Just how are such projects to be viewed again without prejudice?

One thing is common to the views of my three co-authors. Where Liszt fails, he fails grandly, not trivially, a victim of over-ambition, of the excesses prompted by virtuosity and the poetic. And he often succeeds. Of the bravura etudes, the second and tenth exhibit a near-perfect balance between invention and disposition. Yet elsewhere questions may be asked about either the invention or the disposition. The excitements of the *Mazeppa* theme are real, but a critic may well ask if they can be sustained through so many near-literal repetitions of a single closed unit, however much the accompaniment is diversified, so that bridges are of necessity insertions rather than outgrowths? In contrast, the working-through of material in *Eroica* is in many ways subtly contrived, but for our critic the material itself may seem over-insistent, inflated, working rather too hard at its heroism. Of the more lyrical etudes, *Paysage* skilfully conceals its calculated unpredictabilities – and especially its intricate play of rhythms – within an apparently bland surface texture, an 'inspired simplicity' that satisfies at several levels. It invites repeated hearings, as does *Ricordanza*, whose seamless melodic flow effortlessly merges cumulative ornamental variation and sequential development to embrace a remarkably wide range of expression. On the other hand, *Vision* and *Harmonies du Soir*, for all the magic of their variegated sonorities and the strength and delicacy of their principal themes, may be marred for our critic by a surfeit of sequential repetition, and a consequent over-working of certain well-worn harmonic shifts. Lisztians will protest, but in each case of adverse criticism here, the gist of our critic's complaint is a tendency towards the kind of rhetorical overstatement of which Chopin is seldom accused.

This is not the first time I have broached a comparison between Liszt and Chopin in this book. Their reception histories tell an interesting story, where the high ambition of the one was cut down to size in the twentieth century, while the achievement of the other was elevated beyond what were really deceptively modest aims. I have already suggested (in chapter 4) that an ideological shift within Olsen's practice (of appreciating Western art music) benefited Chopin at the expense of Liszt. I am now prepared to venture that among many of the properly backgrounded listeners of that practice the judgement that Chopin could attain a level of greatness that was more rarely afforded to Liszt is – as far as this can ever be possible – without prejudice to differences in style or shifting paradigms of taste. We should not be overly nervous of recognising what Steiner calls 'plainly lit excellence', even if we are usually forced to concede that the various criteria designed to demonstrate it somehow fall short of an adequate explication. One might indeed salute Leonard B. Meyer in this context. His essay of 1967, all too easily criticised for its narrowness of focus, still offers a powerful insight into the models of aesthetic appreciation that operate within the practice.[41] In Meyer's terms, the repetitions and sequences of some of the Liszt etudes, and even the blatancy of some of their themes, quite simply amount to insufficient 'information',

---

[41] Leonard B. Meyer, 'On Value and Greatness in Music', in *Music, the Arts and Ideas* (Chicago and London, 1967), pp. 22–41.

to an element of redundancy defined by the probability system that is tonal music. Such judgements can never be a science. At root they can do no more than attempt to conceptualise judgements that will have been made initially without the benefit of concepts; finding 'bad reasons', as T. S. Eliot cynically put it, 'for what we believe upon instinct'. Yet that is not to demote them from judgements to preferences. The aberrations of yesterday may also be the aberrations of today and tomorrow.

Meyer's model fleshes out and nuances criteria of value – notably formal efficiency – that are explicit in Kant, and indeed have a rather prestigious lineage. His argument is Kantian in its neglect of the contextual, but it departs from Kant in its reliance on concepts, which (in Kantian terms) of necessity take us outside the sphere of art itself.[42] Thus (again in Kantian terms) Meyer's observations, like those of my three co-authors and like my own in the paragraph before last, reduce art to another sphere, and leave an uncomfortable space between the commentary of the connoisseur and the experience of aesthetic engagement, an experience that is somehow compromised by its own avowal, as also by attempts to rationalise it. There is indeed something wonderfully radical about Kant's proposal that there may be a disinterested aesthetic judgement, a judgement of the beautiful, of which art is a privileged but not an exclusive instantiation. And it is by no means unthinkable that we might cultivate the residue of this; that we might want to bring the aesthetic home, as it were, after its period of disparagement at the hands of one ideology after another, seeking, with Niecks, some trace of a 'natural, gracious, persuasive beauty'.[43] That said, it is hard to keep the concepts at bay, and once engaged they not only qualify any hope that our judgement might be disinterested, but also register an underlying and inexorable historical shift towards authenticity, rather than beauty, as the primary criterion of value within the practice. Of my co-authors, it is only Dahlhaus who fully acknowledges this shift and tries to make room for it within his value-judgement. He incorporates, in other words, some element of historical fitness in his placement of *Mazeppa*, and of Liszt's music in general.

It is true that in one sense Liszt was very much a figure of his time. As noted earlier, his putative unification of absolute music and the poetic – the idea rather more than its realisation, perhaps – was a project aptly caught in its historical moment. Yet in other respects he was positioned oddly in relation to the canons of taste and the expectations of audiences in the late nineteenth century. His was neither the remoteness of the avant-garde artist (his modernity had an element of modishness in it) nor yet the proximity of the popular culture icon (his populism was tempered by a pronounced streak of Idealism). If there is a single quality that expresses his achievement, it is one that perhaps embraces these contradictions. Significantly it is a quality shared with Victor Hugo. Hugo has been credited (or debited) with the commodification of Romanticism for the world of letters.[44] And Liszt, it seems to me, might sustain a very similar claim in the musical world. Spanning the two halves of the century, both men appropriated the idealised imagery and topoi associated with early Romantic elites and made them available to a much wider catchment area, with the

---

[42] Given Kant's criterion of formal efficiency, this may seem self-contradictory. But he refers here to a general intellectual model of music, meaning that formal properties (and thus beauty rather than mere pleasing sensations) are enabled by the mathematical proportions underlying the vibrational ratios of tones.

[43] *Programme Music in the last Four Centuries*, p. 537.   [44] Graham Robb, *Victor Hugo* (London, 1997), p. 313.

attendant danger that the heroic will translate to the vulgar, the expressive to the sentimental, the dramatic to the melodramatic. In doing so they both somehow (miraculously) sustained a claim to Modernist ambition, while remaining very much alive to populist prejudices about just what might reasonably be expected of art. If there is an Achilles's heel, at least where Liszt is concerned, it lies precisely in the near-impossibility of straddling such apparently irreconcilable positions. Ultimately it is a challenge to nothing less than the authenticity of the artwork, to its 'genuine-ness'. For, ironically enough (and the scare-quotes are inescapable), it may be easier for today's listener to 'believe in' some of the 'authentically trivial' music of the later nineteenth century than to accept the credentials of a popular Modernism.

That very suggestion takes our discussion to another plane, for it reminds us that what were once perceived as chinks in an armour-plated practice have since been recognised as alternative practices. If we live, work and think within the Western cultural tradition, we have some experiential basis from which to evaluate its products. In seeking a ground for such evaluations we may appeal to a global category of disinterested beauty, perhaps formulated in the terms of one, or even all, of a familiar triad of aesthetic qualities.[45] Alternatively we may appeal to a 'contextual beauty', where both subject and object are recognised as importantly contingent; and here we may already feel that beauty is no longer the *mot juste*, and that authenticity better serves the purpose.[46] In any case, whatever our criteria, we judge from within the practice, and the integrity of our judgement is not prejudiced by any views we may hold about the historical nature of that practice. We may accept, for instance, that the universalist ambitions of Western bourgeois culture were founded on a myth, but argue at the same time that the myth was valuable, glorious, even necessary, and above all that it was conducive to the creation of great art. It is from just this 'insider' perspective that Chopin emerges for many of us as a central figure within the Western tradition, transforming an imposing Bachian inheritance into a generous legacy for Debussy. And it is from this same perspective that Liszt is recognised by many of us as significant but problematical, a figure at the margins.

There is, however, another, possibly fanciful, way of looking at it. In considering those features that have worked to marginalise Liszt's music, notably the performative and the poetic, we may be struck that they are highly valued qualities in other practices: in today's popular music, for instance, and in the music of several non-Western traditions. Maybe Liszt is located on the margins, then, in the almost literal sense that his music occupies a border territory where a Western – specifically an Austro-German – tradition begins to dissolve into at least some of its others. Edges, after all, have their own interest and their own merit, not least as privileged sites from which to look critically at a centre, if not indeed

---

45 In discussing what he calls a 'modern theory of value', Roger Seamon allows the possibility of an additive (rather than a mutually exclusive) approach to the triad of mimesis, expression and form. See 'The Conceptual Dimension of Art and the Modern Theory of Artistic Value', *Journal of Aesthetics and Art Criticism*, 59, 2 (Spring 2001), pp. 139–52. For a more elaborate, if perhaps eccentric, typology, see the ten criteria listed by Elder Olson in 'On Value Judgments in the Arts', published in his collection *On Value Judgments in the Arts and Other Essays* (Chicago, 1976), pp. 307–26.

46 See Marcia M. Eaton, 'Kantian and Contextual Beauty', a contribution to the symposium 'Beauty Matters' in *Journal of Aesthetics and Art Criticism*, 57, 1 (1999), pp. 11–15. Also Brian Rosebody, 'The Historical Contingency of Aesthetic Experience', *British Journal of Aesthetics*, 40, 1 (January 2000), pp. 73–88.

to probe the stability and durability – even the very idea – of that centre (it goes without saying that demolishing centres also removes peripheries). Virtuosity, in this reading, is a kind of immanent critique of the work-concept, the canon, and the idea of absolute music. Its contention – if it could embody a contention – would be that a sense of event and situation, fundamental to many musical traditions, might re-enter a cultural world from which it has been dislodged; and here the historical placement (and posture) of the virtuoso tradition in the late nineteenth and early twentieth centuries has some explanatory value: a last-ditch stand for the phenomenal in a culture of conservation? Likewise an appropriation and dignifying of the poetic – of the 'extra-musical', to invoke again that problematical term – might be taken as implicitly critical of an autonomy principle that took its origins in German thought but was later universalised, not least through the institutionalisation of musicology in Europe and America. It was, after all, at least partly through an embrace of the poetic that colour and sonority, together with new concepts of metre and rhythm, were liberated – not to say animated – in the music of non-German composers at the *fin-de-siècle*, in the process finding some common cause with musics from non-Western traditions. Liszt may have something to teach us, then, about the defining edges – they are elusive and shadowy, perhaps even in dissolution, but no less defining – of a Western canon to which he has himself been granted only a grudging admittance. And in our present age, when the kudos attaching to a European cultural tradition seems hard to sustain, when familiar categories have been destabilised, and when (paradoxically) the global dissemination of Western art music creates an ever more deep-seated anxiety and insecurity about its isolation in the world, we may well look with a renewed, if valedictory, historical interest at those edges. Where Liszt is concerned, any loss to art may yet prove to be history's gain.

Bibliography

Abbate, Carolyn. 'Outside Ravel's Tomb', *Journal of the American Musicological Society*, 52, 3 (Fall 1999).

Adorno, Theodor W. *Philosophy of Modern Music*, trans. Anne G. Mitchell and Wesley V. Bloomster (London, 1973; orig. edn, 1948).

    Aesthetic Theory, ed. Gretel Adorno and Rolf Tiedemann, trans. Christian Lenhardt (London, 1983).

    'On the Problem of Music Analysis', ed. and trans. Max Paddison, *Music Analysis*, 1, 2 (July 1982).

Agawu, Kofi. *Playing with Signs: A Semiotic Interpretation of Classic Music* (Princeton and Oxford, 1991).

    'Formal Perspectives on the Symphonies', *The Cambridge Companion to Brahms*, ed. Michael Musgrave (Cambridge, 1999).

Altenburg, Detlef. 'Franz Liszt and the Legacy of the Classical Era', *19th-Century Music*, 18, 1 (Summer 1994).

    (ed.). *Liszt und die Weimarer Klassik* (Laaber, 1997).

Antokoletz, Elliott. *The Music of Béla Bartók* (Berkeley and Los Angeles, 1984).

Bailey, Robert. 'The Structure of the "Ring" and Its Evolution', *19th-Century Music*, 1 (1977).

Baker, James. 'The Limits of Tonality in the Late Music of Franz Liszt', *Journal of Music Theory*, 34, 2 (1990).

Bárdos, Lajos. 'Modale Harmonien in den Werken von Franz Liszt', in Klára Hamburger (ed.), *Franz Liszt: Beitrage von ungarischen Autoren* (Budapest, 1978).

    'Ferenc Liszt, the Innovator', *Studia Musicologica*, 17 (1975).

Barth, George. *The Pianist as Orator: Beethoven and the Transformation of Keyboard Style* (Ithaca and London, 1992).

Barthes, Roland. *Image – Music – Text* (London, 1977).

Bartók, Béla. *Béla Bartók Essays*, ed. Benjamin Suchoff (London, 1976).

Bass, Richard. 'From Gretchen to Tristan: The Changing Role of Harmonic Sequences in the Nineteenth Century', *19th-Century Music*, 19, 3 (Spring 1996).

Beach, David. 'Schubert's Experiments with Sonata Form: Formal-Tonal Design versus Underlying Structure', *Music Theory Spectrum*, 15, 1 (1993).

    'Harmony and Linear Progression in Schubert's Music', *Journal of Music Theory*, 38 (1994).

Bellman, Jonathan. 'Frédéric Chopin, Antoine de Kontski and the *carezzando* Touch', *Early Music*, 29, 3 (2001).

Benjamin, Walter. *Ursprung des deutschen Trauerspiels*, in *Schriften*, vol. I, ed. T. W. Adorno (Frankfurt, 1955).

Bent, Ian. 'Heinrich Schenker, Chopin and Domenico Scarlatti', *Music Analysis*, 5, 2–3 (1986).

(ed.). *Music Analysis in the Nineteenth Century, Volume 2: Hermeneutic Approaches* (Cambridge, 1994).

Bergfeld, Joachim. *Die formale Strucktur der Symphonische Dichtungen Franz Liszt* (Eisenach, 1931).

Bernstein, Susan. *Virtuosity of the Nineteenth Century: Performing Music and Language in Heine, Liszt and Baudelaire* (Stanford, 1998).

Boissier, Mme Auguste. *Liszt pédagogue: Leçons de piano données par Liszt à Mlle. Valérie Boissier en 1832* (Paris, 1927).

Bolte, Theodor. 'Liszt als Orchesterkomponist', *Neue Zeitschrift für Musik*, 42 (October 1911).

Brantlinger, Patrick. *Bread and Circuses: Theories of Mass Culture and Social Decay* (Ithaca and London, 1983).

Burger, Ernst. *Franz Liszt: A Chronicle of his Life in Pictures and Documents*, trans. Stewart Spencer (Princeton, 1989).

Busoni, Ferruccio. *The Essence of Music*, trans. Rosamund Ley (London, 1957).

    Sketch of a New Aesthetic of Music, trans. Theodore Baker, in *Three Classics in the Aesthetics of Music* (New York, 1962; orig. edn, 1911).

Celenza, Anna H. Harwell. 'Death Transfigured: The Origins and Evolution of Franz Liszt's *Totentanz*', in Jim Samson and Bennett Zon (eds.), *Nineteenth-Century Music: Selected Proceedings of the Tenth International Conference on Nineteenth-Century Music* (Aldershot, 2002).

Chanon, Michael. *Musica Practica: The Social Practice of Western Music from Gregorian Chant to Postmodernism* (London, 1994).

Chester, Andrew. 'Second Thoughts on a Rock Aesthetic: The Band', *New Left Review*, 62 (1970).

Chopin, Fryderyk. *Collected Correspondence of Fryderyk Chopin*, collected and annotated B. S. Sydow, trans. and ed. Arthur Hedley (London, Melbourne and Toronto, 1962).

Chua, Daniel. *Absolute Music and the Construction of Meaning* (Cambridge, 1996).

Cinnamon, Howard. 'Tonic Arpeggiation and Successive Equal Third Relations as Elements of Tonal Evolution in the Music of Franz Liszt', *Music Theory Spectrum*, 8 (1986).

Clark, Suzannah. 'From Nature to Logic in Schubert's Instrumental Music' (Diss., Princeton University, 1997).

Clark, Suzannah and Alexander Rehding (eds.). *Music Theory and Natural Order from the Renaissance to the Early Twentieth Century* (Cambridge, 2001).

Cohn, Richard. 'Maximally Smooth Cycles, Hexatonic Systems, and the Analysis of Late-Romantic Triadic Progressions', *Music Analysis*, 15, 1 (1996).

Conway, James Bryant. 'Musical Sources for the Liszt 'Etudes d'exécution transcendante: A Study in the Evolution of Liszt's Compositional and Keyboard Techniques' (Diss., University of Arizona, 1969).

Cook, Nicholas. *Music, Imagination and Culture* (Oxford, 1990).

Cumming, Naomi. 'Analogy in Leonard B. Meyer's Theory of Musical Meaning', in Jamie C. Kassler (ed.), *Metaphor: A Musical Dimension* (Sydney, 1991).

Czerny, Carl. *Erinnerungen aus meinem Leben*, ed. Walter Kolneder (Strassburg, 1968; orig. MS, 1842); Eng. trans. by Ernest Sanders: 'Recollections from my Life', *Musical Quarterly*, 42, 3 (July 1956).

    A Systematic Introduction to Improvisation on the Pianoforte, Op. 200, trans. and ed. A. Mitchell (New York, 1983; orig. edn, 1829).

    Complete Theoretical and Practical Pianoforte School, Op. 500, trans. J. H. Hamilton (London, 1839).

    Umriss der ganzen Musikgeschichte (Mainz, 1851).

Letters on Thorough-Bass, with an Appendix on the Higher Branches of Musical Execution and Expression, trans. J. A. Hamilton (London, n.d., orig. edn, *c*. 1840).

Dahlhaus, Carl. *Between Romanticism and Modernism*, trans. Mary Whittall (Berkeley, Los Angeles and London, 1974).

'Liszts Bergsymphonie und die Idee der symphonischen Dichtung', *Jahrbuch des Staatlichen Institut für Musikforschung* (1975).

Esthetics of Music, trans. William Austin (Cambridge, 1982; orig. edn, 1967).

Analysis and Value Judgement, trans. Siegmund Levarie (New York, 1983; orig. edn, 1970).

Schoenberg and the New Music, trans. Derrick Puffett and Alfred Clayton (Cambridge, 1987).

Nineteenth-Century Music, trans. J. B. Robinson (Berkeley and Los Angeles, 1989).

The Idea of Absolute Music, trans. Roger Lustig (Chicago and London, 1989; orig. edn, 1978).

Damschroder, David Allen. 'The Structural Foundations of 'The Music of the Future': A Schenkerian Study of Liszt's Weimar Repertoire' (Diss., Yale University, 1981).

Davies, Stephen. 'Transcription, Authenticity and Performance', *British Journal of Aesthetics*, 28 (1988).

Deaville, James. 'The Controversy Surrounding Liszt's Conception of Programme Music', in Jim Samson and Bennett Zon (eds.), *Nineteenth-Century Music* (Aldershot, 2002).

Delacroix, Eugène. *The Journal of Eugène Delacroix*, ed. Hubert Wellington, trans. Lucy Norton (New York, 1948).

Denis Diderot, '*Rameau's Nephew* (with *d'Alembert's Dream*)', trans. Leonard Tancock (Harmondsworth, 1966; orig. MS, *c*. 1761–*c*. 1779).

Dolar, Mladen. 'The Object Voice', in Renata Salecl and Slavoj Žižek (eds.), *Gaze and Voice as Love Objects* (Durham, NC, and London, 1996).

Dreyfus, Lawrence. *Bach and the Patterns of Invention* (Cambridge, MA, 1996).

Dessauer, Hans. *John Field: sein Leben und seine Werke* (Langensalza, 1912).

Eaton, Marcia M. 'Kantian and Contextual Beauty', *Journal of Aesthetics and Art Criticism*, 57, 1 (1999).

Eckhardt, Mária. *Liszt's Music Manuscripts in the National Széchényi Library* (Budapest, 1968).

'Liszt à Marseille', in *Studia Musicologica Academiae Scientarum Hungaricae*, 24 (1982).

Eco, Umberto. *Interpretation and Over-interpretation*, ed. Stefan Collini (Cambridge, 1992).

Empson, William. *Some Versions of Pastoral* (New York, 1974).

Fay, Amy. *Music Study in Germany* (London, 1886).

Forte, Allen. 'Liszt's Experimental Idiom and Music of the Early Twentieth Century', *19th-Century Music*, 10, 3 (1987).

Foucault, Michel. *The Archaeology of Knowledge and the Discourse on Language*, trans. A. M. Sheridan Smith (New York, 1972).

Ganz, Peter Felix. 'The Development of the Etude for Pianoforte' (Diss., Northwestern University, 1960).

Gárdonyi, Zoltán. 'Neue Tonleiter- und Sequenztypen in Liszts Fruhwerken (Zur Frage der "Lisztchen Sequenzen")', *Studia Musicologica*, 11 (1969).

Gavoty, Bernard. *Liszt: Le virtuose* (Paris, 1980).

Glasenapp, Franzgeorg von. *Georg Simon Löhlein* (Halle, 1937).

Goehr, Alexander. 'Poetics of my Music', in *Finding the Key: Selected Writings of Alexander Goehr*, ed. Derrick Puffett (London, 1998).

Goehr, Lydia. *The Imaginary Museum of Musical Works: An Essay in the Philosophy of Music* (Oxford, 1992).

'The Perfect Performance of Music and the Perfect Musical Performance', *new formations*, 27 (Winter 1995–6).

Gooley, Dana. 'Warhorses: Liszt, Weber's *Konzertstück*, and the Cult of Napoléon', *19th-Century Music*, 24, 1 (Summer, 2000).

Grabócz, Márta. *Morphologie des Oeuvres pour Piano de Liszt* (Paris, 1996).

Guhr, Charles. *L'Art de jouer du violon de Paganini* (French trans: Paris, 1830).

Gut, Serge. *Franz Liszt* (Paris, 1989).

  (ed.). *Liszt-Studien 2: Kongress-Bericht Eisenstadt 1978* (Munich and Salzburg, 1981).

Habermas, Jürger. *The Structural Transformation of the Public Sphere*, trans. Thomas Burger and Frederick Lawrence (Cambridge, MA, 1991).

Hahn, Arthur. *Franz Liszt: Symphonische Dichtungen* (Leipzig, 1920).

Hall, Helen. 'The Evolution of Liszt's Compositional Style as Reflected in the Three Versions of the Transcendental Etudes' (Diss., University of Victoria, 1983).

Hamilton, Kenneth. *Liszt Sonata in B Minor* (Cambridge, 1996).

  'Liszt', in Kern Holoman (ed.), *The Nineteenth-Century Symphony* (New York, 1997).

Hanslick, Eduard. *On the Musically Beautiful*, trans. and ed. Geoffrey Payzart (Indianapolis, 1996; orig. edn, 1854).

Hatten, Robert. *Musical Meaning in Beethoven: Markedness, Correlation, and Interpretation* (Bloomington and Indianapolis, 1994).

Hawkins, John. *A General History of the Science and Practice of Music* (London, 1853).

Heine, Heinrich. *Lutèce: Lettres sur la vie politique, artistique et sociale de la France*, vol. 19 of *Heines Werke, Säkularausgabe* (Berlin and Paris, 1977; orig. edn, 1855).

Hepokoski, James. *Sibelius Symphony No. 5* (Cambridge, 1993).

Heuss, Alfred. 'Eine motivisch-thematische Studie über Liszts symphonische Dichtung "Ce qu'on entend sur la montagne" ', *Zeitschrift der Internationalen Musikgesellschaft*, 13 (1911–12).

Hildebrandt, Dieter. *Pianoforte: A Social History of the Piano*, trans. Harriet Goodman (London, 1988).

Howe, Michael. *The Origins of Exceptional Abilities* (Oxford, 1990).

Hunkemöller, Jürgen. 'Perfektion und Perspektivenwechsel: Studien zu den drei Fassungen der "Etudes d'exécution transcendante" von Franz Liszt', *Archiv für Musikwissenschaft*, 51 (1994).

Huschke, Wolfram. *Musik im klassischen und nachklassischen Weimar* (Weimar, 1982).

Ingarden, Roman. *The Work of Music and the Problem of its Identity*, trans. A. Czerniawski, ed. J. G. Harrell (Berkeley and Los Angeles, 1986; orig. edn, 1928).

Iser, Wolfgang. *The Act of Reading: A Theory of Aesthetic Response* (Baltimore and London, 1978).

Janáček, Leos. *Janácek's Uncollected Essays on Music*, ed. and trans. Mirka Zemanová (London and New York, 1989).

Jankélévitch, Vladimir. *Liszt et la Rhapsodie: Essaie sur la Virtuosité* (Paris, 1979, repr. 1989). *Maurice Ravel* (Paris, 1939).

Jauss, Hans Robert. *Towards an Aesthetic of Reception*, trans. T. Bahti (Minneapolis, 1982).

Jiránek, Jaroslav. 'Franz Liszts Beitrag zur Musiksprache der Romantiker', *Studia Musicologica*, 28 (1986).

Johns, Keith T. 'The Music of the Future and the Berlin Critics: Franz Liszt Returns to the Singakademie, December 1855', *Journal of the American Liszt Society*, 23 (1988).

  The Symphonic Poems of Franz Liszt, rev. and ed. Michael Saffle (New York, 1996).

Jung, Hermann. *Die Pastorale: Studien zur Geschichte einer musikalischen Topos* (Bern and Munich, 1980).

Kallberg, Jeffrey. 'Chopin in the Market-Place', *Notes*, 39, 3–4 (March–June 1983).

Kallberg, Jeffrey. 'Small "Forms": in Defense of the Prelude', in Jim Samson (ed.), *The Cambridge Companion to Chopin* (Cambridge, 1992).

Kárpáti, János. *Bartók's String Quartets* (Budapest, 1967).

Kinderman, William and Harold Krebs (eds.). *The Second Practice of Nineteenth-Century Tonality* (Lincoln, Nbr, and London, 1996).

Kivy, Peter. *The Fine Art of Repetition* (Cambridge, 1993).

Kramer, Lawrence, 'Franz Liszt and the Virtuoso Public Sphere: Sight and Sound in the Rise of Mass Entertainment'; in *Musical Meaning: Towards a Critical History* (Berkeley and Los Angeles, 2002).

Kullak, Adolph. *The Aesthetics of Pianoforte-Playing* (New York, 1972; based on the 3rd edn, 1889).

Kurth, Ernst. *Selected Writings*, ed. Lee A. Rothfarb (Cambridge, 1991).

Laster, Arnaud. 'Victor Hugo, la Musique et les Musiciens', in Victor Hugo, *Oeuvres Complètes*, gen. ed. Jean Massin (Paris, 1967–71), vol. 5 no. 1.

Lendvai, Ernö. *The Workshop of Bartók and Kodály* (Budapest, 1983).

Leppert, Richard and Stephen Zank. 'The Concert and the Virtuoso', in James Parakilas (ed.), *Piano Roles: Three Hundred Years of Life with the Piano* (New Haven, 1999).

Levy, Janet. 'Texture as a Sign', *Journal of the American Musicological Society*, 35, 3 (1982).

Liszt, Franz. *Letters of Franz Liszt*, coll. and ed. La Mara, trans. Constance Bache, 2 vols. (London, 1894).

Des Bohémiens et de leur musique en Hongrie (Leipzig, 1881).

An Artist's Journey, trans. and annotated Charles Suttoni (Chicago and London, 1989; orig. letters, 1835–41).

F. Chopin (Paris, 1852).

Correspondance de Liszt et de la comtesse d'Agoult, ed. Daniel Ollivier (Paris 1933–40).

The Letters of Franz Liszt to Olga von Meyendorff, 1871–1886, trans. William R. Tyler, with introduction and notes by Edward N. Waters (Washington, 1979).

Gesammelte Schriften, ed. Lina Ramann (Leipzig, 1881–99).

Sämtliche Schriften, ed. Detlef Altenburg (Leipzig, 1989–).

MacIntyre, Alasdair. *After Virtue* (London, 1981).

Mäkelä, Tomi. *Virtuosität und Werkcharakter* (Munich and Salzburg, 1989).

Maus, Fred Everett. 'Music as Drama', *Music Theory Spectrum*, 10 (1988).

Mersmann, Hans. *Angewandte Musikästhetik* (Berlin, 1926).

Metzner, Paul. *Crescendo of the Virtuoso* (Berkeley, Los Angeles and London, 1998).

Meyer, Leonard B. *Music, the Arts and Ideas* (Chicago and London, 1967).

Style and Music: Theory, History and Ideology (Philadelphia, 1989).

Micznik, Vera. 'Music and Narrative Revisited: Degrees of Narrativity in Beethoven and Mahler', *Journal of the Royal Musical Association*, 126, 2 (2001).

Miller, Norbert. 'Elévation bei Victor Hugo und Franz Liszt: Über die Schwierigkeiten einer Verwandlung von lyrischen in symphonische Dichtungen', *Jahrbuch des Staatlichen Instituts für Musikforschung Preussischer Kulturbesitz* (Berlin, 1975).

Milliot, Sylvette. 'Le virtuose international: un création du 18ᵉ siècle', *Dix-huitième siècle*, 25 (1993).

Monelle, Raymond. *The Sense of Music: Semiotic Essays* (Princeton and Oxford, 2000).

Morgan, Robert P. 'Coda as Culmination: The First Movement of the *Eroica* Symphony', in Christopher Hatch and David W. Bernstein (eds.), *Artistic Theory and the Exploration of the Past* (Chicago, 1993).

'Dissonant Prolongations: Theoretical and Compositional Precedents', *Journal of Music Theory*, 20, 1 (1976).

Mueller, Rena Charnin. 'Liszt's *Tasso* Sketchbook: Studies in Sources and Chronology' (Diss., New York University, 1986).

Nägele, Rainer. *Echoes of Translation: Reading between Texts* (Baltimore and London, 1997).

Nattiez, Jean-Jacques. *Music and Discourse: Towards a Semiology of Music*, trans. Carolyn Abbate (Princeton, 1990).

Newcomb, Anthony. 'Once More "Between Absolute Music and Programme Music"', *19th-Century Music*, 7 (1984).

  'Schumann and Late Eighteenth-Century Narrative Strategies', *19th-Century Music*, 2 (1986).

Niecks, Frederick. *Programme Music in the Last Four Centuries: A Contribution to the History of Musical Expression* (London and New York, [1907]).

Novack, Saul. 'Aspects of the Creative Process in Music', *Current Musicology*, 36 (1983).

Olsen, Stein Haugom. 'The Canon and Artistic Failure', *British Journal of Aesthetics*, 41, 3 (July 2001).

Olson, Elder. *On Value Judgments in the Arts and Other Essays* (Chicago, 1976).

Paddison, Max. *Adorno's Aesthetics of Music* (Cambridge, 1993).

Penesco, Anne (ed.). *Défense et illustration de la virtuosité* (Lyon, 1997).

Perle, George. *Twelve-Tone Tonality* (Berkeley and Los Angeles, 1977).

Pincherle, Marc. *Le Monde des Virtuoses* (Paris, 1961).

Pousseur, Henri. 'Webern's Organic Chromaticism', *Die Reihe*, 2 (Eng. edn, London, 1958).

Proctor, Gregory. 'Technical Bases of Nineteenth-Century Chromatic Tonality: A Study in Chromaticism' (Diss., Princeton University, 1978).

Puffett, Derrick. 'Transcription and Recomposition: The Strange Case of Zemlinsky's Maeterlinck Songs', in Craig Ayrey and Mark Everist (eds.), *Analytical Strategies and Musical Interpretation: Essays on Nineteenth- and Twentieth-Century Music* (Cambridge, 1996).

Raabe, Peter. *Liszts Schaffen* (Tutzing, 1968; orig. edn, 1931).

Ramann, Lina. *Franz Liszt als Künstler und Mensch*, 2 vols. (Leipzig, 1880).

Ratner, Leonard. *Classic Music: Expression, Form, and Style* (New York, 1980).

Reeve, Katherine Kolb. 'Primal Scenes: Smithson, Pleyel, and Liszt in the Eyes of Berlioz', *19th-Century Music*, 18, 3 (1995).

Reich, Nancy B. *Clara Schumann: The Artist and the Woman* (New York and London, 1985).

Revitt, Paul J. 'Franz Liszt's Harmonizations of Linear Chromaticism', *Journal of the American Liszt Society*, 13 (1983).

Riemann, Hugo. *Musikalische Dynamik und Agogik* (Leipzig, 1884).

Rink, John. *Chopin: The Piano Concertos* (Cambridge, 1997).

Robb, Graham. *Victor Hugo* (London, 1997).

Rosebody, Brian. 'The Historical Contingency of Aesthetic Experience', *British Journal of Aesthetics*, 40, 1 (January 2000).

Rosen, Charles. *Sonata Forms* (New York, 1988).

  The Romantic Generation (London, 1995).

  'Schubert's Inflections of Sonata Form', in Christopher Gibbs (ed.), *The Cambridge Companion to Schubert* (Cambridge, 1997).

Rosenthal, Albi. 'Franz Liszt and his Publishers', *Liszt-Saeculum*, 2, 38 (1986).

Rowland, David (ed.). *The Cambridge Companion to the Piano* (Cambridge, 1998).

Rummenholler, Peter. 'Die verfremdete Kadenz. Zur Harmonik Franz Liszts', *Zeitschrift für Musiktheorie*, 9 (1978).

Sachania, Millan. 'The Arrangements of Leopold Godowsky: An Aesthetic, Historical, and Analytical Study' (Diss., University of Cambridge, 1997).

Saffle, Michael and James Deaville (eds.). *New Light on Liszt and his Music* (New York, 1991).

Said, Edward W. *Musical Elaborations* (London, 1991).

Samson, Jim (ed.). *The Cambridge History of Nineteenth-Century Music* (Cambridge, 2001).

'Chopin and Genre', *Music Analysis*, 8, 3 (1989).

The Music of Chopin (London, 1985).

Satyendra, Ramon. 'Chromatic Tonality and Semitonal Relationships in Liszt's Late Style' (Diss., University of Chicago, 1992).

Schoenberg, Arnold. *The Musical Idea and the Logic, Technique, and Art of its Presentation*, ed. Patricia Carpenter and Severine Neff (New York, 1995).

Style and Idea: Selected Writings of Arnold Schoenberg, ed. Leonard Stein, trans. Leo Black (London, 1975; orig. edn, 1946).

Schottky, Julius Max. *Paganinis Leben und Treiben als Künstler und als Mensch* (Prague, 1830).

Schumann, Robert. *Gesammelte Schriften über Musik und Musiker* (Leipzig, 1888). For a selection in English translation: Robert Schumann, *On Music and Musicians*, trans. P. Rosenfeld, ed. K. Wolff (London, 1946).

Schütz, Georg. 'Form, Satz- und Klaviertechnik in den drei Fassungen der *Grossen Etüden* von Franz Liszt', in Zsoltán Gárdonyi and Siegfried Mauser (eds.), *Virtuosität und Avantgarde: Untersuchungen zum Klavierwerk Franz Liszts* (Mainz, 1988).

Schwab, Heinrich W. 'Formen der Virtuosenehrung und ihr Sozialgeschichtlicher Hintergrund' in Henrik Glahn, Søren Sørensen and Peter Ryom (eds.), *Book of the International Musicological Society Congress* (Copenhagen, 1972), vol. 2.

Scruton, Roger. *The Aesthetic Understanding* (London, 1983).

Seamon, Roger. 'The Conceptual Dimension of Art and the Modern Theory of Artistic Value', *Journal of Aesthetics and Art Criticism*, 59, 2 (Spring 2001).

Searle, Humphrey. *The Music of Liszt*, rev. edn (New York, 1966).

Seidel, Wilhelm. 'Über Figurationsmotive von Chopin und Liszt', in Henrik Glahn, Søren Sørenson and Peter Ryom (eds.), *Book of the International Musicological Society Congress* (Copenhagen, 1972), vol. 2.

Sennett, Richard. *The Fall of Public Man* (Cambridge, 1977).

Sipe, Thomas. *Beethoven: 'Eroica' Symphony* (Cambridge, 1998).

Skoumal, Zdenek. 'Liszt's Androgynous Harmony', *Music Analysis*, 13, 1 (March 1994).

Sogny, Michel. *L'Admiration Créatrice chez Liszt* (Paris, 1975).

Somfai, László. 'Die musikalischen Gestaltwandlungen der Faust-Symphonie von Liszt', *Studia musicologica*, 2 (1962).

Sontag, Susan. *A Susan Sontag Reader*, ed. Elizabeth Hardwick (London, 1983).

Steblin, Rita. *A History of Key Characteristics in the Eighteenth and Early Nineteenth Centuries* (Ann Arbor, 1983).

Stradel, August. 'Liszts Mazeppa-Werke', *Neue Zeitschrift für Musik*, 43 (October 1911).

Streets, Randall Keith. 'The Piano Sonatas of Carl Czerny' (Diss., University of Maryland, 1987).

Strohm, Reinhard. *The Rise of European Music 1380–1500* (Cambridge, 1993).

Supičič, Ivo. *Music in Society: A Guide to the Sociology of Music* (New York, 1987).

Talbot, Michael (ed.). *The Musical Work: Reality or Invention?* (Liverpool, 2000).

Tanner, Mark. 'The Power of Performance as an Alternative Analytical Discourse: The Liszt Sonata in B Minor', *19th-Century Music*, 24, 2 (2000).

Tanner, Michael. *Wagner* (Princeton, 1996).

Tarasti, Eero. *A Theory of Musical Semiotics* (Bloomington, 1994).

Taruskin, Richard. 'Chernomor to Kashchei: Harmonic Sorcery; or, Stravinsky's "Angle"', *Journal of the American Musicological Society*, 38, 1 (1985).

Text and Act (Oxford, 1995).

Thomson, C. W. *Victor Hugo and the Graphic Arts (1820–1833)* (Geneva, 1970).

Todd, Larry. 'The "Unwelcome Guest" Regaled: Franz Liszt and the Augmented Triad', *19th-Century Music*, 12, 2 (Fall 1988).

Tyson, Alan. 'A Feud Between Clementi and Cramer', *Music & Letters*, 54 (1973).

Wagner, Richard. *Richard Wagner's Prose Works*, ed. William Ashton Ellis, 8 vols. (London, 1897).

The Diary of Richard Wagner, 1865–1882: The Brown Book, ed. Joachim Bergfeld, trans. George Bird (London, 1980).

Walker, Alan. *Franz Liszt: The Virtuoso Years 1811–1847* (London, 1983).

Franz Liszt: The Weimar Years 1848–1861 (London, 1989).

Wallace, Robin. *Beethoven's Critics: Aesthetic Dilemmas and Resolutions during the Composer's Lifetime* (Cambridge, 1986).

Wangermée, Robert. 'Tradition et innovation dans la virtuosité romantique.' *Acta Musicologica*, 42 (1970).

Wason, Robert W. 'Progressive Harmonic Theory in the Mid-19th Century', *Journal of Musicological Research*, 8 (1988).

Weber, Max. *The Rational and Social Foundations of Music*, trans. and ed. D. Martindale, J. Riedel and G. Neuwirth (Illinois, 1958; orig. edn, 1921).

Weber, William. 'The History of Musical Canon', in Nicholas Cook and Mark Everist (eds.), *Rethinking Music* (Oxford and New York, 1999).

Webster, James. 'Schubert's Sonata Form and Brahms's First Maturity', *19th-Century Music*, 2 (1978).

Wegman, Rob C. 'From Maker to Composer: Improvisation and Musical Authorship in the Low Countries, 1450–1500', *Journal of the American Musicological Society*, 49 (1996).

Weitz, Morris. 'The Role of Theory in Aesthetics', *Journal of Aesthetics and Art Criticism*, 15 (1956).

The Opening Mind: A Philosophical Study of Humanistic Concepts (Chicago, 1977).

Williams, Adrian. *Portrait of Liszt by Himself and his Contemporaries* (Oxford, 1990).

(ed.). *Franz Liszt: Selected Letters* (Oxford, 1998).

Williams, Peter. *The Chromatic Fourth during Four Centuries of Music* (Oxford, 1997).

Wintle, Christopher. 'Kontra-Schenker: *Largo e Mesto* from Beethoven's Op. 10 no. 3,' *Music Analysis*, 4 (1985).

Zamoyski, Adam. *Paderewski* (London, 1982).

Zeke, Lajos. '"Successive Polymodality" or Different Modes Based on the Same Final in Liszt's Works', *Studia Musicologica*, 28 (1986).

Ziehn, Bernhard. *Canonic Studies*, ed. Ronald Stevenson (New York, 1977; orig. edn, 1912).

Index

Index

Made in the USA
Monee, IL
26 May 2020